# EAVESDROPPING

## — ON —

# HEAVEN

## UNCOVERING THE HIDDEN ORDER
## IN REVELATION

### NICK JOHNSTON

By Nick Johnston

First paperback edition March 2025
Second paperback edition September 2025

ISBN: 978-1-966708-01-8

Book Cover by Miblart.com
Published by Never Unprepared Publishing
All Bible verses cited were sourced from Biblehub.com
Author's Website: https://Neverunprepared.org

# Acknowledgements

There are several people who had an impact on this book that I want to thank.

First, I want to thank my late mother. Though she didn't get to experience the Rapture as she had so deeply hoped, her influence played a crucial role in my eventual commitment to Christ and my pursuit of a deeper understanding of the true sequence of the end times.

To my dad, Lyle Johnston, thank you for reading and refining several drafts of this book with such enthusiasm and care. Your unwavering sense of urgency that this message needed to reach the world was a great encouragement to me.

To Harold Suggs, my longtime pastor friend, thank you for walking with me through my early days as a new believer and for continuing to sharpen me along my journey. Your encouraging words and thoughtful feedback on my draft gave me inspiration to see this project through.

To Jack Hoey Jr., my friend and the smartest man I know, thank you for your discerning comments on my early draft. Your insights and penetrating questions sharpened my work and compelled me to strengthen the details.

To my nephew, Andrew Sneed, thank you for lending your innate talent to the editing process. Answering your insightful questions gave me confidence that I was on the right track.

And finally, to my sweet wife, Terry, you are the heart of this project. You supported what became my all-consuming drive to find these answers with unwavering patience and love. You never complained about the countless sacrifices you made, allowing me to spend late nights and weekends at the church, dedicating nearly every available moment of the past three years to this journey. You selflessly took on many of my responsibilities so I could continue my research uninterrupted, and you read more drafts than I can count. Terry, your belief in me, your encouragement, and your steadfast support made this book possible. I can never fully express my gratitude. From the depths of my heart, thank you.

# Contents

# Introduction

I am not a theologian, so this book does not aim to explain specific doctrines or belief systems.[1] I'm simply a believer who has spent time nearly every day for the past thirty seven years studying and marveling at the beauty and depth of God's word. As an analyst and retired Colonel, I've applied my interpretive skills to search Scripture and discern what God wants me to understand about the last days. Each time I discovered something new, I would ask myself, just as my pastor asks at the end of each sermon, "What does God want me to do about it?"

I didn't set out to challenge the core elements of the conventional end-time timeline, which traditionally begins with the opening of the seven seals, followed by the seven trumpets, followed by the seven bowls. I was simply searching through every published

---

[1] It seems there is a lot of scriptural support for Premillennialism, so I will explain it. It is the belief that Jesus will return before his 1,000 year reign. Within Premillennialism lie at least 4 different views, primarily concerned with the point in the timeline during which all believers will be escorted to heaven:
1) Pre-tribulation: believers go to heaven **before** the final 7 years begin and they completely escape tribulation
2) Mid-tribulation: believers go to heaven at the 3½ year––**the midpoint** of the final 7 years.
3) Pre-wrath: believers go to heaven at an unknown point between 3½ years and 7 years, but **before the wrath** of God is released.
4) Post-tribulation: believers go to heaven **at the very end** of the final 7 years.

timeline chart I could find, hoping to locate one that accounted for all of the prophetic verses I had collected from the Bible. When I couldn't find any that took these thousands of end-time verses into account, I had no choice but to make my own chart. This started me down a path of intense, verse-by-verse examination in search of clues to the sequence of end-time events.

Revelation is unique in many ways, but I found one aspect especially fascinating: it is the only book in the Bible that describes people being in heaven. I carefully analyzed each of the five distinct instances of humans arriving in heaven, along with details about what some had endured on earth. Hidden within these accounts are clues to the end-time timeline that are not found anywhere else in Scripture. By piecing together these clues and connecting them to events on earth, I was able to fill in critical gaps in the end-time puzzle. Throughout this detailed process, I kept Solomon's wise advice at the forefront of my mind as I searched for connections throughout the rest of Scripture.

> *What has been is what will be, and what has been done is what will be done, and there is nothing new under the sun.* (Ecclesiastes 1:9 ESV)

By scrutinizing parallels between events in the Old Testament and events in John's vision in Revelation, I began to make the connection that the seven plagues of Revelation are strikingly similar to the ten plagues of Exodus and that some of the powers of the seven trumpets of Revelation are similar to the powers Satan was given in the book of Job.

The timeline that unfolds chapter by chapter in this book is assembled from clues found in dozens of overlooked verses whose meanings have been hiding in plain sight. I include these and other more widely recognized verses to support each chapter. In the few parts of the timeline where I found no specific Scripture to rely on, I leaned heavily on the events that occurred before and after, as well as on historically similar events in the Bible, as guides. This approach allowed me to make an educated guess about what likely happened to connect one prophesied event to the next.

As each prophetic Scripture started to fall into place naturally, fitting together in a timeline so different from the standard narrative, I felt the exhilaration that comes from solving a difficult part of a puzzle. But that excitement was quickly tempered by the cautionary words of a good friend, "why would you be the only person to arrive at this understanding?" I took his advice to heart as I analyzed each word of God's Bible with even greater reverence and thoughtfulness.

The more I learn from God's Word, the more I realize just how much information can be contained within a single verse. So profound is God's message that no one will ever fully grasp every meaning and nuance he has woven within it. I think I now understand a small portion of the big picture, and even that small glimpse has given me a unique understanding of how most of the major end-time events fit within it.

The traditional views of the end-times are deeply entrenched. Well-intentioned writers, commentators, teachers, and ordinary believers will always look at end-time passages through the lenses with which they were taught, whether in seminary or by their denominational creeds.[2] [3] Holding tightly to those glasses gives

---

[2] "Topic: Denominations," *Christianity Today*, https://www.christianitytoday.com/ct/topics/d/denominations/. As of 2001, *Christianity Today* reports that there are at least 33,830 different Christian denominations in the world.

[3] Donavyn Coffey, "Why does Christianity have so many denominations?" *Live Science*, July 29, 2022, https://www.livescience.com/christianity-denominations.html. *Live Science* says there are more than 200 Christian denominations in the United States. Denominations are based on different interpretations of the same

them a sense that they are in good company. I know because I wore a pair faithfully for over 20 years and confidently shrugged off all the Scriptures that didn't seem to conform.

If this describes you, I sincerely pray that in the interest of stress-testing your understanding—or even challenging mine—you will take the uncomfortable step of removing those glasses, if only for long enough to consider these new insights from verses that most Bible readers pass right over.

> For now we see through a glass, darkly; but then face to face: now I know in part; but then shall I know even as also I am known. (1 Corinthians 13:12 KJV)

As we edge closer to the opening of the 1st seal, God will inspire spirit-filled people with new insight into even more verses that have been right before us but whose deeper meaning has been hidden until the appointed time.

---

Bible. People were so dogmatic in their specific interpretation that they divided themselves according to their own interpretation of specific Scriptures, in the same way that The Tower of Babel event ended up dividing humans based on how they could or could not interpret each other's speech.

# How to Read This Book

Here's a friendly suggestion on how best to read this book:

If you are completely new to the topic of the end times and unfamiliar with concepts like the 7 seals, 7 trumpets, or 7 bowls, I invite you to visit my website: http.www//neverunprepared.org. There, you can watch a short introductory video or read a brief overview of the end times. Either option will provide a foundation in what is currently being taught by seminaries and end-times authors.

A basic background will help you better appreciate just how groundbreaking the perspective presented in this book is, a perspective built by meticulously connecting every verse in the Bible related to the end times.

To get the full picture of the end times and discover what's driving them, start from the beginning of the book... and resist the urge to skim through the Bible passages. I've included over 900 verses, allowing the Word to speak directly to you and present its own case.

But if you're pressed for time or just want to get to the point of the book quickly to see if this is really anything different from the traditional end-time message, I suggest taking a sneak peak of Chapter 16: Seal 5. This is the first time we eavesdrop on people in heaven. You can continue to read a few more pages until the second eavesdropping moment, which is even more revealing. There are three more such moments throughout the book, but if the first two do not make you question what you thought you knew about Revelation, you might not yet be ready for the deeper insights that come to light in this book.

You'll notice that the Table of Contents is detailed and a bit lengthy. That's intentional; it's designed to double as the end-times timeline, guiding you through events in the order they'll likely unfold. Think of it as a cross-referenced roadmap for navigating the last days.

I pray that as you read, your heart and mind remain open to the promptings of the Holy Spirit. Be like the Bereans and double-check what is presented here against the Scriptures.[4]

---

[4] Acts 17:11 NIV, "Now the Berean Jews were of more noble character than those in Thessalonica, for they received the message with great eagerness and examined the Scriptures every day to see if what Paul said was true.

# Part One:

## What Is the Meaning of All This?

# 1 Don't Leave the Difficult Passages to the Bible Scholars

The 1970s was an exciting time to be an adolescent. Some of the hippie spirit of The Sixties had carried over and was still front and center in the news, but in this decade it manifested through protests against the Vietnam War or in support of women's liberation or gay rights (LGBTQ wouldn't appear for decades). Television viewers endured seemingly endless "we interrupt our regularly scheduled programming..." to give us live feeds of the Watergate hearings. Oh, for the simpler days when lying about the recording of a conversation was considered so evil it caused a president to resign! But overshadowing all of this, the ever-present possibility of imminent nuclear war enveloped our thoughts like a persistent fog. America's leaders and newscasters warned us about what Ronald Reagan later would brand "the Evil Empire." The threat of total nuclear destruction by the Soviet Union was a constant possibility. The thought of it was so horrible that most of us chose not to dwell on it and carried on with our lives.

I found solace in dreaming about a future living in space, unmoored from the concerns of this world. I escaped into the magically perfect world of science fiction, reading books on artificial intelligence, interstellar space travel, robots, and otherworldly life. One day in middle school, as I searched for another book to feed my endless sci-fi appetite, I came across a worn paperback copy of Hal Lindsay's *The Late Great Planet Earth*. I was drawn to the title, assuming it was apocalyptic science fiction, one of my favorite genres. While the title attracted me, the straightforward, authoritative message of what would happen to those alive during the end-times kept me turning its pages. By the time I was through, I knew exactly what was going to transpire and learned that it could happen at any moment. Although I'd only been to church a few times, I believed I would be one of those lucky ones taken away before all the bad stuff started.

Hal Lindsay's book gave me so much hope that I confidently told friends what was going to happen and what to watch for before that day. Though it would be 14 years before my faith journey brought me to a relationship with Jesus, God still used my young, unsaved soul that had never read more than a verse or two from the Bible to tell others about his plan for the end-times. I found that most people had a thirst to know what the future held.

When I accepted Jesus, I quickly got hooked on the wisdom I found in his Word. I set aside my secular books and began reading the Bible and books about the Bible. I soon discovered that there were lots of authors writing about the end-times. The theme was always the same: watch for the warning signs, then there would be a catching away of the saints, and then the wrath of God would break loose on the rest of the unfortunate, unsuspecting, and unbelieving world. That end-time theme was the lens through which I read the Bible over the next 20 years.

My analytical nature led me to methodically read through the entire Bible each year. When I came to a verse related to the end-times, I would subconsciously categorize it as either a verse that pertained to me or a verse I could breeze through because it would only apply to those poor souls who would be left behind. I put my trust in the end-time authors and Bible scholars who could devote more time to decipher all of those difficult verses scattered throughout the Bible. I simply adopted their conclusions and didn't see a need to research the matter myself.

Twenty years into my systematic annual Bible-reading plan, I adjusted the timing so that I would complete the Bible every three years. This allowed me the freedom to spend more time researching passages that were still puzzling. By this point, I had a strong enough baseline knowledge of the Bible that I felt it was safe to begin to learn about different world religions. I wanted to understand the faith of others so that I could better relate to and possibly reach them.

This three-year reading program allowed me time to focus on the many verses I had previously categorized as only pertaining to those who would be left behind. Yet, as I collected more and more of those "nonapplicable" verses, it eventually became evident that something wasn't adding up. Who did all those verses apply to? According to most authors I had read, once the tribulation began, the Christians would be gone. So, how would the people who had been left behind get their hands on a Bible, let alone understand enough of what they were reading to find their way to God?

One day, while talking with a missionary friend, he casually mentioned that he had just renewed his yearly commitment to his ordaining denomination. However, he was feeling a bit frustrated with one of its core beliefs. He explained that he could find just as many Bible verses supporting a post-tribulation rapture as he could for a pre-tribulation rapture. This made him question why his denomination required all ministers to affirm this single point of view. The uncertainty of this learned man of God added water to the seed of doubt that had already been germinating in my mind. And that seed grew a little more each time I came to yet another verse that seemed to support one philosophy over another. The end-time message was not as clear-cut as all these writers and pastors I admire made it seem. So, I decided that I could no longer naively accept their narratives and would research the matter myself.

What I discovered is that the last days are far more than a series of unfortunate events drawn neatly on a timeline chart. The big picture is the "why." Why does there have to be a Great Tribulation at all? Once I discovered that amazing answer, everything else—the who, what, where, and when—fell into place more easily. Then as I applied what I learned from eavesdropping on the conversations in heaven, every end-times event began to align, unveiling a timeline of breathtakingly clear simplicity. But it also became clear that the final seven years, the last "week" of Daniel 9:27, affect more than just humans. As Revelation 5:13b indicates, *"every creature in heaven and on earth and under the earth..."* has an existential stake in the outcomes. Some will be rewarded with *"everlasting life and some to shame and everlasting disgrace"* (Daniel 12:2 NLT).

# 2 In Search of the Box Cover for the End-Times Puzzle

Nearly every book in the Bible has at least an allusion to the last days. I found over 5,000 verses in 62 out of the 66 books that dealt with some aspect of the latter days, so it's clear God did not intend for us to skim-over those end-time verses. But if he wants us to understand it, why did he make it such a complicated puzzle? Why did he inspire 36 different writers across 1,500 years to explain different pieces of the end-times using perplexing imagery like beasts, horns, horses, goats, locusts, dragons, mountains, and a multitude of other symbols? Why didn't the prophets just come out and say what God wanted us to know in clear, unmistakable language, or at least use parables and then explain them like Jesus did?

Biblical prophecies are meant to be understood at just the right time. God reveals them in a way that only becomes clear when the moment arrives, and sometimes only after the moment has happened. This ensures that his people remain devoted to following him in the present, rather than assuming they have plenty of time to put off following him simply because they believe the end-time events won't happen in their lifetime. Yet, God also tells us ahead of time what is to come so that when it happens, that generation will recognize that nothing surprises him—that he has known from the beginning what will come.

Day by day, he calls us to continue to grow his kingdom, to *"be fruitful and multiply,"* to *"go into the world and make disciples of all nations. . ."*[5] Ultimately, God desires that we lead others to a relationship with him right up until our own last day.

---

[5] Genesis 1:28 ESV: *And God blessed them. And God said to them, "Be fruitful and*

Once we have a firm foundation and understanding of God's Word, we can start to look at the end-time pieces he carefully placed throughout the Bible and begin to put the puzzle together. But no matter how deeply we search, some of the pieces will, by God's design, remain obscure until we get closer to the events. That's one of the great marvels of God's word; after each prophecy has been fulfilled, we find that it had been right in front of us in the Bible, but we just couldn't understand its deeper meaning until the proper time.

Analysts understand that before diving into the details, you must first grasp the big picture. Without it, knowing what specifics to tackle can become overwhelming and inefficient. While this concept may seem straightforward, achieving a full understanding of a problem is often more challenging than simply jumping into the minutiae.

Consider my wife's experience with puzzles. She has completed dozens of 1,000-piece puzzles, typically taking her 15 to 20 hours. But when she attempted a 1,500-piece puzzle, the pieces were much smaller which increased the difficulty exponentially. She quickly realized she couldn't just start with a quick glance at the box cover and then begin fitting the pieces together. Instead, she spent time carefully studying the box cover, intricately examining the entire image to identify very subtle distinctions in colors and patterns. Only then did she begin sorting the pieces into sections that corresponded with those patterns, allowing her to work efficiently and with purpose.

You can special-order 5,000-piece puzzles, but their tiny pieces make their complexity exponentially greater, likely requiring a week

---

*multiply and fill the earth and subdue it, and have dominion over the fish of the sea and over the birds of the heavens and over every living thing that moves on the earth."* Matthew 28:19 ESV: *"Go therefore and make disciples of all nations, baptizing them in the name of the Father and of the Son and of the Holy Spirit"*

or more for the most dedicated puzzle enthusiast to solve. But what if your 5,000-piece puzzle arrived with most of the picture on the box cover torn away? And, what if, unbeknownst to you, the seller withheld 70 key pieces to ensure it would not be completely solved until he sent them to you? Trying to assemble it by meticulously fitting each tiny, dime-sized piece with another with no picture to follow would be virtually impossible. To put it simply, the box cover, the big picture, is crucial to solving a complex puzzle.

Finding the big picture is rarely as simple as locating the box cover of a puzzle. But you must have *something* to use as a guide so that you can begin to map out the general color schemes and start to sift through the pile of 4,930 pieces and begin to sort them. Many end-time authors and creators of timelines gave up trying to find the big picture and dove right into examining the individual Scripture pieces and tried their best to force them to fit together.

In the case of the end-times, where would you start to look for the big picture? Most would guess Revelation, Matthew 24 or Daniel 9. While each is a critical part of the puzzle, none of them provide a complete picture. Even re-reading every end-time verse by category did not help me find the big picture. For example, is the *"falling away"* of the believers part of the seven-year timeline? Or does it occur as a birth pang before the timeline begins?

As I started creating my own chart, I needed to identify each end-time event and start plotting the dots, beginning with what seemed to be the most unmistakable events in the timeline. A few passages are certain: the signing of the covenant initiates the final seven-year countdown, the abomination of desolation occurs at the midpoint, and the Day of the Lord comes at the end. With so many differing views on when believers will be removed from earth, I decided not to focus on that aspect initially, opting to see where it might naturally fit as the timeline took shape.

However, there are critical events in biblical prophecy for which the timing is either unclear or appears contradictory. One of the most pivotal questions is: when does the Wrath of God actually begin? Does it start with the opening of the seven seals, the sounding of the seven trumpets, the pouring of the seven bowls of plagues, or at some other point in the timeline? While many commentators agree on the timing of God's wrath, the prophetic verses I've gathered strongly indicate that this consensus is flawed. As this book progresses, I will demonstrate how the Wrath of God actually begins during a different, pivotal, though often overlooked, event, at a point that changes our entire understanding of the end-times timeline.

Since Revelation was the last book of the Bible penned, I started from the premise that John was inspired to write his letter to tie-up many loose ends in other prophetic Scripture. A deep analysis of Revelation unveiled many surprising clues but didn't answer enough questions to allow me to put all the end-time pieces together. Understanding the big picture turned out to be much more challenging than I had expected.

I soon realized that gaining this perspective required looking beyond just the end-times passages. So, I went back to the beginning of the Bible, setting aside my preconceptions and reexamining each verse with fresh eyes.

*"Truly, I say to you, unless you turn and become like children, you will never enter the kingdom of heaven."* (Matthew 18:3 ESV)

# 3 Creating a Free Spirit

*For thus saith the LORD that created the heavens;*
*God himself that formed the earth and made it; he*
*hath established it, he created it not in vain, he formed*
*it to be inhabited: I am the LORD; and there is none*
*else.* (Isaiah 45:18 KJV)

There is a beautiful order in nature. We are designed to appreciate that order and to know when something is out of order. We recognize disorder.

God created order on the first day because he *is* order. His universe, with its immutable physical laws, served as the embroidery lattices upon which wondrous threads were fantastically woven, inspiring and sustaining life within his well-ordered framework. God created all life, and it was marvelous and beautiful.

*And God saw everything that he had made, and*
*behold, it was very good. And there was evening and*
*there was morning, the sixth day.* (Genesis 1:31 ESV)

But God intended more than just life and beauty for his own delight. He wanted part of his creation to have the ability to truly marvel at what he had made, experiencing awe and a genuine reverence for him as their Creator.

*Worthy are you, our Lord and God, to receive glory and*
*honor and power, for you created all things, and by your*
*will they existed and were created.* (Revelation 4:11 ESV)

The God of order did not desire subjects who mindlessly recite praises out of fear, like those who flatter a dictator under threat. Instead, he sought true, heartfelt love—people capable of genuinely admiring him, understanding him, and marveling at his creation. His desire was not to demand adoration but to inspire it, inviting a worship that was authentic, unforced, and rooted in awe. By granting humanity the freedom to question, explore, and seek understanding, God allowed each person to encounter him on their own terms and, through that journey, to recognize his worthiness. He wanted people who would choose, with open eyes and open hearts, to offer him their love and praise.

God established a set of laws within which the universe operates to maintain order. Yet, for freedom to be real, alternatives must exist—specifically, the freedom to break those laws. Herein lies the inherent risk: order is a precise, harmonious balance, and any alternative to it inevitably leads to disorder. Disorder breeds chaos, and as more laws are disregarded, chaos intensifies. Left unchecked, this chaos threatens to unravel creation itself, spiraling toward destruction and even annihilation.

> . . . but of the tree of the knowledge of good and evil you shall not eat, for in the day that you eat of it you shall surely die. (Genesis 2:17 ESV)

Yet God understood that this risk was essential to elicit a sincere, uncoerced decision from his creation. He granted people the freedom to choose, fully aware of the immense cost this freedom would one day place at his Son's feet, who would willingly bear the ultimate sacrifice to redeem those who came to believe in and truly love God but were lost and held captive in the chaos of Satan's kingdom. These repentant people, having come to understand and genuinely revere their Creator and yearning to return to the perfect order of his embrace, could now do so because Jesus made a way.

# 3.1 Paradise Lost: The Antagonist

God created one of his beings with such perfection that this highest of angels eventually came to believe that he deserved to be equal to or even above God and, through his pride, became the antagonist, the alternative to God's perfect plan.

> *You were blameless in your ways from the day you were created, till* unrighteousness was found in you. (Ezekiel 28:15 ESV)

> *You said in your heart, 'I will ascend to heaven; above the stars of God I will set my throne on high; I will sit on the mount of assembly in the far reaches of the north; I will ascend above the heights of the clouds;* I will make myself like the Most High.' (Isaiah 14:13–14 ESV)

God was not surprised when Eve succumbed to this traitorous angel's temptation. He already knew that man would not be able to resist exploring chaos. So, *"since the foundation of the world,"* which means even before he created humans, God designed an elaborate plan to bring those future humans who were willing back into fellowship with him. Some parts of this plan were revealed through his prophets, but the full meaning of those prophecies would remain hidden until the right time. The time came about 2,000 years ago to reveal a major portion of that plan, which allowed people to rediscover God and provided a way, through his Son, to be reconciled to him. However, portions of this plan remain obscure because the proper time has not yet come for their revelation.

*This was to fulfill what was spoken by the prophet: "I will open my mouth in parables; I will utter what has been hidden since the foundation of the world."* (Matthew 13:35 ESV)

God's plan still depends on people freely choosing to follow his plan and accept him.

## 3.2 Good Order Requires Good Bookkeeping

As the God of order, he documented many things from day one in several books, one of which is the Lamb's Book of Life, containing the names of all who would freely choose him.

> . . . and all who dwell on earth will worship it [the beast], everyone whose name has not been written before the foundation of the world in the book of life of the Lamb who was slain . . . (Revelation 13:8 ESV)

This is probably the same book mentioned in Psalms:

> Let them be blotted out of the book of the living; let them not be enrolled among the righteous. (Psalm 69:8 ESV)

Malachi told us there is also a Book of Remembrance.

> Then those who feared the LORD spoke with one another. The LORD paid attention and heard them, and a book of remembrance was written before him of those who feared the LORD and esteemed his name. (Malachi 3:16 ESV)

Daniel mentions the book of life above, but he also mentions another book, the book of truth:

> But I will tell you what is inscribed in the book of truth: there is none who contends by my side against these except Michael, your prince. (Daniel 10:21 ESV)

But the book that is most important for deciphering the last days is the book sealed with 7 seals. That book lists the events and rules necessary to become ruler of the Kingdoms of the World.[6] The presence of this rulebook in the right hand of God is a major part of the big picture.

> *And I saw in the right hand of him that sat on the throne a book written within and on the backside, sealed with seven seals.* (Revelation 5:1 KJV)

The 7-sealed book describes the main characters who must arise and what each of them will do. Amazingly, it gives us glimpses of what will happen in heaven during portions of the last 3½ years of the end-times. It also provides a relative framework for the timing of the events that will precede the Day of the Lord, the day on which Jesus will bring an end to Satan's kingdom of chaos and take his place as the new King of the World. Jesus will finally restore order to creation, something that creation has longed for ever since order was lost when Adam forfeited his dominion.

> *We know that the whole creation has been groaning as in the pains of childbirth right up to the present time.* (Romans 8:22 NIV)

We'll discuss this 7-sealed book in more detail later.

---

[6] "The roll, or book, appears from the context to be 'the title-deed of man's inheritance' [De Burgh] redeemed by Christ, and contains the successive steps by which He shall recover it from its usurper and obtain actual possession of the kingdom already 'purchased' for Himself and His elect saints. . . Re 20:12, 'Another book was opened. . . the book of life'; Re 22:19. None is worthy to do so save the Lamb, for He alone as such has redeemed man's forfeited inheritance, of which the book is the title-deed" (Bible Hub. "Revelation 5:1." Jamieson-Fausset-Brown Bible Commentary. https://biblehub.com/commentaries/revelation/5-1.htm.).

# 3.3 God Keeps His Promises

God's plan was established from the very beginning and will never need revision. There is no need for a Plan B. He has chosen to reveal key parts of this plan through his prophets over the centuries, not only to prove that he is a God of order and justice but also to demonstrate that his plan will unfold exactly as he told us it will, no matter what.

> "For the Lord GOD does nothing without revealing his secret to his servants the prophets." (Amos 3:7 ESV)

Once God makes a proclamation through a prophet, he cannot lie and so has obligated himself to ensuring it comes to pass. God isn't surprised by the decisions we make, including Adam's. Neither our choices nor Satan's can derail his master plan.

Sometimes, God must even bring things back into existence to keep his plan on track. For example, his prophecies tell us that the country of Israel will play a key role in the end-times.

> "Behold, I am with you and will keep you wherever you go, and will bring you back to this land. For I will not leave you until I have done what I have promised you." (Genesis 28:15 ESV)

> "I will surely assemble all of you, O Jacob; I will gather the remnant of Israel; I will set them together like sheep in a fold, like a flock in its pasture, a noisy multitude of men." (Micah 2:12 ESV)

Until a few decades ago, the fulfillment of that prophecy seemed absolutely impossible because Israel had been utterly destroyed about forty years after Jesus was crucified. For nearly 1,900 years, there was no such thing as Israel and its former citizens, the Jews, were scattered across dozens of nations spanning multiple continents. For centuries, theologians struggled to make sense of the prophecies about a future Israel because no country, once destroyed and disbanded, had ever reappeared. How could these prophecies possibly be fulfilled? Then, against all odds, on May 14, 1948, the state of Israel was miraculously re-established, teaching us that God's plan could not be derailed.[7] His Word will be fulfilled, even when it seems impossible from our perspective.

We also see God's immovable plan in Jesus' first coming. Jesus' mission was impossibly precise, and specific events had to happen at exactly the right moment to fulfill the dozens of detailed prophecies and allow God's grand plan to unfold exactly as foretold in each prophecy.

> *"From that time Jesus began to show his disciples that he must go to Jerusalem and suffer many things from the elders and chief priests and scribes, and be killed, and on the third day be raised."* (Matthew 16:21 ESV)

As much as it surely pained God (and Jesus), Jesus knew the plan had to be fulfilled exactly as published in the Word. He said as much here:

> *"Do you think that I cannot appeal to my Father, and he will at once send me more than twelve legions of angels? But how then should the scriptures be fulfilled, that it must be so?"* (Matthew 26:53-54 ESV)

---

[7] https://www.history.com/this-day-in-history/state-of-israel-proclaimed

While God allows us free will, giving us the ability to make our own choices, he has also established boundaries to prevent our actions from derailing his plan. Just like he set limits for the oceans, saying, *"This far you may come, but no farther, and here your proud waves must stop!"* (Job 38:11 NKJV), he has set limits on how far evil and chaos can spread.

This means that God sometimes intervenes in the affairs of rulers to ensure his plan stays on course.

> *"The king's heart is a stream of water in the hand of the LORD; he turns it wherever he will."*
> (Proverbs 21:1 ESV)

An example of these boundaries is seen in Kim Jong Un, the dictator of North Korea. While he holds unchecked power and uses his free will to sometimes commit horrific acts, there are limits to how far he can go. For instance, he can't simply decide to detonate all his nuclear weapons and destroy the earth's atmosphere in a moment of rage. This isn't because we trust in his rationality, but because God has promised that life on earth will endure, even through the darkest times of the Great Tribulation.

> *"While the earth remains, seedtime and harvest, cold and heat, summer and winter, day and night, shall not cease."* (Genesis 8:22 ESV)

God's promises act as guardrails for creation, and understanding them brings great comfort. If more people truly believed his promises, there would be far less fear and anxiety in the world.

## 3.4 When Free Will Goes Out of Bounds

Here are several examples of God stepping in to ensure his plan remains on track when mankind began to try to push the boundaries God placed on his creation.

1. After Satan succeeded in tempting the humans to eat the fruit from the Tree of Knowledge of Good and Evil, God stepped in and made man and his offspring eternal enemies of Satan so they could not conspire together again.

   > The LORD God said to the serpent, *"Because you have done this, cursed are you above all livestock and above all beasts of the field; on your belly you shall go, and dust you shall eat all the days of your life. 15 I will put enmity between you and the woman, and between your offspring and her offspring; he shall bruise your head, and you shall bruise his heel."* (Genesis 3:14–15 ESV)

2. Later, God limited man's life to 120 years to give him less opportunity to descend into chaos (Genesis 6:3).
3. When mankind had become so evil that almost every person had spiraled into sin and his creation was heading for total chaos, God stepped in and destroyed them all in the Great Flood, save Noah's family, and started mankind over (Genesis 6:13).
4. After that great cleansing flood, God guaranteed the earth wouldn't become too warm or too hot, and the sun wouldn't fail.

*While the earth remains, seedtime and harvest, cold*
*and heat, summer and winter, day and night,* shall not
cease. (Genesis 8:22 ESV)

5. Several hundred years later, when men conspired together to circumvent God and make their way directly to heaven by building the colossal Tower of Babel, God again stepped in because by working together, they were advancing faster than the timeline. He slowed them down by dividing their language, which made it very difficult for them to conspire (Genesis 11:6–8).

6. Over a thousand years later, under Nebuchadnezzar, the city of evil rose again, and again defied God's authority. When Nebuchadnezzar claimed to be as mighty as God, he was humbled and cast into the wilderness, where he lived like an animal, eating grass like a cow.[8] John reveals that Babylon will rise one final time in the last days, becoming the center of the antichrist's ultimate attempt to defy and overthrow God's authority. Yet, as in every act of rebellion throughout its history, God will destroy Babylon, but this time forever.

7. In the future, at the end of the Great Tribulation, when Satan is on the brink of totally destroying the earth, John tells us that God will step in again so that his people, *"the elect,"* will be saved.

---

[8] Daniel 4:29-33 (ESV) *"At the end of twelve months he was walking on the roof of the royal palace of Babylon, 30 and the king answered and said, "Is not this great Babylon, which I have built by my mighty power as a royal residence and for the glory of my majesty?" 31 While the words were still in the king's mouth, there fell a voice from heaven, "O King Nebuchadnezzar, to you it is spoken: The kingdom has departed from you, 32 and you shall be driven from among men, and your dwelling shall be with the beasts of the field. And you shall be made to eat grass like an ox, and seven periods of time shall pass over you, until you know that the Most High rules the kingdom of men and gives it to whom he will." 33 Immediately the word was fulfilled against Nebuchadnezzar. He was driven from among men and ate grass like an ox, and his body was wet with the dew of heaven till his hair grew as long as eagles' feathers, and his nails were like birds' claws."*

*And if those days had not been cut short, no human being would be saved. But for the sake of the elect those days will be cut short.* (Matthew 24:22 ESV)

When he steps in to *"cut short"* the destruction of the earth, which we'll read about in the 6th seal chapter, God's sudden presence will be dramatic and unmistakable.

# 4 Key Books of the Bible Are Not in Order

You would expect most books to convey information in chronological order. While that's generally true for most books of the Bible, there are many exceptions. Psalms and Proverbs come to mind as two books that are not in chronological order. Proverbs is a collection of wise sayings. Psalms are prayers that cover different periods in the lives of several authors who sought help from the Lord, lamented over the wicked getting away with something, or just wanted to marvel at the Lord's goodness. About half of the Psalms are attributed to David, but they are not in any definable order and certainly are not arranged chronologically. You can argue that many of the Psalms are loosely grouped by theme, but there are many exceptions. What's more, there are Psalms from other writers intermixed among those believed to be written by David. But this lack of order doesn't make Psalms any less important in helping us understand the heart of God or providing the words to pray for something we may be going through at the moment.

Daniel is another book that reads as though it's in order, but it's not. It's probably the most essential Old Testament book for understanding key parts of the end-times. It's Daniel who tells us about the sequence of dynasties who would each take their turn ruling over the region containing Jerusalem. And it's Daniel who tells us that the final empire will be the *"toes of iron mixed with clay."*[9] He's also the prophet who explained that it would be seventy weeks between the time of the commandment to restore the temple in

---

[9] Daniel 2:32–33 ESV: "2:32 *The head of this image was of fine gold, its chest and arms of silver, its middle and thighs of bronze, 33 its legs of iron, its feet partly of iron and partly of clay."*

Jerusalem and the *"coming of the anointed one"* (Jesus).[10] Daniel is also the one who tells us the end-times will last seven years (*"one week"*).[11] In Revelation, John assumes that his readers already know about this 70th week when he begins his descriptions of what will happen during that final seven-year period.

When I organized Daniel's chapters into a matrix and aligned them based on the event each verse describes, the results were eye-opening. The matrix revealed that Daniel describes the same events in multiple chapters. For example, the first verses of Chapter 10 are almost a repetition of Chapter 9, but they use different wording and imagery. Similarly, Chapter 8 describes the same events as Chapter 7 but presents them with different language and symbolism. This method of modified reiteration is similar to the way in which the Pharaoh was given two different dreams, one about seven cows and another about seven stalks of grain. As Joseph interpreted those dreams, he told the Pharaoh that God had given the same message in two different ways to confirm that it would happen.[12] Since Psalms, Proverbs, and Daniel demonstrate that it's not unusual for the contents of books of the Bible to be out of chronological order, we should not be surprised that Revelation does not follow a chronological order.

---

[10] Daniel 9:24–25 ESV: *"Seventy weeks are decreed about your people and your holy city, to finish the transgression, to put an end to sin, and to atone for iniquity, to bring in everlasting righteousness, to seal both vision and prophet, and to anoint a most holy place. 25 Know therefore and understand that from the going out of the word to restore and build Jerusalem to the coming of an anointed one, a prince, there shall be seven weeks. Then for sixty-two weeks it shall be built again with squares and moat, but in a troubled time."*

[11] Seven days (one week) is symbolic for seven years. Daniel 9:27 NET *"He will confirm a covenant with many for one week. But in the middle of that week he will bring sacrifices and offerings to a halt. On the wing of abominations will come one who destroys, until the decreed end is poured out on the one who destroys."*

[12] Genesis 41:1-46 Describes the Egyptian Pharaoh's dream and Daniel's interpretation.

# 4.1 Revelation is Not in Order, but is Purposefully Structured

Many readers and authors assume that the events in Revelation are described in the order that they will happen, believing that the events in Chapter 6 will occur before those in Chapter 8, and the events in Chapter 9 will happen before those in Chapter 16. However, even a casual reader will quickly notice that many significant events don't make sense in the order in which they are recorded in Revelation. But Revelation does have a kind of order. When John describes a particular group of things, such as 7 seals or 7 bowls, he's conveying that each element within that group will appear in the order he describes. But he's not telling us that the entire group will be complete before the next group of elements he describes will happen. An easy way to demonstrate this is through the grouping of the three flying angels, which I refer to later as Whispering Angels One, Two, and Three.

> *6 Then I saw another angel* [the first] *flying directly overhead, with an eternal gospel to proclaim to those who dwell on earth, to every nation and tribe and language and people. 7 And he said with a loud voice, "Fear God and give him glory, because the hour of his judgment has come, and worship him who made heaven and earth, the sea and the springs of water."*

> *8 Another angel, a second, followed, saying, "Fallen, fallen is Babylon the great, she who made all nations drink the wine of the passion of her sexual immorality."*

*9 And another angel, a third, followed them, saying with a loud voice, "If anyone worships the beast and its image and receives a mark on his forehead or on his hand, 10 he also will drink the wine of God's wrath, poured full strength into the cup of his anger, and he will be tormented with fire and sulfur in the presence of the holy angels and in the presence of the Lamb."* (Revelation 14:6–10 ESV)

These circumnavigating angels don't herald their warnings to humans on earth until the 14th chapter of Revelation when, if you subscribe to the sequential order of Revelation, most of the bad things have already happened. It would be pretty cruel of God to send these warnings to people one right after the other when it was already too late for them to do anything in response. By this time, if Revelation were written in order, the 7 seals would have already been opened by Chapter 8, and the trumpets would have been finished by Chapter 11, where more than 1/3rd of humans were killed. Yet somehow, God doesn't see fit to send his first angel to alert the unchurched world to the message of the gospel until Chapter 14, after all those billions of people have died horrible deaths.[13] I find that difficult to believe.

Additionally, if one subscribes to the literal order of Revelation, one would have to believe that God had a mean streak to allow a billion or more people to be enticed or coerced into accepting the mark of the beast in Chapter 13, and then, in the middle of Chapter 14, finally, sends his angel to warn everyone <u>not</u> to get the mark of the beast. Because at the point that the second angel flies to warn

---

[13] Matthew 24:14 tells us the gospel will be preached to the whole world just before the end comes. While missionary work is critical and commanded, I'm certain Jesus was referring to this first Whispering Angel who will preach to every single person at the same time, in their own language, customized to their own ability to understand.

the world, most of the unchurched world would have already taken the mark because they didn't know any better.

This means that there would be billions of non-Christians who had no idea who the God of the Bible was, let alone that God forbade them from getting the mark. If these three angels deliver their messages at the point they appear in Revelation, they would be too late to make any lifesaving difference. In fact, their messages would serve no purpose except to make God appear calculatingly heartless.

But we know that "heartless" is the antithesis of our God. God always warns us, usually over and over, and always in time to change our ways. In fact, God told us that if the people are not warned, he will hold the watchman, or in this case, the three angels, responsible for their deaths.

> But if the watchman sees the enemy coming and doesn't sound the alarm to warn the people, he is responsible for their captivity. They will die in their sins, but I will hold the watchman responsible for their deaths. (Ezekiel 33:6 NLT)

At that late point (Chapter 14), he's effectively telling those on earth: "I know it's too late for you, but I just wanted to let you know that you're all going to hell." This is contrary to the character of God because he does not want anyone to go to hell.

> The Lord is not slow to fulfill his promise as some count slowness, but is patient toward you, not wishing that any should perish, but that all should reach repentance. (2 Peter 3:9 ESV)

I maintain that by grouping these three angels, John is telling us that at three totally different points in his vision, he saw flying angels doing similar things: proclaiming important messages. So, he grouped the flying angels together in the order he saw them, but not at the exact time in the sequence of events that he saw them. It looks like he did the same thing with just about every other grouping he describes, including the trumpets and the bowls.

My point is that Revelation is organized, but it is not describing end-time events in order, as readers expect. Readers expect Revelation to unfold like a story in sequence. When you ask many Christians what they think of Revelation, most say it is confusing, hard to follow, and they couldn't get through it. I wholeheartedly agree that it is confusing, until you understand the systematic and orderly way John narrates the major events of his fast-moving and detailed vision. His reporting method worked well to describe all the events he saw in a way that was as concise as possible. Providing a specific order of events would have required much more explanation and would have made Revelation a much longer letter.

The primary reason we can infer that John was giving us lists rather than writing in chronological order is by his prolific use of the word "*and*" to begin most of his thoughts.[14][15] *And,* or its Greek equivalent, *kai,* is a conjunction tying two thoughts together.[16] *And* does not imply any particular order. Here's a specific and very consequential example:

---

[14] I use the word *thoughts* rather than *verses* because, technically, the language John used, Greek, has no verses or even punctuation. Verse and chapter divisions were added much later ("Question: Who divided the Bible into chapters and verses?" Got Questions, last updated January 4, 2022. https://www.gotquestions.org/divided-Bible-chapters-verses.html).

[15] Of the 404 verses (KJV) of Revelation, 265 verses begin with *and*, 14 begin with *and when*, and 8 begin with *after*.

[16] Vine's Expository Dictionary of New Testament Words, Blue Letter Bible, "Kai," https://www.blueletterbible.org/search/Dictionary/viewTopic.cfm?topic=VT0003445

*And I saw the seven angels which stood before God; and*
*to them were given seven trumpets.* (Revelation 8:2 KJV)

This verse begins with *kai*, which, as we've noted previously, is the word John uses to document another group of things he sees in his vision. Yet nothing in verse 8:2 ties it to the previous verse:

*And when he had opened the seventh seal, there was*
*silence in heaven about the space of half an hour.*
(Revelation 8:1 KJV)

Even though verse 8:2 deals with an entirely different subject than the previous verse, many translators attempt to relate it to the previous verse by substituting the ill-suited adverb *'then'* for *'and'* (*kai*).[17] This substitution is misleading and indicates that the translators were influenced by their own preconceived idea of the order because verse 8:2 is just another one of the 265 Revelation verses that begin with *kai (and)*.

John uses a distinct methodology in Revelation. *"And"* meant that John was moving on to describe another group of things, a group of 7 trumpets in this case. John conveyed an order when he thought it important. He occasionally begins his thoughts with *"and when"* or *"after,"* which is what you would use if you wanted to denote an order. When John wants to say, *"and when,"* he uses the Greek *hote* or *hotan*.[18] He starts thoughts with *hote* or *hotan*

---

[17] Several versions substitute *then* for *and*. These are some of the versions which translate *kai* as *then* instead of the normal *and* in this verse: ESV, Amplified Bible, Christian Standard, Good News Translation, NET, and Weymouth.

[18] Blue Letter Bible, "ὅτε," https://www.blueletterbible.org/lexicon/g3753/kjv/tr/66-1/#lexResults. "When:--after (that), as soon as, that, when, while." Blue Letter Bible, "G3753--*hote*--Strong's Greek Lexicon (kjv)." Accessed 12 Apr, 2024. https://www.blueletterbible.org/lexicon/g3753/kjv/tr/66-1/#lexResults

only 14 times (from over 400 verses), so whenever it occurs, it merits particular attention (see Exhibit 1). When John meant to say, *"after this,"* he used *meta*.[19] There are only eight verses where he began his thoughts with *meta, and they* can be seen in Exhibit 2.

There are 22 verses that use language that could indicate an order, but only one appears to be useful in showing how any major event fits together.[20] In other words, on its surface, John gives us no indication of whether the two witnesses appear before or after the abomination, if the 7 seals are opened before the 7 trumpets, if the three angels fly before or after their warnings would be effective, and so on. Though John's letter filled in many gaps, it seems he deliberately avoided overtly conveying the order of events. There could be several reasons why John chose not to clearly reveal the sequence:

1. John wanted to obscure the order for current political reasons,
2. He did not think the order was relevant,
3. He believed that prior authors of the Bible already provided all that we needed to know,
4. He wove clues into his letter that, at the appointed time, would be found and would establish the order.

I believe it was the latter reason.

---

[19] Blue Letter Bible, "Meta," Strong's #G3326. "Biblical usage: with, after, behind." https://www.blueletterbible.org/lexicon/g3326/kjv/tr/66-1/#lexResults. Blue Letter Bible, "meta," Strong's Greek Lexicon (kjv). Accessed 12 Apr, 2024. https://www.blueletterbible.org/lexicon/g3326/kjv/tr/66-1/#lexResults

[20] There is one exception. In 7:1, *after this* helps confirm that heavenly and earthly silence immediately follows the 6th seal events described in the verses immediately preceding 7:1. If *after this* was not used, we would think the silence was just another thing happening in no particular order.

# 4.1 (A) Chronology in Revelation is Not What it Seems

Once you've read Revelation completely a few times, several things become apparent:

1. The reader is unlikely to understand much of what John describes unless they are already familiar with many Old Testament prophecies about the latter days, and John assumes they are. For example, when John uses a specific period of time, such as 1,260 days and 3½ years, he assumes that his readers are familiar with Daniel's prophecy of the 70 weeks of 7 in Daniel 9:24, so he doesn't waste words explaining them.

2. John recalls and expands upon descriptions from Old Testament prophets so that his readers will understand that his portrayals are not replacing those of the prophets, they are adding information and filling in gaps. For example, the fantastic celestial events that John describes as occurring when the 6th seal is opened would have already been familiar to the Jews and Christians who knew Joel's apocalyptic descriptions of the end-times. John was just letting his readers know that he was providing more context to many of the latter-day events.

3. John groups similar events together to keep his letter systematic, like a catalog of lists, and makes almost no overt attempt to provide an order of those events. Some of the most notable groupings are lists of seven: seven churches, candlesticks, spirits,

heads, crowns, horns, seals, and trumpets.[21] There are more than 50 occurrences of the number 7 in Revelation.[22]

One possible explanation for Revelation's unique structure, which lists events followed later by further details sprinkled throughout the letter, is that John was organizing a large amount of information and was trying to keep the letter reasonably short. For instance, when John describes the seals, he quickly summarizes the first 6 seals in succession. However, it's obvious that what is transpiring in most of those seals will take months to unfold. In subsequent chapters, John returns to some of those seals and provides more details.

Let's take the 5th seal as a clear example of how John introduces an event and then gradually provides more details across several chapters. In Chapter 6, John presents a powerful and somber image of countless martyred souls gathered under the altar in heaven, but he doesn't explain why they were martyred or the manner in which they were killed. He doesn't begin to reveal the answer until Chapter 13, in which he describes how everyone is forced to accept the mark of the beast on their right hand or forehead. Then, in Chapter 14, the third angel warns humanity that God's judgment will fall on anyone who accepts the mark of the beast. Finally, in Chapter 20, John reveals the specific details: those who refuse to renounce their faith in Jesus and thereby reject the mark of the beast are beheaded, becoming the martyred souls John first introduced back in Chapter 6.

---

[21] By cataloging one group of elements after another, with no obvious indication of order, an uninformed reader, such as John's captor, would be hard-pressed to make much sense of his letter.

[22] "The List of Sevens in Revelation," agapebiblestudy.com, https://agapebiblestudy.com/charts/Chart%20of%207s%20in%20Revelation.htm

| Order event will happen | Martyr Verses Listed in the **Order in Which the Events will Happen** | | Order verse Appears in Revelation | |
|---|---|---|---|---|
| ⬇ 1 | The third Whispering Angel warns everyone not to get the mark of the beast. | | 14:9-10 | 3rd |
| 2 | The mark of the beast is forced upon everyone. | | 13:16-17 | 2nd |
| 3 | We find out what happens to those who refused the mark: they are beheaded. | | 20:04 | 4th |
| 4 | The 5th seal martyrs arrive in heaven. They have been "*slain. . . for the witness they had borne*," (but we don't yet know how or why they were slain) | | 6:09 | 1st |

| Order event will happen | Martyr Verses Listed in the **Order in Which the Verses Appear in Revelation** | | Order verse Appears in Revelation | |
|---|---|---|---|---|
| 4 | The 5th seal martyrs arrive in heaven. They have been "*slain. . . for the witness they had borne*," (but we don't yet know how or why they were slain) | | 6:09 | ⬇ 1st |
| 2 | The mark of the beast is forced upon everyone. | | 13:16-17 | 2nd |
| 1 | The third Whispering Angel warns everyone not to get the mark of the beast. | | 14:9-10 | 3rd |
| 3 | We find out what happens to those who refused the mark: they are beheaded. | | 20:04 | 4th |

Listing the verses in this manner makes it clear that John did not present the events which led to the deaths of the martyrs of the 5th seal in chronological order. As we'll see in future chapters, this was not the only instance where he recounted events out of sequence.

## 4.2 Jesus' End Time Conversation (the Olivet Discourse) is in Order

Jesus often retreated to the Mount of Olives when he needed to get away to pray. One day, Peter, James, John, and Andrew were alone with Jesus, making encouraging conversation by pointing out the temple's splendor.[23] But Jesus responded that the beautiful temple was going to be destroyed in such a complete and devastating manner that not even one stone block would be left standing on another. This response from Jesus alarmed them, so they prodded him to *tell us, when shall these things be? And what shall be the sign of thy coming and of the end of the world?"*[24]

Matthew wrote down what happened that day in his gospel and theologians now refer to this dialog as the Olivet Discourse. Mark, who doesn't list himself among those present that day, probably recorded his version of the conversations from that day based on what Peter remembered. Luke, whom we know wasn't there, also compiled a well-researched version.

Matthew records Jesus' explanation of what will happen in 24:4-31. Unlike John, who, in Revelation, describes different groups and events in an order that is not easy to figure out, Matthew presents the events in the order in which Jesus explained them. What can be confusing, however, is that while in the middle of explaining the order, Matthew reports that Jesus pauses a few times to warn his followers about how to tell the difference between him and the

---

[23] Mark 13:3–4.ESV *"And as he sat on the Mount of Olives opposite the temple, Peter and James and John and Andrew asked him privately, 4 "Tell us, when will these things be, and what will be the sign when all these things are about to be accomplished?"*

[24] Matthew 24:3 KJV—which is the beginning of Matthew's account of the Olivet Discourse.

fake messiahs who will show up in the last days, and then he gets back to his clear timeline in verse 29.

Mark's version is like Matthew's because he, too, includes the breaks in the order where Jesus warns about not being fooled by people pretending to be Christ.[25]

Luke's version is a bit different. Always a thorough investigator, Luke focuses on delivering all the details he gathered in order and without breaking the train of thought. And who doesn't love the message of exhilarating hope, which only Luke records, *"And when these things begin to come to pass, then look up, and lift up your heads: for your redemption draweth nigh?"*[26]

It's no accident that we have all three of their perspectives. It demonstrates just how critical this particular teaching from Jesus truly is to his church. To fully understand everything Jesus conveyed in his Olivet Discourse, I recommend reading all three accounts in harmony, which I share in Exhibit 3.

The Olivet Discourse provides the crucial framework of events in the order in which they will occur leading up to the Day of the Lord, but there are many events that were not mentioned that we still need to fit within and after that framework.

[25] Olivet Discourse of Mark 13:1–27.
[26] Olivet Discourse of Luke 21:28 KJV

# 5 The Rules of Engagement (The 7-Sealed Book)

> *And I saw in the right hand of him that sat on the throne a book written within and on the backside, sealed with seven seals.* (Revelation 5:1 KJV)

God is holding a book of such immense value and significance that, until this point, not a single being in all of creation has been found worthy to open it. Its contents remain sealed, waiting for the moment when someone will be deemed worthy to open it.

> *2 And I saw a strong angel proclaiming with a loud voice, Who is worthy to open the book, and to loose the seals thereof? 3 And no man in heaven, nor in earth, neither under the earth, was able to open the book, neither to look theron.* (Revelation 5:2–3 KJV)

The 7-sealed book isn't just sitting idly on a shelf or displayed as a showpiece on a golden table. It's held in God's right hand—an unmistakable sign of its immense importance. Surely, God wouldn't guard it so carefully if its contents weren't critical to him and the eternal fate of his beloved creation, humanity.[27] The fact that God

---

[27] Genesis 48:17–18 ESV. When Jacob put his right hand on the younger grandson's head to bless him, it displeased Joseph, because the right hand conveys the greater blessing: *"When Joseph saw that his father laid his right hand on the head of Ephraim, it displeased him, and he took his father's hand to move it from Ephraim's head to Manasseh's head. 18 And Joseph said to his father, "Not this way, my father; since this one is the firstborn, put your right hand on his head."*

holds this book so closely shows that no one can access it until the appointed time.

As the *"possessor of heaven and earth,"* God has the absolute authority to entrust the kingdom of the earth to whomever he wills.

> *And Melchizedek king of Salem brought out bread and wine. (He was priest of God Most High.) 19 And he blessed him and said, "Blessed be Abram by God Most High, Possessor of heaven and earth;* (Genesis 14:18-19 ESV)

This book contains the rules, details, and boundaries that govern each inning of a very consequential contest. A contest that will determine who will be the next King of the Earth. As Jesus opens each seal, John describes an image that summarizes the essence of that chapter.[28] Then, where applicable, John describes the powers that will be granted to Satan or his antichrist by God, as well as the limitations set upon those powers.

Because the events or actions of one seal must be completed before the next seal is broken, the very presence of the seals regulates the speed at which the contest can advance. In other words, the consequences of each seal are restricted to a precise pace, a pace that ensures two or more seals won't be released at once, and at a tempo that ensures the Great Tribulation will last the 3½ years that God ordained.

Why are we given glimpses into the awe-inspiring 7-sealed book? Why does God need this book and these rules in the first place? Why doesn't God just let things unfold as he wants and let us find out "in the moment?" After all, God doesn't have to prove or justify anything to anyone, right? This may surprise you, but

---

[28] This does not apply to the 7th seal, which is Jesus' seal. John sees nothing when that seal is opened, but he tells us there was silence in heaven for about half an hour.

that's not true. In this case, he does need to justify his actions for a specific group in heaven.

Here's what I mean by that. God's nature is one of justice and order. By revealing glimpses of his plan thousands of years ahead, he proves that he is all-knowing, not acting arbitrarily in the Great Tribulation, but acting as justice requires. He ensures that, in the end, every being *"in heaven and on earth and under the earth"* will understand and accept that his actions are always just, purposeful and ordained.[29] I'll refer to this core theme throughout this book.

God is a God of order. Destroying everything without warning would be impulsive and chaotic, which is the opposite of order. That's why he laid out his plan in the 7-sealed book. However, revealing its full contents before the proper time would cause confusion and chaos, not just on earth but in heaven as well. So, God keeps the details secure in his right hand until the right time.

There are several reasons humans, as well as angels, have a vested interest in the outcome of the last days:

1. The 7-sealed book explains God's plan to return creation back to the order he originally intended. That promise of restoration has given hope to every generation of humans as well as the angels.
2. By making these warnings accessible to us sinners, it demonstrates that he is a just God because he plainly shows what will happen to each of us if we freely choose not to return to him.

> *The Lord is not slow to fulfill his promise as some count slowness, but is patient toward you, not wishing that any should perish, but that all should reach repentance.*
> (2 Peter 3:9 ESV)

---

[29] Revelation 5:13b

3. By putting his prophecies in writing using multiple prophets spanning 1,500 years, God demonstrates his supreme confidence that his Word will be proven true.[30] He tells us what to watch for, most of what will happen, and gives us general indicators of when it could happen. God is sure of himself. God is order and cannot lie.

4. After the Day of the Lord, God will invite those who make it into the Millennial Kingdom to examine the prophecies which by then they will have seen unfold before their eyes. If that doesn't convince them that he is truly God and is worthy to be praised, then there is no hope for them.

> . . . *knowing this first of all, that no prophecy of scripture comes from someone's own interpretation. For no prophecy was ever produced by the will of man, but men spoke from God as they were carried along by the Holy Spirit.* (2 Peter 1:20-21 ESV)

5. As we'll see in Chapter 6, "The Big Picture Found," God really does have to lay out these rules and oversee a fair contest to maintain order among heavenly beings.

---

[30] Jay Smith asserts that "It is possible that Job is the oldest of any book of the Bible, written approximately 2100–1800 B.C." Jay Smith, "Job Summary," biblehub.com, https://biblehub.com/summary/job/1.htm.

# 5.1 Is it a Book or a Scroll?

Sometimes interpreters of different Bible versions translate the words *book* and *scroll* interchangeably within their respective Bibles. For example, both the English Standard Version and the New International Version chose to convey the Greek word *Biblion* as *scroll* in this passage:[31]

> *Then I saw in the right hand of him who was seated on the throne a scroll written within and on the back, sealed with seven seals.* (Revelation 5:1 ESV)

> *Then I saw in the right hand of him who sat on the throne a scroll with writing on both sides and sealed with seven seals.* (Revelation 5:1 NIV)

But those same interpreters chose to translate the same Greek word as *book* in other passages, such as John 21:25b: "*I suppose that the world itself could not contain the books that would be written*" (ESV), *and "I suppose that even the whole world would not have room for the books that would be written*" (NIV).

The distinction between *book* and *scroll* doesn't really matter in most instances, but it is very important in this instance for several

---

[31] Thayer's Greek Lexicon, "Biblion," Strong's G975, biblehub.com, https://biblehub.com/thayers/975.htm. Biblion means a small book or a scroll. Biblion is used in 28 verses in the New Testament. Strong's G975, "βιβλίον," or "biblion," blueletterbible.org, https://www.blueletterbible.org/lexicon/g975/niv/mgnt/0-1/. In the KJV, biblion is always translated as book except in Revelation 6:14, where the context is clearly a scroll. However, in the ESV version, it is translated as a scroll 12 of those 28 times and in the NIV 19 times. I think this inconsistent treatment introduces confusion.

reasons. Think about writing a lengthy letter on both sides of a 6-foot-long piece of paper, then rolling it up and applying seven blobs of hot wax along the seam to keep it secure. Then, imagine using a metal or clay seal to press a unique image into each blob of wax. You would end up with a rolled-up scroll of paper sealed along the seam with seven blobs of wax, each stamped with an impression. Breaking the first wax seal wouldn't let you open the scroll, and neither would breaking the second or the third. No, that scroll could only be unrolled and read after all seven wax seals were broken.

A book with seven chapter dividers, each secured with a separate wax seal covering the edge of the pages within that divider and the next divider solves the intractable problem of how the wax seal alone could possibly convey more information than just a few characters or symbols. It explains how opening one seal gave Jesus access to the pages of information that had been secured by that seal. See Exhibit 4 for additional evidence that it is a book, not a scroll.

As Revelation unfolds, it also becomes clear that there is far more information in that seven-sealed book than what John was allowed to see.

# 6 The Big Picture Found

The 7-sealed book is an essential key to understanding the order in which the end-time prophecies will unfold. But just as consequential as that book are some very detailed conversations we get to hear in heaven: two in the book of Job, which we'll discuss later, and five in the book of Revelation. In a departure from John's normal way of grouping similar things together, these conversations in Revelation are interspersed between events occurring on earth. Each time John sees people doing something or saying something in heaven, he reports it to us, much like a sportscaster verbally illustrates to listeners what's happening in the game. John tells us who just made it in, what condition they were in, and what they were celebrating or lamenting. Their conversations indicate what event just happened on earth or, in the case of the fifth conversation, what they are getting ready for in heaven.

I have read those dialogues of people in heaven dozens of times, but because of the lens I used, I read them as though they were not applicable to me. Their profound meaning only became apparent once I removed that lens.

The remainder of this book will reveal how the 7-sealed book, together with these crucial conversations in heaven and the Olivet Discourse, provides the picture I was searching for. Now that I had the essential big picture, I could start organizing all the pieces, but I still needed to understand more about what this 7-sealed book contained and why it was necessary.

# 6.1 The Contest for the Kingdom

Very specific conditions must be met before this 7-sealed book can be opened, let alone read *("look into it")*.

> *And I saw a mighty angel proclaiming with a loud voice, "Who is worthy to open the scroll and break its seals?" 3 And no one in heaven or on earth or under the earth was able to open the scroll or to look into it* (Revelation 5:2–3 ESV)

We're not yet told what those conditions are, but John introduces an interesting fact here. Apparently, anyone from the three realms of existence—heaven, earth, or under the earth—could have potentially qualified to open the book. *"Under the earth"* indicates that even Satan was eligible.[32] What? That's a horrifying thought, but who else could be contenders in this epic contest besides an entity from heaven or from the underworld?

Verse 3 indicates that a grand contest to prove worthiness to open the scroll had been playing out, but no winner had been declared; no one was *"worthy."* To be considered worthy, the winner must have had to perform something so impossible that John wept as he considered the consequences of the world continuing without a winner: no one could pay our ransom. Later, as each seal of the seven-sealed book is broken and the pages of its corresponding chapter are read aloud, we discover that it holds the rules governing the second half of this contest.

---

[32] "... **no one in the heaven, or on the earth** (Revised Version). That is, no one in all creation--in heaven, or on earth, or in the place of departed spirits. No one was able "to look thereon" (that is, "to read therein") as a consequence of no one being fit to open the book." Bible Hub, "Revelation 5," Pulpit Commentary, https://biblehub.com/commentaries/pulpit/revelation/5.htm.

*4 and I began to weep loudly because no one was found worthy to open the scroll or to look into it. 5 And one of the elders said to me, "Weep no more; behold, the Lion of the tribe of Judah, the Root of David, has conquered, so that he can open the scroll and its seven seals."* (Revelation 5:4–5 ESV)

John had the privilege of witnessing the exact moment in verse 7 when the victor of the first half of the contest, Jesus, claimed his hard-won reward! Jesus took the book from the right hand of God, and the elders fell down before him, declaring Jesus as *"worthy!"* Once you understand the gravity of this contest, it should make you want to shout praises to the Lord!

*6 And between the throne and the four living creatures and among the elders I saw a Lamb standing, as though it had been slain, with seven horns and with seven eyes, which are the seven spirits of God sent out into all the earth. 7 And he went and took the scroll from the right hand of him who was seated on the throne. 8 And when he had taken the scroll, the four living creatures and the twenty-four elders fell down before the Lamb, each holding a harp, and golden bowls full of incense, which are the prayers of the saints. 9a And they sang a new song, saying, "Worthy are you to take the scroll and to open its seals,"* (Revelation 5:6–9a ESV)

Finally, we find out in verse 9b the impossible thing that Jesus had to do to win the first part of the contest.

*...for you were slain, and by your blood you ransomed people for God from every tribe and language and people and nation* (Revelation 5:9b ESV)

There is so much packed into that partial sentence; it's essentially the entire Gospel! There was only one way to break Satan's right as king of the world to hold believers who die (Paul calls them the dead in Christ) ransom. Someone had to live a life without sin and then, after doing so, willingly offer their perfect self as a sacrifice. Jesus was born of a virgin, so he didn't inherit the sin of Adam, then he lived his entire life, *"tempted in every way, just as we are—yet he did not sin."*[33] Since his blood was perfect (without sin), when he willingly laid down his life, his blood could serve as a perfect substitute for our sinful blood.

Without someone doing that, living a human life without sin and then willingly dying in our place, no one had any chance to be saved from Satan's kingdom. It was an impossible mission, against impossible odds, but Jesus did the impossible.

Jesus was slain and offered his blood as a ransom. For there to be a ransom, there must be a prisoner.[34] For there to be a prisoner, there must be a prison and a prison warden. This verse means that someone is holding souls captive, and we instantly understand who those prisoners are and who their captor is. The reason they are being held captive will be discussed later.

---

[33] Hebrews 4:15 NIV

[34] Revelation 5:9b (displayed above) *and also 1John 1:7 ...and the blood of Jesus, his Son, purifies us from all sin. (NIV)*
Though this verse is in the past tense, something important still must happen, and we'll find out what that is when the 7th trumpet sounds.

## 6.2 The Current King of the World

God created Adam and gave him dominion over men and animals. Adam was king of his domain, which at first was Eden, but extended over the whole earth.

> *And God blessed them. And God said to them, "Be fruitful and multiply and fill the earth and subdue it, and have dominion over the fish of the sea and over the birds of the heavens and over every living thing that moves on the earth."* (Genesis 1:28 ESV)

God told Adam not to eat the fruit of one specific tree, the tree of the knowledge of good and evil:

> *16 And the LORD God commanded the man, saying, "You may surely eat of every tree of the garden, 17 but of the tree of the knowledge of good and evil you shall not eat, for in the day that you eat of it you shall surely die."* (Genesis 2:16–17 ESV)

The serpent persuaded Eve and then Eve convinced Adam that God didn't really want the best for them because he had prohibited them from eating the fruit of the Tree of the Knowledge of Good and Evil. It's implied that the serpent convinced Eve that he was really the one who loved them and cared for them because it was he who wanted this precious knowledge for them, and it was God who wanted to keep that knowledge from them.[35] The serpent

---

[35] "Satan alleges that the real motive for God's command is that he's self-serving, so intent on holding exclusive power that he can't risk giving freedom to others.

convinced Eve that God didn't want them to be as powerful as him and that God was lying that the repercussion of having this great knowledge was death.

> Now the serpent was more crafty than any other beast of the field that the LORD God had made. He said to the woman, "Did God actually say, 'You shall not eat of any tree in the garden'?" 2 And the woman said to the serpent, "We may eat of the fruit of the trees in the garden, 3 but God said, 'You shall not eat of the fruit of the tree that is in the midst of the garden, neither shall you touch it, lest you die.'" 4 But the serpent said to the woman, "You will not surely die. 5 For God knows that when you eat of it your eyes will be opened, and you will be like God, knowing good and evil." (Genesis 3:1–5 ESV)

By choosing to believe Satan was right and God was wrong and then choosing to disobey God's one simple command, Adam forfeited his God-given right of kingship, and the serpent became the king of the earth. Yes, Satan gained the kingdom through deception, but just as God, ten generations later, officially recognized the birthright that Jacob swindled from Esau by deceiving their father, God also officially recognized the transfer of power from Adam to Satan. The forfeiture of both birthrights was the legitimate consequence of using their free will to choose to do something other than obey God's Word.

So, when we look at the temptation and fall of Adam as the cause of us all becoming mortal and sinful, we must realize that this wasn't the worst part of his fall. Arguably, the worst part of his fall

---

. . God is not interested in the well-being of his creatures, only in protecting his own status." Dennis McCallum, *Satan and His Kingdom: What the Bible Says and How It Matters to You* (Bethany House Publishers, 2009), 30.

was that Satan gained dominion over the kingdoms of the world. Part of the privilege of being king is that he has control over what happens to the souls of those who die in his kingdom. Souls are immortal, so he can't destroy them, but he can keep them under lock and key in Hades, or, as the Jews call it, Sheol. However, Jesus comforted us in the parable of Lazarus and the Rich Man by letting us know that the souls of believers are in a good section of Sheol called Abraham's Bosom while the souls of unbelievers are kept in a completely isolated and terrible section.[36]

God cursed the serpent for his treacherous deception and implied that there was still a chance that Satan would lose his newfound dominion with the prophecy that man's offspring would one-day *"bruise"* the Serpent's head.

---

[36] 19 *"There was a rich man who was clothed in purple and fine linen and who feasted sumptuously every day. 20 And at his gate was laid a poor man named Lazarus, covered with sores, 21 who desired to be fed with what fell from the rich man's table. Moreover, even the dogs came and licked his sores. 22 The poor man died and was carried by the angels to Abraham's side. The rich man also died and was buried, 23 and in Hades, being in torment, he lifted up his eyes and saw Abraham far off and Lazarus at his side. 24 And he called out, 'Father Abraham, have mercy on me, and send Lazarus to dip the end of his finger in water and cool my tongue, for I am in anguish in this flame.' 25 But Abraham said, 'Child, remember that you in your lifetime received your good things, and Lazarus in like manner bad things; but now he is comforted here, and you are in anguish. 26 And besides all this, between us and you a great chasm has been fixed, in order that those who would pass from here to you may not be able, and none may cross from there to us.' 27 And he said, 'Then I beg you, father, to send him to my father's house— 28 for I have five brothers—so that he may warn them, lest they also come into this place of torment.' 29 But Abraham said, 'They have Moses and the Prophets; let them hear them.' 30 And he said, 'No, father Abraham, but if someone goes to them from the dead, they will repent.' 31 He said to him, 'If they do not hear Moses and the Prophets, neither will they be convinced if someone should rise from the dead.'* (Luke 16:19–31 ESV)

*The LORD God said to the serpent, "Because you have done this, cursed are you above all livestock and above all beasts of the field; on your belly you shall go, and dust you shall eat all the days of your life. I will put enmity between you and the woman, and between your offspring and her offspring; he shall bruise your head, and you shall bruise his heel."* (Genesis 3:14–15 ESV)

When Jesus appeared on earth thousands of years later, Satan, and later, several demons were caught off guard. They immediately recognized his spirit as Jesus, the Son of God, but were confused. Based apparently on their understanding of the Scriptures, they didn't expect Jesus to arrive on earth until the end-times and seemed confident that was supposed to be further in the future. Since Satan and his demons aren't all-knowing, their confusion likely stemmed from their interpretation of specific events that the Scriptures said would happen before Jesus' return.

When Satan confronted Jesus in the desert, it became clear that he didn't understand why Jesus was on earth this early. He tried various clever ploys, attempting to get Jesus to reveal his purpose. I don't believe the devil was deluded enough to think Jesus would give up his lordship for anything Satan had to offer, no matter how hungry Jesus was. Instead, Satan was trying to provoke Jesus into overreacting and thus give away some clue about why he had come to earth earlier than expected. But, as we see in Luke 4:1-11, Jesus didn't fall for any of Satan's schemes and didn't give even the slightest hint of the reason for his return to earth earlier than expected.

Satan failed to learn anything about Jesus' reason for being on earth early. However, he did learn that Jesus did not exhibit the power he had when he was in heaven. We, however, learned something very important during their exchange. Satan's second attempt to manipulate Jesus revealed that, even after all the thousands of years since Adam's fall, Satan was still in control of the kingdoms of the world.

> *And the devil took him up and showed him all the kingdoms of the world in a moment of time, 6 and said to him, "To you I will give all this authority and their glory, for it has been delivered to me, and I give it to whom I will. 7 If you, then, will worship me, it will all be yours." 8 And Jesus answered him, "It is written, 'You shall worship the Lord your God, and him only shall you serve.'"* (Luke 4:5–8 ESV)

When the devil offered Jesus this shortcut to gaining the kingdoms of the world, tellingly, Jesus didn't respond that the kingdoms were not the devil's to give. This was not just a simple omission by Jesus because later, after Jesus had begun his ministry, he acknowledged that Satan did indeed have dominion over the earth when he referred to him as *"the ruler of this world."*

> *I will no longer talk much with you* [his disciples], *for the ruler of this world is coming. He has no claim on me* (John 14:30 ESV)

Jesus revealed that Satan had *"no claim"* on him. This would have been a puzzling statement to the disciples. They could not have understood that Jesus meant Satan had *"no claim"* on him because he had not sinned up to that point in his life and that he wouldn't sin for the rest of his life. But Jesus makes sure this is recorded here because it is a key: Satan is the ruler of this world and thus has the right to *"claim"* everyone because *"all have sinned."* But Satan too was ignorant of the fact that Jesus had never sinned.

Now that we understand Satan's dominion over the world, it becomes clear why God kept the purpose of sending his Son to earth hidden from Satan. Because Satan would have tried to circumvent God's plan, it was critical that Satan not understand what Jesus was planning to do. If Satan had figured it out and not acted to kill Jesus, it would have thwarted the sophisticated plan God had set in motion from the beginning.

> *7 But we impart a secret and hidden wisdom of God, which God decreed before the ages for our glory. 8 None of the rulers of this age understood this, for if they had, they would not have crucified the Lord of glory.* (1 Corinthians 2:7-8 ESV)

By dying as an innocent and sinless human, Jesus became the perfect sacrifice and, at the same time, proved that Satan was a liar. How? Remember when Satan implied to Eve that God must not really care about her since he didn't want her to have all that knowledge? That day on the cross, Jesus proved to the world that he cared for his sheep so much that he willingly exchanged his own life as the ransom for them and thus exposed Satan's lie that God was uncaring.[37]

But for his life to work as a ransom, Jesus had to resist every temptation and sin for his entire 33-year life. If he had committed even one small sin, Satan would have had him dead to rights. Satan would have exercised his right as king of this world to hold him in Sheol, along with every other sinner who has ever lived, and God's

---

[37] *For God so loved the world that he gave his one and only Son, that whoever believes in him shall not perish but have eternal life. (John 3:16 NIV)*

plan would not have worked.[38] Since Jesus died sinless, Satan had no authority to hold him captive, which is how Jesus was the only human ever to rise from the dead and ascend to heaven. This is why Jesus was declared the victor of the first half of this contest and why only he was worthy to open the 7-sealed book.

Jesus' death and resurrection did not tear the kingship from Satan instantly, but Jesus put him "in check," to use a chess metaphor.

*The reason the Son of God appeared was to destroy the works of the devil.* (1 John 3:8b ESV)

*Now is the judgment of this world; now will the ruler of this world be cast out.* (John 12:31 ESV)

To this day, Satan is planning some "surprise" moves to extricate himself and avoid the "checkmate," the triumphal return of Jesus. But we know, because we've read the end of Revelation, that Satan, the greatest deceiver, has deceived himself.

God is the God of order, so his intricate plan couldn't be accomplished all at once. God's prophetic Scriptures about the first return of Jesus were ingeniously obscured so that no one, not the Pharisees or even Satan, could anticipate it.[39] Satan must have concluded that since Jesus was in his domain, the earth, and in a human body, with no apparent powers, that he was under his

---

[38] With the exceptions of Enoch and Elijah who did not die, but were transferred directly to heaven.

[39] "God's plan to redeem humanity, reclaim the nations. . . had to be expressed in sophisticated and cryptic ways to ensure that the powers of darkness would be misled." Michael S. Heiser, *The Unseen Realm: Recovering the Supernatural Worldview of the Bible* (Lexham Press, 2015), 243.

domain just like every other person and so conspired to kill Jesus.[40] Not by his own hand, of course, but indirectly by the hands of the Pharisees and Romans. Satan was arrogantly ignorant of the fact that God understood his nature so well that he knew that this was exactly how Satan would respond to Jesus' presence in a vulnerable human form. Imagine Satan's horror when he not only couldn't hold Jesus captive in hell, but he couldn't even restrict his activities once he arrived there, so Jesus spoke to the imprisoned spirits.[41]

> *wherefore, he saith, 'Having gone up on high he led captive captivity, and gave gifts to men,' 9 and that, he went up, what is it except that he also went down first to the lower parts of the earth? 10 he who went down is the same also who went up far above all the heavens, that He may fill all things –* (Ephesians 4:8-10 Young's Literal Translation)

---

[40] Satan thoroughly tested Jesus in the desert (Matthew 4:1-11) to determine if he possessed any of the powers he had in heaven, but Jesus did not display any. Satan could not have known that Jesus had voluntarily laid aside his powers to fulfill this impossible mission. Jesus... *"Who, being in very nature God, did not consider equality with God something to be used to his own advantage; 7 rather, he made himself nothing by taking the very nature of a servant, being made in human likeness.8 And being found in appearance as a man, he humbled himself by becoming obedient to death—even death on a cross!"(Philippians 2:6-8 NIV)*

[41] The imprisoned spirits were not the souls of departed non-believers. They were the Watcher Angels, whom God had imprisoned for sinning by sleeping with human women: *"For if God did not spare angels when they sinned, but cast them into hell and committed them to chains of gloomy darkness to be kept until the judgment"* (2 Peter 2:4 ESV). We can be fairly certain it is these fallen watcher angels that Jesus visited in Hades, because they were in chains in Hades, and Jude tells us the watcher angels were kept in chains. From Jude 1:6 ESV: *"And the angels who did not stay within their own position of authority, but left their proper dwelling, he has kept in eternal chains under gloomy darkness until the judgment of the great day."*

Seeing Jesus move freely between the good part of Sheol and the bad part to give a message to the *"spirits in prison"* must have been terrifying to Satan. That was the moment he understood that his actions that had led to Jesus' death played right into God's plan and he had unwittingly lost the crucial first half of the contest.

> *For Christ also suffered once for sins, the righteous for the unrighteous, that he might bring us to God, being put to death in the flesh but made alive in the spirit, 19 in which he went and proclaimed to the spirits in prison, 20 because they formerly did not obey, when God's patience waited in the days of Noah, while the ark was being prepared, in which a few, that is, eight persons, were brought safely through water.* (1 Peter 3:18–20 ESV)

We'll discuss Paradise more in the next chapter.

## | 6.3 The King's Ransom

As long as Satan remains king of the earth, he can legitimately hold human souls in Sheol as ransom, even those who are *"dead in Christ"*. [42]

> *Like sheep they are appointed for Sheol; death shall be their shepherd, and the upright shall rule over them in the morning. Their form shall be consumed in Sheol, with no place to dwell. 15 But God will ransom my soul from the power of Sheol, for he will receive me.* Selah. (Psalm 49:14–15 ESV)

But a ransom implies a trade for something. What does Satan want in exchange for the souls he's holding? Satan has been playing the long game since the moment he interjected himself into God's work in Eden by deceiving Eve. He construes love for man as God's soft spot and his plan is to exploit that perceived weakness in a negotiation. He has toiled in the eons since that fateful day in the Garden to deceive men into rejecting God and by now holds billions of souls of unbelievers and probably hundreds of millions of souls of believers captive in Sheol. Those numbers grow each day.

Hosea lets us know that God has no intention of redeeming the souls of unbelievers from the bad part of Sheol because they chose their fate and got what they deserved.

---

[42] The "dead in Christ" are Christians who have died or will die before the Great Tribulation begins. *"For the Lord himself will come down from heaven, with a loud command, with the voice of the archangel and with the trumpet call of God, and the dead in Christ will rise first."* (1 Thessalonians 4:16 NIV)

*The punishment of Ephraim has been decreed; his punishment is being stored up for the future.13 The labor pains of a woman will overtake him, but the baby will lack wisdom; when the time arrives, he will not come out of the womb! 14 Will I deliver them from the power of Sheol? No, I will not! Will I redeem them from death? No, I will not! O Death, bring on your plagues! O Sheol, bring on your destruction! My eyes will not show any compassion!* (Hosea 13:12–14 NET)

But the souls of believers in the Paradise section of Sheol—now that's a completely different story. Satan knows that Jesus will one day come for the souls of his believers, so he is betting his life that Jesus will agree to exchange them in return for the release of his Watcher angels, his demons, and, of course, himself from the punishment he knows awaits them when Jesus wins the kingdom.[43]

But God has a perfect plan that already circumvented Satan and negated his great plans for an exchange. In a roundabout way, a way that completely blindsided Satan, the ransom was paid by Jesus.

*For even the Son of Man came not to be served but to serve, and to give his life as a ransom for many."* (Mark 10:45 ESV)

Even though the ransom was paid in full by his sinless death on the cross, Jesus couldn't take his kingdom at that moment. Yes, we will eventually be able to go to heaven with him, but he must

---

[43] Watcher Angels are the angels of Genesis 6:1-4 ESV who fell for human women. They are also mentioned in Daniel 4. Jude 1:6 ESV brings them up again and says, "And the angels who did not stay within their own position of authority, but left their proper dwelling, he has kept in eternal chains under gloomy darkness until the judgment of the great day"

wait until the time God has designated–"*when the full number of Gentiles has come in*"–before he will be officially declared the victor of the first half of the contest and thus deemed worthy to open the 7-sealed book and begin the second half of the contest.

> *For I do not want you to be ignorant of this mystery, brothers and sisters, so that you may not be conceited: A partial hardening has happened to Israel until the full number of the Gentiles has come in. 26 And so all Israel will be saved, as it is written: "The Deliverer will come out of Zion; he will remove ungodliness from Jacob. 27 And this is my covenant with them, when I take away their sins."* (Romans 11:25–27 NET)

The opening of the 7-sealed book marks the kick-off of the second half of this cosmic contest. This is not merely a symbolic moment; it signifies the beginning of the final stage of a cosmic battle with eternal consequences. Jesus' ultimate victory, his 'checkmate,' will come when he, adhering to all the rules of engagement outlined in the 7-sealed book, triumphs in this second half.

Until victory is achieved, Jesus cannot simply bypass this 7-sealed book and preemptively seize the *"dead in Christ"* from Paradise to bring them to heaven. God, being a God of order, will not permit such chaos, so the dead remain under the jurisdiction of the reigning legitimate king. The stakes of this contest could not be higher: the ultimate fate of Christian souls hinges on Jesus' triumph. That is why Jesus called us to fervently pray, "...*Thy Kingdom Come...*" [44] Every prayer brings us closer to the opening of the 7-sealed book and, in turn, to Jesus defeating Satan and winning the kingdom.

---

[44] Matthew 6:9-10 ESV, "*Pray then like this: "Our Father in heaven, hallowed be your name. 10 Your kingdom come, your will be done, on earth as it is in heaven."*

I found this discovery to be jolting, one that challenged everything I had assumed and it demanded a complete shift in my understanding. It's a lot to take in. If you're reacting to this news about Paradise the way I did, you're probably questioning its truth. I immediately asked myself, *If we don't go directly to heaven, then what about the criminal to whom Jesus promised, "Today you will be with me in paradise"?*[45] The answer I found clearly supported the idea that we go to Paradise, but that it is temporary and a place of comfort.

Paradise was another name for Abraham's Bosom, the comfortable part of Hades (Hades is called Sheol in Hebrew), where the souls of the 'saved' wait in comfort for the final outcome of this epic contest.[46] [47] It's no coincidence that Jesus chooses this precise moment—on the cross, at the edge of his death—to mention Paradise for the first time. Throughout his ministry, Jesus spoke extensively about heaven and the Kingdom of Heaven, as recorded dozens of times in the Gospels.[48] Yet, he reserves mentioning *Paradise* for this single, pivotal instance, right as he is about to die.

---

[45] Luke 23:43 ESV, "*And he said to him, "Truly, I say to you, today you will be with me in paradise.*"

[46] "In the Septuagint, Genesis 2:8, of the garden of Eden. In the Jewish theology, the department of Hades where the blessed souls await the resurrection; and therefore equivalent to Abraham's bosom (Luke 16:22, Luke 16:23). It occurs three times in the New Testament: here; 2 Corinthians 12:4; Revelation 2:7; and always of the abode of the blessed." Bible Hub, "Luke 23," Vincent's Word Studies, https://biblehub.com/commentaries/vws/luke/23.htm.

[47] "3. that part of Hades which was thought by the later Jews to be the abode of the souls of the pious until the resurrection: Luke 23:43. . ." Bible Hub, "STRONGS NT 3857: παράδεισος," Thayer's Greek Lexicon, https://biblehub.com/greek/3857.htm.

[48] Based on a keyword search of the KJV, heaven is mentioned 75 times in Matthew, 17 times in Mark, 32 times in Luke, and 17 times in John. However, Paradise is only mentioned three times in the entire New Testament: in Luke 23:43 (*"today thou shalt be with me in paradise"*), 2 Corinthians 12:4 [Paul] *"was snatched away to Paradise and heard things that cannot be expressed in words, things that no human being has a right even to mention."* (ISV) and in Revelation 2:7 "...

His choice of words here carries profound significance: as he consoles the repentant thief, Jesus reveals a glimpse of the immediate and personal comfort and rest awaiting those who trust in him.[49] Unlike his eternal teachings on the Kingdom of Heaven, which, as we learn in Revelation, is accessed only after Judgment Day, Paradise here serves as an immediate (*"today you will be with me"*) promise of peace and presence with God at the moment of death. [50]

Understanding the difference between Paradise and heaven brings a whole new depth to this passage in John.

> *Jesus then said, "I will be with you a little longer, and then I am going to him who sent me. 34 You will seek me and you will not find me. Where I am you cannot come." (John 7:33-34 ESV)*

The belief that Christians who die go to Paradise has not been widely taught by the church in recent generations, but it turns out the belief was held by several early Church Fathers, including Irenaeus.[51] The founder of the Methodist denomination,

---

*I will give the privilege of eating from the tree of life that is in God's paradise.* (ISV)

[49] Solomon shared that once you are dead you will have no more worries. He said all feelings and emotions (good or bad) cease. There is nothing further you can do to improve or worsen your ultimate fate (*"no more reward"*) and all contact with the world of the living is cut off (*"no more share in all that is done"*). Ecclesiastes 9:5-6 (ESV): *"For the living know that they will die, but the dead know nothing, and they have no more reward, for the memory of them is forgotten.6 Their love and their hate and their envy have already perished, and forever they have no more share in all that is done under the sun."*

[50] Heaven is accessed after Judgment Day for those believers who die before the Great Tribulation. However, believers who die after the Great Tribulation begins receive a "special blessing": bypassing Paradise and going directly to heaven. (see chapter 11.3 *Special Promise for Believers who die From Now On.*

[51] Irenaeus, *Against Heresies 5.5.1*, trans. Alexander Roberts and W.H. Rambaut, in *Ante-Nicene Fathers, Vol. 1*, ed. Alexander Roberts and James Donaldson (Buffalo,

John Wesley, made an even more granular distinction regarding different sections in Hades, teaching that souls of the righteous waited in Paradise.[52] The Eastern Orthodox Church still teaches that Paradise is a "middle state," a place of comfort where the souls of Christians await Resurrection Day, which I refer to as the Day of the Lord in Chapter 25.[53]

When Jesus arrived on earth fully human and just as vulnerable as everyone else, Satan smugly assumed that, like every other human since Adam, Jesus must have sinned at some point in his life. If that were true, he would be confined in Sheol (the Paradise section) under Satan's authority as king. But to his utter shock, Jesus moved freely between Paradise and the darkest parts of Sheol, completely unhindered by Satan's boundaries.

In that moment, Satan grasped the devastating truth: Jesus had just exploited the only way to escape his grasp: He had done the impossible by living a life completely free of sin, therefore Jesus was not only able to move freely to any part of Sheol he wished, but he was also free to leave when he was ready to ascend to show himself alive to his disciples. And when that 40 days on Earth was finished, he was free to ascend to the right hand of his Father in heaven.

---

NY: Christian Literature Publishing Co., 1885), revised ed., New Advent, accessed 12/1/2024, https://www.newadvent.org/fathers/0103.htm. Here's the key excerpt on Paradise: "Wherefore also the elders who were disciples of the apostles tell us that those who were translated were transferred to that place (for paradise has been prepared for righteous men, such as have the Spirit; in which place also Paul the apostle, when he was caught up, heard words which are unspeakable as regards us in our present condition 2 Corinthians 12:4), and that there shall they who have been translated remain until the consummation [of all things], as a prelude to immortality."

[52] "Christian Views on Hades," Wikipedia: The Free Encyclopedia, last modified 12/1/2024, accessed , https://en.wikipedia.org/wiki/Christian_views_on_Hades.

[53] "What Happens After We Die?" Saint John Orthodox Church, accessed 12/1/2024, https://www.saintjohnchurch.org/what-happens-after-death.

But as Jesus tells us in John 7:34, we cannot follow him to heaven just yet (*"you cannot come"*).

It's not essential that you believe you will go to Paradise, but it's important to understand Paradise the way believers of Jesus' day understood it. Understanding what and where Paradise is, and who currently holds people ransom there, unlocks how several key pieces of prophecy fit into the end-times puzzle. If Paradise doesn't exist, those pieces remain impossible to fit.

Revelation 2:7 tells us the Tree of Life is in Paradise, which implies that the rest of the Garden of Eden is there too. Between that detail and Luke's account that Lazarus was living well while the rich man was in torment, we can be assured Paradise is a comfortable place to abide a while.

For more information on Paradise, see Exhibit 5.

That was the first half of this epic contest; now we'll explore the second half, which begins after the church age is over and Jesus takes the 7-sealed book from God's right hand.

## 6.4 Conditions are Right: Time to Open the 7-Sealed Book

We know now that at least 2,000 years will pass after the resurrection of Jesus before the end-time appointed by God will come. At some point, *"the lamb who was slain"* will be declared *"worthy"* to look on and open the 7-sealed book. At that pre-ordained moment, Jesus will take that 7-sealed book from God's right hand and the last half of the contest will begin.[54] No eternal being will be able to deny that Jesus won the first half of the contest fair and square, which is why even those spirits *"under the earth"* have no choice but to acknowledge that he was worthy to open the book.[55]

> *And I heard every creature in heaven and on earth and under the earth and in the sea, and all that is in them, saying, "To him who sits on the throne and to the Lamb be blessing and honor and glory and might forever and ever!"* (Revelation 5:13 ESV)

We don't know what event will cause Jesus to break open the 1st seal, but we know from prophecies that there will be natural disasters, war, diseases, and other pestilences and that they'll

---

[54] The moment Jesus takes the 7-sealed book into his hand is when the Day of the Lord begins. However, most prophecies about the Day of the Lord focus on the activities Jesus carries out after the 7th trumpet sounds.

[55] Bible Hub, "Revelation 5:13," Pulpit Commentary, biblehub.com, https://biblehub.com/commentaries/pulpit/revelation/5.htm. "Those under the earth are probably the 'spirits in prison' of 1 Peter 3:19, though Vitringa understands the expression to be used of the devils 'who unwillingly obey Christ,' and even declare his glory, as in Mark 1:24 KJV, 'I know thee who thou art, the Holy One of God.'

come in waves that will occur closer and closer together like the contractions preceding childbirth.

From the Olivet Discourse, we learn that many Christians will abandon their faith in Jesus. Debauchery, immorality, and outright evil will be openly celebrated. Many will brazenly claim to be the savior, and a widespread fear of another world war will grip humanity.

We can infer that some type of global calamity plunges most, if not all, countries into turmoil. Regardless of the triggering event, when the conditions and timing are precisely right, Jesus breaks open the 1st seal.

# Part Two:

# He's a Smooth Operator: Building a World Coalition

# 7 Seal 1: The Charismatic Silver-tongued Grand Caliph

*Now I watched when the Lamb opened one of the seven seals, and I heard one of the four living creatures say with a voice like thunder, "Come!" 2 And I looked, and behold, a white horse! And its rider had a bow, and a crown was given to him, and he came out conquering, and to conquer.* (Revelation 6:1–2 ESV)

A white horse is ideal for a leader because it stands out. Napoleon rode one, as did General George Washington. The Babylonian King Xerxes, also known as Ahasuerus in the Book of Esther, held white horses in high regard, considering them sacred. Therefore, it is not unusual to see a leader riding a white horse, as it symbolized power, sanctity, and authority in many ancient traditions. What is unusual is that we're told this leader also *"had a bow."* However, this was not a bow without arrows, as most commentators confidently convey. While the Greek word *"Toxon"* can be translated that way, it can also refer to a shape like a rainbow or a crescent made of fabric.[56] So imagine this leader astride a white horse, accompanied by his flag-bearer who is proudly holding aloft his distinctive royal standard. Prominently emblazoned on that white flag is the image of a rainbow or a crescent, which is intended to give the impression that he comes in peace and tolerance, but we'll learn later that his real intention is *"to conquer."*

---

[56] Strongs Concordance: Toxon. From the base of Tikto, a bow (apparently as the simplest fabric) – bow.

This rider is trying to fool people into thinking that he is someone else. He's making his triumphal entry in the same way Jesus will when he rides a white horse on the Day of the Lord.[57] This impersonator has thought long and hard about the initial impression he wants to convey: that of a loving savior. His image is a well-choreographed, deceptive, subliminal message. This is the leader that Christians will later come to identify as the antichrist.[58]

We know this leader does not rise to power in the normal manner. He isn't a ruler by birth, a democratic election, or even a coup. Instead, the crown of a kingdom is described as being literally *"given"* to him, and he rides in on a white horse, making the impression he has come to save the world.[59]

John is making a connection to a description penned six hundred years earlier when Daniel wrote that the antichrist would be given his kingdom through *"flatteries"* and deceit.

> *In his place shall arise a contemptible person to whom royal majesty has not been given. He shall come in without warning and obtain the kingdom by flatteries. 22 Armies shall be utterly swept away before him and broken, even the prince of the covenant. 23 And from the time that an alliance is made with him he shall act deceitfully, and he shall become strong with a small people.* (Daniel 11:21–23 ESV)

---

[57] Revelation 19:11 ESV. *"Then I saw heaven opened, and behold, a white horse! The one sitting on it is called Faithful and True, and in righteousness he judges and makes war."*

[58] "Many expositors make this rider the Lord Jesus or some power which represents him. It is positively incorrect. The rider here is a great counterfeit leader... (Daniel 7:1-28)" (Bible Hub, "Revelation 6:1-2," Gaebelein's Annotated Bible, biblehub.com, https://biblehub.com/commentaries/gaebelein/revelation/6.htm.)

[59] Revelation 6:2 ESV

This man will imply he's somebody they've been expecting through prophecy, and the king from the smallest of the ten aligned kingdoms will completely fall for his deception and flatteries and bestow on him his own throne. But then, this newly ascended king will soon take over or *"put down"* two more kings and thus expand his power over three kingdoms.

> *As for the ten horns, out of this kingdom ten kings shall arise, and another shall arise after them; he shall be different from the former ones, and shall put down three kings. 25 He shall speak words against the Most High and shall wear out the saints of the Most High, and shall think to change the times and the law; and they shall be given into his hand for a time, times, and half a time.* (Daniel 7:24–25 ESV)

After consolidating these first three kingdoms, he either intimidates the remaining seven nations in his alliance or has some kind of powerful weapon or capability that the seven leaders desire. Alternatively, these leaders may trust him so completely that they're willing to simply hand over control of their armies and governments. It's extremely rare for a country to willingly give up its sovereignty, but when seven leaders do so, they must be incredibly desperate and out of options. Or perhaps this new leader has presented a vision that seems so enticing that they're willing to give him everything he asks for, at least for a while, all in the name of a greater cause. And for a time, it will seem like a brilliant decision.

> *. . . for God has put it into their hearts to carry out his purpose by being of one mind and handing over their*

*royal power to the beast, until the words of God are fulfilled.* (Revelation 17:17 ESV)

He will be a conqueror. Though he's a deceiver, he turns out to be a brilliant military leader. He will *"become strong"* through unstoppable military victories.[60] Even Israel, *"the prince of the covenant,"* will be knocked off its feet and soon seek to make a treaty.[61]

> *He shall honor the god of fortresses instead of these. A god whom his fathers did not know he shall honor with gold and silver, with precious stones and costly gifts. 39 He shall deal with the strongest fortresses with the help of a foreign god. Those who acknowledge him he shall load with honor. He shall make them rulers over many and shall divide the land for a price.* (Daniel 11:38–39 ESV)

He enlists *"the help of a foreign god"*. This may be one of the dark princes like the Prince of Persia or Greece.[62] With this foreign god's help, he defeats mighty nations no matter how strong their armies. Those he's conquered and who pledge their loyalty and worship, he will honor publicly and give them parcels of the conquered territories.

---

[60] *"And they worshiped the dragon, for he had given his authority to the beast, and they worshiped the beast, saying, "Who is like the beast, and who can fight against it?"* (Revelation 13:4 ESV). This implies that the antichrist has some special weapon or new undefeatable tactic, similar to how Hitler's Blitzkrieg method was virtually impossible to defend against.

[61] Daniel 11:22.

[62] *"The prince of the kingdom of Persia withstood me twenty-one days, but Michael, one of the chief princes, came to help me, for I was left there with the kings of Persia, 14 and came to make you understand what is to happen to your people in the latter days. For the vision is for days yet to come."* (Daniel 10:13–14 ESV).

# 7.1 "It's a Miracle!" Finally, a Middle East Peace Treaty

Israel is not one of the ten nations of this confederacy led by the Grand Caliph (I'll use this name for the man who will later be revealed as the antichrist), but they will want to get in on this "Pax Persiana" that is bringing stability and superficial peace to the ten nations in the confederacy.[63] [64] It's not clear whether Israel entreats the Grand Caliph or whether he approaches Israel, but either way, a historic treaty will be made. But it will be a treaty the Jews will come to regret.

The great prophet of the Jews, Isaiah, warned them 2,500 years before not to make a covenant with the Grand Caliph.

> *And your covenant with death shall be disannulled, and your agreement with hell shall not stand; when the overflowing scourge shall pass through, then ye shall be trodden down by it.* (Isaiah 28:18 KJV)

But they do not heed God's prophecies and sign it anyway. This tells us that when this covenant is signed, Israel's leader will be a

---

[63] The antichrist will restore the former Ottoman/Persian Empire. Their leaders were usually called Sultans, but this time the revived empire will be called a Caliphate, because that's a stated goal of Islam. A recent example of the attempted fulfillment of this goal is ISIS, Islamic State of Iraq and Levant. ISIS has tried, unsuccessfully so far, to revive the Caliphate. The leader would be called the Caliph, but since this leader has designs for a worldwide Caliphate, I think his followers will bestow on him the more far-reaching title of Grand Caliph, or something similar

[64] Like the Pax Romana, I posit that there will be a temporary peace after the antichrist revives the Caliphate, which will include most of the former Ottoman Empire and Persian Empire. That's why I termed this peace the Pax Persiana. But the peace will be short-lived.

non-religious Jew who doesn't know the Torah. Because not only will this leader not know Isaiah's warning, but he will also not know that another famous Jew, Joshua, made a similarly grave mistake 3,500 years earlier. As Joshua was conquering his way through the land of Canaan, he was deceived by the Gibeonites into signing a treaty of protection with them.[65] He didn't seek God's approval before doing so and the Gibeonites became a thorn in the nation of Israel's side. The future leader of Israel will not see a reason to seek God's approval and will, therefore, sign this *"agreement with hell."*[66]

Part of the agreement will guarantee Israel's protection and part will likely guarantee land for the Palestinians.[67] But security is not the real reason the Grand Caliph establishes the treaty.

The Grand Caliph has a vision that will require a technological quantum leap. To bring it to fruition, he needs the brightest minds in banking and network security to develop and implement the technology. He has likely concluded that his best chance to successfully create and launch his vision of a completely closed, members-only economy is to enlist the foremost experts in global finance, leveraged buyouts, and secure verification technology: the Jewish banking elite. With these unparalleled titans of banking such as the Rothschilds, Goldmans, Finks (BlackRock), Soros (Soros

---

[65] Joshua 9:1–27.

66 It's a safe bet that the long-serving Benjamin Netanyahu will not be the Prime Minister when that disastrous agreement is signed, because based on his writings, he's well versed in the Torah and would not willingly ignore it.

[67] I assume it's at this point in time that Israel will be partitioned between Palestinians and Israelis because, at Jesus' return, one of the wrongs that he's going to make right will be to restore Israel to its full land area, because it had been subdivided: *"For behold, in those days and at that time, when I restore the fortunes of Judah and Jerusalem, 2 I will gather all the nations and bring them down to the Valley of Jehoshaphat. And I will enter into judgment with them there, on behalf of my people and my heritage Israel, because they have scattered them among the nations and have divided up my land,"* (Joel 3:1–2 ESV).

Fund), and Icahns leading its creation and publicly transferring their own fortunes to his new secure digital exchange, global adoption of the system will be all but guaranteed. Who could be more qualified to spearhead this unprecedented technology than these financial powerhouses? The exchange will be virtually unhackable, as it will rely on bio-electric verification. We'll discuss this revolutionary exchange in more detail after the 3rd seal is opened.

But why would these already incredibly wealthy Jewish banking industry titans agree to such a thing? They will probably be offered something money can't buy, something that their forebearers have prayed for since their last temple was destroyed in 70 AD: a new Jewish temple on holy ground in Jerusalem.

The earth-shattering nature of this treaty cannot be overemphasized. Some of the greatest diplomats in the world have tried and failed to negotiate peace in the Middle East. Many experts have declared it impossible, but this Grand Caliph will do the impossible. Not only will he negotiate peace, he will guarantee it. But even more monumental than peace in the Middle East will be the promise to Israel that they can begin building their temple immediately!

Once this covenant is signed, the Grand Caliph establishes himself on the world stage as the man who did the impossible. Since he's conquered virtually everyone in the region and has negotiated a peace that was thought impossible, there will appear to be peace on earth, or at least peace in that portion of the earth. His status in the world will exceed that of any rockstar, and some will begin using god-like adjectives to describe him. Some people will start referring to him as a savior, but he will meekly demure, which will make him all the more appealing to the media and the masses.

As part of the peace guarantee, the Grand Caliph will position some of his troops around Jerusalem and Israel will begin to take down their defensive barriers so that it once again becomes "*an unwalled village*."[68] Joyful shouts of "*peace, peace*" will resound in its streets. But that peace will be short-lived.

---

[68] Ezekiel 38:11 ESV: "*. . . and say, 'I will go up against the land of unwalled villages. I will fall upon the quiet people who dwell securely, all of them dwelling without walls, and having no bars or gates. . .'*"

# 7.2 The Jews Get a Temple at Last

> *Then I was given a measuring rod like a staff, and I was told, "Rise and measure the temple of God and the altar and those who worship there, 2 but do not measure the court outside the temple; leave that out, for it is given over to the nations, and they will trample the holy city for forty-two months.* (Revelation 11:1–2 ESV)

This is a land-for-peace agreement with Muslims. John is told to measure just enough space for a new temple and altar, then he is told not to bother measuring anything else because it's all *"given over to the nations."* The Muslims will trample the rest of the space on the Temple Mount only for as long as the Great Tribulation lasts, which is *"forty-two months."*

> *In that day will I raise up the tabernacle of David that is fallen, and close up the breaches thereof; and I will raise up his ruins, and I will build it as in the days of old:* (Amos 9:11 KJV)

Amos tells us the temple won't just be thrown together without a plan. It will be magnificent, like Solomon's temple, *"as in the days of old."*

The mission of the Temple Institute in Jerusalem is to prepare everything for the next temple, which they believe is prophesied to once again stand on Mt Moriah.[69] Where exactly it will be built

---

[69] "The Temple Institute is dedicated to every aspect of the Holy Temple of Jerusalem, and the central role it fulfilled, and will once again fulfill, in the spiritual well-being of both Israel and all the nations of the world." ("About the Temple Institute," The Temple Institute, https://templeinstitute.org/about-us/.)

is not yet known. Maybe during some of the worldwide natural disasters or wars, the Dome of the Rock will be destroyed, or maybe a new space is found for God's third temple. But the temple will exist again before the start of the Great Tribulation. We know this because the antichrist will defile the temple, which begins the period called the Great Tribulation.

The Grand Caliph will post soldiers around the building site to keep anyone from hindering the construction of this new temple. He wants this temple built as much as the Jews because, secretly, the Grand Caliph has big plans for it in the near future.

# 8 Seal 2: The Whitewashed Horse Fades Back to Red

*When he opened the second seal, I heard the second living creature say, "Come!" And out came another horse, bright red. Its rider was permitted to take peace from the earth, so that people should slay one another, and he was given a great sword.* (Revelation 6:3–4 ESV)

The rules God established in this book *"permitted"* this Rider on the Red Horse to take peace from the earth. This demonstrates one of the things the 7-sealed book does: it documents that God grants specific powers to end-time antagonists at precise and carefully controlled times. The book is separated into 7 chapters, and each chapter has its own seal. Which means the book acts as a regulator, not allowing any event to advance before its time. For instance, the 3rd seal won't be opened until everything outlined in this 2nd seal transpires.

To *"take peace"* means war. Since it's the *"earth"* and not a specific region, this means it's another World War. It's too soon to know whether at that point in the future this war will be called WW3 or WW4. There will be battles in many places throughout the world, but since *Revelation* is Jerusalem-centric, it's a safe bet that most of the largest battles will occur in the areas formerly controlled by the Ottoman Empire as the antichrist works to quickly expand his domain (see Exhibit 6).

Writers of many of the commentaries that I consulted think the first rider is Jesus bringing peace on earth and that this second rider symbolizes the rejection of Jesus or the rejection of his gospel, which causes peace to leave the earth.[70] They have to take great extra-Biblical leaps to come to those conclusions, but I think they have one part right: it's the same rider. This rider is probably the deceptive hero who was introduced in the 1st seal riding on a white horse under the banner of peace, but now his true colors are starting to show. The horse wasn't genuinely white, it was a bright red horse all along that had just been carefully painted white to fool everyone. Now the ruse that he came in peace can't be maintained any longer and the horse's white color is beginning to wear off to expose what was really there all along: a bright red horse. Red is

---

[70] According to Clarke's Commentary, the first rider is "Supposed to represent Jesus Christ." (Bible Hub, "Revelation 6," Clarke's Commentary, biblehub.com, https://biblehub.com/commentaries/clarke/revelation/6.htm).

From Ellicott's Commentary for English Readers, concerning the first rider: "It was thus their hopes saw Christ: through ascended He went forth in spiritual power conquering." Concerning the second rider: "The seal puts in pictorial form the warning of Christ that wars and rumours of wars would be heard of." (Bible Hub, "Revelation 6," Ellicott's Commentary for English Readers, biblehub. com, https://biblehub.com/commentaries/ellicott/revelation/6.htm).

According to the Geneva Study Bible, the first and second rider are God. Concerning the first rider, "God will invade the world: and first of all will suddenly, mightily, and gloriously. . . triumph over it as conquer." Concerning the second rider: "God being provoked to wrath by the obstinacy and hard heartedness of the world, not repenting for the former plague: as setting on the same at hand, will cause disputes among men, and will destroy the inhabitants of this world, by the swords of one another." (Bible Hub, "Revelation 6," Geneva Study Bible, biblehub.com, https://biblehub.com/commentaries/gsb/revelation/6.htm).

Gill's Exposition says the first rider is the gospel and the second rider is the rejection of the gospel. The first rider: ". . . may design the swift progress of the Gospel in the world. . ." and the second rider ". . . perhaps may point out a decrease in the Gospel ministry. . ." (Bible Hub, "Revelation 6," Gill's Exposition, biblehub.com, https://biblehub.com/commentaries/gill/revelation/6.htm).

According to the Jamieson-Fausset-Brown Bible Commentary, the first rider is Christ or his angel and the second rider is "man's perversion of the gospel. . ." (Bible Hub, "Revelation 6," Jamieson-Fausset-Brown Bible Commentary, biblehub.com, https://biblehub.com/commentaries/jfb/revelation/6.htm).

the color of the devil, the dragon.[71] The devil, Satan, has been the secret behind the Grand Caliph's success. His deceptive arrival on the white-washed horse served its purpose. He fooled the people long enough to rise to the pinnacle of the revived Caliphate, which now encompasses the nations of the former Ottoman Empire. By the time this 2nd seal is opened, a year or more has probably passed, and some people are starting to understand that the white horse's arrival was a ruse; he never intended to bring peace. Some have suspected all along that he is the antichrist, but they have probably been branded as "conspiracy theorists."

The rider was "*given*" a great sword. It's probably not actually a sword, but a powerful weapon of some kind and its power may be unique since it was "*given*." We aren't told who gave this weapon to him, but it's either God or Satan. Since it's mentioned in this 7-sealed book, it's most likely a power authorized by God. The implication here is that this special weapon is the key to his unstoppable victories.

> . . . *they worshipped the beast, saying, "Who is like the beast, and who can fight against it?"* (Revelation 13:4b ESV)

All this widespread warring will destroy productive land and kill or displace many farmers who work the land, which sets the stage for the 3rd seal.

---

[71] "*And another sign appeared in heaven: behold, a great red dragon, with seven heads and ten horns, and on his heads seven diadems.*" (Revelation 12:3 ESV)

# 9 Seal 3: The Logistics Genius and his Grand Plan

> *When he opened the third seal, I heard the third living creature say, "Come!" And I looked, and behold, a black horse! And its rider had a pair of scales in his hand. And I heard what seemed to be a voice in the midst of the four living creatures, saying, "A quart of wheat for a denarius, and three quarts of barley for a denarius, and do not harm the oil and wine!"*
> (Revelation 6:5–6 ESV)

The rider on the black horse is the person Christians will eventually identify as the false prophet. He is false because Jesus has already told us that whatever this rider proclaims will not be true. I will share my thoughts on who he will probably be after I tell you what he's going to do.

He will be a skilled but corrupt logistics genius who takes control of a major portion of the war-torn world economy and deals out scarce food among survivors who are aligned with the Grand Caliph. Once again, God is setting limitations in his 7-sealed book, dictating that the basic foods essential for man's survival, barley and wheat, will remain available during this portion of the crisis, but they will be staggeringly expensive. It will take a whole day's labor to earn one day's worth of this tasteless food, which means this is dire, subsistence-level poverty.[72] Working an entire

---

[72] "During Roman times, there was a period when a denarius was worth about a day's wages" ("The History of Currency – What is a Denarius Worth?" Small Biz Viewpoints, April 4, 2017, https://www.smallbizviewpoints.com/2017/04/04/

day in exchange for only a day's worth of basic food is essentially slavery, and we're told this slave master, the false prophet, is the one who's holding the scales, making sure he gets a day's labor for a day's sustenance.

We have an earlier instance of God setting a price for wheat and barley in 2 Kings.[73] There had been a famine in Samaria, and on top of that, the king of Assyria had laid siege to Jerusalem. That siege dragged on for so long that all food was gone and the besieged Jews had turned to cannibalism to survive. The king was so beside himself that he ordered the prophet Elisha be killed, believing he had something to do with causing this unbearable deprivation. When the king entered Elisha's room to have him executed, Elisha prophesied an event would occur the next day which was absolutely impossible in their current siege situation. All of their farms outside the walls had been destroyed and picked clean by the massive, ravenous Assyrian army, yet Elishah prophesied this:

> But Elisha said, "Hear the word of the LORD: thus says the LORD, Tomorrow about this time a seah of fine flour shall be sold for a shekel, and two seahs of barley for a shekel, at the gate of Samaria." (2 Kings 7:1 ESV)[74]

While Elisha prophesied flour and barley would be cheap and plentiful the next day, John prophesied flour and barley would be

---

the-history-of-currency-what-is-a-denarius-worth/.)

[73] 2 Kings 6:24 – 7:20

[74] A seah would be about three 5-pound packages of flour and a shekel is just over ½ oz of silver, which would be worth about $12 in today's market. (James Wilson, "Converting Old Testament Shekel To Dollar Amounts," Chronicle Collectibles, September 29, 2023, https://www.chroniclecollectibles.com/old-testament-shekel-to-dollar/).

available but so expensive that every cent a person earned would be spent on that day's food ration.

The 7-sealed book also specifies that Satan will not be allowed to *"harm the oil and wine."* Oil and wine is a mystery, but it is likely that they are symbolic of foods that give variety and enjoyment to life. While these enjoyable things may not remain affordable to the common man, the 7-sealed book assures us that they will remain unharmed.[75]

---

[75] Bible Hub, "Revelation 6," Cambridge Bible for Schools and Colleges, bible-hub.com, https://biblehub.com/commentaries/cambridge/revelation/6.htm).

# 9.1 Two sets of Scales: "One for You and Two for Me"

The people of the world will be in dire straits due to the war(s), plagues, famine, disease, and pestilence. People will be miserable and desperate and looking for someone to save them from these unimaginable calamities and deprivations for which most are not prepared.

The rider on the black horse holds a pair of scales in his right hand. In John's day, scales were a balance mechanism used to measure the weight of goods being sold. But why would this rider be carrying two sets ("*a pair*") of scales? The answer is indisputable. One set must be accurate and the other rigged in favor of the merchant, or in this case the false prophet. This practice must have been common among the merchants because God called-out the cheating practice of using "*dishonest*" scales on a couple of different occasions:

> *The businessmen love to cheat; they use dishonest scales* (Hosea 12:7 NET)

> *The LORD abhors dishonest scales, but an accurate weight is his delight* (Proverbs 11:1 NET)

Notice how these two verses use the singular "*scales*?" This is why a "*pair of scales*" stands out.[76] The New Babylon exchange system started during the 1st seal is the rigged set of scales, benefitting those in that closed system to the detriment of everyone outside of

---

[76] In all the books and commentaries I searched, I could find none that recognized that there were two different sets (a pair) of scales. Everyone I reviewed, without exception, treated "pair" as though it was only "one" scale. This is another example of reading a verse with a preconceived lens.

its system. Famine across the world has made food scarce and most people are barely surviving on grains normally fed to livestock and whatever else they can beg for or scavenge. It's very possible that the false prophet will use food to entice people to join the Grand Caliph's fledgling economic exchange system. He will offer access to better food (oil and wine) from the reserves that the Grand Caliph has seized during his conquests.

> *Without warning he shall come into the richest parts of the province, and he shall do what neither his fathers nor his fathers' fathers have done, scattering among them plunder, spoil, and goods. He shall devise plans against strongholds, but only for a time.* (Daniel 11:24 ESV)

Many will voluntarily sign up for the Grand Caliph's new economic system and accept his unusual and megalomaniacal terms. These early adopters will be given special privileges, including access to better food, but this is one time when they had better read the 'terms of service' carefully. Because in order to be part of his closed economic exchange, they must first agree to take his permanent security mark physically on their right hand, pledge their loyalty, and bow down to him, much like North Koreans must bow down to the image of their leader.[77] It's a deal with the devil and can't be undone.

> *And see to it that no one becomes an immoral or godless person like Esau, who sold his own birthright for a single meal.* (Hebrews 12:16 NET)

---

[77] The mark's symbol itself will in some way indicate that you "belong" to or are the property of the antichrist.

Many early adopters will gladly accept this deal, not only because they are tired of working to barely feed their families but because cybercrime will be rampant and out of control. The false prophet's closed exchange system with 100% physical bio-electric verification will be almost completely immune from cybercrime. Such an impregnable security feature will be touted as an enticement in its early days.

Citizens from many countries, including those in the West, will push their leaders to join this exclusive economic system, seeing it as the only way to escape poverty and reap its attractive benefits. The promise of prosperity and security will be too compelling to resist, driving most nations to align themselves economically with this new world order.

It's clear that this system will rapidly dethrone whatever world reserve currency system is in place at the time. If it occurs while the US dollar remains the world's reserve currency, it will send the United States into an economic tailspin, at least for a time. There will undoubtedly be U.S. politicians who will try to sell out and sign up for this system despite many of their citizens recognizing it as the infamous mark of the beast.

We'll expand on this New Babylon system after the 4th seal is opened, which is when taking the mark becomes mandatory.

## 9.2 "Did you hear? Jesus has appeared in Syria": The False Prophet's Masquerade

The false prophet will be Satan's masterpiece. Satan has been working for the past 1,400 years to ensure that all the pieces will fall into place for this exact moment, so when this remarkable man arrives on the scene, the stage will already be set for much of the world to instantly accept him as genuine.

All Muslims have been prepared by specific Quranic verses to accept this miracle-working man as a true prophet of Allah. Sadly, however, Jesus warned that many Christians will also eagerly accept him. Not because any verses in the Bible support his authenticity (quite the contrary), but because they are unfamiliar with end times Scriptures and Christ's warnings about the appearance of false Christs.[78]

John calls him the *"false"* prophet for a specific reason: to tie him directly to Jesus' warning of false christs in the Olivet Discourse. Jesus knew that this man would be a very convincing imposter. He would be so convincing that Jesus prophesied that many Christians would be deceived. In his Olivet Discourse, as Jesus told his disciples about the signs that would portend his next coming, he kept repeating this specific warning. In the same way that Jesus warned Peter that he would deny that he knew Christ three times before the rooster crowed, in Matthew 24 he also warned us three times to not be deceived by those who will come saying they are Christ.[79]

---

[78] Eschatology is the study of prophecies regarding events about the end of the age.

[79] *"Jesus said to him, 'Truly, I tell you, this very night, before the rooster crows, you will deny me three times.'"* (Matthew 26:34 ESV)

1. *3 As he sat on the Mount of Olives, the disciples came to him privately, saying, "Tell us, when will these things be, and what will be the sign of your coming and of the end of the age?" 4 And Jesus answered them, "See that no one leads you astray. 5 For many will come in my name, saying, 'I am the Christ,' and they will lead many astray."* (Matthew 24: 3-5 ESV)

2. *11 And many false prophets will arise and lead many astray.* (Matthew 24:11 ESV)

3. *23 Then if anyone says to you, 'Look, here is the Christ!' or 'There he is!' do not believe it. 24 For false christs and false prophets will arise and perform great signs and wonders, so as to lead astray, if possible, even the elect. 25 See, I have told you beforehand. 26 So, if they say to you, 'Look, he is in the wilderness,' do not go out. If they say, 'Look, he is in the inner rooms,' do not believe it. 27 For as the lightning comes from the east and shines as far as the west, so will be the coming of the Son of Man. 28 Wherever the corpse is, there the vultures will gather* (Matthew 24:23-28 ESV)

Yes, the third rider will claim to be Jesus, the lamb.

*Then I saw another beast rising out of the earth. It had two horns like a lamb and it spoke like a dragon. 12 It exercises all the authority of the first beast in its presence, and makes the earth and its inhabitants worship the first beast, whose mortal wound was healed.* (Revelation 13:11-12 ESV)

You and I know it won't be Jesus, but a large percentage of the world is already being primed to fall for his elaborate deception. The arrival of "Jesus" at his headquarters will add even more believability to the carefully choreographed beneficent façade of the Grand Caliph. The endorsement of a beloved leader like the Grand Caliph will fan the flames of mass hysteria and groupthink, rapidly accelerating the widespread acceptance of this imposter as Jesus.[80] Word of the miracles he performs will spread and be exaggerated with each retelling. And in case you think that sounds farfetched, you need only look at cases of mass Christian hysteria, such as the Salem Witch Trials, to understand how easily many Christians could be swayed by his convincing miracles and false claim.[81]

This false Jesus will be highly compelling, performing miraculous signs and wonders likely similar to those of the real Jesus. However, there is a guaranteed way to confirm that this Jesus is false: he will not call us to worship himself or God. We know this because the phrase *"he spoke like a dragon"* indicates that he is aligned with the dragon, (the devil) and his antichrist. Unlike the real Jesus, this false Jesus will instead exhort us to give homage to the Grand Caliph, whom he will proclaim as the Mahdi. [82]

---

[80] "Transformational leaders can sometimes produce this same [GROUP THINK] effect because group members are more willing to buy into their vision for the group" (Kendra Cherry, "How Groupthink Impacts Our Behavior," Verywellmind.com, June 19, 2024, https://www.verywellmind.com/what-is-groupthink-2795213).

[81] Khalid Elhassan, "12 of History's Most Baffling Mass Hysteria Outbreaks," *History Collection,* November 28, 2017, https://historycollection.com/12-historys-baffling-mass-hysteria-outbreaks/

[82] The false prophet, who claims to be Jesus, will perpetuate the contention Muslims make today: that the Bible has been altered and that the Quran is, instead, the true word of god (Allah). This false prophet will assert that Allah has kept him alive in heaven and brought him back to earth at this exact moment to inform Jews and Christians that they have it all wrong. Furthermore, he will warn that if they do not repent and worship Allah, he will have no choice but to

The Grand Caliph, however, is not yet ready to reveal his true intentions, so he will continue to humbly deny this esteemed designation. It's not that he is truly humble; rather, he must wait for a specific event he has been meticulously planning before he can tip his hand and reveal his next false persona.

put them to death.

## 9.3 "Why Can't We All Just Get Along and Worship the Same God?"

The false Jesus will claim that our Bible has been corrupted. Sound familiar?[83] Virtually all Muslims will believe the antichrist is really the Mahdi, who has been prophesied in their Quran and Hadiths. For a well-researched and convincing explanation of this deception, I recommend two excellent books by Joel Richardson.[84]

The false Jesus will use the world-wide food and shelter shortage to denigrate all world religions except one. He'll diplomatically ask, "where are your gods now?" He'll advocate that for the good of humanity, we should all make theological concessions and purge the flaws from our respective faiths; a process I believe Revelation chapter 17 illustrates through its degrading imagery. He will convince the leaders of all the major world religions to come together and set aside their differences and see just how similar each other's pathways to heaven are. He'll say that together we can make the dream of the coexist slogan a reality.[85]

---

[83] Islam claims that the Bible has been corrupted, that the Current New Testament is NOT the same Gospel given by Jesus, so even though the Quran praises the Bible, they "conclude that what the Quran praises are not the same books included in today's Bible." (Alaa M. Abdou, "What does the Quran say about the Bible?" Explore Islam, November 26, 2023, https://explore-islam.com/what-does-the-quran-say-about-the-bible/).

[84] Joel Richardson, *Mideast Beast: The Scriptural Case for an Islamic antichrist* (WND Books, 2012), and *The Islamic Antichrist: The Shocking Truth about the Real Nature of the Beast* (WND Books, 2015).

[85] "The 'C' is typically represented by the Islamic crescent moon and star, symbolizing Islam. The 'o' is represented by the peace symbol, which is universally recognized and associated with 1960s counterculture movements. The 'e' is represented by a male and female gender symbol intertwined, representing gender equality and LGBTQ+ rights. The 'x' is represented by a Jewish Star of David, symbolizing Judaism. The 'i' is represented by a pagan or Wiccan pentacle, symbolizing nature-based spirituality. The 's' is represented by a Taoist

He'll appeal to the whole world with a speech that goes something like this: "Can we all agree to cooperate for the sake of those billions suffering in the world? Let's join spirits behind the one true god of the universe and agree that there's more than one way to reach god. Religion has been behind so much of this fighting and religious dogmas are literally killing us. Come, let us work together to take only the best of each of these great and esteemed religions and then let's team up to spread this new inclusive message of acceptance and begin to heal the wounds created by eons of needless conflict."

Keep in mind that the antichrist and his false Jesus both radiate charisma and charm. All major religions, including, sadly, many Christian denominations, will eagerly join this effort to be "inclusive" for the "greater good" of mankind. These Christian leaders will compromise their core beliefs that Jesus is the only way to God, that you must be born again, the Trinity, the virgin birth, and a host of other foundational tenets. Interestingly, while initially appearing like they were going along with all the other religious leaders, the Muslim representatives ultimately will not compromise, forcing every other major faith to compromise even more of their core beliefs to establish a new, ecumenical doctrine

yin yang symbol, representing balance and harmony. Finally, the 't' is represented by a Christian cross, symbolizing Christianity" (Anjana Sahney Thakker, "Unveiling The Deeper Meaning Behind The Coexist Symbol: A Message Of Unity And Tolerance," shunspirit.com, July 19, 2023, https://shunspirit.com/article/coexist-symbol-meaning).

that everyone can accept.[86] This brand new, world-unifying religion will, unsurprisingly, considering their representatives negotiate in bad faith, look and sound a whole lot like Islam.

Those who've read the Quran will tell you that the first portion of the Quran sounds somewhat like the Bible, and it even has stories revolving around many of the main characters in our Bible, from Adam to Isaac and Ishmael. But its message diverges radically from the Bible. One consequential example of their diametrically opposed message is that the Quran says Jesus is a prophet but not a deity. To them, he's not the Son of God, and his death on the cross was faked.[87]

Sadly, it will be easy to deceive many Christians with this "new" Bible. Lacking a deep familiarity with key verses in their current Bible, many will fail to notice the subtle, yet deadly changes craftily woven into this new, inclusive version, likely named something like *The Universal Testament*.[88]

---

[86] Within Islam, neither Shia nor Sunni will compromise. I agree with Joel Richardson's theory that these two factious sects of Islam are the final kingdom, the toes of the statue which Daniel saw which were part iron and part clay. "its legs of iron, its feet partly of iron and partly of clay " (Daniel 2:33 ESV ) "Despite the fact that most down throughout Church history have interpreted the legs of Iron in Daniel 2 to be referring to the Roman Empire, instead, as we have seen, a far more solid case is made for the Islamic Caliphate as the fulfillment of this passage. If one understands the legs of iron to be the Roman Empire, then this causes a significant tension with numerous other passages throughout the prophets. But if the legs of iron represent the Islamic Caliphate, then the message of Daniel 2 is seen to flow together seamlessly with all of the other passages throughout the prophets that speak of Jesus judging Muslim nations and Israel's neighbors on the Day of the LORD." Joel Richardson, *Mideast Beast: The Scriptural Case for an Islamic Antichrist* (WND Books, 2012), 82–83

[87] "And for boasting, 'We killed the Messiah, Jesus, son of Mary, the messenger of Allah.' But they neither killed nor crucified him--it was only made to appear so. Even those who argue for this 'crucifixion' are in doubt. They have no knowledge whatsoever--only making assumptions. They certainly did not kill him" (Quran. com, "An-Nisa, Verse 157," https://quran.com/an-nisa/157).

[88] Since the word "Bible" is closely associated with Christianity and "the book" is acknowledged within the Quran, this new doctrine may be called something slightly different, like the "The Universal Testament" or "The Testament of

*For the fool speaks folly, and his heart is busy with iniquity, to practice ungodliness, to utter error concerning the LORD, to leave the craving of the hungry unsatisfied, and to deprive the thirsty of drink.* (Isaiah 32:6 ESV)

The representatives of each major religion that meet for this First Council of Babylon to hash out the doctrine and basic tenets for this new religion will become ambassadors or bishops preaching the new unifying doctrine from their new bibles.

There will be those who resist, but to ensure its adoption, all of their legacy religious works, such as Bibles, Torahs, Buddhist teachings, Hindu Vedas, the Book of Mormon, and so on, will be banned as non-inclusive and divisive.

The banning of Bibles should come as no surprise to anyone familiar with church history. There were hundreds of years during the Middle Ages that people, especially in Europe, were prohibited, some even tortured and killed, for possessing a Bible or even parts of a Bible. One of the more infamous examples was William Tyndale, who, for the crime of translating the Bible into English, was burned at the stake.[89]

---

the Enlightened." Key passages will be removed or ever-so-slightly changed, just as when Satan ever-so-slightly changed what God told Adam. So, this new adulterated bible will be totally worthless spiritually and will not lead anyone to a saving faith in Christ, which is exactly what the antichrist wants.

[89] Church history unfortunately has many hundreds of examples of the church (both Catholic and, for a period of time, Anglican) banning Bibles and executing people for possessing one or translating one into another language for more than 1,000 years in Europe. People got good at concealing their Bibles, such as the example cited below of one Huguenot family who baked theirs in a loaf of bread to hide it from state soldiers on a search and destroy mission.
Emma Muscat, "Hidden In Plain Sight: The Fascinating Huguenot Practice Of Bible Concealment," Huguenot Museum, April 26, 2018, https://huguenotmuseum.org/about/news/hidden-in-plain-sight-the-fascinating-huguenot-practice-of-bible-concealment/.
John Foxe, Foxe's Book of Martyrs (n.p.: n.p., n.d.), https://ia600802.us.archive.org/14/items/foxesbookofmartyrs_201708/Foxes-Book-of-Martyrs.pdf.

## 9.4 The Whispering Angel Round One – *"For God so Loved the World"*

> *Then I saw another angel flying directly overhead, with an eternal gospel to proclaim to those who dwell on earth, to every nation and tribe and language and people. 7 And he said with a loud voice, "Fear God and give him glory, because the hour of his judgment has come, and worship him who made heaven and earth, the sea and the springs of water."* (Rev 14:6–7 ESV)

Despite the false prophet's efforts to subvert the Bible by rewriting important verses and renaming it *The Universal Testament*, and then banning genuine Bibles, our Lord will demonstrate to the world that his Word is supreme and unfailing. He will broadcast critical portions of it supernaturally. God uses scores of angels in Revelation to explain to John what he is seeing, sound trumpets, pour out bowl judgments, and make pronouncements. Several of the angels are sent flying around the world to make proclamations at specific times. This is the first of three circumnavigating angels, which I refer to as whispering angels because their voices will sound like whispering in your head.

Each angel travels across the entire globe to deliver their messages to all of humanity, and they aren't just shouting at people who happen to be outside. For their messages to reach and be understood by everyone on earth ("*every nation and tribe and language*") at almost the same time, they will be communicated directly inside each person's mind in a clear and understandable way. This will happen whether the person is indoors or outdoors,

---

"List of Protestant Martyrs of the English Reformation," Wikipedia, https://en.wikipedia.org/wiki/List_of_Protestant_martyrs_of_the_English_Reformation.

awake or asleep, or even deaf. The message will come as an audible voice or whisper uniquely tailored to each person's way of learning, their level of understanding and in their own language and dialect.

> *But I say, Have they not heard? Yes verily, their sound went into all the earth, and their words unto the ends of the world.* (Romans 10:18 KJV)

This first angel will probably not be visible because the principalities of the unseen world, both good and evil, are still concealed from people until the Great Tribulation begins in just a little while. The angel will proclaim the gospel and maybe even some of the Old Testament prophecies which would help them better understand the gospel and they may even customize the message to each person depending on their familiarity with the Bible. After this first supernatural message, everyone will probably be asking each other, "Did you just hear that, or am I imagining things?" and chatter will spread throughout the world, with each person comparing what they heard. The message will be instantly impressed in our memories.

> *And this gospel of the kingdom shall be preached in all the world for a witness unto all nations: and then shall the end come.* (Matthew 24:14 KJV)

In broadcasting this universally clear message, God makes his final plea to persuade unsaved men and women to accept the truth while still respecting their freedom to choose to believe what they want.

The antichrist's propaganda machine will move swiftly to discredit the message, claiming, 'It was merely an attempt by Satan, or some other scapegoat, to derail the progress we've made in uniting the world.

Ignore what you think you heard and place your faith in the *Universal Testament.*' Yet, some people, still grieving the loss of their 'old' Bibles, will treasure the angel's message in their hearts and find comfort in it.

It's possible this final preaching of the gospel turns into a mass-conversion event because many from other religions in all areas of the world who had never heard the gospel, or never heard it presented in an understandable way, will now consider the truth of God's word and will accept Jesus as their Savior. It's also possible that many who had considered themselves Christians, but who had never read much of the Bible and had not fully grasped God's message will now understand it and truly accept Jesus as their Lord and Savior.

Tragically, however, the majority of people will still reject Jesus. Even after hearing the gospel presented with supernatural clarity, customized by the first whispering angel so that they understand it perfectly, they will, by their own free will, still choose to reject God, thereby sealing their own fate.

But even more tragic, many self-proclaimed Christians will *"refuse to love the truth"* and will *"believe what is false."*[90] They will believe the lie that the false Jesus and his new religion is the real religion that God originally intended but which had been corrupted. The false Jesus will testify that the Bible has been corrupted by the Jews and early Christians and that he should know because it was his own words that inspired the original Scriptures. He will claim that Allah kept him safe in paradise and restored him to earth for this very reason. The false Jesus may even produce some ancient artifact or document to make his case, but it will all be a well-orchestrated ruse thousands of years in the making.[91]

---

[90] *and with all wicked deception for those who are perishing, because they refused to love the truth and so be saved.11 Therefore God sends them a strong delusion, so that they may believe what is false,"* (2 Thessalonians 2:10-11 ESV)

[91] "In one final very interesting series of traditions regarding the Mahdi we find that he is said to produce some previously undiscovered Bible scrolls—even the

## 9.5 The Whispering Angel Round Two – "Babylon's Days are Numbered"

*Another angel, a second, followed, saying, "Fallen, fallen is Babylon the great, she who made all nations drink the wine of the passion of her sexual immorality."* (Revelation 14:8 ESV)

This is a fair warning to the world: the newly created, suddenly wealthy, and stunningly beautiful, yet utterly corrupt, Babylon will fall. However, as we will see in the coming chapters, many events must still unfold before that day arrives.

This angel's prophecy to the world will seem ridiculous and outlandish because the Grand Caliph's New Babylon City, fueled by its exclusive and secure financial exchange system, is experiencing meteoric growth. This city's beauty will rival that of Paris, its immense wealth will dwarf that of Riyadh, and the excesses it celebrates will make Las Vegas look like a modest county fair. As discussed in Seal 1, the world's top financiers will likely be the architects behind this sophisticated, closed economic system. And it won't just work, it will exceed all expectations, with early adopters amassing fortunes beyond anything they could have imagined. But how is all this wealth generated so quickly?

The answer lies not only in the economic system's design but also in the seductive allure of what New Babylon represents. It's an unstoppable financial empire built on global dependence on and personal faith in the Caliph. The Grand Caliph seems uninterested in accumulating personal wealth. Instead, he cultivates an image of selflessness by distributing his share of the profits to all his loyal subjects

---

Ark of the Covenant itself" (Joel Richardson, *The Islamic Antichrist, 30*).

in the New Babylon economy. This fosters a sense of shared prosperity and further enhances his allure and mystique as a benevolent leader. But this is far more than an impressive economic boom; it's a silent and insidious revolution. This brilliant system is designed to quietly siphon wealth—and with it, power—from every other nation, depositing global influence in the hands of the Grand Caliph.

As the world remains captivated by and jealous of its success, the very foundations of international power are being drained, leaving all other countries weakened and under the shadow of New Babylon's growing dominance. Babylon will rise as the only economic superpower, offering financial aid to struggling nations, but at a heavy cost. In exchange for this lifeline, these nations will be forced to pledge their allegiance and comply with Babylon's religious mandates, effectively submitting themselves and their citizens to its authority and control.

> *And the woman that you saw is the great city* [Babylon] *that has dominion over the kings of the earth."* (Revelation 17:18 ESV)

Babylon exerted some form of control over (*"she...made"*) *every* nation, not necessarily by fully dominating their governments but likely through economic influence, using its closed exchange system. Part of the cost of doing business with Babylon and sharing in its wealth was the requirement to participate in its lavish and immoral lifestyle.

However, as we'll later see, several powerful nations will grow increasingly resentful of their economic enslavement and the dark truths they uncover about the antichrist's sinister agenda. In defiance, they will unite and launch a massive ground assault against the antichrist's forces in Israel, igniting the final world war.

But how is such rapid accumulation of wealth possible? It seems almost unbelievable that a newly established city with an untried economic system could surpass every other city to become the world's largest economy in just a year or so. One source of this rapid wealth accumulation is the Grand Caliph's ruthless pillaging of unsuspecting nations and seizing their most valuable assets. By stripping these countries of their finest resources, he channels their wealth directly into New Babylon, enriching those who worship him while expanding his global dominance.

> *Without warning he shall come into the richest parts of the province, and he shall do what neither his fathers nor his fathers' fathers have done, scattering among them plunder, spoil, and goods. He shall devise plans against strongholds, but only for a time.* (Daniel 11:24 ESV)

To those paying attention, Babylon's sudden rise to wealth and power will seem baffling but irresistibly alluring. Wealth attracts more wealth, and many of the world's richest people will eagerly abandon their struggling homelands to join this new paradise. Drawn by the allure of Babylon's opulence, the wealthy will relocate, bringing their fortunes with them to escape the crushing taxes of their home countries. Back home, governments are straining under mounting burdens, desperately trying to rebuild and feed their suffering populations. The Grand Caliph will warmly welcome these immigrants of means, asking only one thing in return: their total and irreversible veneration.

But there's more to it than meets the eye, for this is no ordinary reverence. To partake in Babylon's seemingly magical economy, they must take his mark, publicly acknowledge the miracle he has created, and pay homage to him as their savior of the world. It's a form of baptism publicly acknowledging that they're now on his team! Babylon, now filled with his loyal followers, becomes a city of his minions, all bound to him by wealth, submission, and his brand emblazoned on their right hand. In return for their undying fealty, the Grand Caliph generously dispenses power and fortune from the vast riches his new economic empire has amassed.

> *Those who acknowledge him he shall load with honor. He shall make them rulers over many and shall divide the land for a price.* (Daniel 11:39b ESV)

After all, the Grand Caliph doesn't have the desires of a normal rockstar, billionaire, or dictator. He's not after money. He's been consolidating power and has everything he needs for his next step. What he needs now is for as many people as possible to reject Jesus as their Savior.

> *36 And the king shall do as he wills. He shall exalt himself and magnify himself above every god, and shall speak astonishing things against the God of gods. He shall prosper till the indignation is accomplished; for what is decreed shall be done.* (Daniel 11:36 ESV)

This second whispering angel is also trying to wake up the Christians and Jews who've started enjoying the life of luxury in Babylon a little too much. Yes, we know there will be Christians and Jews living there because a few chapters after this angel's proclamation and just before Jesus destroys Babylon, another angel gives a final warning in Revelation 18, saying, "*Come out of her, my people.*" Some Christians and Jews may be there for employment and haven't submitted to the Grand Caliph by taking his mark, yet.

But in the same way that Lot and his wife started enjoying the easy life of luxury in Sodom even though they could see the depravity all around them, so some Christians and Jews will indulge in the luxuries and debaucheries of Babylon and will be swept away when it is finally destroyed at the 7th bowl.

The Pax Persiana around Babylon will seem to be heaven on earth, but the trap has been set and those inside won't believe it until it's too late.

# 9.6 Those Troublesome Jews and their Inhumane Animal Sacrifices

*In that day will I raise up the tabernacle of David that is fallen, and close up the breaches thereof; and I will raise up his ruins, and I will build it as in the days of old* (Amos 9:11 KJV)

By this time, 3½ years after they signed the covenant with the Grand Caliph, the Jewish temple has been rebuilt. The Jews are required to offer sacrifices carefully and ceremonially on specific occasions. On the Day of Atonement, a specially selected animal will be honorably sacrificed on the altar as an atonement for sin. At other times, there will be offerings of grain, oil, small birds, and occasionally a special animal.

To the civilized world and even to nonpracticing Jews, the sacrifice of animals will be abhorrent. There will be a lot of bad publicity and protests against the inhumanity of the Jews. At just the right time, the Grand Caliph will find it expedient to direct his media's attention to that "barbaric" practice.

They will not like being the subject of protests, but the Jews will be living their dream, offering sacrifices to God in their beautiful temple after a forced hiatus of almost 2,000 years. But one fateful day, as they celebrate their good fortune and the peace and safety they've experienced while under the sworn protection of the Grand Caliph, they will be oblivious to what's about to hit them.

*For when they shall say, Peace and safety; then sudden destruction cometh upon them, as travail upon a woman with child; and they shall not escape.* (1 Thessalonians 5:3 KJV)

# 10 The Archangel Michael is Hindering Satan's Grand Plan

There are likely several archangels in God's heavenly kingdom, but only two are mentioned by name in the Protestant Bible: Gabriel and Michael.[92] Michael is known as the protector of Israel. He once came to the aid of Gabriel, who was detained in a weeks-long battle with the *"Prince of Persia"* while on a mission from God to bring an answer to one of Daniel's prayers. Gabriel had been sent with answers for Daniel, who had asked God how he was to understand what had just been revealed to him about what would happen in the last days.

Michael performs his work entirely in the unseen world except for a few instances. He is one of the rule enforcers that God assigned over Israel to protect the Jews and their temple from Satan and other demonic entities. Those demonic entities sometimes push against the boundaries and the archangels have to fight back. Michael constantly protected Israel from the dark actors, such as the Prince of Persia and the prince of Greece mentioned in the next verse, who are evil entities who also exist in that unseen realm.

> *And he* [The Archangel Gabriel] *said, "O man greatly loved, fear not, peace be with you; be strong and of good courage." And as he spoke to me, I was strengthened and said, "Let my lord speak, for you have strengthened me."* 20*Then he said, "Do you know why I have come to you? But now I will return to*

---

[92] A third Archangel, Raphael, is mentioned in the Catholic Bible in Tobit 12:15, an apocryphal book.

> *fight against the prince of Persia; and when I go out,*
> *behold, the prince of Greece will come. 21 But I will*
> *tell you what is inscribed in the book of truth: there*
> *is none who contends by my side against these except*
> *Michael, your prince.* (Daniel 10:19–21 ESV)

The 3½ years since the Grand Caliph signed the protective covenant with the Jews has gone amazingly well for Satan. He has guided and empowered his human puppet, the Grand Caliph, to become the most powerful and respected leader in the world. But Satan's rapid success has led him to believe that his ultimate goal is within reach. Satan wants much more than a ten-nation coalition. He wants everything. Satan desires the heavens and the earth.

The Grand Caliph's good-guy façade is becoming increasingly difficult to maintain, so Satan thinks the time is right to strike. He's going to circumvent the 7-sealed book and surprise God with the rebellion he's been plotting for eons. Satan must quickly take the battle to the next level, but he can't as long as Michael is protecting the temple. Michael is the *"hedge"* of protection around Israel.

> *And now go to; I will tell you what I will do to my*
> *vineyard: I will take away the hedge thereof, and it*
> *shall be eaten up; and break down the wall thereof,*
> *and it shall be trodden down* (Isaiah 5:5 KJV)

Once Michael, *"he who now restrains it,"* is out of the way, the antichrist will make his move to challenge God. The Earthly part of that challenge, called the abomination of desolation, will reveal to the believing world that the Grand Caliph has been the antichrist all along.

*And you know what is restraining him now so that he may be revealed in his time. 7 For the mystery of lawlessness is already at work. Only he who now restrains it will do so until he is out of the way.* (2 Thessalonians 2:6-7 ESV)

In the unseen realm, Satan had been carefully observing the archangel Michael's daily routine, watching for just the right moment to execute his arrogant plan. He waited until Michael was distracted or, even better, called away to help with some problem far from the temple. Satan's patience is rewarded when Michael, for some inexplicable reason, completely leaves his watchman's post in Jerusalem.

# 10.1 Michael Rises

*At that time shall arise Michael, the great prince who has charge of your people...* (Daniel 12:1a ESV)

Satan has no idea why Michael suddenly leaves his post in Jerusalem; he just knows it's the fortuitous opportunity he's been watching for to usher his Grand Caliph inside the temple without a fight in the unseen world.[93] By the time Satan learns that it was God who recalled Michael to heaven, it will be too late for Satan.

Three things will happen virtually simultaneously:
1. Michael leaves earth and goes up to heaven
2. On earth, the antichrist brazenly claims God's Earthly temple for himself
3. In heaven, Satan leads millions of disillusioned angels to mutiny against God's heavenly temple

As soon as Satan's rebellions are finished, the Great Tribulation begins.

---

[93] The Book of Daniel gives us a surreal glimpse into the unseen spiritual world that surrounds us, though it remains invisible—at least for now (see chapter 11.2 when the unseen world begins to operate openly in our world). In the Archangel Gabriel's dramatic account, he tells Daniel that he was sent from heaven by God to deliver an urgent answer to Daniel's fervent prayer, and would have been there three weeks ago, but something terrible happened to him on his way. Gabriel goes on to say that he was captured and restrained by a formidable being he calls the Prince of Persia. This mysterious figure, clearly not human, is powerful enough to hold back an archangel, locking him in a cosmic standoff for three weeks. The stalemate is only broken because the mightiest of Archangels, Michael, arrives to battle alongside Gabriel and finally frees him to complete his divine mission. *"The prince of the kingdom of Persia withstood me twenty-one days, but Michael, one of the chief princes, came to help me, for I was left there with the kings of Persia,"* (Daniel 10:13 ESV)

## 10.2 Defiling all that is Sacred: Hijacking God's Temple

The first prong of Satan's two-prong attack is on God's Earthly temple, but he will make this part seem like his antichrist is doing the civilized world a favor.

Still trying to maintain his benevolent pretense, the Grand Caliph enters God's earthly temple. His next act will finally *"reveal"* his true identity to the world.

> And *then the lawless one will be revealed,* whom the Lord Jesus will kill with the breath of his mouth and bring to nothing by the appearance of his coming. (2 Thessalonians 2:8 ESV).[94]

While Scripture is silent on the details, one can imagine the scene unfolding like this. As part of his grand plan, The Grand Caliph and his entourage of reporters, laden with broadcasting equipment, push their way past the now-enraged Jewish priests assembled in the temple courtyard, who are ceremoniously preparing an animal for sacrifice. The Grand Caliph, adorned with all the splendor of a triumphal king, motions for the reporters to remain in the courtyard and observe from there, ostensibly to show concern for

---

[94] The lawless one is the antichrist, not Satan. The antichrist has been mentored, guided, and steered by Satan, and Satan gives him some of his power. He is empowered *"by the activity of Satan"* to work some impressive miracles to deceive those who don't know or understand God's warnings.

> The coming of the lawless one is *by the activity of Satan* with all power and *false signs and wonders,* 10 and with all wicked deception for those who are perishing, because they refused to love the truth and so be saved. (2 Thessalonians 2:9–10 ESV)

their lives should mere mortals dare to enter with him, while they continue broadcasting. He alone, with audacious resolve, takes the risk of crossing the threshold into the sacred room, the Holy of Holies, where no ordinary human dares to trespass for fear of God's retribution in being immediately struck dead.[95]

As the entire world watches through the doorway, a foreboding hush of anticipation settles over the temple. The majesty of this sacred inner sanctum, paneled in glistening 24-carat gold, is revealed in all its glory to the world for the first time.

Having survived that first blasphemous step, now taking on the aura of a victorious conqueror, the Grand Caliph ascends to take his seat at the altar, crafted in the image of God's altar in heaven, and declares that all animals will be freed and there will be no more sacrifices. And he, by his very presence, will take their place, implying that his mere existence now fulfills the demands of heaven.

As Paul foretold in Thessalonians, this act of calculated irreverence must occur in order for the Christian and Jewish world to see the Grand Caliph's true colors and motive.

> Let no man deceive you by any means: for that day shall not come, except there come a falling away first, and that man of sin be revealed, the son of perdition; 4 Who opposeth and exalteth himself above all that is called God, or that is worshipped; so that he as God sitteth in the temple of God, shewing himself that he is God. (2 Thessalonians 2:3–4 KJV)

If there had been any doubt about the Grand Caliph's true identity, this sacrilegious act makes it clear to Christians and Jews

---

[95] Only the specifically chosen and anointed priest, ritually cleansed and wearing specific garments, dares to enter God's throne room, the Holy of Holies.

familiar with prophecy that the Grand Caliph, this highly popular and idolized leader, is indeed the antichrist. His desecration of the temple is a blatant violation of the rules of engagement in God's 7-sealed book, and it unfolds exactly as predicted in Scripture. The official term for this ultimate rebellion against God's temple is *"the abomination of desolation."*

> *... then they shall take away the daily sacrifices and place there the abomination of desolation. 32 Those who do wickedly against the covenant he shall corrupt with flattery...* (Daniel 11:31b–32a NKJV)

> *So when you see the abomination of desolation spoken of by the prophet Daniel, standing in the holy place (let the reader understand), 16 then let those who are in Judea flee to the mountains.* (Matthew 24:15-16 ESV)

While this abomination and blasphemy sends a shockwave through the religious Jewish world and Christian communities, the rest of the world rejoices! They celebrate that those barbaric Jews have been forced to stop their outrageous cruelty to animals and, if he hasn't already achieved it, this will launch the Grand Caliph to celebrity status.

To the Muslims, with this bold act, usurping the God of the Jews, the Grand Caliph takes on a supernatural mantle; one that places him just slightly lower than Allah himself. Muslims will worship no one but Allah, but they can and will give homage and reverence to one specific person: the Mahdi. They now recognize that the Grand Caliph is the Mahdi for which they've all been praying.[96] This is what the Grand Caliph's prophet, the fake Jesus,

---

[96] Joel Richardson, *The Islamic Antichrist.*

whom the Muslims have been acknowledging as the real Jesus, but whom John tells us is the false prophet, has been proclaiming all along to anyone who would listen. But now, after this public demonstration, the Grand Caliph humbly acknowledges that yes, he is the Mahdi. He'll say that he could not acknowledge that fact earlier because his time had not yet come.

The world's newfound respect and admiration for the Mahdi will not extend to knowledgeable Christians, who will now be certain of what many long suspected. There is no longer any doubt about the true identity of this Grand Caliph. This person who did the impossible and allowed the Jews to live in peace without fear of missiles and suicide bombers from their Palestinian neighbors and who had allowed and even encouraged them to build their temple again on the Temple Mount was the deceiver. This person whom the banking experts had willingly helped to establish the sophisticated economic exchange system was the antichrist, the *"Assyrian"* that Isaiah warned about!

> *In that day the Lord will shave with a razor that is hired beyond the River-with the king of Assyria-the head and the hair of the feet, and it will sweep away the beard also.* (Isaiah 7:20 ESV)

The religious Jews will pour dust on their heads and pull hair out of their beards as they ask themselves how they could have been so blind as to not understand that this Grand Caliph was the antichrist!

> *Behold, their valiant ones shall cry without: the ambassadors of peace shall weep bitterly.* (Isaiah 33:7 KJV)

This event is one of the clearest markers on the end-times timeline. The 70th week of Daniel starts with the signing of the covenant, and according to Daniel's terminology, a week is 7 years. When the abomination of desolation occurs, we know we are in the *"midst,"* or middle, of that final seven-year period. This means that even if we were unaware of the date that the peace agreement was signed, once this event occurs, we can be sure that there will be 3½ years remaining in the final half of the contest. As soon as this abomination of desolation occurs, the Great Tribulation, also known as the time of Jacob's trouble, begins and will last 3½ years.

> *And he shall confirm the covenant with many for one week: and in the midst of the week he shall cause the sacrifice and the oblation to cease, and for the overspreading of abominations he shall make it desolate, even until the consummation, and that determined shall be poured upon the desolate.* (Daniel 9:27 KJV)

> *Alas! for that day is great, so that none is like it: it is even the time of Jacob's trouble; but he shall be saved out of it.* (Jeremiah 30:7 KJV)

But why would Satan incite God by having his antichrist sit on God's earthly altar? The answer is that this is about much more than just angering God. This has been a lifelong ambition, if you can say lifelong when talking about an immortal being. Satan has been dreaming, *"you said in your heart,"* and plotting to usurp God from his throne for thousands of years.

> *How you have fallen from the heavens, O shining one, son of the dawn! You have been cut down to earth, O*

*weakener of nations. 13 And you said in your heart: "I go up into the heavens, I raise my throne above the stars of God, And I sit on the mountain of meeting in the sides of the north. 14 I go up above the heights of a thick cloud, I am like to the Most High."15 Only- you are brought down to Sheol, To the sides of the pit.* (Isaiah 14:12–15 Literal Standard Version)

Most authors and commentators acknowledge this is the desecration of God's earthly temple, but because they are locked into a specific end-time narrative, they misunderstand the true sequence of Revelation and, therefore, miss its connection to a larger, full-scale revolution. The antichrist's rebellion against God's earthly throne is merely the earthly front of a far greater and more reckless war, a war rooted in Satan's irrational and insatiable ambition to overthrow God and elevate himself above all.

The antichrist's desecration of the temple reveals his arrogance, but the second front of this war: a revolution Satan has been simultaneously orchestrating in the heavenly realm, showcases just how blinded and delusional Satan has become in his egotistical ambition to exalt himself above God and thus nullify the end-times plan God laid out in his 7-sealed book.

# 10.3 A Fifth Column in Heaven: The Disillusioned Angels

*Now war arose in heaven* (Revelation 12:7a ESV)

How many angels did God have before this war in heaven began? Jeremiah tells us there are so many that they cannot be numbered.

> *As the host of heaven cannot be numbered and the sands of the sea cannot be measured, so I will multiply the offspring of David my servant, and the Levitical priests who minister to me.* (Jeremiah 33:22a ESV)

John described that he saw many more than 100 million angels in heaven.[97] A war, then, would require close to a similar number of angels on Satan's side. So, how many angels does Satan have?

Satan has an untold number of demons, but only angels participate in this war in heaven. The only angels we know of who are aligned with Satan are the former Watchers of Genesis 6:1–4. Those Watcher angels were condemned by God for *"lusting after"* and *"going into"* the daughters of men and having children with them.[98] The majority of them were subsequently chained in hell, awaiting their latter-day judgment.[99] Even if Satan were to jail-break

---

[97] "And I beheld, and I heard the voice of many angels round about the throne and the beasts and the elders: and the number of them was ten thousand times ten thousand, and thousands of thousands;" (Revelation 5:11, KJV). In other words, it sounds like billions of angels.

[98] The Book of Enoch is not part of the Bible, though concepts from it are referenced by Peter and Jude (Michael S. Heiser, *The Unseen Realm*). The most complete version of it remains canon in the Ethiopian Bible.

[99] "The two hundred angels take an oath to descend to Mt Hermon, find women

every fallen angel that God chained, there are far too few for John to call that a "*war.*"[100] John would more likely have called that tiny number of rebels a skirmish or a guerilla action.

Therefore, as incredible as this may sound, this is a civil war among God's holy angels, led by that great dragon, Satan. Satan deceived these angels using the same playbook he used to deceive Eve, and with thousands of years of 24-hour-a-day ("*day and night*") access to heaven, he's had plenty of time to work his wiles on them.

> . . . *for the accuser of our brothers has been thrown down, who accuses them day and night before our God.* (Revelation 12:10b ESV)

How did he accomplish this? Over the past several millennia, Satan has personally groomed each angel he sensed was either sympathetic to his cause of advocating for their fellow Watcher angels, resentful of humanity's special place in God's heart above the angels, or still in awe of his former glory as God's chief angel.

Day by day, Satan will eventually convince tens of millions of God's angels, using every vestige of his incomparable charisma and power of deception, that one wrong word or action from them and it could just as easily be they who would be confined in chains forever, just like the Watcher angels.

He succeeded in fully indoctrinating them into believing that he and the fallen angels he's caring for are being treated unjustly by

---

to marry and have children with them. 1 Enoch 6:7–8 lists the names of the leaders of these angels. Most have names with some reference to God (Remashel, "evening of God," or Kokabel, "star of God"). (Phillip J. Long, "The Fallen Angels – 1 Enoch 6–8," Reading Acts, readingacts.com, May 31, 2016, https://readingacts.com/2016/05/31/the-fallen-angels-1-enoch-6-8/).

[100] The Book of Enoch indicates that there were 200 Watchers. (Michael S. Heiser, *The Unseen Realm*).

God. These disillusioned angels who are now convinced that God doesn't love them will form a fifth column in heaven.[101] They will remain interspersed within the ranks of God's faithful angels like tares among the unsuspecting wheat.[102] Those angels will continue performing their duties in heaven, waiting for the day they will hear the rallying cry from Satan.

Daniel tied these two events together, the desecration of the temple on earth and the war in heaven, 600 years before John, but it seemed more like another one of Daniel's surreal dreams until John affirmed it and fleshed it out in Revelation 12. The small horn, the antichrist, grew powerful on earth and "*its power reached to the heavens*," where it attacked God's angels and succeeded in vanquishing some of them.

> *Then from one of the prominent horns came a small horn whose power grew very great. It extended toward the south and the east and toward the glorious land of Israel. 10 Its power reached to the heavens, where it attacked the heavenly army, throwing some of the heavenly beings and some of the stars to the ground and trampling them.* (Daniel 8:9–10 NLT)

When the antichrist walked into the Holy of Holies and stopped the animal sacrifices, it was an affront to the Archangel Michael, who would have fought back had God not recalled him to heaven, which "*restrained* [Michael] *from responding*." The antichrist, "*the horn*," succeeded in desecrating the earthly temple.

---

[101] "A 'fifth column' is a group which operates in secret, usually within enemy lines, in order to help further a cause which they secretly support." (Taegan Goddard, "Fifth Column," Political Dictionary, https://politicaldictionary.com/words/fifth-column/).

[102] Matthew 13:24-30, the parable of the wheat and the tares.

*11 It even challenged the Commander of heaven's army by canceling the daily sacrifices offered to him and by destroying his Temple. 12 The army of heaven was restrained from responding to this rebellion. So the daily sacrifice was halted, and truth was overthrown. The horn succeeded in everything it did.* (Daniel 8:11–12 NLT)

As further support for the angels becoming disillusioned, Peter told us that angels lack the same freedom as humans to research anything that piques their interest. Angels long to research certain things, for instance, the process of salvation in 2 Peter, but for some reason, God does not allow them to.

*It was revealed to them that they were serving not themselves but you, in the things that have now been announced to you through those who preached the good news to you by the Holy Spirit sent from heaven, things into which angels long to look.* (1 Peter 1:12 ESV)

Just how many angels sided with Satan in this civil war? We don't know a number, but we know the ratio. In Revelation 12:4, we're told it's the ratio we always see Satan restricted to by God: 1/3$^{rd}$.

*His tail swept down a third of the stars of heaven and cast them to the earth...* (Revelation 12:4a ESV)

Satan must have believed that way more than a third of God's angels were on his side; otherwise, he wouldn't have thought he stood any chance of victory. When we get to the trumpets, we will see that Satan's authority in nearly everything is restricted to 1/3$^{rd}$, and we see that restrictive fraction 1/3rd here again.[103] The presence of that ratio here implies that God knew about these rebellious angels, and he thwarted Satan by restraining him to just 1/3rd.

> *. . . Michael and his angels fought against the dragon, and the dragon and his angels fought back. 8 But the dragon was not strong enough to prevail, so there was no longer any place left in heaven for him and his angels. 9 So that huge dragon––the ancient serpent, the one called the devil and Satan, who deceives the whole world––was thrown down to the earth, and his angels along with him. 10 Then I heard a loud voice in heaven saying, "The salvation and the power and the kingdom of our God, and the ruling authority of his Christ, have now come, because the accuser of our brothers and sisters, the one who accuses them day and night before our God, has been thrown down. 11 But they overcame him by the blood of the Lamb and by the word of their testimony, and they did not love their lives so much that they were afraid to die. 12 Therefore you heavens rejoice, and all who reside in them! But woe to the earth and the sea because the devil has come down to you! He is filled with terrible anger, for he knows that he only has a little time!"* (Revelation 12: 7–12 NET)

---

[103] Here's a thought about Satan's number: 666. Throughout Revelation, Satan has been limited to 333 (1/3rd = 0.333). Though he desperately desires it all, he's not allowed to have the remaining 2/3rds (2/3rds = 0.666). Therefore 666 is the portion that he can't have, which may be why John tells us his number is 666, because Satan has always lusted after, and is trying to attain, the 666 he can never have. That means Satan is labeled by how much he falls short of the glory of God. Imagine if each of us was labeled by exactly how much we fall short of the glory of God. Thank God we are not labeled by our shortcomings and instead are labeled as complete, 100%, in Jesus.

The minute the antichrist makes his grand entrance into the temple and takes possession of God's earthly throne, Satan launches a coordinated attack against God's throne in heaven. He has carefully masterminded every detail of this rebellion and has been grooming his angelic acolytes for thousands of years for this very moment.

A crucial aspect of Satan's plan is the element of surprise. But instead of catching heaven off guard, Michael and his loyal angels are ready and waiting for *"the dragon"* and his angelic rebels. Satan has no idea that he has lost the battle before it has even begun. He has no idea that the reason the archangel Michael left his guardian post at Jerusalem was because God knew what Satan was planning and recalled him to heaven at precisely the right moment.

At the exact moment Satan arrives in heaven and shouts the rallying cry to his secret followers to begin the attack, Michael is ready and waiting. The tares that Satan has been sowing among God's angels suddenly spring forth, separating themselves from God's faithful angels as they answered Satan's cry.[104] Michael and his most loyal angels can then easily distinguish which angels have defected and then round them up and cast them out of heaven.

Michael had the advantage of God's foreknowledge, so Satan and his angels were forced into defensive positions, which is what *"fought back"* means.

> *...Michael and his angels fighting against the dragon. And the dragon and his angels fought back* (Revelation 12:7b ESV)

---

[104] Tares are the evil—the weeds—sewn or dispersed among the wheat, which are the good seed. Matthew 13:25-26 (KJV): *"but while men slept, his enemy came and sowed tares among the wheat and went his way. 26 But when the blade was sprung up, and brought forth fruit, then appeared the tares also."*

It appears some of God's faithful angels are injured during the war.

> . . . *where it* [the dragon] *attacked the heavenly army, throwing some of the heavenly beings and some of the stars to the ground and trampling them.* (Daniel 8:10 NLT)

For the angels who sided with Satan, the loss is devastating. These tens of millions of rebel angels will now be chained alongside Satan's Watcher angels.[105]

> . . . *8 but he was defeated, and there was no longer any place for them in heaven. 9 And the great dragon was thrown down, that ancient serpent, who is called the devil and Satan, the deceiver of the whole world-he was thrown down to the earth, and his angels were thrown down with him.* (Revelation 12:8–9 ESV)

I really feel pity for these deceived and vanquished angels, even more than the pity I feel for the deceived Adam and Eve. The fate of these mutinous angels will now be the same as the fate of the Nephilim of Genesis 6: there will be absolutely no opportunity for forgiveness.

> . . . *'Depart from me, you accursed, into the eternal fire that has been prepared for the devil and his angels!* (Matthew 25:41b NET)

---

[105] While I could find no specific reference to the fate of these rebel angels, it's clear that they do not remain free on earth with Satan, because the havoc they could wreak upon men and the earth would be indescribable. It is likely that God will treat them the same way he treated the earlier rebel angels, by chaining them in a pit in hell.

As a result of Satan's failed rebellion, he will no longer be able to converse with God or commune with other heavenly angels because he will never again have access to heaven. The news of Satan's permanent eviction from heaven fills the occupants of heaven with joy!

> *12 Therefore, rejoice, O heavens and you who dwell in them!* (Revelation 12:12a ESV)

Having failed in his rebellious attempt to bypass the rules of engagement in the 7-sealed book, Satan is furious that he has no choice but to continue participating and adhering to the rules for the second half of the contest. He knows, according to that book, that his time is short. He must overcome Jesus' challenge to his rule over the kingdoms of the world, and starting from this defining moment, he has been allotted exactly 3½ short years to try to do it.

> *"But woe to you, O earth and sea, for the devil has come down to you in great wrath, because he knows that his time is short!"* (Revelation 12: 12b ESV)

The second half of the verse that started this dual rebellion sequence confirms that the 3½-year-long Great Tribulation, also known as the Time of Jacob's Trouble, will begin after Michael arises to heaven and vanquishes the rebel angels.

> *At that time shall arise Michael, the great prince who has charge of your people. And there shall be a time of trouble, such as never has been since there was a nation till that time* (Daniel 12:1a ESV)

# Part Three:

## The Great Tribulation Begins

# 11 The Antichrist is Authorized Power

The abomination of desolation is the unmistakable signal that the world has reached the halfway point of the final seven years before the return of Jesus, which is called the Day of the Lord. The antichrist fully understands that his abominable act has fired the starter's gun and he must now move quickly to find a way to thwart God's plan in just 3 ½ years.

> *The beast was given a mouth speaking proud words and blasphemies, and he was permitted to exercise ruling authority for forty-two months. 6 So the beast opened his mouth to blaspheme against God--to blaspheme both his name and his dwelling place, that is, those who dwell in heaven. 7 The beast was permitted to go to war against the saints and conquer them. He was given ruling authority over every tribe, people, language, and nation. . .* (Revelation 13:5–7 NET)

Though it sounds inconceivable, once the Grand Caliph is revealed to the Christian world as the antichrist, God will grant him so many powers and permissions that it takes three verses to describe them all.[106] Here are some of the powers God grants the antichrist:

a. *"He is given a mouth,"* which means that he will be allowed to control the media, the internet (or its future replacement), and the messaging.

---

[106] Only those familiar with end-time Scripture will understand that he's the antichrist. Everyone else will see him as a type of savior. The Muslims will acknowledge him as their long-awaited Mahdi.

b. The antichrist is permitted *"to blaspheme both his name and his dwelling place."* His message will be to constantly blame and curse God, his angels, and the Christians and Jews for all calamities.

c. He will speak *"proud words,"* which means that he will boast that there is no god greater than himself, so everyone should unite with him. He will say that together, they can defeat God and put an end to all the calamities God has brought on.

d. He is given permission to *"go to war against the saints and conquer them."* He'll now go on full attack against Christians and kill as many as he can who won't take his mark.

e. *"He was given ruling authority."* He won't necessarily rule the world, but there is no part of the world that God will shield or exempt from his rule.

f. As proof that it is God and his 7-sealed book who is allowing and authorizing this, God tells us exactly how long the antichrist will be suffered to rule the nations: he'll have *"authority for forty-two months."*

g. 2 Thessalonians 2:11 tells us that those who refuse to accept Jesus by this point will be sent a *"strong delusion."* There will be no hope of saving them.

Revelation 13:5-7 serves as a powerful confirmation of Daniel 11:36. It amazes me that God not only foresees these events (and shares them with us in these passages) but also permits them to unfold. As this book progresses, you'll see that this is because God is a God of perfect justice and divine order.

> *"And the king* [the antichrist] *shall do as he wills. He shall exalt himself and magnify himself above every god, and shall speak astonishing things against the God of gods. He shall prosper till the indignation is accomplished; for what is decreed shall be done. (Daniel 11:36 ESV)*

Satan has been preparing for this moment for 2,000 years, since his humiliating loss in the first half of the contest. Now, for his prodigy, the antichrist, the charade is over.[107] The "Mr. Nice Guy" mask is off, and there is no more holding back, no more negotiating with world leaders, no more building coalitions, and no more enticing religious leaders to compromise their faith, because he's about to cancel and replace the one-world religion he recently finished negotiating. With his true nature revealed through his desecration of the temple, the antichrist now has one overriding goal: to win the second half of the contest. To achieve this, he must forcibly convince the majority of the world to reject Jesus and accept him as their savior instead.

He knows exactly how much time remains to win this contest: 1,260 days, or 42 months, or 3½ years. The 7-sealed book gives him authority to rule during this period, but his reign—known as the Time of Jacob's Trouble, or the Great Tribulation—will be a time of unparalleled suffering and darkness.

As the Great Tribulation begins, at least a dozen significant events will unfold in rapid succession, with some potentially commencing on the very first day. We'll devote a chapter to exploring each of these events in detail.

1. God hardens the hearts of those who refuse to believe God's gospel.
2. The unseen world begins to operate in the open.
3. Paradise closes to new arrivals because the "Special Blessing" for believers begins for those who die from this point forward.

---

[107] I use the word prodigy loosely. Satan probably isn't personally training and mentoring the antichrist or pulling the antichrist's strings like a puppet, but he is providing the antichrist his plan and probably making the antichrist think he's doing it all on his own.

4. Jacob's Trouble. Immediately, an order is given regarding the Jews in Jerusalem, for them to be killed or rounded up and hauled away to other countries to be imprisoned.

5. The Grand Caliph declares himself the savior or the Mahdi and abruptly dissolves the world religion he and his prophet had worked so carefully to hammer together.

6. The words of God and Jesus will be outlawed: no longer just banned, they will be searched out in every form and format and destroyed.

7. The infamous mark of the beast will now become mandatory. It's no longer just a requirement to buy, sell, or own property but will now serve as a visible sign of fealty to the new savior. Any who refuse this visible act of worship will be beheaded. Many Christians will refuse to accept the mark.

8. The third Whispering Angel warns everyone in the world, "Don't take the mark!"

9. Taking up your cross to follow Jesus gets real.

10. The Holy Spirit warns believers that taking the mark is the "Unforgiveable Sin"

11. People must choose whom they will serve: God or the antichrist. Everyone must make a choice.

12. For Christians and Jews, their friends and families will grow cold and turn on them.

13. The two witnesses appear on a street in Jerusalem, possibly on the steps of the recently desecrated temple.

14. 144,000 Jews who have already been carefully selected by God will be "*sealed*" with the mark of God by an angel and led away to a secret location somewhere outside of Israel where Jesus will keep them safe for the entire 3½ years.

# 11.1 God Hardens the Hearts of Those Who Rejected Him

People will have an opportunity to repent and turn to Jesus until the antichrist reveals his true identity by desecrating the temple. After that momentous event, *"the coming of the lawless one,"* it will be too late to accept Jesus as their Savior. God will send those who haven't yet accepted him a *"strong delusion."* They will fall for the antichrist's miracles and believe he is the hope of the world.

> *9 The coming of the lawless one is by the activity of Satan with all power and false signs and wonders, 10 and with all wicked deception for those who are perishing, because they refused to love the truth and so be saved. 11 Therefore God sends them a strong delusion, so that they may believe what is false, 12 in order that all may be condemned who did not believe the truth but had pleasure in unrighteousness.* (2 Thessalonians 2:9–12 ESV)

The above passage seems to indicate that everyone from this point forward who is not a believer will fall for the miracles of the antichrist and will thus be condemned in the end. There's a nuance, though, that will cover those in the middle. Those who are not believers but don't fall for the antichrist's persuasive miracles and antics and who took no *"pleasure in unrighteousness"* will not necessarily fall for the strong delusion. These are the people who, if they remain decent and hospitable toward the persecuted Jews and Christians and if they survive the tribulation, may get a second chance by being allowed to enter the Millennial Kingdom. We'll cover these exceptions in detail in the Sheep and Goat Separation chapter.

## 11.2 The Unseen World Begins to Operate Openly in Our World

Most spiritual activity occurs in a hidden dimension the Bible calls the unseen realm. Based on several verses in Revelation, it's clear that at a certain point, once Satan loses the war in heaven, things that used to be hidden will begin happening in full view. For instance, as we'll see in the following chapters, demonic spirits will operate in full view of the *"kings of the whole world."*[108]

---

108    Revelation 16:14a, *"For they are demonic spirits, performing signs, who go abroad to the kings of the whole world. . ."*

## 11.3 Blessing for Believers who Die *"from now on"*

> *And I heard a voice from heaven saying, "Write this: Blessed are the dead who die in the Lord from now on." "Blessed indeed," says the Spirit, "that they may rest from their labors, for their deeds follow them!"* (Revelation 14:13 ESV)

The Great Tribulation will be the darkest 3½ years in human history, when unprecedented terror will be unleashed upon the world. Yet, as this horror begins, a profound blessing is bestowed upon Christians *"who die in the Lord from now on."* What could this mean other than that their souls will now bypass the wait in the Paradise section of Sheol and go directly to heaven instead?[109]

This indicates Satan has had yet another colossal, humiliating setback! Let me break it down a little better. We know that at the end of the Great Tribulation the seventh trumpet will sound signifying Jesus has been crowned King of the World and the kingdom will be instantly transferred from Satan to Jesus. The loss of the kingdom means Satan loses his authority to hold the souls of dead Christians in the Paradise portion of Sheol from that point on. Jesus' very first act as King will be to shout a command to his angels to free the *"believers who have died"* from Paradise and raise them to meet him in the air.

> *First, the believers who have died will rise from their graves. (1 Thessalonians 4:16b NLT)*

---

[109] This is different than the promise for those who die as martyrs for Jesus and for his Word. Those who die as martyrs during the Great Tribulation will also bypass the Paradise portion of Sheol, but in addition to that, they will be given the amazing honor of reigning with Christ during the Millennium.

So this phrase *"from now on,"* which means from the start of the Great Tribulation forward, reveals that by trying to bypass the rules of engagement laid out in God's 7-sealed book, Satan was dealt this crushing penalty! From the moment he is cast out of heaven, he loses the right to hold the souls of believers who die from that point forward, a full 3½ years earlier than he otherwise would have at the 7th trumpet!

And there's at least one more huge consequence of his failed revolution that we don't find out about until just before the 5th trumpet sounds: Satan has been permanently locked out of heaven's gates!

The verse below indicates that, while people who die from that point onward will *"rejoice"* that they will now *"dwell"* in heaven, the tide has turned against Satan. His delusional plan (*"...I will ascend to the heavens; I will raise my throne above the stars of God..."* Isaiah 14:13b NIV) is crumbling around him, but he will never concede defeat.

> *Therefore, rejoice, O heavens and you who dwell in them! But woe to you, O earth and sea, for the devil has come down to you in great wrath, because he knows that his time is short!"* (Revelation 12:12 ESV)

From this point forward, he is confined to earth, (*"the devil has come down to you,"*) and now, consumed with anger and desperation, (*"in great wrath;"*) things are only going to get worse for him in the *"short"* 3 ½ years he has left before that glorious 7th trumpet sounds! Satan's failed revolution not only marks the end of Satan's access to heaven but in losing his ability to hold the souls of believers who die during the Great Tribulation ransom, he has also lost a large portion of his bargaining chip for any potential deal with God. This means his failed rebellion stripped him of much of the power he, as king, was once authorized to wield over death itself.

*O death, where is your victory? O death, where is your sting?* (1 Corinthians 15:55 ESV)

This Special Blessing, *"Blessed are the dead who die in the Lord from now on,"* is the very reason this book could be written.[110] Because of this amazing promise, those believers who die after the Great Tribulation begins are granted the unique privilege of bypassing Paradise and going directly to heaven. While, since the time of Adam, the faithful who die typically go to the Paradise part of Sheol, this Special Blessing will change everything. From the start of the Great Tribulation, John gives us his firsthand account of believers who die and are immediately given incorruptible bodies and brought into heaven.[111] Each time John sees a group of these newly arrived saints, he shares their stories with us, revealing the remarkable fulfillment of this divine promise.[112]

By learning the stories of these new arrivals to heaven, we can piece together how each group met its demise and link the cause of their deaths to specific events occurring on earth, thereby discerning the true end-time timeline. The knowledge of this Special Blessing will give hope and courage to Christians suffering persecution and deprivation during the Great Tribulation.

---

[110] There are no verses in the Bible which indicate there are people in heaven right now. The first place we're told about humans in heaven is Revelation 6:9, after the start of the Great Tribulation, which is exactly when this Special Blessing kicks-in. Prior to this Special Blessing, Christians who die are in the Paradise area of Sheol, which Luke 16:22 identified as Abraham's Bosom.

[111] This verse is also the reason most churches teach that believers go directly to heaven when they die. It's an understandable misinterpretation if you don't know what *"from now on"* means. They unknowingly took a verse that specifically deals with the start of the Great Tribulation and interpreted it as though it applied at all times.

[112] This means that there are no people in heaven now and there won't be any until the first Christians (and Christian martyrs) begin to die or be killed in the Great Tribulation. The notable exceptions to this rule are those humans who were taken directly to be with God: Enoch, Elijah, and probably Moses (since he was seen at the transfiguration).

## 11.4 "The Final, Final Solution": Eliminating Jews and Christians Too

When they hear of this abomination that just occurred in their temple, religious Jews will instantly understand what this means and what to do. Even though they will be in shock from the desecration of their new temple, they must drop everything and run to the hills!

> *The songs of the temple shall become wailings in that day,"*
> *declares the Lord GOD. "So many dead bodies!" "They are*
> *thrown everywhere!" "Silence!"* (Amos 8:3 ESV)

The Grand Caliph's first move after the abomination of desolation event will be to turn his peacekeeping soldiers posted in Jerusalem inward to hem-in all of the Jews and keep them from fleeing. They will instantly turn against the Jews and kill, rape, and load about half of them up and haul them away as prisoners among the nations.

The barbarism of the soldiers that day will make the killers and rapists of October 7, 2023, look like amateurs.[113]

> *For I will gather all the nations against Jerusalem to*
> *battle, and the city shall be taken and the houses plundered*
> *and the women raped.* (Zechariah 14:2a ESV)

---

[113] Lucy Williamson, "Israel Gaza: Hamas raped and mutilated women on 7 October, BBC hears," BBC, December 5, 2023, https://www.bbc.co.uk/news/world-middle-east-67629181).

Half of Jerusalem's citizens will be killed or hauled to other countries to be abused and imprisoned, but for some unexplained reason, about half of the Jews will be allowed to remain.[114]

> *Half of the city shall go out into exile, but the rest of the people shall not be cut off from the city.* (Zechariah 14:2b ESV)

Christians familiar with end-time prophecies have been forewarned of this by Mark and Paul:

> *But when ye shall see the abomination of desolation, spoken of by Daniel the prophet, standing where it ought not, (let him that readeth understand,) then let them that be in Judaea flee to the mountains: And let him that is on the housetop not go down into the house, neither enter therein, to take any thing out of his house: And let him that is in the field not turn back again for to take up his garment.* (Mark 13:14–16 KJV)

> *Let no one deceive you in any way. For that day will not come, unless the rebellion comes first, and the man of lawlessness is revealed, the son of destruction, 4 who opposes and exalts himself against every so-called god or object of worship, so that he takes his seat in the temple of God, proclaiming himself to be God. 5 Do you not remember that when I was still with you I told you these things? 6 And you know what is restraining*

---

[114] It seems that one of the roles of the two witnesses who will make their appearance at any moment will be to immediately protect the remaining ½ of the Jews who survived the initial Blitzkrieg attack by the antichrist's forces. A less likely explanation would be that about ½ of the secular Jews in Jerusalem accepted the mark and so were already on the antichrist's side.

*him now so that he may be revealed in his time.* (2
Thessalonians 2:3-6 ESV)

God implores the Jews in Judea to flee to the mountains without
hesitation and Jews in other areas will attempt to do the same.

It will be unimaginably horrible for these Jews, but there is
hope for some of them who survive to the end of the Tribulation.
At that time, after he wins the epic battle, Jesus himself will release
the survivors and personally lead them back to Jerusalem.

> *"At that time, declares the LORD, I will be the God of all
> the clans of Israel, and they shall be my people." 2 Thus
> says the LORD: "The people who survived the sword
> found grace in the wilderness; when Israel sought for rest,
> 3 the LORD appeared to him from far away. I have loved
> you with an everlasting love; therefore I have continued
> my faithfulness to you."* (Jeremiah 31:1–3 ESV)

This is a bit of a sidebar, but it appears that some devout Jews
and maybe some Christians may use guerrilla warfare to remain a
thorn in the side of the antichrist.

> *. . . but the people that do know their God shall be
> strong, and do exploits.* (Daniel 11:32b KJV)

This Time of Jacob's Trouble is an unbelievably bad time for
the Jews of Jerusalem and around the world. It is tragic that they
did not heed Isaiah's prophecy.[115] The next verse in 1 Thessalonians

---

[115] *And your covenant with death shall be disannulled, and your agreement with
hell shall not stand; when the overflowing scourge shall pass through, then ye shall be
trodden down by it.* (Isaiah 28:18 KJV)

indicates that the Jews, as well as the Christians (*"brethren"*), should have seen this coming but chose instead to remain ignorant of the signs.

> *But ye, brethren, are not in darkness, that that day should overtake you as a thief. 5 Ye are all the children of light, and the children of the day: we are not of the night, nor of darkness. 6 Therefore let us not sleep, as do others; but let us watch and be sober.* (1 Thessalonians 5:4–6 KJV)

Most end-time authors believe that God will not let Christians suffer the experience of the tribulation. But nowhere in Scripture are Christians promised exemption from persecution. While most Christians in the West have not experienced significant religious trials, Timothy reminds us that facing such challenges is something we can be certain of.

> *Indeed, all who desire to live a godly life in Christ Jesus will be persecuted,* (2 Timothy 3:12 ESV)

## 11.5 "My Only Demand is that You Worship Me."

The Grand Caliph no longer has time for the elaborate pretense, so he stops maintaining his peacemaker persona. He now demands to be honored and praised as the savior of the world, or, as the Sunni Muslims will most likely call him, the Mahdi.[116]

God permits this blasphemy because it's *"decreed"* by the rules of the 7-sealed book. This is one of the many rules or decrees of the 7-sealed book which isn't read aloud in Revelation but has been provided by other Prophets.

> *And the king shall do as he wills. He shall exalt himself and magnify himself above every god, and shall speak astonishing things against the God of gods. He shall prosper till the indignation is accomplished; for what is decreed shall be done. 37 He shall pay no attention to the gods of his fathers, or to the one beloved by women. He shall not pay attention to any other god, for he shall magnify himself above all.* (Daniel 11:36–37 ESV)

Although it's a fairly safe bet he'll choose to go by the title 'The Mahdi,' we will, from this point forward in this book, refer to him by the term the Bible uses: the antichrist. He will issue an edict that will eliminate all other religions, even the one-world religion he co-founded. The antichrist will no longer share the stage with any world or religious leaders. He will be pre-eminent, and every other leader, pope, and priest will either take his mark and bow to him or die. All must now pay homage to the antichrist or be executed as an infidel. Worldwide antisemitism will know no bounds. He will

---

[116] Joel Richardson, *The Islamic Antichrist.*

lead a sanctioned wholesale eradication of every Jew he can find. It will be another Holocaust, but this time it's worldwide.

There will be an all-out demonically inspired effort to round up Christians and others who refuse the mark or won't worship the beast. The government may, however, try to "re-educate" some of the less committed Christians and use these turncoats to infiltrate and root-out other Christians. To instill widespread loathing of Christians and Jews, the antichrist and false prophet may accuse them of "causing" all the calamities or of being parasites on the scarce resources of the economy.

## 11.6 "I Give You My Word: Corrected Bibles for Everyone"

The antichrist will now allow only himself to be worshipped. When he desecrated the temple, he declared that no one gets to heaven except through him, so, by definition, all other religions are false, including the universal religion he and his false Jesus forged. For some reason, that one-world religion, *"the prostitute,"* whose priests are headquartered in Babylon, now disgusts him.

> *And the ten horns that you saw, they and the beast will hate the prostitute. They will make her desolate and naked, and devour her flesh and burn her up with fire* (Revelation 17:16 ESV)

Now that he has dropped all pretenses, he uses his dictatorial power to eradicate any remaining religions in the parts of the world he controls or influences. The deep compromises the leaders of each religion had to make in order to join his now-banned new-world religion rendered all of their own literature and teachings erroneous, including their formerly holy books. Because these religious leaders completely sold out their own religions, they now have no credibility with which to argue that the antichrist's new religion is any better than the one-world religion that they had just worked so hard to water down. So the antichrist will eliminate all the false doctrines in one fell swoop and destroy any other religion besides his.

But this time, it will be more than a book ban. This will be a seek-and-destroy order backed by the full force of international law. We're talking about door-to-door searches in every country where he holds economic influence or has radicalized followers empowered with search warrants. There will be burn piles in the streets all across the world. In the areas the antichrist doesn't control, his religious minions will carry out his bidding with fervor and terrorism. He's not just burning genuine Bibles, but any book or media format deemed Christian, including the one you're reading now. Oh sure, they'll throw a few Buddhist or Hindu books in the fires for good measure if they happen to come across them, but the search and destroy order will only be for the eradication of anything Christian or Jewish because those are the only threats to Satan.

The punishment for having Christian 'contraband' is extreme and horrifyingly brutal. John reveals that those who hide Bibles, *"the Word of God,"* will face execution by beheading, alongside those who refuse to accept the mark. They will die as martyrs for their unwavering faith.

> *Then I saw thrones, and seated on them were those to whom the authority to judge was committed. Also I saw the souls of those who had been beheaded for the testimony of Jesus and for the word of God, and those who had not worshiped the beast or its image and had not received its mark on their foreheads or their hands. They came to life and reigned with Christ for a thousand years.* (Revelation 20:4 ESV)

But what about the promise of Matthew 5:18, that not one letter from my word shall disappear? Look carefully at the end of that verse. There is a caveat, *"until."* The Literal Emphasis Translation captures the actual word-for-word meaning of that verse, *"until everything should happen."*

*For truly I say to you, until the heaven and the earth shall pass away, not one iota nor one apostrophe shall pass away from the law until everything should happen.*
(Matthew 5:18 Literal Emphasis Translation)

It's likely that the abomination of desolation is the *"everything,"* because it is what kicks off the Great Tribulation, which is when the antichrist will work to adulterate God's Word. But doesn't Isaiah tell us God's Word will continue?

*Grass has withered, the flower faded, But a word of our God rises forever.*
(Isaiah 40:8 Literal Standard Version)

Most translations say, *"the word"* of God which implies the Bible. I selected the Literal Standard Version of this verse to point out that Isaiah literally says it is *"a word"* of God. Not necessarily his entire Bible.

It's unlikely that you will be able to hide a Bible somewhere and retrieve it later because this search and destroy mission will be supernaturally assisted. In this dual-meaning prophecy, Amos tells us that after this purge is finished, no one will be able to find the Word of God anywhere.[117]

---

[117] "This shall be the bitterness at the end; they had rejected the warnings of the prophets (Amos 8:12, etc.); now the Word of God and the light of his teaching should fail them." (Bible Hub, "Amos 8," Pulpit Commentary, biblehub.com, https://biblehub.com/commentaries/pulpit/amos/8.htm). "They who will not now hear His word, as proclaimed by the prophets, will then cherish the greatest longing for it. Such hunger and thirst will be awakened by the distress and affliction that will come upon them." (Bible Hub, "Amos 8," Keil and Delitzsch Commentary, biblehub.com, https://biblehub.com/commentaries/kad/amos/8.htm).

*"Behold, the days are coming," declares the Lord GOD, "when I will send a famine on the land--not a famine of bread, nor a thirst for water, but of hearing the words of the LORD. 12 They shall wander from sea to sea, and from north to east; they shall run to and fro, to seek the word of the LORD, but they shall not find it.* (Amos 8:11–12 ESV)

Just as in the prophetic movie, *The Book of Eli*, the Word of God in any form will be successfully eradicated.[118] That should give you chills and spur you to memorize the most important passages now, just as Denzel Washington's character had memorized the entire Bible.

Notably, it's likely that the Quran will be exempt from destruction. The antichrist's most zealous followers will be Muslims due to reasons I discussed earlier. They will believe the antichrist is their Mahdi, even if they think he did go a little too far in declaring himself worthy of worship during the abomination of desolation. His killing of Jews and Christians who refuse to convert aligns perfectly with their prophecies of the Mahdi.

Anyone who refuses to cooperate and allow their homes to be searched—or, worse, if a search uncovers a hidden Bible, Christian symbols, music, or books—will be immediately seized. Those caught spreading the now-outlawed Christian message face the same fate. Some who are caught may decide that their survival is more important and will renounce Christ and submit to the mark. Those who don't renounce Christ will be sent to the processing centers or summarily executed.

---

[118] Dalton Norman & Tom Russell, "The Book of Eli Ending & Meaning Explained," ScreenRant, July 28, 2024, https://screenrant.com/book-of-eli-ending-meaning-eli-blind/.

## 11.7 "I Give You My Mark, I Absolutely Insist"

The mark on the forehead or right hand, which allows people to maintain access to their civilized lives, has already been in place for months.[119] The technological advancement behind this mark and its tie to a secure exchange system will probably be rolled out with great fanfare. Still, its technical workings will be shrouded in mystery. Up to this point, getting the mark was voluntary, and it would just be the early adopters who showed off their marks and their love for the antichrist with pride. From its beginning, the early adopters had to swear allegiance to and pay homage to the antichrist, the creator of this amazing system and mark. But that seemed innocuous enough to those who really wanted it.

Now that it is clear that this mark will demonstrate that you're a worshiper of the antichrist, it becomes evident that it was not just a secure, hi-tech, cult-like thing to do but was really a religious litmus test. A very public test. There will be no hiding that you don't have the mark. The mark will quickly become the most divisive thing mankind has ever faced.

> *Also it [the false prophet] causes all, both small and great, both rich and poor, both free and slave, to be marked on the right hand or the forehead, 17 so that no one can buy or sell unless he has the mark, that is, the name of the beast or the number of its name. 18 This calls for wisdom: let the one who has*

---

[119] In our current state of technology, this would mean that without the mark of the beast, you will have no access to email accounts, bank accounts, brokerage accounts, social media accounts, or shopping. In the future, as technology evolves, it's difficult to know what other forms of communication and commerce a person would be deprived of unless they took the mark.

*understanding calculate the number of the beast, for*
*it is the number of a man, and his number is 666.*
(Revelation 13:16–18 ESV)

We're not told what this mark will look like, and no, it most likely won't be an actual 666, but that is a clue. There's little use in trying to figure out the symbol of this mark because, rest assured, those who understand the Word of God will know it when they hear about it, let alone see it.

But what about the rest of the unchurched world? How could they possibly know about the mark of the beast and that, if they accept it, they are accepting eternal damnation?

God is a fair and compassionate God. He's going to let everyone in the world know, in no uncertain terms, what will happen to them if they take the easy, logical, popular road and accept the mark. God will ensure that everyone will know in time and thus have no excuse on Judgment Day.

## 11.8 The Whispering Angel Round Three –"Don't Take the Mark!"

The first two whispering angels were invisible, but ever since the abomination of desolation, the unseen spiritual realm has become visible to everyone. As a result, when this final whispering angel circumnavigates the globe, it will be seen by the entire world.

> *And another angel, a third, followed them, saying with a loud voice, "If anyone worships the beast and its image and receives a mark on his forehead or on his hand, 10 he also will drink the wine of God's wrath, poured full strength into the cup of his anger, and he will be tormented with fire and sulfur in the presence of the holy angels and in the presence of the Lamb. 11 And the smoke of their torment goes up forever and ever, and they have no rest, day or night, these worshipers of the beast and its image, and whoever receives the mark of its name."* (Revelation 14:9–11 ESV)

Could the angel have been any clearer? As we've seen with the previous two circumnavigating angels, there will be no way to avoid hearing and understanding these angels no matter what language you speak, whether you know nothing of God, whether you work deep underground in a coal mine, or even if you are deaf. God will ensure everyone hears and understands his message. Even if your heart is hardened and you refuse to listen, there will be no way to block out the message. Therefore, on Judgment Day, no one who took the mark will have an excuse.

*For as the rain and the snow come down from heaven and do not return there but water the earth, making it bring forth and sprout, giving seed to the sower and bread to the eater, 11 so shall my word be that goes out from my mouth; it shall not return to me empty, but it shall accomplish that which I purpose, and shall succeed in the thing for which I sent it.* (Isaiah 55:10–11 ESV)

## 11.9 "But Surely God Doesn't Want Me to Give up all He's Blessed Me With?"

At first, the false prophet will likely try to appear civil while forcing everyone to get the mark. If his administrators sense that someone who is refusing the mark has a weak Christian foundation, they may be sent to short-term re-education camps, where they will be presented with passages from *The Universal Testament,* the revised bible created by the antichrist's team of religious leaders for his new *Enlightened Way* Religion. Just as Satan deceived Eve in Genesis 3:4 with a slight variation on God's Word, this corrupted scripture will mimic God's Word so closely that Christians who haven't memorized key Bible verses will fail to recognize the subtle but crucial distortions. Many will be persuaded to accept the mark, and some of these converts will be used as spokespeople to convince other unprepared Christians who are still undecided.

But for prepared Christians who know God's Word and his prophecy, the administrators won't waste time. They will be sent to processing centers, where a sham legal appointee, such as a Guardian ad Litem, will declare them incompetent.[120] Since they rejected the antichrist's "generous offer" to cooperate and continue to enjoy their civilized lives, they will be declared unfit to manage their own affairs. With that ruling, all of their possessions, homes, bank accounts, personal businesses, retirement accounts, and more, will be seized and absorbed into the antichrist's world economy, the center of which Is Babylon.[121]

---

[120] A Guardian ad Litem is someone appointed by the court to represent a person who is deemed incapable or incompetent, in this case a Christian, to represent themselves.

[121] I presume that the antichrist and those with the mark will steal everything from those who refuse the mark from two facts. First, Babylon––for reasons

The currency of Babylon's new economic system, which the Jewish financiers so skillfully designed, will quickly become the world's reserve currency. The Babylonian economy will eclipse every economy in the world, growing so unimaginably wealthy that it will defy description. Through the operation of these processing centers, it will seize control of vast amounts of the world's land, homes, and a significant share of businesses, acquiring stocks that were "processed" (stolen) from those who refuse to accept the mark, whom I call "Refuseniks." The term *Refusenik* was originally a derogatory slur coined in the Soviet Union to describe Jewish individuals who applied to emigrate to Israel, the Promised Land, but were "refused" permission by the Soviet regime.[122] It will once again be a derogatory term.

---

not explained—grows immensely wealthy in 3½ years, and that wealth has to come from somewhere. Second, after the trumpets are finished, men still don't repent of a whole list of things, including their *"thefts"*: *"nor did they repent of their murders or their sorceries or their sexual immorality or their thefts" (Revelation 9:21ESV)*. It's very likely they are stealing the belongings of those who refused the mark.

[122] "The Six-Day War in 1967 initiated a new phase in Jewish consciousness in the Soviet Union.... While Soviet media pumped out anti-Zionist propaganda, declaring that all who supported the Zionist cause were enemies of the people, Soviet Jews began to feel not only pride in being Jewish but to acknowledge a common national fate.

Many Soviet Jews dreamed of moving to Israel, but making that dream a concrete reality was almost an impossibility. To emigrate from the USSR, one needed approval from the Soviet government. Most Jews who applied to leave were rejected. These rejections were generally given without explanation, although some applicants were told that they knew "state secrets" that could be divulged to the West. The applicants were then in a "state of refusal" and became known as "Refuseniks." This period lasted months, usually years, and sometimes even decades... Having made the request to leave, the Refuseniks were treated as enemies of the state: they lost their jobs or were demoted, they lost their homes, and they were continually followed and bullied by the secret police. Many were arrested and imprisoned on imaginary or trumped-up charges (prisoners who were arrested for Jewish practice or pro-Zionist activities are called 'Prisoners

Nations who do not join Babylon and refuse to adopt its currency will quickly become severely impoverished as their wealth is drained into Babylon if they don't quickly take steps to stop it. This is what the two sets of scales which the false prophet holds indicate. One indicates the economy of Babylon (the corrupted scale), while the other represents the economy of what's left of the rest of the world.

The last step of the processing centers will be the beheading of the offenders, probably similar to what occurred during the French Revolution, but more likely as it occurs this very day in Saudi Arabia.[123] But we'll discuss more about the beheadings in the next section, when the 5th Seal is opened.

of Zion')." (The Refusenik Project, "Historical Overview," refusenikproject.org, https://www.refusenikproject.org/history/)

[123] "When they [death row prisoners] get to the execution square, their strength drains away. Then I read the execution order, and at a signal I cut the prisoner's head off," al-Beshi said." (Umberto Bacchi, "Execution Central: Saudi Arabia's Bloody Chop-Chop Square," *International Business Times*, April 3, 2013, https://www.ibtimes.co.uk/saudi-arabia-chop-square-beheading-453240)

## 11.10 Mayday from the Holy Spirit: "This Sin Absolutely Cannot be Forgiven"

Christians with something to lose, such as their home, a retirement account, bank accounts, or even just a job, may try to convince themselves that God wouldn't want them to give up all that he's blessed them with. They may say to themselves that God would understand that they need to keep access to their bank accounts so they can pay their mortgages because God wouldn't want them to be homeless. God wouldn't want them to give up their job because he understands how much they need their health insurance and how they must be able to provide for their children. They will justify to themselves that God will understand that they have no choice but to accept the mark to maintain access to all of their resources.

The agonizing choice everyone must make, whether to take the mark and preserve their civilized lifestyle or reject it to remain faithful to Jesus, losing everything, including their very life, depending on how far along this is in the Great Tribulation, will separate the wheat from the chaff.[124] This will be their defining moment: they must choose between comfort or, like Job, unwavering devotion to God even though it costs them everything, even their life. The choice will distinguish those whose spiritual foundations are deeply rooted in firm soil from those who merely go through the motions of attending church or Mass without truly growing in their understanding of God's Word.

---

[124] "Simon, Simon! Listen! Satan has received permission to test all of you, to separate the good from the bad, as a farmer separates the *wheat* from the *chaff*. 32 But I have prayed for you, Simon, that your faith will not fail. And when you turn back to me, you must strengthen your brothers." (Luke 22:31-32 Good News Translation)

*And they have no root in themselves, but endure for*
*a while; then, when tribulation or persecution arises*
*on account of the word, immediately they fall away.*
(Mark 4:17 ESV)

However, the Holy Spirit will urgently work within each Christian who may be attempting to justify in their mind why they should take the mark, warning them in their spirit that they are deceiving themselves with thoughts that seem rational on the surface but will guarantee their damnation. The Holy Spirit will remind them that this is the loyalty test for which we've been preparing all our Christian lives. Is your master Jesus or is it your family and possessions?

*And behold, a man came up to him, saying, "Teacher,*
*what good deed must I do to have eternal life?" 17*
*And he said to him, "Why do you ask me about what*
*is good? There is only one who is good. If you would*
*enter life, keep the commandments." 18 He said to him,*
*"Which ones?" And Jesus said, "You shall not murder,*
*You shall not commit adultery, You shall not steal, You*
*shall not bear false witness, 19 Honor your father and*
*mother, and, You shall love your neighbor as yourself."*
*20 The young man said to him, "All these I have kept.*
*What do I still lack?" 21 Jesus said to him, "If you*
*would be perfect, go, sell what you possess and give to*
*the poor, and you will have treasure in heaven; and*
*come, follow me." 22 When the young man heard this*
*he went away sorrowful, for he had great possessions.*
*23 And Jesus said to his disciples, "Truly, I say to*
*you, only with difficulty will a rich person enter the*

*kingdom of heaven. 24 Again I tell you, it is easier for a camel to go through the eye of a needle than for a rich person to enter the kingdom of God."* (Matthew 19:16–24 ESV)

When many of us in the Western world accepted Jesus, we didn't face real danger or sacrifice. Maybe we lost a few friends who didn't believe or let go of some bad habits, but our lives mostly carried on as before, just pointed in a better direction. But in the last days, these following passages will take on a terrifying reality. People will be forced to make a gut-wrenching decision if they want to continue following Christ: take the mark or abandon everything they've ever known and face the high probability of being executed.

*Let us hold fast the confession of our hope without wavering, for he who promised is faithful.* (Hebrews 10:23 ESV)

*Peter began to say to him, "See, we have left everything and followed you." 29 Jesus said, "Truly, I say to you, there is no one who has left house or brothers or sisters or mother or father or children or lands, for my sake and for the gospel, 30 who will not receive a hundredfold now in this time, houses and brothers and sisters and mothers and children and lands, with persecutions, and in the age to come eternal life. 31 But many who are first will be last, and the last first."* (Mark 10:28–31 ESV)

*But those who desire to be rich fall into temptation, into a snare, into many senseless and harmful desires that plunge people into ruin and destruction. For the love of money is a root of all kinds of evils. It is through this craving that some have wandered away from the faith and pierced themselves with many pangs.* (1 Timothy 6:9–10 ESV)

The Holy Spirit warns each follower of Christ about their sins, usually by a prompting or "check" in their spirit that something's not right. But this time it's different. This time it will be more than a subtle feeling or voice. The Holy Spirit will be sounding a clear and unmistakable alarm within the hearts of Christians, leaving no room for doubt about the right course of action. The dire warning from the Holy Spirit within them will be impossible to ignore. It will be warning Christians tempted to take the mark in order to keep enjoying the comforts of Sodom, that by doing so, they will be in direct opposition to the Holy Spirit, calling the Holy Spirit a liar, and thus will be blaspheming against him. Those who refuse to heed the warning of the third whispering angel and now reject the Holy Spirit's warning and take the mark will be committing the infamous, and previously mysterious, unpardonable sin. There will be no forgiveness from this ultimate apostasy.

*Therefore I tell you, every sin and blasphemy will be forgiven people, but the blasphemy against the Spirit will not be forgiven. 32 And whoever speaks a word against the Son of Man will be forgiven, but whoever speaks against the Holy Spirit will not be forgiven, either in this age or in the age to come.* (Matthew 12:31–32 ESV)

*There is sin that leads to death; I do not say that one should pray for that.* (1 John 5:16b ESV)

Whenever I read those verses, I used to wonder how someone would go about committing a sin against the Holy Spirit, even if they wanted to. Isn't Jesus able to forgive every sin? Yes, Jesus can and will forgive all sins for those who seek forgiveness and truly repent. But there is one exception. As far as I can tell, accepting the mark is the one sin Jesus will not forgive because once it's done, there is no turning back. There is absolutely no chance for repentance. Once you take the mark, it's indelible, irreversible, forever. It's a permanent and public baptism into the religion of Satan, and once you accept it, you are counted among the wicked forever.

Just as the third circumnavigating angel warned, accepting the mark is a complete and final rejection of Jesus as Lord and it signifies to all who see it that Satan is your lord. It is so egregious to Jesus and the Holy Spirit that Jesus will not forgive it, which is why his angelic warning against it could not be any clearer.

> "... *If anyone worships the beast and its image and receives a mark on his forehead or on his hand, 10 he also will drink the wine of God's wrath, poured full strength into the cup of his anger, and he will be tormented with fire and sulfur in the presence of the holy angels and in the presence of the Lamb"* (Revelation 14:9–10 ESV)

This will be the hour that your eternal destiny will hang in the balance. There will be no trick questions. You will either pass or fail this test.

Will you love Jesus enough to reject the great things you've worked hard for in this world?

Will you make the sacrifice and give up your earthly possessions, and maybe even your life, to remain a follower of Jesus?

*Whoever loves his life loses it, and whoever hates his life in this world will keep it for eternal life. 26 If anyone serves me, he must follow me; and where I am, there will my servant be also. If anyone serves me, the Father will honor him.* (John 12:25–26 ESV)

## 11.11 Unbelievably Tough Love: You Must Choose This Day Whom You Will Serve

As if losing your hard-earned possessions, including your home, social security benefits, and retirement savings, was not bad enough, these Refuseniks, once declared incompetent by the state, will also have their children taken away and placed under state custody. I can't imagine how difficult that will be or how many people will choose not to trust in God, instead accepting the mark just to stay with their children.

But Jesus warned us beforehand that we may face this dilemma. The verse below has multiple applications, but in this context, it warns believers not to put protecting our loved ones (by taking the mark upon ourselves to maintain access to our normal lives) above our love for Jesus:

> *Whoever loves father or mother more than me is not worthy of me, and whoever loves son or daughter more than me is not worthy of me. 38 And whoever does not take his cross and follow me is not worthy of me. 39 Whoever finds his life will lose it, and whoever loses his life for my sake will find it.* (Matthew 10:37–39 ESV)

We must be prepared to face the ultimate test of faith that God knows best, just as Abraham demonstrated his willingness to sacrifice his son Isaac.

> *He said, "Take your son, your only son Isaac, whom you love, and go to the land of Moriah, and offer him there as a burnt offering on one of the mountains of which I shall tell you."* (Genesis 22:2 ESV)

Though in Abraham's case the angel stopped Abraham after he passed the test, those parents will not have any last-minute rescue.

> He said, "Do not lay your hand on the boy or do anything to him, for now I know that you fear God, seeing you have not withheld your son, your only son, from me." (Genesis 22:12 ESV)

If you think there is a way to accept the mark while crossing your fingers behind your back, there isn't. And if you think anyone will be able to claim ignorance about the mark on Judgment Day, they won't; because, as we've explained above, the Holy Spirit's warning within them will be impossible to ignore.

You may ask, "What about people who don't know anything about God, let alone his prohibition of accepting the mark of the beast?" The answer is that God already sent an angel to broadcast the penalty to the world in unmistakable language. They will now know better when faced with the decision.

There will be no excuse for accepting the mark. Accepting the mark means you reject Jesus and choose instead to worship the antichrist.

But this is not all doom and gloom! There is a spectacular reward for those who choose Jesus instead of their wealth, their children, or their own lives. It's a reward that has never been offered to any believer in history. It's a reward that only those martyred during the tribulation will receive: they will be the only Christians resurrected during the Millennium. And if that were not enough, they will also be given the esteemed privilege of reigning with Jesus Christ!

> Then I saw thrones, and seated on them were those to whom the authority to judge was committed. Also

*I saw the souls of those who had been beheaded for the testimony of Jesus and for the word of God, and those who had not worshiped the beast or its image and had not received its mark on their foreheads or their hands. They came to life and reigned with Christ for a thousand years.* (Revelation 20:4 ESV)

Jesus exhorts us to persevere, to endure this tribulation to the end.

*Here is a call for the endurance of the saints, those who keep the commandments of God and their faith in Jesus.* (Revelation 14:12 ESV)

And Jesus gives us the new promise, which we discussed in chapter 11.3: *"from now on,"* believers who die will go directly to heaven.

*13 And I heard a voice from heaven saying, "Write this: Blessed are the dead who die in the Lord from now on." "Blessed indeed," says the Spirit, "that they may rest from their labors, for their deeds follow them!"* (Revelation 14:13 ESV)

Those who were beheaded for refusing the mark of the beast and maintaining their faith in Jesus and their *"testimony of Jesus and for the word of God"* are the only souls resurrected during the Millennium. They are given the esteemed privilege of not just receiving their new immortal bodies 1,000 years earlier than everyone else, but Jesus loves them so much for making the ultimate sacrifice in his name that he will give them the unimaginable privilege of sharing his throne. Their resurrection is called the First Resurrection. The second resurrection, when the rest of the dead will be resurrected to face Judgment, won't occur until after the Millennium is over.

> *...They came to life and reigned with Christ for a thousand years. 15 The rest of the dead did not come to life until the thousand years were ended. This is the first resurrection. 16b Blessed and holy is the one who shares in the first resurrection! Over such the second death has no power, but they will be priests of God and of Christ, and they will reign with him for a thousand years.* (Revelation 20:4b–6 ESV)

If you knew all of this already, I'm impressed. I've read the Bible cover to cover at least 25 times over the past 37 years before I started this research and I never understood the real meaning of these verses until I forced myself to take my blinders off and read the Bible through twice more. If you believe in the pre-tribulation rapture theory, it follows that you would not be among those who will live and reign with Christ during the Millennium. That unique honor is reserved for those who endure the trials of the Great Tribulation, remaining faithful to Christ *"even unto death."*[125] This means that those who pass away (or are raptured) *before* the Tribulation begins are not eligible for that honor; it is granted exclusively to those who are executed for holding on to their faith in Jesus *during* the Great Tribulation.

---

[125] Psalm 48:14 (KJV) *"For this God is our God for ever and ever: he will be our guide even unto death."*

## 11.12 You're as Cold as Ice: Betrayed by Family and Friends

The processing centers administering the mark and seizing the Refuseniks' property will be going full steam ahead by this point. The sheer number of people accepting the mark will be hard to fathom. Processing those people with the mark and plugging them into the Babylon economy will require a sophisticated logistics process. The false prophet, who is the person who arrives with the antichrist claiming to be Jesus, is the mastermind behind this worldwide process:

> *Also it* [the 2nd beast/false prophet] *causes all, both small and great, both rich and poor, both free and slave, to be marked on the right hand or the forehead, 17 so that no one can buy or sell unless he has the mark, that is, the name of the beast or the number of its name.* (Revelation 13:16-17 ESV)

When word spreads that those who refuse the mark will forfeit everything they own to New Babylon, people who have family members with assets will panic and try to prevent that loss. They will preemptively turn in parents, grandparents, aunts, and uncles to secure those homes or bank accounts for themselves. The following verse is certainly applicable today, but it will be even more relevant when the marking begins.

> *Do not think that I have come to bring peace to the earth. I have not come to bring peace, but a sword. 35 For I have come to set a man against his father, and a daughter*

*against her mother, and a daughter-in-law against her mother-in-law. 36 And a person's enemies will be those of his own household.* (Matthew 10:34–36 ESV)

How difficult it will be to know that it was your own son or daughter that sent you to the processing center. But parents will also turn in their own children.

*And brother will deliver brother over to death, and the father his child, and children will rise against parents and have them put to death. 13 And you will be hated by all for my name's sake. But the one who endures to the end will be saved.* (Mark 13:12–13 ESV)

Why would someone turn-in a loved one so heartlessly? They may justify their actions by convincing themselves that their relatives are hopeless conspiracy theorists, religious fanatics, or are certifiably crazy for refusing to take the mark. They will probably think that as much as it hurts, they are doing the smart and responsible thing by keeping the family house or other assets in the family. And they may even be rewarded by the antichrist.

For those faithful Christians who are turned in by their family and beheaded because their faith in Jesus will not allow them to take the mark, their reward will be great. While the following is not a prophetic verse, its promise applies to those who stand up with honor and face the consequences of refusing the mark:

*Blessed are those who are persecuted for righteousness' sake, for theirs is the kingdom of heaven. 11 Blessed are you when others revile you and persecute you and utter all kinds of evil against you falsely on my account. 12 Rejoice and be glad, for your reward is great in heaven, for so they persecuted the prophets who were before you.* (Matthew 5:10–12 ESV)

In this next verse, John warns believers that they *"are about to suffer,"* but there will be a crown for them in the next life.

*Do not fear what you are about to suffer. Behold, the devil is about to throw some of you into prison, that you may be tested, and for ten days you will have tribulation. Be faithful unto death, and I will give you the crown of life.* (Revelation 2:10 ESV)

Peter, too, warned us that in this world, you may suffer for following Christ, but you should always be ready to make a case for why you follow him.

*But even if you should suffer for righteousness' sake, you will be blessed. Have no fear of them, nor be troubled, 15 but in your hearts honor Christ the Lord as holy, always being prepared to make a defense to anyone who asks you for a reason for the hope that is in you; yet do it with gentleness and respect, 16 having a good conscience, so that, when you are slandered, those who revile your good behavior in Christ may be put to shame. 17 For it is better to suffer for doing good, if that should be God's will, than for doing evil.* (1 Peter 3:14–17 ESV)

Matthew adds a caveat, however, that will be applicable in the last days, when you are delivered to the tribunal processing centers for refusing to reject Christ. He tells us that at just the right moment, the Holy Spirit will give you the words to speak.

> *But when they deliver you up, take no thought how or what ye shall speak: for it shall be given you in that same hour what ye shall speak.* (Matthew 10:19 KJV)

# 11.13 Déjà vu: Two Politically Incorrect Witnesses all Over Again

Immediately after the abomination of desolation, the two witnesses appear. There are exactly 1,260 days between the abomination of desolation and the Day of the Lord. Malachi tells us in this dual prophecy that he will send the prophet Elijah before the Day of the Lord.

> *Behold, I will send you Elijah the prophet before the great and awesome day of the LORD comes.* (Malachi 4:5 ESV)

John tells us that the witnesses will prophesy for 1,260 days. This means they will make their appearance shortly after the antichrist desecrates the temple.

When the antichrist desecrated the sanctuary, it caused a monumental shift in this contest for the kingdom. The battles that had previously been occurring in the unseen realm now come out in the open as God exposes the real forces at work. While Michael the Archangel was on earth he operated in the unseen realm, but his successors, these two witnesses, will be flesh and blood. After the abomination took place, God handed over the temple court to the antichrist to *"trample"* for the next forty-two months, a period that, not surprisingly, matches the exact duration for which the witnesses are granted their power.

> *. . . but do not measure the court outside the temple; leave that out, for it is given over to the nations, and they will trample the holy city for forty-two months. 3 And I will grant authority to my two witnesses,*

*and they will prophesy for 1,260 days, clothed in sackcloth." 4 These are the two olive trees and the two lampstands that stand before the Lord of the earth. 5 And if anyone would harm them, fire pours from their mouth and consumes their foes. If anyone would harm them, this is how he is doomed to be killed. 6 They have the power to shut the sky, that no rain may fall during the days of their prophesying, and they have power over the waters to turn them into blood and to strike the earth with every kind of plague, as often as they desire.* (Revelation 11:2–6 ESV)

The role of protector of Israel passes from the Archangel Michael to these two witnesses. They will be like unstoppable superheroes to the Jews and Christians, but absolute enemies to the antichrist, who will try everything in his arsenal to kill these two thorns in his side, but they cannot be harmed. They are here for the duration of the Great Tribulation and they are protected by a supernatural force and cannot be killed until their mission is complete, which we're told will take the exact length of time the Great Tribulation will last: 1,260 days.

During their 3½ years on earth, their mission is to testify to the world that the antichrist and his false prophet are imposters. The witnesses will present evidence and give testimony that they are not who they claim to be but are, in fact, puppets of Satan. The two witnesses may also be here to help protect the 144,000 Jews specifically selected by God to be set apart and marked with the Seal of God. Most importantly, by directing the bowls of plagues to counter the worst effects of each trumpet power granted to the antichrist, they will prove that the God they serve is more powerful than the antichrist.

You may be curious to know who the two witnesses will be. They are called witnesses because they will be biblical prophets, familiar figures from Scripture who knew Jesus personally and can provide firsthand testimony that the false prophet, who claims to be Jesus, is a liar and deceiver. Since people can only die once, the fact that these two witnesses will be killed by the antichrist at the conclusion of their mission definitively rules out prophets who have died.

> *And just as it is appointed for man to die once, and after that comes judgment* (Hebrews 9:27 ESV)

There are just three prophets who, it seems, did not die: Enoch, Moses, and Elijah.[126] From what I can tell, Enoch never met Jesus on earth. So it seems only the last two prophets meet both qualifications because they didn't die and they appeared to Jesus and talked to him as he was transfigured in front of Peter, James, and John.

> *And after six days Jesus took with him Peter and James, and John his brother, and led them up a high*

---

[126] There's a possibility it could be Moses, even though we're told he died: "*5 So Moses the servant of the LORD died there in the land of Moab, according to the word of the LORD, 6 and he buried him in the valley in the land of Moab opposite Beth-peor; but no one knows the place of his burial to this day*" (Deuteronomy 34:5-6 ESV). Satan, asserting his authority as the king of this world, sought to claim Moses' soul and bring it to Sheol (the Paradise section). However, when he could not find Moses's body, he engaged in a heated argument with the archangel Michael, questioning where God had concealed it. "*But when the archangel Michael, contending with the devil, was disputing about the body of Moses, he did not presume to pronounce a blasphemous judgment, but said, 'The Lord rebuke you'*" (Jude 1:9 ESV). Moses' reported death may have been a divine strategy to deceive the deceiver, Satan. His appearance at the Transfiguration further supports the idea that Moses did not die. If that is the case, Moses would be a strong candidate to be one of the two witnesses.

*mountain by themselves. 2 And he was transfigured before them, and his face shone like the sun, and his clothes became white as light. 3 And behold, there* appeared *to them* Moses *and* Elijah, *talking with him.*
(Matthew 17:1–3 ESV)

But there's no need to be dogmatic about their identity, as they will be easy to recognize. They will appear as though they've stepped right off a biblical movie set, dressed in crude garments made of goat hair, known as sackcloth, symbolizing that both they and God are in mourning for all who have rejected him despite the many warnings.[127] However, don't be deceived by their primitive attire; they will be armed and dangerous!

They're not armed with weapons in the traditional sense. Instead, they have access to God's full arsenal of plagues; the same plagues represented by the seven angels in Revelation 15:6 and probably others as well.

It's easy to understand why most authors and commentators never make the connection between the plagues of the two witnesses and those of the seven angels. John doesn't introduce the group of seven angels and their bowls of plagues until four chapters after discussing the two witnesses. This is yet another example of John's structured, thematic approach, where he presents related events without following a strict chronological order. Once you recognize this pattern, it becomes clear that the plagues controlled by the two witnesses are the same as the seven plagues held by the angels.

---

[127] Sackcloth is a coarse material made of goat hair: *"And I will grant authority to my two witnesses, and they will prophesy for 1,260 days, clothed in sackcloth"* (Revelation 11: 3 ESV).

# 11.14 The Who's Who of the Twelve Tribes: Safeguarding 144,000 Jews

An angel with authority shouts to the four angels who are poised to *"harm earth and the sea"* to delay their terrible duty until 144,000 chosen Jews can be individually marked with the seal of God by another angel.[128] We know from the following text that these Jews are sealed before the land, sea, or trees are harmed. The land and the trees are harmed in the 1st trumpet and the sea in the 2nd trumpet, which means they are sealed before the 1st trumpet sounds:

> *And I saw another angel ascending from the east, having the seal of the living God: and he cried with a loud voice to the four angels, to whom it was given to hurt the earth and the sea, 3 Saying, Hurt not the earth, neither the sea, nor the trees, till we have sealed the servants of our God in their foreheads.4 And I heard the number of them which were sealed: and there were sealed an hundred and forty and four thousand of all the tribes of the children of Israel.* (Revelation 7:2–4 KJV)

Many commentators and some denominations believe that these Jews are really Christians. Their rationale goes like this: Since Christians have been grafted into the vine, which represents Christ, then we are all now included with the Jews as his chosen people.

> *17 But if some of the branches were broken off, and you, although a wild olive shoot, were grafted in*

---

[128] This gives us a little more insight into the working of the trumpets. In this 1st trumpet a single angel will sound, but 4 angels will actually carry out the deed.

*among the others and now share in the nourishing root of the olive tree, 18 do not be arrogant toward the branches. If you are, remember it is not you who support the root, but the root that supports you. 19 Then you will say, "Branches were broken off so that I might be grafted in." 20 That is true. They were broken off because of their unbelief, but you stand fast through faith. So do not become proud, but fear. 21 For if God did not spare the natural branches, neither will he spare you.* (Romans 11:17–21 ESV)

It's true that for much of the New Testament, Christians inherit the blessings that belong to Jews because we've been grafted in like adopted brothers and sisters. But John makes it very clear that in this instance, he's talking about 144,000 Jews and not Christians. He devotes the next three verses to counting out exactly how many Jews will come from each of the twelve tribes he names.[129] Though we've lost track of most of their descendants, God hasn't. If God knows the number of hairs on each person's head, we can be sure that he knows each person's DNA.[130] There is nothing that will keep him from gathering the selected children of Abraham at the proper time.

*Bear fruits in keeping with repentance. And do not begin to say to yourselves, 'We have Abraham as our father.' For I tell you, God is able from these stones to raise up children for Abraham.* (Luke 3:8 ESV)

---

[129] There may be some significance to John naming the tribe of Joseph and the tribe of one of his sons, Manasseh, but not the other son, Ephraim. Normally, both sons are named in place of Joseph. There is also significance to the tribe of Dan being excluded from this list.

[130] "Why, even the hairs of your head are all numbered. Fear not; you are of more value than many sparrows" (Luke 12:7 ESV).

I've heard ministers refer to these 144,000 as "super evangelists" who will be able to preach during the tribulation without fear of harm from anyone because of their supernatural protection. While it's true that they will be supernaturally protected, I could find no verse to indicate they can move around as individuals or travel anywhere. The scriptural evidence indicates instead that they will remain as a group in a safe hiding place, "*a place prepared by God*," for the duration of the Great Tribulation, 1,260 days.

> *She* [Israel] *gave birth to a male child* [Jesus], *one who is to rule all the nations with a rod of iron, but her child was caught up to God and to his throne, 6 and the woman* [the sealed remnant of 144,000] *fled into the wilderness, where she has a place prepared by God, in which she is to be nourished for 1,260 days.* (Revelation 12:5–6 ESV)

In marking them with his personal protection, God is keeping the covenant he made thousands of years earlier. God will supernaturally protect these chosen ones whom he has called by name:

> *But now thus says the LORD, he who created you, O Jacob, he who formed you, O Israel: "Fear not, for I have redeemed you; I have called you by name, you are mine. 2 When you pass through the waters, I will be with you; and through the rivers, they shall not overwhelm you; when you walk through fire you shall not be burned, and the flame shall not consume you.* (Isaiah 43:1–2 ESV)

Near the middle of Revelation, we learn more about these 144,000 Jews because, as promised, they survived the Great Tribulation and will emerge unscathed as Jesus leads them to Mt Zion:

> *Then I looked, and behold, on Mount Zion stood the Lamb, and with him 144,000 who had his name and his Father's name written on their foreheads.* (Revelation 14:1 ESV)

> *It is these who have not defiled themselves with women, for they are virgins. It is these who follow the Lamb wherever he goes. These have been redeemed from mankind as first fruits for God and the Lamb, 5 and in their mouth no lie was found, for they are blameless.* (Revelation 14:4-5 ESV)

These are very special Jews, the holiest among each of the twelve tribes, handpicked by God for a divine purpose. Each one was personally marked by an angel with the seal of God, granting them supernatural protection during the Great Tribulation. This seal assures them that they will survive Satan's furious attempt to exterminate every Jew and will enter the Millennium to repopulate the Jewish people.

## Part Four:

# The Real Mother of All Wars

Saddam Hussein famously said the First Gulf War (1991) would be "the mother of all battles."

Har Maggeddon will be The Mother of All Wars

# 12 Seal 4: Death and the Grave Make Their Big Debut: The Deadly Volleys Begin

*When the Lamb broke the fourth seal, I heard the fourth living being say, "Come!" 8 I looked up and saw a horse whose color was pale green. Its rider was named Death, and his companion was the Grave. These two were given authority over one-fourth of the earth, to kill with the sword and famine and disease and wild animals.* (Revelation 6:7–8 NLT)

By this time, you've probably figured out that, with the exception of the first horse and rider, the next three are not actual horses and riders. The next three seals serve as vivid images that God uses to summarize the essence of chapters two, three and four of the seven chapters of the 7-sealed book. The rider of this 4th horse is named Death, and he's traveling alongside *"the Grave,"* so that's not a literal horse and rider, but a striking image that leaves no doubt about its meaning. This indicates that the antichrist's reign has entered a gruesome phase: the systematic extermination of those who will not bow to him. The rider and his companion *"were given authority"* in accordance with the rules of the 7-sealed book, but their authority is limited to 1/4th of the earth. That doesn't necessarily mean the antichrist's forces will kill all the people on a quarter of the earth, just that their authority extends to a quarter of the earth. They have the authority to kill by multiple means: *"with the sword, famine and disease and wild animals."* That last one, wild animals, or some translations say beasts, indicates that they are given authority to control or direct wild animals to kill people.

Killing with the sword doesn't necessarily mean war. Considering the exterminations that are about to begin, it's more likely that it means he's given the authority to use the edge of the sword to behead those who refuse the mark. Soon after this 4th seal is opened, the large scale killing events will begin.

# 12.1 Seals, Bowls and Trumpets: The Septet Sequence is an End-Time Deception

The seals, trumpets, and bowls of the Book of Revelation are often described by end-time authors and end-time chart creators as signs of God's judgment or wrath. However, this interpretation highlights another example of viewing Scripture through the lens of a particular doctrine. Because, while all 7 bowls are "filled with the wrath of God...", only one trumpet (the 7th) and one seal (the 6th) mention wrath; and these are distinct types of wrath.[131]

---

[131] 28 The 7th trumpet mentions wrath (*orge*), but it means a measured, controlled anger. Just as there are 4 different Greek words for love (*Eros, Philia, Agape,* and *Storge*),(Pastor Darryl T. Cuffie, "The 4 Greek Words for 'Love' Used In The New Testament," Blessing of Heaven, February 14, 2023, http://www.blessingofheaven.org/blog/the-4-greek-words-for-love-used-in-new-testament), there are 4 main Greek words for anger or wrath. *Parorgismos* (Strong's #3950): Irritated, provoked anger, *Orge* (#3709): Anger under control, Orgizo (#3710): Provoke, arouse anger, and *Thumos* (# 2372): Anger forthwith boiling up and soon subsiding again. (Koine Greek, "*parorgismos,*" "*orge,*" "*orgizo,*" & "*thumos,*" https://www.koinegreek.com/koine-greek-dictionary). John uses the Greek word *thymou* (a form of *thumos*) to describe the specific kind of wrath the bowls represent, which Thayer's Greek lexicon says means passionate anger boiling forth violently.

> *And one of the four living creatures gave to the seven angels seven golden bowls full of the wrath [thymou] of God who lives forever and ever* (Revelation 15:7 ESV)

John uses that same Greek word when he recounts the wrath Jesus will personally be exhibiting in Revelation 14:19 as he harvests the grapes (the wicked) and throws them into God's winepress because his righteous indignation has passed the boiling point.

> *So the angel swung his sickle over the earth and gathered the grapes from the vineyard of the earth and tossed them into the great winepress of the wrath [thymou] of God.* (Revelation 14:19 NET)

Most authors group the seals, trumpets, and bowls together, asserting that they occur one after another in a continuous sequence and treating them all as part of God's wrath.

The chart below illustrates the traditional sequence that most commentators believe the 7 seals, 7 trumpets, and 7 bowls will follow.

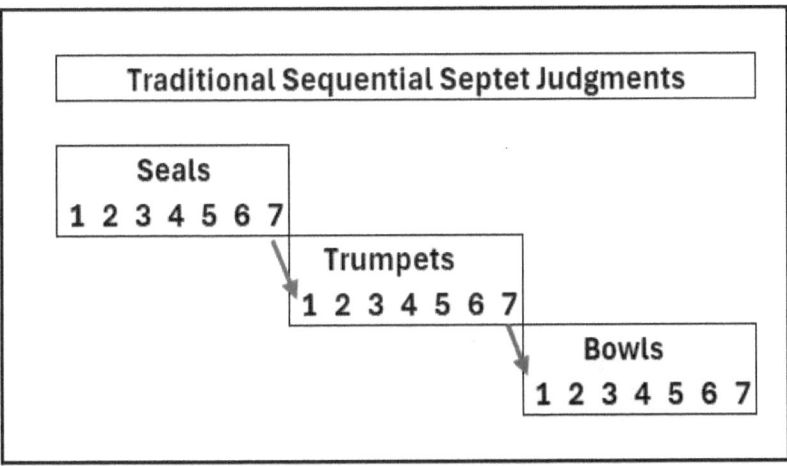

But as we'll cover in subsequent chapters, John gives us several clues to let us know that this is not the true sequence, and the exact point when Jesus' wrath will be poured out is part of the key.

## 12.2 An Important Pattern of Three Sixes

Though some authors allow for a slight variation, nearly every end-time author I've read assumes that the 7 seals are opened one right after the other, then the 7 trumpets sound one right after the other, and then the 7 bowls are poured out in succession. This sequence is sometimes referred to as the three septet sequence, where septet means a group of seven.

But as John recounts the seals, trumpets, and bowls, he lists each as a series of 6. After the 6th of each, he breaks the series to describe something else and then returns to describe the 7th of each.

Specifically, John recounts the first 6 seals in an unbroken sequence, then there is a break in the sequence as other events are described, and then he gets back to describing the 7th seal. Later, he describes the first 6 trumpets in an unbroken sequence, then breaks to explain something else, before getting back to the 7th trumpet. He does the same thing with the first 6 bowls, with a break to describe other events before coming back to the 7th bowl.

Through this pattern, John is conveying that there is something different about the 7th Seal, the 7th trumpet, and the 7th bowl and that they should not be grouped in with the first series of six of each set. He is communicating an unmistakable pattern; that the 7th of each set stands apart from the first 6 in each set. The 7th of each is not part of the same sequence. When you read only the 7th of each of those together, you'll experience an "aha" moment, just as I did. Let me attempt to recreate that "aha" moment for you by demonstrating how each 7th works together to proclaim the glorious news that Jesus is King.

1. The 7th seal is 30 minutes of silence. Creation is rendered motionless in order to pay homage to God and build suspense for an announcement which will come from heaven immediately after that pause.

2. That long silence is broken by the sounding of 7th trumpet, which heralds the long-awaited glorious announcement from great voices in heaven: "The kingdom of the world has become the kingdom of our Lord and of his Christ, and he shall reign forever and ever."[132] This is the long-awaited Day of the Lord.

3. Once all of the events of the Day of the Lord are completed, the 7th bowl is poured out and a pronouncement is made from the temple of God that "*It is done.*" The contest is over.

God reserved the 7's for himself. He could have accomplished his work using 3, 5, or 10 of each, but he chose 7 for a sacred reason. The 7th of each is dedicated to Jesus, just as the 7th day of the week is set apart as the Sabbath for the Lord.

> *Six days you shall labor, and do all your work, 10 but the seventh day is a Sabbath to the LORD your God.* (Exodus 20:9–10a ESV)

When the 7th of each set is treated as something set aside for God, then a few more pieces of the end-time puzzle instantly fall into place.

---

[132] Revelation 11:15b (ESV)

## 12.3 Satan is Allotted Powers: Each Preceded by a Loud Trumpet Blast

The book of Job is probably the oldest book in the Bible.[133] Most know it as the story of Job's nearly unbearable suffering and the double blessing he receives because he stayed faithful to God through his entire painful, traumatic, and extraordinary tribulation. But the book of Job offers much more—it is rich with insights into how God governs the universe.

It's one of the most fascinating books of the Bible to me and it gives us a rare glimpse into the interaction between God and Satan. Remarkably, Job's suffering begins with what is portrayed as just another normal day in heaven with God and Satan having a conversation:

> *6 Now there was a day when the sons of God came to present themselves before the LORD, and Satan also came among them.*
>
> *7 The LORD said to Satan, "From where have you come?" Satan answered the LORD and said, "From going to and fro on the earth, and from walking up and down on it."*
>
> *8 And the LORD said to Satan, "Have you considered my servant Job, that there is none like him on the*

---

[133] While scholars haven't reached a consensus on the age of the book of Job, I believe that it predates the writings of Moses, given a variety of historical information included in the book. Commentator Jay Smith writes that "It is possible that Job is the oldest of any book of the Bible, written approximately 2100–1800 B.C." (Jay Smith, "Job," Bible Book Summary, biblehub.com, https://biblehub.com/summary/job/1.htm)

*earth, a blameless and upright man, who fears God and turns away from evil?"*

*9 Then Satan answered the LORD and said, "Does Job fear God for no reason?*

*10 Have you not put a hedge around him and his house and all that he has, on every side? You have blessed the work of his hands, and his possessions have increased in the land.*

*11 But stretch out your hand and touch all that he has, and he will curse you to your face."*

*12 And the LORD said to Satan, "Behold, all that he has is in your hand. Only against him do not stretch out your hand." So Satan went out from the presence of the LORD.* (Job 1:6–12 ESV)

We learn several things in this passage:

1.  Surprise! Satan, has access to heaven and can enter the throne room of God and even converse with him at certain times.
2.  Satan is constantly roaming the earth, looking for people to turn away from God.
3.  God can put "*a hedge around*" those who love him, which prevents Satan from doing the harm he'd like to do.
4.  Satan really wants to have control of some of God's power.
5.  God could not let Satan call him a liar regarding Job's faithfulness, so he permitted Satan to put Job's faith to a supernatural test by using heavenly powers against him and his family.

6. Satan was convinced that Job only loved God because God had so richly blessed him and that he would buckle and curse God immediately if he lost his wealth and children.

7. God was right about Job's faith and was also right that Satan, *"the accuser of our brothren,"* was lying as usual.

8. Since Satan couldn't make Job curse God even after focusing some of God's power against him, the entire heavenly audience saw for themselves that it was Satan who was the liar, not God.

This answers the question of why God would allow the antichrist to wield these trumpet powers against believers. God allowed Satan to use his powers on Job and his family to test Job's faith, but in the end it strengthened it. Suffering can serve a purpose in proving and building-up one's reliance on prayer and strengthen one's devotion to Jesus. But, and this is crucial to understanding the first 6 trumpets, God placed specific limits on the power he allowed Satan to temporarily wield.

> 15 *And the Sabeans fell upon them, and took them away; yea, they have slain the servants with the edge of the sword; and I only am escaped alone to tell thee. 16 While he was yet speaking, there came also another, and said, The fire of God is fallen from heaven, and hath burned up the sheep, and the servants, and consumed them; and I only am escaped alone to tell thee. 17 While he was yet speaking, there came also another, and said, The Chaldeans made out three bands, and fell upon the camels, and have carried them away, yea, and slain the servants with the edge of the sword; and I only am escaped alone to tell thee. 18 While he was yet speaking, there came also another, and said, Thy sons and thy daughters were eating and drinking wine in their eldest brother's house: 19 And, behold, there*

*came a great wind from the wilderness, and smote the four corners of the house, and it fell upon the young men, and they are dead; and I only am escaped alone to tell thee.* (Job 1:15–19 KJV)

What were the powers Satan was allowed to wield in Job 1:15-19?

1. God removed his protection from Job's property, so Satan used his power of persuasion to incite two different enemy forces to kill, steal, and destroy Job's property. The Sabeans (an infamous marauding force) stole Job's asses and his 1,000 oxen and killed their handlers. The Chaldeans (a different enemy force) then stole Job's 3,000 camels and killed their handlers.
2. Satan was allowed to use the *"fire of God,"* so he directed it to fall from heaven and burn up all 7,000 of Job's sheep and their shepherds. We'll see this fire again in the 1$^{st}$ trumpet.
3. Satan was allowed to control one aspect of the weather, so he aimed a *"great wind"* at the home of Job's son that was so powerful it knocked the house down and killed Job's sons and daughters and their families inside.

But also note that the power which Satan was allowed to exercise was severely restricted. Did you notice it affected only Job's property, Job's children, Job's servants, and Job's livestock? We can infer this because the three friends who visited Job after those catastrophes did not mention even one neighboring property or town that was touched. The raiding parties did not touch any other ranch but were supernaturally restricted to only Job's property. Nor was Satan permitted to harm Job...at first.

We get our second view into the workings of heaven when Satan comes before God once more in Job 2:1–6. God brings up the subject of Job to Satan and it is clear that Satan is irritated that he has not been able to turn Job away from God. He thought that if he was allowed to inflict physical pain on Job, that would surely cause him to curse God.

> ... *He* [Job] *still holds fast his integrity, although you incited me against him to destroy him without reason. 4 Then Satan answered the LORD and said, "Skin for skin! All that a man has he will give for his life.*
>
> *5 But stretch out your hand and touch his bone and his flesh, and he will curse you to your face."*
>
> *6 And the LORD said to Satan, "Behold, he is in your hand; only spare his life." 7 So Satan went out from the presence of the LORD and struck Job with loathsome sores from the sole of his foot to the crown of his head.* (Job 2:3–7 ESV)

We know the beautiful end of this tragic story. Job suffers immensely from the sores, is tempted by his wife to curse God, and must continuously defend his innocence against each of his three friends, who falsely accuse him of committing some sin that brought this calamity upon him. In the end, God exonerates Job and blesses him with twice what he lost.

Tellingly, God never justifies to Job why he allowed all of these tragedies to befall his faithful servant. One reason the story of Job is included in the Bible was to give us a window into heaven and inform us about this ongoing contest between God and Satan. This window gives us valuable insight into the trumpets of the end-time.

# 12.4 The First Six Trumpets

There are seven reasons why we can be sure it is God who authorizes the powers of the first 6 trumpets to Satan and that Satan then empowers his human avatar, the antichrist, to direct some of them.[134]

1. Satan has controlled one of these powers before. In Job chapter 1, God allows Satan to control the *"fire of God,"* which fell from heaven and burned up all Job's sheep and shepherds:

   > *While he was yet speaking, there came also another, and said, The fire of God is fallen from heaven, and hath burned up the sheep, and the servants, and consumed them...* (Job 1:16a ESV)

   This power is nearly identical to the power unleashed during the 1ˢᵗ trumpet.

   > *The first angel blew his trumpet, and there followed hail and fire, mixed with blood, and these were thrown upon the earth. And a third of the earth was burned up, and a third of the trees were burned up, and all green grass was burned up.* (Revelation 8:7 ESV)

   In Revelation 8, John informs us that the antichrist will be given access to the same kind of power that he was given in Job 1.

---

[134] An avatar in this context is a man who thinks and acts like Satan and is inspired to carry out his desire. The actual definition of avatar is "an image that represents you in online games, chatrooms, etc. and that you can move around the screen." (Cambridge Dictionary, s.v. "avatar," https://dictionary.cambridge.org/dictionary/english/avatar).

2. Just as in Job 1, the antichrist's power, doled out to him one power at a time via each of the first 6 trumpets, will be limited to a specific target, effect, and duration. The 7-sealed book gives the antichrist specific powers that are drastically limited, in most cases, to 1/3$^{rds}$. In other words, the antichrist is only allotted 1/3$^{rd}$ of the authority he really desires. Each trumpet releases a little more power and crescendos with the 6$^{th}$ trumpet when the antichrist is given control of 200 million horsemen, who could destroy much of humanity. But once again, even with all of that destructive power, he will be limited to killing "only" 1/3$^{rd}$ of all men.

3. Some trumpets harness demonic powers. Trumpets 5 and 6 release wicked demonic powers on the earth, something God would never do if it were his wrath. Think about this; wouldn't it show that God is limited if he had to rely on demons to demonstrate his wrath? He didn't do it in Egypt; in fact, he countered the black arts of Pharaoh's magicians as they duplicated his first two plagues. So why would God change tactics and start relying on demons in the last days? As further evidence that God is allowing the antichrist to wield the power of the trumpets, a being in heaven has to first give permission for the 5$^{th}$ and 6$^{th}$ trumpets. Specifically, in the 5$^{th}$ trumpet, the demonic stinging locusts led by Apollyon are so destructive that they have been kept restrained in hell with a lock. Someone in heaven must first give a fallen angel a key before they can be unlocked.

*And the fifth angel blew his trumpet, and I saw a star fallen from heaven to earth, and he was given the key to the shaft of the bottomless pit. 2 He opened the shaft of the bottomless pit, and from the shaft rose smoke*

*like the smoke of a great furnace, and the sun and the air were darkened with the smoke from the shaft.*
(Revelation 9:1–2 ESV)

Additionally, in trumpet 6 a voice from heaven must first give verbal permission saying *"release the four angels who are bound"* [135] before the 200 million cavalry can wreak their havoc on the world.

4.  None of the trumpets are specifically directed at the wicked. In fact, it's quite the opposite. The horrifying demon-locusts of the 5th trumpet are specifically commanded not to harm the wicked. Contrast that with the bowl judgments, two of which are aimed solely at the wicked: bowl 1 inflicts oozing sores only on those with the mark, and bowl 5, utter darkness, only affects the antichrist's kingdom.

5.  God is a God of order and justice. Though Satan used deception and trickery to wrest the kingdom from Adam, God will not forcefully seize the kingdom back from Satan. God is going to follow the very specific rules of engagement he set forth in the 7-sealed book. God wants the world to see, and maybe more importantly, God wants his angels to witness for themselves that he is going above and beyond to give Satan a fair chance to hold on to his kingdom. And this apparently includes *"permitting"* him, through his antichrist, to wield some specific powers (*"authority"*) once again.

> *The beast was permitted to go to war against the saints and conquer them. He was given ruling authority over every tribe, people, language, and nation, 8 and*

---

[135] Revelation 9:13-14 ESV " Then the sixth angel blew his trumpet, and I heard a voice from the four horns of the golden altar before God, 14 saying to the sixth angel who had the trumpet, "Release the four angels who are bound at the great river Euphrates."

*all those who live on the earth will worship the beast, everyone whose name has not been written since the foundation of the world in the book of life belonging to the Lamb who was killed.* (Revelation 13:7–8 NET)

Each trumpet allots the antichrist (*"the beast"*) very specific, limited powers which he is *"permitted"* to use to *"go to war against the saints."* It's as if God is responding to the antichrist's challenge to a cosmic duel. In his omniscience, God foresaw the challenge at *"the foundation of the world"* and so created the 7-sealed book to prepare the terms and instruments for the battle, the dueling pistols and ammunition, to guarantee an equitable contest. The trumpets represent the antichrist's ammunition, while the bowls signify God's. As the God of order, he allows the antichrist to take the first shot, but only within the boundaries he has set.

John concludes this passage with an admonition that this is important; we should pay attention to what he just told us:

*If anyone has an ear, he had better listen!*
(Revelation 13:9 NET)

The world and, more importantly, the angels will also observe that Satan followed the rules up until the point he realized he was going to lose. The angels will see with their own eyes that Satan will flagrantly and violently break the rules. But we'll discuss that in the Chapter 21.1, "Satan's Final Move."

6.  The prayers of the saints who wear the full armor of God. Many people apparently heed John's admonition in Revelation 13:9 that they *"had better listen,"* and they fervently pray before

each trumpet is sounded. In Revelation 8:2-5 John gives us his fascinating firsthand account of how prayers are gathered and sent before God.[136] It's no coincidence that the only detailed description of how prayers reach God occurs just as the seven angels are handed their trumpets, which signifies Satan is about to receive his first allotment of God's power.

> *Then I saw the seven angels who stand before God, and seven trumpets were given to them. 3 And another angel came and stood at the altar with a golden censer, and he was given much incense to offer with the prayers of all the saints on the golden altar before the throne, 4 and the smoke of the incense, with the prayers of the saints, rose before God from the hand of the angel. 5 Then the angel took the censer and filled it with fire from the altar and threw it on the earth, and there were peals of thunder, rumblings, flashes of lightning, and an earthquake.* (Revelation 8:2–5 ESV)

This demonstrates that God hears the prayers of the prepared saints who have been asking him for protection from the impending trumpet powers. The prepared saints will know from their study of end-time Scriptures that the trumpets will soon be released on the world. They know God has promised that he will not leave Christians defenseless. The spiritual armor God gave us to defend against the devil and *"against the authorities, against the cosmic powers over this present darkness, against the*

---

[136] In Revelation 5:8 ESV we learn a little about prayers, ". . . golden bowls full of incense, which are the prayers of the saints," but we're not told how they are handled or processed by God. The detailed account of prayers coming before God occurs only in Revelation 8:4, where we are told specifically how the smoke of the incense reaches God.

*spiritual forces of evil in the heavenly places"* were given to defend ourselves against each of the trumpet and bowl powers, too!

By the time John sees this event, millions of Christians are experts with their armor and have been fervently praying for protection.

> *Finally, be strong in the Lord and in the strength of his might. 11 Put on the whole armor of God, that you may be able to stand against the schemes of the devil. 12 For we do not wrestle against flesh and blood, but against the rulers, against the authorities, against the cosmic powers over this present darkness, against the spiritual forces of evil in the heavenly places. 13 Therefore take up the whole armor of God, that you may be able to withstand in the evil day, and having done all, to stand firm. 14 Stand therefore, having fastened on the belt of truth, and having put on the breastplate of righteousness, 15 and, as shoes for your feet, having put on the readiness given by the gospel of peace. 16 In all circumstances take up the shield of faith, with which you can extinguish all the flaming darts of the evil one; 17 and take the helmet of salvation, and the sword of the Spirit, which is the word of God, 18 praying at all times in the Spirit, with all prayer and supplication. To that end, keep alert with all perseverance, making supplication for all the saints* (Ephesians 6:10-18 ESV)

Viewing these two passages together (Revelation 8:2-5 and Ephesians 6:10-18) reveals that each spiritual warrior's *"prayer and supplication"* is gathered by a special angel and then all those gathered prayers, together *"with much incense...rose before God from the hand of the angel"* at this exact moment, just before the trumpets begin to sound.[137][138] God will answer their prayers by empowering his two witnesses to counter many of the effects of the trumpets.

7. Trumpets are not God's judgments or wrath. How many times have you read or looked at end-time charts that indicated the trumpets are God's wrath or God's judgments, or both? We're explicitly told that the bowls are God's wrath and God's judgments (Rev. 16:5 and 16:7). However, nowhere in the Bible do we find the trumpets referred to as either judgments or wrath. The absence of either word is further indication that the trumpets are simply powers that have been allotted to the antichrist to test men in the same way Satan was allotted power to test Job. Satan and his antichrist will torment men to try to get them to reject Christ and accept him and his mark.

---

[137] Ephesians 6:18 ESV
[138] Revelation 8:3b & 4b ESV

## 12.5 The Bowl Judgments: Plagues Again

The bowls and trumpets may seem novel to us as John describes them in Revelation, but there is nothing new under the sun. God left us with an account of when he used similar powers by similar witnesses for similar reasons in the past.

In the book of Exodus, God used his witnesses, Moses and Aaron, to call down 10 plagues upon Egypt. In addition to the case I presented in the Déjà Vu chapter for Moses being a strong candidate to be one of the witnesses, he is one of the few people in Scripture who has had direct conversations with God and visibly encountered him, or at least an aspect of him, first at the burning bush on Mt. Horeb, and later on Mount Sinai.

> And Moses said, "I will turn aside to see this great sight, why the bush is not burned." 4 When the LORD saw that he turned aside to see, God called to him out of the bush, "Moses, Moses!" And he said, "Here I am." 5 Then he said, "Do not come near; take your sandals off your feet, for the place on which you are standing is holy ground." 6 And he said, "I am the God of your father, the God of Abraham, the God of Isaac. . ." (Exodus 3:3–6 ESV)

God then sent Moses and Aaron to Egypt with instructions that when the Egyptians asked who sent them, Moses would inform the people that *"I am"* sent him. Moses and Aaron were, therefore, serving as God's ambassadors and witnesses.

Why didn't God prove his superiority by sending one giant, devasting plague on Egypt to terrorize everyone, and then have

Moses shepherd his people out of the land? Why, instead, did he take the time to put them through 10 consecutive plagues with a pause in between each? The answer is that God wasn't just freeing his people from enslavement; he was also giving everyone, both the Jews and the Egyptians, a chance to learn who he was. God gave the Egyptians and the Jews the opportunity to see and experience firsthand that he wasn't just another god. He was the God above all gods. Giving people a chance to understand and repent is God's modus operandi; it's his heart.

The Israelites had been enslaved for about 400 years, and by that time, it's likely that few of them knew much about God. And it's certain the Egyptians knew almost nothing about God. They worshipped dozens of gods, not the least of which was the Pharaoh. Pharaoh believed himself to be a god, but God was patient with him and allowed him time after each plague to reflect on his own inferior abilities and consider repenting before sending each subsequent plague. To substantiate this point, we're told about the state of Pharaoh's heart between each of the plagues:

> *But when Pharaoh saw that there was relief, he hardened his heart and did not listen to them, just as the LORD had predicted* (Exodus 8:15 NET)

God knew that Pharaoh wasn't going to repent. He said so to Moses at the burning bush, and God subsequently hardened Pharaoh's heart. But through the process of administering ever more deadly plagues, the Israelites and the Egyptian people came to know firsthand that the God of the Israelites was mightier than the dozens of Egyptian deities combined. We'll never know for sure if any of those Egyptians threw away their idols and started worshipping God, but we do know that God cared just as much for the Egyptian laborer as for the Pharaoh, and we know that God is a God of second chances.

A number of Egyptians came along with the Jews on their desert journey, and we're given a few indications that some Egyptians became convinced of the power of God. As God warned about the plague of hail, which would kill the livestock and people outside, we're told that some of these people were convinced that it would really happen.

> *Then whoever feared the word of the LORD among the servants of Pharaoh hurried his slaves and his livestock into the houses* (Exodus 9:20 ESV).

God will once again demonstrate to an unbelieving world that he is the God of the universe. And, once again, he will use two witnesses to call down the plagues. But this time, the witnesses will administer the plagues by directing angels to release the contents of their bowls.

There are five key reasons to support the claim that the plagues called down by the two witnesses are the same plagues as those poured out by the seven angels.[139]

1. Using two witnesses to wield his power and call down plagues is not new. King Solomon shared many observations toward the end of his storied life: One of his observations, *"What has been is what will be, and what has been done is what will be done, and there is nothing new under the sun,"* is relevant for understanding the end-times.[140]

---

[139] As we'll discuss in a later chapter, the witnesses control 6 of the plagues. The 7th is set aside for the Lord.

[140] Ecclesiastes 1:9 ESV

God didn't announce and deliver the ten plagues on Egypt[141] himself. In the same way that he used his two witnesses, Moses and Aaron, to call down the plagues on Egypt, God will use two witnesses to call down plagues during the Great Tribulation.[142] Using Moses and Aaron to administer his plagues against Egypt was highly effective and God has told us he *"will seek to do again what has occurred in the past."*

> . . . *whatever will be has already been; for* God *will seek to do again what has occurred in the past.* (Ecclesiastes 3:15b NET)

2. John's wording ties the witnesses' plagues to the angels' plagues. He makes it clear that the two witnesses are in control of *"every kind of plague,"* which would include the plagues poured out in Revelation 15 and 16, and it implies that there may even be additional plagues about which we don't know. There are at least three Greek words that mean plague or pestilence, but John uses the same one, *plege*, for the plagues which the two witnesses control and the plagues released by the seven angels. This is compelling corroboration that the plagues of the two witnesses and the plagues of the seven angels are one and the same.

3. A voice from heaven says, *"And I will give power unto my two witnesses. . ."* (Revelation 11:3a KJV). So, they're not just here to testify and witness, they are also here to wield God's power. Three verses later, the voice specifies what kind of power: *"they*

---

[141] Exodus Chapters 7–11 describe the 10 plagues on Egypt

[142] There are 7 plagues, but the 7th is set apart for the Lord. This means the two witnesses control the first six plagues. Once they complete the 6th plague, their mission will be complete, and they can then be killed by the antichrist.

*have power. . . to strike the earth with every kind of plague, as often as they desire"* (Revelation 11:6b ESV).

4.  John tells us that two of the plagues which the witnesses call down are identical to the plague released by the second angel, which turns the oceans into blood, and the plague released by the third angel, which turns the rivers and fountains into blood.[143] [144] And the fifth angel releases a plague of total darkness on the antichrist's kingdom, which is identical to the plague of total darkness which Moses and Aaron direct upon the Egyptians.[145]

| Parallels between Revelation Bowls/Plagues and Exodus Plagues | | | |
|---|---|---|---|
| # | Bowls (Revelation) | # | Plagues (Exodus) |
| 1 | Festering sores on men (16:02) | 6 | Festering boils on men (9:8–12) |
| 2 | Sea turns to blood. All sea creatures die (16:03) | 1 | Rivers and drinking water turn to blood (7:20–21) |
| 3 | Rivers and drinking water turn to blood (16:04) | 1 | Rivers and drinking water turn to blood (7:20–21) |
| 4 | Sun scorches and burns people (16:8–9) | | |

---

[143] Revelation 16:3

[144] Revelation 16:4

[145] "21 Then the LORD said to Moses, "Stretch out your hand toward heaven, that there may be darkness over the land of Egypt, a darkness to be felt." 22 So Moses stretched out his hand toward heaven, and there was pitch darkness in all the land of Egypt three days. 23 They did not see one another, nor did anyone rise from his place for three days, but all the people of Israel had light where they lived" (Exodus 10:21–23 ESV).

| 5 | Liquid darkness on land of the antichrist (16:10–11) | 9 | Liquid darkness on land of Egyptians (10:21-23) |
|---|---|---|---|
| 6 | Water in the Euphrates River runs dry. All nearby land affected (16:12–14) | 2 | Nile River clogged with frogs. All land infested with frogs (8:2–7) |
| 7 | Lightning, thunder, hail, severe earthquake (16:17–21) | 7 | Lightning, thunder, hail (9:22–25) |
|  | Protection of the Jews sealed by the mark of God (the 144,000) (7:04) |  | Protection of the Jews with God's seal on their door posts (12:12–13) |

How strange would it be if the two witnesses called down plague after plague, and then, if you subscribe to a chronological order of Revelation, a couple of weeks or months later, the 2nd and 3rd angels release those very same plagues again? It would not only be chaotic, which is the antithesis of God, but it would be anticlimactic. Yes, the ocean turning to blood is undeniably devastating, but one has to wonder how many times does this particular calamity need to happen? Surely, an all-powerful God could have chosen from countless other apocalyptic signs without resorting to repetition. And what about the confusion in heaven? Are we to believe that the second angel, who holds the bowl containing the plague that turns the oceans into blood, will stand idly by as another angel has to go and do the exact same thing when the two witnesses decide to call for the oceans to turn to blood? No. God is the God of order and he's placing that order in the hands, or maybe the staffs, of the two witnesses to let them direct when and where each of those angels release their plagues.

5.  In addition to the plagues, the witnesses can stop the rain *"during the days of their prophesying,"* which takes 1,260 days, or 3½ years.

> *They have the power to shut the sky, that no rain may fall during the days of their prophesying, and they have power over the waters to turn them into blood and to strike the earth with every kind of plague, as often as they desire.* (Rev 11:6 ESV)

The last time we read of a prophet holding back the rain for 3½ years was Elijah, in the years preceding his contest with Jezebel's prophets of Baal.

> *Elijah was a man with a nature like ours, and he prayed fervently that it might not rain, and for three years and six months it did not rain on the earth.* (James 5:17 ESV)

This is another indicator that God may be using the same playbook as before and that Elijah may be one of the two witnesses.

For the antichrist, everything will seem to be going according to his plan. When he excitedly thinks it's about time for God to release the power of the first trumpet to him, he will grow impatient. But God will keep him waiting, as he has no intention of granting the first angel permission to sound that trumpet until one crucial detail is completed: identifying 144,000 specific Jews and placing his mark of supernatural protection upon them, as we discussed in the "Who's Who of the Twelve Tribes of Israel" chapter.

# 12.6 Trumpet and Bowl Similarities

If you believe the bowls of plagues can only begin after all seven trumpets have sounded, then ask yourself: why are five of the bowls of plagues so strikingly similar to five of the trumpets?[146] More specifically, why would God send the 2nd trumpet to turn 1/3rd of the sea to blood, then wait until the next five trumpets are carried out, plus wait for the first bowl to finish, and then during the 2nd bowl turn the sea to blood again? Only this time, more of the sea is turned to blood than was during the 2nd trumpet. If you follow this line of thought and compare the 3rd trumpet to the 3rd bowl, and the 4th trumpet to the 4th bowl, then the sequential septet theory to which most end-time authors subscribe becomes incoherent.

| Similarities between certain Trumpets and Bowls | | | |
|---|---|---|---|
| # | Trumpets (Revelation 8:6–9:21) | # | Bowls (Revelation 16:1–12) |
| 2 | 1/3rd of the sea turns to blood | 2 | Sea turns to blood and every living thing in the sea dies |
| 3 | 1/3rd of the rivers and springs turn to wormwood (poison) | 3 | Rivers and springs turn to blood, people have no choice but to drink the blood |
| 4 | 1/3rd of the sun, 1/3rd of the moon, and 1/3rd of the stars go dark and will not give their light | 4 | The sun scorches men with fire and great heat |

---

[146] Recall that the 7th trumpet and the 7th bowl belong to the Lord, along with the 7th seal, so there is no similarity between them.

| | | | |
|---|---|---|---|
| 5 | Satan releases demonic stinging locusts to inflict pain on men | 5 | The beast's kingdom is thrown into pitch darkness and his followers gnaw on their tongues in pain from the dreadful sores inflicted on them in the first bowl |
| 6 | Four angels bound at the Euphrates River are released to allow 200 million horsemen to prepare for war. They are allowed to kill 1/3rd of men | 6 | The Euphrates River is dried up to prepare a way for the kings of the East to gather for the coming war |

The sequential septet theory—that the 7 seals are followed by the 7 trumpets, which are followed by the 7 bowls—makes the end-time timeline disjointed and, more importantly, impossible to reconcile harmoniously with many key end-time passages.

You may recall from Exodus that when God directs Moses to transform his staff into a snake, the pharaoh's magicians use their secret occultic arts to duplicate that miracle. When Moses turns the Nile into blood, they again duplicate that miracle with their occultic powers. Even when Moses calls down a plague of an overwhelming number of frogs, we're told that they matched it using the power of the occult. It was not until Moses turned the dust of Egypt into a plague of gnats that the magicians acknowledged they couldn't duplicate that power, so they declared it was clearly *"the finger of God."* Even though the magicians conceded that they were powerless against God after the first two plagues, it would require eight more plagues before the Pharaoh would begrudgingly concede defeat and let the Hebrews leave Egypt with all their possessions. God used those final eight plagues to demonstrate that Pharaoh was no match for him, and he will once again use multiple plagues to demonstrate to the world that the antichrist is no match for him either.

Scripture forewarns that the occult will thrive openly in the last days, as evidenced by the antichrist and his false prophet performing deceptive "miracles" designed to deceive Christians (*"the elect"*) into believing he is the "god" who truly cares for them and is worthy of their worship. But in an even more brazen deception, one calculated to convince world leaders to fear and respect his power, the antichrist will boast that the trumpet powers released to him are his own supernatural powers. Yet God will expose this lie. After each trumpet sounds, signaling the antichrist has been given another specific and limited power, the two witnesses will respond by calling down a plague that not only reduces much of the harm the antichrist intends to cause but also proves their plagues are far more powerful than anything the antichrist can do.

The antichrist is going to despise the fact that everyone in the world will be able to hear the sound of each trumpet as each new power is released and carefully doled out to him by God. Much like the way in which the prophet Elijah mocked the prophets of Baal when their god couldn't perform the simple task of lighting the sacrifice on fire, the two witnesses may exploit the sound of each trumpet to mock and taunt the antichrist and let the world know that he has no power of his own but must wait for each trumpet of God to grant it to him.

> *25 Then Elijah said to the prophets of Baal, "Choose for yourselves one bull and prepare it first, for you are many, and call upon the name of your god, but put no fire to it." 26 And they took the bull that was given them, and they prepared it and called upon the name of Baal*

*from morning until noon, saying, "O Baal, answer us!"
But there was no voice, and no one answered. And they
limped around the altar that they had made. 27 And at
noon Elijah mocked them, saying, "Cry aloud, for he is
a god. Either he is musing, or he is relieving himself, or
he is on a journey, or perhaps he is asleep and must be
awakened."* (1 Kings 18:25–27 ESV)

The antichrist will know from Scripture the order and the *relative* time that he should expect each of the first 6 trumpets to sound and release power to him, but he won't know the *exact* time they'll sound. The two witnesses, however, will know exactly when the trumpets will sound and will be ready to call down their countermeasure plagues. These countermeasures will demonstrate God's superiority and concern for the Christians and Jews.

The antichrist wants the world to think he has supreme power. Just as Satan specifically targeted Job's land, the antichrist will strategically select the countries and cities where he will wield the one-third powers he is granted. But the two witnesses are going to proclaim the truth, that the antichrist has limited powers and that they, as representatives of God, will counter the antichrist's trumpet powers with plagues from God which are not limited to 1/3rd of anything.

## 12.7 God's Word is Your Superpower: Prepare Your Armor Now

*12.7 (A) God's Wrath, not Vengeance*

Why would God pour out his bowls of wrath on everyone, the good and the evil, the just and the unjust? Well, Scripture is filled with examples of God's blessings--as well as his judgments--affecting all people.

> *But I say to you, Love your enemies and pray for those who persecute you, so that you may be sons of your Father who is in heaven. For he makes his sun rise on the evil and on the good, and sends rain on the just and on the unjust. (Matthew 5:44-45 ESV)*

God's intention in sending the bowls of wrath is not indiscriminate punishment or blind fury. Rather, like the plagues Moses called down on Egypt, these bowl plagues display his supreme power over all false gods, the antichrist in this instance, and call his people to deeper faith and resilience. These trials offer an opportunity for Christians "untested" in faith, those who have not prepared for The Great Tribulation, to grow stronger. It is a second chance, a refining fire that will reveal where faith truly lies and who has the resolve and faith to endure in the name of Jesus when times become almost unbearably difficult.

> *Many will be purified, cleansed, and refined by these trials. But the wicked will continue in their wickedness,*

*and none of them will understand. Only those who are*
*wise will know what it means.* (Daniel 12:10 NLT)

Historically, we've seen that when Christians face extreme persecution, their faith grows stronger and often attracts others to Christ. For example, during the persecution under the Roman Empire, the more Christians were thrown to the lions for refusing to recant their belief in Jesus and worship Caesar, the more others became convinced that Christians possessed something extraordinary, leading to the growth of the Christian movement. Similarly, in modern times, Christians in countries hostile to the faith, such as Iran, continue to grow in numbers despite threats of imprisonment, torture, or death. It's under pressure that faith is purified, refined, and made more resolute.

God is allowing the world, especially lukewarm or unprepared believers who ignored Jesus' warning in the Olivet Discourse, an opportunity to strengthen their commitment and deepen their dependence on him, much like the multiple chances he gave Pharaoh to turn from his ways.

These bowls of wrath are a series of nightmarish events for those who bear the mark. But for believers, the bowls are not about punishment; they are about purification.

*Those whom I love, I reprove and discipline, so be*
*zealous and repent. (*Revelation 3:19 ESV)

The bowls act as a divine crucible, revealing and refining the hearts of unprepared Christians, offering them a second chance to prepare, to get more oil for their lamps and be ready to meet the bridegroom, the Lord, when he returns in triumph.

The parable of the ten virgins is Jesus' admonition to constantly work to keep your faith (*"oil for our lamps"*) strong and prepare your armor for the Great Tribulation because if you don't, then when you need to use it in this crisis it may be too late to practice. Like the five virgins who ran out of oil, unprepared believers are those who do not take Jesus' warning in Matthew 24 seriously. If you are unprepared when that 7-sealed book is opened, there is a possibility you will fall for the sensational and convincing deceptions of the antichrist and his false prophet.

> *"Let no one deceive you in any way."*
> (2 Thessalonians 2:3a ESV)

If you fall prey to the antichrist's great deception, against which we are all warned, before you have a chance to make up for being unprepared by getting *"purified, cleansed, and refined by these trials,"* you risk hearing the five most terrifying words on Judgment Day: *"I do not know you."*[147] The time to prepare is now, before it's too late, because spiritual readiness cannot be gained overnight and we do not know when that hour will come.

> *Then the kingdom of heaven will be like ten virgins who took their lamps and went to meet the bridegroom. 2 Five of them were foolish, and five were wise. 3 For when the foolish took their lamps, they took no oil with them, 4 but the wise took flasks of oil with their lamps. 5 As the bridegroom was delayed, they all became drowsy and slept. 6 But at midnight there was a cry, 'Here is the bridegroom! Come out to meet him.' 7 Then all those virgins rose and trimmed their lamps. 8 And the foolish*

---

[147] *Many will be purified, cleansed, and refined by these trials. But the wicked will continue in their wickedness, and none of them will understand. Only those who are wise will know what it means.* (Daniel 12:10 NLT)

*said to the wise, 'Give us some of your oil, for our lamps are going out.' 9 But the wise answered, saying, 'Since there will not be enough for us and for you, go rather to the dealers and buy for yourselves.' 10 And while they were going to buy, the bridegroom came, and those who were ready went in with him to the marriage feast, and the door was shut. 11 Afterward the other virgins came also, saying, 'Lord, lord, open to us.' 12 But he answered, 'Truly, I say to you, I do not know you.' 13 Watch therefore, for you know neither the day nor the hour.* (Matthew 25:1–13 ESV)

It's important to point out that Jesus gave this parable during the Olivet Discourse, just after he told us, "See, *I have told you ahead of time.*" He told us ahead of time so that we could practice ahead of time using our full armor of God. Jesus warned us to put oil in our lamps and keep topping it off daily, not just when we think the end is near. In Luke's Olivet Discourse account, Jesus told us these events *"will overtake all who live,"* so we should pray that we *"have the strength to escape all these things,"* which means pray for the strength of faith to get through everything he warned about.

*But be on your guard so that your hearts are not weighed down with dissipation and drunkenness and the worries of this life, and that day close down upon you suddenly like a trap. 35 For it will overtake all who live on the face of the whole earth. 36 But stay alert at all times, praying that you may have strength to escape all these things that must happen, and to stand before the Son of Man.* (Luke 21:34–36 NET)

God's ultimate wrath, his retribution upon those who worship the antichrist, will come later, at the 7$^{th}$ trumpet. At the sound of that last trumpet, Jesus will personally carry out the Wrath of God and take vengeance on those who rejected his love, chose to align with evil, and took the mark. We'll cover this in chapter 26.3, *The Second Harvest.*

## 12.7 (B) Prepared Christians Prepare Their Armor

Spiritually prepared Christians will endure pain, suffering, and deprivation as well, but it will be tempered by their foreknowledge of each event that will unfold. They will draw strength from donning their spiritual armor, lifting their prayers to God, and standing firm in the assurance that the final stage of God's plan for justice is unfolding in their lifetime and that Jesus Christ will ultimately prevail.

> *Behold, I have created the smith who blows the fire of coals and produces a weapon for its purpose. I have also created the ravager to destroy; 17 no weapon that is fashioned against you shall succeed, and you shall refute every tongue that rises against you in judgment. This is the heritage of the servants of the LORD and their vindication from me, declares the LORD."* (Isaiah 54:16–17 ESV)

> *He does not fear bad news. He is confident; he trusts in the LORD. 8 His resolve is firm; he will not succumb to fear before he looks in triumph on his enemies.* (Psalm 112:7–8 NET)

What does it mean to be prepared for the Great Tribulation? Throughout the Bible, we are repeatedly urged to ready ourselves for the end-times, as they could begin at any moment. For example, the end of the Olivet Discourse, Jesus specifically tells us, *"see I have told you ahead of time."*[148] Was Jesus trying to make sure we are

---

[148] Matthew 24:25 NIV "See, I have told you ahead of time."

prepared to be whisked away?[149] Why would being taken to heaven require any kind of preparation for a Christian? Or do you think, as many prophecy authors do, that Jesus was simply warning us not to be found committing a sin during the moment of the rapture?

No. We're given so many warnings and *"told. . . ahead of time"* so that we can prepare our spiritual armor by wearing it, testing it, and sharpening our skills with it before we truly need to defend ourselves with it during the spiritual and physical battle of the Great Tribulation. The author of Chronicles told us that the Lord is ready to help strengthen those who are devoted to him.

> *Certainly the LORD watches the whole earth carefully and is ready to strengthen those who are devoted to him. You have acted foolishly in this matter; from now on you will have war."* (2 Chronicles 16:9 NET)

He has given Christians powerful armor that will work at any time but was specifically designed for this exact time. As Paul says, God provides armor so *"that you may be able to withstand in the evil day."* That *"evil day"* refers to the entire duration of the Great Tribulation.

> *Finally, be strong in the Lord and in the strength of his might. 11 Put on the whole armor of God, that you may be able to stand against the schemes of the devil. 12 For we do not wrestle against flesh and blood, but against the rulers, against the authorities, against the cosmic powers over this present darkness, against*

---

[149] The time will come when Christians will be whisked away, but that won't take any preparation at all on our part; we will be passive participants just holding on for the ride (Revelation 14:17).

*the spiritual forces of evil in the heavenly places. 13 Therefore take up the whole armor of God, that you may be able to withstand in the evil day, and having done all, to stand firm.* (Ephesians 6:10–13 ESV)

Christians who are mindful of the alignment of biblical prophecies to events happening around them should work diligently to prepare themselves for the coming trials.[150] But how do you prepare your armor? You should memorize key Scriptures, practice wearing your armor of God and become confident and proficient in the Word.

When those trials begin, immediately following the antichrist's desecration of the temple, the boldness and unshakable confidence of prepared Christians in the face of persecution will shine like a beacon of hope. Their faith and courage will inspire the bewildered and unprepared believers, drawing them in to learn, grow, and refine their faith through their guidance. In the darkest hours the prepared will rise as leaders, guiding others through the storm and reciting God's Word and prophecies as their map.

---

[150] *"You hypocrites! You know how to interpret the appearance of earth and sky, but why do you not know how to interpret the present time?"* (Luke 12:56 ESV).

## 12.7 (C) Prepared Christians, Prepare Christians

God does not want anyone to perish, so why would he abandon unprepared churchgoers or even unbelievers who have resisted taking the mark of the beast during the Great Tribulation? Far from forsaking them, God will use prepared believers who will step up as his hands and feet to train and guide those around them who are unprepared. These prepared believers will play a vital role in helping others find a deeper relationship with Christ during this time of trial and will be greatly rewarded for their faithfulness when it's over. [151]

> *For the mountains may depart and the hills be removed* [this describes the 7th bowl], *but my steadfast love shall not depart from you, and my covenant of peace shall not be removed," says the LORD, who has compassion on you. 11 "O afflicted one, storm-tossed and not comforted, behold, I will set your stones in antimony, and lay your foundations with sapphires.* (Isaiah 54:10–11 ESV)

These knowledgeable Christians, always ready with an explanation for their confidence in Christ, will be prepared to quickly step-up and teach the unprepared Christians what prophetic events will be coming up and how to protect themselves using their spiritual armor which, arrogantly, they didn't think they'd ever need.[152]

---

[151] See chapter 11.1 God Hardens the Hearts of Those Who Rejected Him

[152] "... but in your hearts honor Christ the Lord as holy, always being prepared to make a defense to anyone who asks you for a reason for the hope that is in you;

*32b But the people who are loyal to their God will act valiantly. 33 These who are wise among the people will teach the masses.* (Daniel 11:32b–33a NET)

Surprisingly, it may not be pastors or priests who are the prepared Christians ready to lead and *"instruct many"* during the Great Tribulation. Many Christian leaders, those Daniel refers to as "the wise," will be caught off guard, confused, and unprepared for what is happening.

They will misunderstand the unfolding events and fail to anticipate each prophetic event to come. As chaos surrounds them, these leaders, who many would expect to be guiding others, will instead find themselves tossed back and forth by every trumpet and bowl.

In their confused desperation, they will seek out prepared Christians, those who do understand the prophetic timeline, to quickly teach them and help them refine their faith. Through this learning under fire, some will be *"refined"* and gain the understanding of God's Word needed to endure and survive until Jesus returns at "the appointed time."

> *35 Even some of the wise will stumble, resulting in their refinement, purification, and cleansing until the time of the end, for it is still for the appointed time.* (Daniel 11:35 NET)

But for Christians who are prepared, there is danger not only from outsiders, but also danger from within the ranks of those they are trying to teach. Some surviving groups of prepared Christians will be infiltrated and betrayed (*"will unite with them deceitfully"*)

---

yet do it with gentleness and respect," (1 Peter 3:15 ESV).

by people who claim to be Christians, some of whom may even believe they are, but they have deceived themselves. The betrayal by these "Christians" causes many true Christians to be killed or imprisoned.

> *33b However, they will fall by the sword and by the flame, and they will be imprisoned and plundered for some time. 34 When they stumble, they will be granted some help. But many will unite with them deceitfully. (Daniel 11: 33b-34 NET)*

## 12.7 (D) Prepared Christians, Prepare to Reach Some Specific Unsaved People

In addition to weak believers seeking further training, there remains a specific but probably very small group of people still reachable with the Gospel. These are desperate souls who have resisted taking the mark of the beast and, importantly, have tried to help persecuted Jews and Christians. Because they have shown compassion and have not worshiped the antichrist, they still have a chance to be saved. They will be confused, questioning why neither science nor their own religion can explain what is happening in the world. But who will evangelize them if not prepared and knowledgeable Christians? They will be open to hearing from Christians who are ready with answers and have memorized key verses (since by this time, true Bibles will have been supernaturally located and destroyed) to explain the truth about what is unfolding around them and how they can accept Jesus Christ as their Savior.

> *. . . but in your hearts honor Christ the Lord as holy, always being prepared to make a defense to anyone who asks you for a reason for the hope that is in you; yet do it with gentleness and respect* (1 Peter 3:15 ESV)

Remember God's overriding concern:

> *The Lord is not slow concerning his promise, as some regard slowness, but is being patient toward you, because he does not wish for any to perish but for all to come to repentance.* (2 Peter 3:9 NET)

## 12.8 The Antichrist gets his First Allotment of Power – "Let the Volleys Begin"

We won't be able to tell for certain the exact moment when Jesus opens any of the first five seals, but we'll be able to recognize that the time for the opening of the fourth seal is drawing near when the Grand Caliph's empire has grown to include ten nations that control approximately one-quarter of the earth. Another indicator will be that Babylon, the seat of the antichrist, is flourishing and it eclipses the wealth, power, and fame of every other city in the world. We can be fairly certain his empire will include most of the territories of the kingdoms mentioned in Revelation and Daniel, countries which were once part of the Turkish/Ottoman empire encompassing the Middle East, northern Africa, and southern Europe.[153] The rest of the world will be at least indirectly affected by the ongoing wars, food shortages, plagues, and millions of beheadings in all his economically aligned nations.

With the first 6 trumpets, God allows Satan, through the antichrist, to have more power than he's ever previously been allowed. However, thankfully, he's limited to $1/3^{rds}$ in most of his powers. Although this war is fought with human adversaries, specifically the antichrist and his false prophet versus the two witnesses, it's really a battle between Satan and God. The antichrist will be hungry for each successive trumpet's power, but as each

---

[153] "The Turkish/Ottoman empire succeeded the Roman empire and ruled over the entire Middle East, including Jerusalem, for nearly five hundred years" (Joel Richardson, *The Islamic Antichrist*, 96). "The Turkish empire existed right up until 1909" (*The Islamic Antichrist*, 12). "Thus we see that the only empire that fulfills the patterns necessary to be considered the seventh empire is the Turkish/Ottoman empire. This of course corresponds perfectly with Ezekiel's list of nations with such a heavy emphasis on Turkey" (*The Islamic Antichrist*, 98).

trumpet is sounded, the two witnesses will counter with a plague that will curb its full effect and foil Satan's plans. Make no mistake, the effects of the trumpets will be terrible, but thanks to the countering plagues called down by the two witnesses, they will not have the devastating effect Satan desires.

The two witnesses won't let the antichrist get away with the lie that the power of the trumpets comes from the antichrist. And they will counter the antichrist at every turn with their *". . . power. . . to smite the earth with all plagues as often as they will"* (Revelation 11:6b KJV). This means that each trumpet the antichrist exploits will be countered by the witnesses smiting the earth with a much more powerful plague.[154]

But just as Satan is tightly restricted when he deals with Job, so too will the antichrist be tightly constrained with each of the trumpets because God is still maintaining order and preventing chaos. For Satan's plan to be successful, the antichrist now needs to deceive mankind into thinking that he really is the Mahdi and that he has supernatural powers to use against his enemies. His enemies are those who have resisted receiving his mark.

In accordance with the 7-sealed book, the antichrist is about to receive his first allowance of power from God. He'll use that 1st trumpet's power to make *"war against the saints."*

---

[154] Revelation 15:6 introduces *"seven angels with the seven plagues",* and then the next verse tells us that the plagues or wrath are contained within seven bowls which those same angels are holding. Therefore, authors use the terms *bowl, plague,* and sometimes *wrath* interchangeably.

# 13 Trumpet Attack #1 (1/3 of the Earth and Trees & All Green Grass Burn)

*The first angel blew his trumpet, and there followed hail and fire mixed with blood, and these were thrown upon the earth. And a third of the earth was burned up, and a third of the trees were burned up, and all green grass was burned up. (Revelation 8:7 ESV)*

When this first trumpet sounds, the antichrist will be given the power and the means to burn the earth, trees, and grass. He'll be allowed to burn all the green grass he wants, but he's strictly limited to burning no more than 1/3rd of the earth and trees. Burning the earth is vague. Dirt doesn't burn, but earth is a general term for what's on the earth, such as houses and farms. If there is a positive side to this 1st trumpet; it's that 2/3rds of the earth and trees as well as the millions of acres of dead grass plains are protected from Satan's pyromaniacal rampage.

This fire sounds just like the fire God allowed Satan to call down onto Job's sheep and shepherds:

*While he was yet speaking, there came also another, and said, The fire of God is fallen from heaven, and hath burned up the sheep, and the servants, and consumed them; and I only am escaped alone to tell thee. (Job 1:16 KJV)*

These fires of the 1st trumpet don't sound as devastating as the later trumpets, but their repercussions will be terrible. Joel tells us in this dual prophecy that all the green grass is burned up and there is nowhere for livestock to graze for a month or more until it regrows.

> *How the beasts groan! The herds of cattle are perplexed because there is no pasture for them; even the flocks of sheep suffer. 19 To you, O LORD, I call. For fire has devoured the pastures of the wilderness, and flame has burned all the trees of the field. 20 Even the beasts of the field pant for you because the water brooks are dried up, and fire has devoured the pastures of the wilderness.* (Joel 1:18–20 ESV)

It's unclear whether these fires will affect 1/3rd of the entire earth indiscriminately or if the antichrist will specifically target enemy territories that collectively cover 1/3rd of the planet. Either way, these fires will be more widespread than anything we've ever seen before.

Fire and smoke will envelop the earth, making it difficult to see or breathe, even in areas far from the burning forests. Hospitals will overflow with respiratory emergencies and burn victims. There will be highway pileups caused by the poor visibility conditions, and collateral problems like widespread blackouts caused by burned power lines. Fire departments won't be able to control such massive fires, so they will attempt to protect only critical infrastructure. Depending on the ground conditions before the fires start, it could be months before they burn themselves out. The dense worldwide smoke would block the sun and lead to drops in temperature and crop failures.

We don't know how long these fires will last, but in response to the 1st trumpet the two witnesses call down their 1st plague. And it's directed where it will affect the antichrist the most: on those who have the mark.

# 13.1 Bowl Countermeasure #1 (The Marked get Forever Sores: Agonizing & Oozing)

> *So the first angel went and poured out his bowl on the earth, and harmful and painful sores came upon the people who bore the mark of the beast and worshiped its image.* (Revelation 16:2 ESV)[155]

These sores are described as similar to the sores Moses inflicted on the Egyptians and their livestock in the 6th plague:

> *So they took soot from the kiln and stood before Pharaoh. And Moses threw it in the air, and it became boils breaking out in sores on man and beast.* (Exodus 9:10 ESV)

But they are probably more like one of the curses God promises in Deuteronomy on those who are disobedient to his commandments and statutes.

> *The LORD will strike you on the knees and on the legs with grievous boils of which you cannot be healed, from the sole of your foot to the crown of your head.* (Deuteronomy 28:35 ESV)

---

[155] It seems like the phrase "*and worshipped its image*" is meaningful. I suspect there may be some people in prison, in slavery, or even in chattel marriage situations who may be forced to take the mark against their will. The Holy Spirit will know if it was a choice or if it was forced upon them. I think this verse demonstrates that, as long as they don't worship the beast, there may be protection for them. There's no way to know that for sure, but we know our God.

The sores of bowl 1 are described as being even worse than boils. They're malignant, festering, oozing sores that, like the Deuteronomy curse, won't ever heal. The pain and oozing of these sores will never go away. We'll see evidence of them never healing during the 5th bowl, when people with the mark are sitting in total darkness, gnashing their teeth in pain because they are still suffering from the oozing sores of this first bowl.

The witnesses will not do this in secret. They will publicly proclaim that they are calling down this plague, so there will be no doubt the sores come from God in response to the antichrist's 1st trumpet. This is part of their "*testimony*." I've read numerous authors who think cable news will cover the witnesses and broadcast everything they do and say. While it's possible that could happen, I doubt the antichrist will allow it. He'll be in control of the media, and besides, the members of the media will have taken the mark, or they would not still be working. As minions of the antichrist, the media will be doing everything they can to block information regarding the actions of the witnesses.

Now that the media will be suffering from these oozing, painful sores that cover every part of their bodies, there will be a window of opportunity for underground amateur reporters to broadcast or post on the dark web that it was the two witnesses who called on God to send the plague of sores.[156] God may even empower the witnesses to supernaturally interrupt programming, but one way or another the world will understand that God's two witnesses

---

[156] The Dark Web is "The set of web pages on the world wide web that cannot be indexed by search engines, are not viewable in a standard Web browser, require specific means (such as specialized software or network configuration) in order to access, and use encryption to provide anonymity and privacy for users." (Merriam-Webster, s.v. "dark web" https://www.merriam-webster.com/dictionary/dark%20web).

have called down this curse of agonizing sores only on those who bear the mark of the beast.

We don't know how soon after each trumpet sounds that the two witnesses respond with their countermeasure bowl. There may be a pause between them, or the countermeasure may be released almost immediately after each trumpet is sounded. But when an angel sounds the 2nd trumpet, the antichrist will turn 1/3rd of the sea into blood, 1/3rd of the sea life will die, and 1/3rd of the ships at sea will be destroyed.

# 14 Trumpet Attack #2 (1/3rd of Sea as Blood, 1/3rd of Sea Life Dies, 1/3rd of Ships Sink)

> *The second angel blew his trumpet, and something like a great mountain, burning with fire, was thrown into the sea, and a third of the sea became blood. 9 A third of the living creatures in the sea died, and a third of the ships were destroyed.* (Revelation 8:8–9 ESV)

*"Something like a great mountain"* could mean that a great volcano erupts in catastrophic fashion, blowing its peak into the water. It hits the sea with such violence or speed that the resulting tsunami waves destroy 1/3rd of the ships. It turns the sea into blood, or at least something that seems like blood to John. True to form, the damage this trumpet can inflict is limited to 1/3rd. Specifically, 1/3rd of the sea is affected, 1/3rd of the sea creatures die, and 1/3rd of the ships are destroyed. God allows only that much and no more. If the antichrist is able to aim and control the powers of this trumpet, he will target only his enemies' coastlands and his enemies' ships, and his targeting will probably be precise. Satan was able to pinpoint his powers specifically to Job's property, so there's a good chance that the antichrist will be allowed to aim the trumpet powers with similar precision.

In response to the 2nd trumpet's effect on 1/3rd of the sea, the two witnesses call down the second plague that will spread the effect to the entire sea and all the sea life.

## 14.1 Bowl Countermeasure #2 (Whole Sea Like Blood, All Sea Life Dies)

> *The second angel poured out his bowl into the sea, and it became like the blood of a corpse, and every living thing died that was in the sea.* (Revelation 16:3 ESV)

The two witnesses will make it abundantly clear to the world that they are the ones calling down the power of God to counter the trumpet powers which the antichrist wields. Satan was restrained from affecting any more than 1/3rd of the sea, but the witnesses will demonstrate that God's power has no limit; it covers the entire sea.

*"Like the blood of a corpse"* is a very precise description. It indicates that the sea dies along with everything in it. It could mean the water is turned into thick blood or something that looks like congealed, thick, and sticky blood. After all, God congealed the sea once before when he parted the Red Sea:

> *At the blast of your nostrils the waters piled up; the floods stood up in a heap; the deeps congealed in the heart of the sea.* (Exodus 15:8 ESV)

Or it may mean the blood-like water will be altered in such a way that it can no longer carry dissolved oxygen the way healthy water does. Either of those possibilities would be deadly to all sea life. Interestingly, unlike at the 2nd trumpet, there is no mention of how it affects ships, so it is most likely not thick. Thick fluid would cause a ship to float higher out of the water and probably topple, not to mention the crushing force waves would have if the fluid was thick. This leads me to believe the water is dark and dead (unable to carry oxygen), rather than congealed.

We don't know how long this will last, but eventually, the 3rd trumpet will sound, giving the antichrist access to another power: poison.

# 15 Trumpet Attack #3 (1/3rd of Fresh Water Turns to Undrinkable Poison)

> *Then the third angel blew his trumpet, and a huge star burning like a torch fell from the sky; it landed on a third of the rivers and on the springs of water. 11 (Now the name of the star is Wormwood.) So a third of the waters became wormwood, and many people died from these waters because they were poisoned.* (Revelation 8:10–11 NET)

This trumpet harms 1/3rd of the freshwater sources. A falling star is a term for a meteor streaking across the sky. For example, when you see a falling star and make a wish, it's actually a meteor blazing as it descends through the earth's protective atmosphere. Again, as in almost all trumpets, God limits the antichrist's power to one-third: 1/3rd of the rivers and 1/3rd of the springs. But even 1/3rd of the fresh water sources would be a widespread event. It sounds as though a very large meteor breaks-up in the upper atmosphere and its pieces scatter across the globe as it falls.

We're only told of its effect on fresh water, but a meteor large enough to distribute its particles across 1/3rd of the earth would be so massive that it would cause a lot of other damage in addition to poisoning the water. Since we are not told about any collateral damage, it could be a meteor made mostly of ice, melting as it enters the atmosphere and scattering poison that falls like deadly raindrops onto surface water and springs. Or it could be a massive meteor shower with millions of small, poisonous fragments that are not large enough to do notable physical damage. The odds are high that some of the rock or ice particles would also hit the oceans, but since people don't drink unprocessed ocean water, it is not mentioned.

The phrase "*. . . many people died from these waters. . .*" suggests that if the deaths were in the millions, it would be worthy of a specific percent or number as is done in other trumpets and bowls. While we're not provided a number or percent, given all the deaths that have occurred in a short time, "*many*" probably indicates a number in the hundreds of thousands.

Sometime after this, the two witnesses publicly call down a plague of blood on all the freshwater sources which renders them drinkable again, if they can just get past this horrible reminder of their guilt.

## 15.1 Bowl Countermeasure #3 (All Fresh Water Made Drinkable Again, But as Blood)

*The third angel poured out his bowl into the rivers and the springs of water, and they became blood. 5 And I heard the angel in charge of the waters say, "Just are you, O Holy One, who is and who was, for you brought these judgments. 6 For they have shed the blood of saints and prophets, and you have given them blood to drink. It is what they deserve!" 7 And I heard the altar saying, "Yes, Lord God the Almighty, true and just are your judgments!"* (Revelation 16:4–7 ESV)

Consider this: The 3rd trumpet poisons one-third of the freshwater, killing those who drink it. But when the two witnesses call down the 3rd bowl, which turns all (not just 1/3$^{rd}$) rivers and springs into blood, they effectively counteract the Wormwood toxin, preventing mass death from poisoning or dehydration.

We know this because it is only after the two witnesses unleash this bowl that we are told people can safely drink again, they are *"given...blood to drink,"* and there is no mention of anyone dying from it.

Though the water now quenches thirst, it comes at a price: psychological torment. The water, thick and dark like blood, offers no comfort. Instead, with every nauseating swallow, the people are haunted by the horrors they tried to forget: the screams, the terror, and the rivers of blood from the beheadings at the processing centers.

Every gag-inducing gulp chokes them with guilt, a bitter reminder of their own role in the roundup and extermination of many of God's people: *"It is what they deserve"—"for they have shed the blood of saints and prophets."*

The mental agony people are experiencing is no accident. It was foretold that the two witnesses would have the power to turn water into blood, and now they are using that power with devastating effect. Through the 2nd and 3rd bowls, they have turned all the world's life-giving waters into rivers of guilt.

> *They* [the two witnesses] *have the power to shut the sky, that no rain may fall during the days of their prophesying, and they have power over the waters to turn them into blood and to strike the earth with every kind of plague, as often as they desire.* (Revelation 11:6 ESV)

The antichrist's false prophet will begin to tighten the screws on the world economy as he distributes the ever-scarcer resources. He and his followers behead non-compliers who don't voluntarily line up to get their hi-tech fealty tattoo (the mark of the beast). But just as Stephen was given elegant words to preach as he was about to be martyred, the Holy Spirit will give these Great Tribulation martyrs the words to proclaim to their judges and executioners in their final moments.

> *And when they bring you before the synagogues and the rulers and the authorities, do not be anxious about how you should defend yourself or what you should say, 12 for the Holy Spirit will teach you in that very hour what you ought to say.* (Luke 12:11–12 ESV)

In the next chapter, when the 5th seal is opened, we will glimpse some of their victims in heaven, the souls of those who had been beheaded for refusing the mark, crying out to Jesus for justice.

# 16 Seal 5: Our First Time Eavesdropping on People in Heaven: How the Contest is Scored

You now understand that Revelation is not written in a way that shows the chronological order that things will happen; it's not meant to present a step-by-step timeline of events. However, John incorporates a special key that he knew would, at the proper time, be used to do just that. Throughout most of Revelation, John is given behind-the-scenes access to heaven, where he shares what he hears and sees. Five of these scenes focus on people in heaven and their actions or words. Because John presents these scenes in the order in which they happen, they provide a window into what is happening on earth at the time of their arrival in heaven. These heavenly conversations, therefore, become a key to decoding the sequence of events.

The first view we're granted of people in heaven is when Jesus breaks this 5th seal. No action occurs in this seal. Its sole purpose is to lift the veil off heaven and provide us a glimpse of the souls who have recently arrived there from earth. John tells us why these souls are there and that more time remains in the 3½ year countdown.

> 9 When he opened the fifth seal, I saw under the altar the souls of those who had been slain for the word of God and for the witness they had borne. 10 They cried out with a loud voice, "O Sovereign Lord, holy and true, how long before you will judge and avenge our blood on those who dwell on the earth?" 11 Then they were each given a white robe and told

*to rest a little longer, until the number of their fellow servants and their brothers should be complete, who were to be killed as they themselves had been.* (Revelation 6:9–11 ESV)

In those three verses, we learn seven amazing and terrifying things about events that are occurring on earth and we learn why God doesn't immediately avenge their deaths.

1.  John sees *"souls,"* not humanlike bodies. This is significant, and we'll talk about that in the First Harvest chapter.
2.  At this specific point in time, people on earth are facing an unimaginably brutal test of their faith. The processing centers are designed to convincingly compel each person to recant their faith, deny Christ, and accept the antichrist as their savior. If they won't give in and take the mark, they are executed for maintaining their belief in Jesus. This means that the antichrist has moved from the voluntary phase to the mandatory phase of his mark (Revelation 13:16). We won't find out until 14 chapters later (Revelation 20:4) that the method of execution for these Christian Refuseniks is decapitation (*"beheaded"*).

*Then I saw thrones, and seated on them were those to whom the authority to judge was committed. Also I saw the souls of those who had been beheaded for the testimony of Jesus and for the word of God, and those who had not worshiped the beast or its image and had not received its mark on their foreheads or their hands. They came to life and reigned with Christ for a thousand years.* (Revelation 20:4 ESV)

We saw in the chapter on the 4th seal that the rider on the deathly horse and his companion were given the authority *"to kill with a sword."* The antichrist and his false prophet have been using that authority to decapitate Christians and others who refuse the mark.

3.  The antichrist's pressure campaign to force people to accept the mark or face execution begins only after he reveals his true identity, which doesn't happen until the abomination of desolation. This means the fifth seal must be opened sometime after this temple desecration occurs. The perfect fit of the fifth seal here in this timeline—immediately following the opening of the first four seals and the countering of the first three trumpets by the first three bowls—shows that this theory, which I call the *trumpet-attack/bowl-countermeasure theory*, provides the most plausible timeline.

4.  The phrase *". . . and told to rest a little longer. . ."* means that the beheadings are not over, they will continue for a little more time. But the chilling line, *"until the number of their fellow servants and their brothers should be complete"* unveils something even more shocking: there is a set, predetermined number of martyred souls that must be reached. This is a bombshell revelation and its significance cannot be overstated. John has just revealed how this contest will be scored. Victory isn't measured by the number of battles won or cities conquered, but by how many Christians choose to remain faithful to Christ and be martyred rather than save themselves by accepting the mark of the antichrist.[157] This war for souls

---

[157] This parallels Satan's challenge to God that Job would reject him if he lost everything dear to him. God stood by Job and told Satan to go ahead and test him. Had God not called Satan on his accusation against Job, no one in *"heaven or on earth or under the earth"* would have known for sure if God's judgment of Job as an *"upright"* man of God was correct (Job 1:6-22).
Just as Satan was given permission and power by God to put Job through terrible

will continue *"until the number...should be complete."* We'll delve into this more when the full number of martyrs is reached just before the 6th seal.

5. Jesus will eventually avenge their deaths, but since he wants the Scripture to be fulfilled, he is powerless to do that until the predetermined number of martyrs is reached.[158] This is a self-imposed limitation, much like the one Jesus accepted when he allowed himself to be falsely accused by the Pharisees and then abused, tortured, and crucified by the Romans. When Peter clumsily tries to defend Jesus, Jesus tells him to restrain himself because there is a much bigger purpose at work.

> *Then Jesus said to him, "Put your sword back into its place. For all who take the sword will perish by the sword. 53 Do you think that I cannot appeal to my Father, and he will at once send me more than twelve legions of angels? 54 But how then should the scriptures be fulfilled, that it must be so?"* (Matthew 26:52–54 ESV)

---

ordeals, Satan will be given permission and power by God to put Christians through terrible ordeals during the Great Tribulation. During the Great Tribulation, God is counting on a specific number of Christians to stand firm in their faith, *"even unto death"*—so that all *"in heaven or on earth or under the earth"* will witness that God was right to love them and, through his Son, make a way for them to be with him in heaven. Just as God was not proven wrong about Job, we know God won't be proven wrong about the number of Christians he declared would die for him.

[158] Jesus is not powerless in that he is not capable of doing anything about it. He's powerless in the sense that if he's going to fulfill Scripture and win this contest, he must adhere to the rules of engagement detailed in the 7-sealed-book. Which means that he must wait until the full number of martyrs is attained before he can use his power

6. They are *"given"* a white robe.[159] Keep this in mind when we get our next view of humans in heaven, where we'll see that the victims of the 4th bowl will not be given white robes when they get to heaven. Instead, we're told that the victims of the 4th bowl must wash their own robes in the blood of the lamb to make them white.

7. This 5th seal is the most obvious indication that rules of engagement (the 7-sealed book) are being followed and Jesus is adhering to it to the letter, in spite of how much it must hurt him to watch this play out. But he's immensely proud of these victors who have passed the ultimate test of their faith and he has a truly special reward in store for them. We'll learn more about this when we next see these martyrs in Revelation 20:4–7, just as the Millennium begins.

Soon after the 5th Seal is broken, the 4th trumpet sounds, which releases another power to Satan.

---

[159] Revelation 6:11 ESV: "Then they were each given a white robe and told to rest a little longer, until the number of their fellow servants and their brothers should be complete, who were to be killed as they themselves had been."

# 17 Trumpet Attack #4 (1/3rd of Sun, Moon, and Stars Go Dark)

*The fourth angel blew his trumpet, and a third of the sun was struck, and a third of the moon, and a third of the stars, so that a third of their light might be darkened, and a third of the day might be kept from shining, and likewise a third of the night.* (Revelation 8:12 ESV)

Once again, the antichrist's power is limited to 1/3$^{rds}$. The light emitted or reflected from the sun, moon and stars is in some way blocked or prevented for 1/3$^{rd}$ of the day. It's likely that a third of the surface of the sun browns-out or develops a gigantic sunspot. Since the moon is simply a reflector of the sun's light, it then reflects 1/3$^{rd}$ less light.

If you assume the typical 12 hours of daylight and 12 hours of night, then this trumpet will shorten the day to 8 hours of daylight and 16 hours of night at the equator. Closer to the earth's poles, however, there would be a much bigger shift towards extended darkness. While this doesn't sound terrible, the cold weather and limited sunlight will interfere with the growing cycle of crops. Temperatures will drop everywhere, but the change will be more drastic the closer one is to the poles of the earth. In addition to shortened growing seasons, darkness has deleterious psychological impacts and can lead to Seasonal Affective Disorder, which disrupts sleep cycles and mood.

It's unclear what Satan hopes to achieve by causing a miniature ice age with this 4th trumpet. Perhaps he's trying to create an ideal climate for the demonic hordes he plans to unleash during the 5th and 6th trumpets. Or perhaps the colder, darker environment helps ease the pain of his marked followers who have been suffering from festering, oozing sores since the first bowl, which would make them more productive for his purposes.

Whatever the antichrist's reason, the two witnesses will soon call down a plague that reverses the cold and darkness, but drastically intensifies the sun's heat and brightness to dangerous, deadly levels.

## 17.1 Bowl Countermeasure #4 (Sun Scorches People with Fire)

> *The fourth angel poured out his bowl on the sun, and it was allowed to scorch people with fire. 10 They were scorched by the fierce heat, and they cursed the name of God who had power over these plagues. They did not repent and give him glory.* (Revelation 16:8–9 ESV)

The sun scorching people with actual fire is much worse than overactive solar flares. It sounds like the sun will eject chunks of its coronal mass, like in The Carrington Event of 1859, which caused sparks in telegraph equipment and endangered some of its operators.[160] But the effects of the 4th bowl will be much, much worse than the 4th trumpet. It will scorch and kill so many people that Isaiah tells us only a *"few men"* will survive.

> *The earth lies defiled under its inhabitants; for they have transgressed the laws, violated the statutes, broken the everlasting covenant. 6 Therefore a curse devours the earth, and its inhabitants suffer for their guilt; therefore the inhabitants of the earth are scorched, and few men are left.* (Isaiah 24:5–6 ESV)

---

[160] Christopher Klein, "A Perfect Solar Superstorm: The 1859 Carrington Event," *History*, August 4, 2023, https://www.history.com/news/a-perfect-solar-superstorm-the-1859-carrington-event. During this event, in some locations, night turned into day, and the northern lights could be observed as far south as Cuba. The solar storm was reported worldwide and caused extensive damage to the new technology of the day, the telegraph system.

In his prophecy about gathering the survivors after the Great Tribulation, Isaiah promises they will never again face the *"scorching wind or sun."* This confirms that they endured and survived the 4th bowl's effects and will never have to face it again.

> . . . *they shall not hunger or thirst, neither scorching wind nor sun shall strike them, for he who has pity on them will lead them, and by springs of water will guide them.* (Isaiah 49:10 ESV)

The big question is: Will the 4th bowl affect Christians? Surprisingly, an often-overlooked but revealing end-time passage from Malachi gives us the answer: Yes, it will.

In this passage, *"evildoers"* clearly refers to non-Christians. However, Malachi also identifies a second group, the *"arrogant,"* and sets them apart from the evildoers. This distinction is a key to their identity.

> 1 *"For behold, the day is coming, burning like an oven, when all the arrogant and all evildoers will be stubble. The day that is coming shall set them ablaze, says the LORD of hosts, so that it will leave them neither root nor branch.* (Malachi 4:1 ESV)

Malachi's distinction between the *"arrogant"* and the *"evildoers"* is purposeful and highly significant. The *"arrogant"* are not labeled as evil, but, as we'll see in Malachi's next verse, they are also not counted among those who obey God (*"fear my name"*). Astonishingly, by comparing this passage with Revelation 7:16, we discover something surprising: the *"arrogant"* are Christians! They are called "arrogant" because they arrogantly thought they didn't need to be spiritually prepared for the end times.

Based on the manner of their deaths, it appears the "*arrogant*" selectively studied only the parts of God's Word they deemed directly relevant to them, disregarding passages concerning the trials of the Great Tribulation. Since they didn't study the end-times or practice using the full armor of God, the "*arrogant*" were no more prepared than the "*evildoers*" and were, therefore, burned up along with them. Yet, as we'll see in the next chapter, John assures us that these "*arrogant*" Christians will still, thankfully, arrive in heaven, though by the narrowest margin.

The third group Malachi addresses, "*you who fear my name,*" or as the Good News Translation puts it, "*you who obey me,*" refers to Christians who have studied the full message of God's Word and are spiritually prepared. These believers take all of God's warnings seriously, including those about the end-times. Malachi tells us that not only will this group survive when everyone else is scorched to death by the 4th bowl, but they will also thrive, "*leaping like calves...*"

> *2 But for you who fear my name, the sun of righteousness shall rise with healing in its wings. You shall go out leaping like calves from the stall. 3 And you shall tread down the wicked, for they will be ashes under the soles of your feet, on the day when I act, says the LORD of hosts.* (Malachi 4:2–3 ESV)

If you are a Christian, I pray that you will be counted among the third group, "*you who fear my name,*" and not among "*the arrogant*" Christians who are shown in the next chapter arriving in heaven pitiful and scorched.

# 18 Second Time Eavesdropping on Heaven: Millions of Scorched Arrive in Heaven

Our second chance to eavesdrop on a conversation in heaven fits precisely here in the timeline, offering further evidence that the *trumpet-attack/bowl-countermeasure theory* remains on track. A huge group of Christians from every nation on earth has just arrived in heaven, but these new arrivals are not martyrs like we saw when the 5th seal was opened. They have lived through the first part of the great tribulation but were not beheaded. They were killed by something we'll learn about a few verses later.

> *9 After this I looked, and behold, a great multitude that no one could number, from every nation, from all tribes and peoples and languages, standing before the throne and before the Lamb, clothed in white robes, with palm branches in their hands, 10 and crying out with a loud voice, "Salvation belongs to our God who sits on the throne, and to the Lamb!" 11 And all the angels were standing around the throne and around the elders and the four living creatures, and they fell on their faces before the throne and worshiped God, 12 saying, "Amen! Blessing and glory and wisdom and thanksgiving and honor and power and might be to our God forever and ever! Amen." (Revelation 7:9-12 ESV)*

This passage is a key pillar of the pre-tribulation belief. Many supporters interpret these first three verses as evidence that masses of people were whisked up to heaven before the tribulation and are now standing before God's throne. However, if they had only read a few verses further, where the elder explains who these people are and how they had just been killed, they would see that these individuals died during the depths of the great tribulation, not before it.

> *13 Then one of the elders addressed me, saying, "Who are these, clothed in white robes, and from where have they come?" 14 I said to him, "Sir, you know." And he said to me, "These are the ones coming out of the great tribulation. They have washed their robes and made them white in the blood of the Lamb. 15 "Therefore they are before the throne of God, and serve him day and night in his temple; and he who sits on the throne will shelter them with his presence." (Revelation 7:13-15 ESV)*

One of the elders in heaven tells John that these poor souls no longer have to fear what killed them, which was the sun striking them and scorching them with intense heat. They were not rescued from the fire like those *"who fear my name"*; they perished in it.

> *16 They shall hunger no more, neither thirst anymore; the sun shall not strike them, nor any scorching heat. 17 For the Lamb in the midst of the throne will be their shepherd, and he will guide them to springs of living water, and God will wipe away every tear from their eyes."* (Revelation 7:16–17 ESV)

This second view into heaven serves as a signpost, telling us exactly where we are in the Great Tribulation timeline: which is immediately after the 4th has been poured out. Here are 10 things we learn in this second conversation in heaven:

1.  This group of people who have recently arrived in heaven is so large that no one could count them, which probably means hundreds of millions.[161]

2.  They have some type of body because they are *"in white robes,"* unlike the souls of the martyrs we saw under the altar of the 5th seal who couldn't wear their robes yet. This is significant and we'll talk about it in due course.

3.  They are from every nation and race, indicating that the overactive sun is affecting the entire world. Incidentally, this also confirms that there will be people from every nation and race in heaven!

4.  They have palm branches in their hands and cry out, *"Salvation belongs to our God..."*

5.  The phrase, *"These are the ones coming out of the great tribulation,"* confirms that this 4th bowl occurs in the midst of the last 3½ years.

6.  Tellingly, this group is not handed robes that are already white, as we saw being done for the martyrs who arrive in heaven before the opening of the 5th seal. Instead, verse 14 tells us that these new arrivals must wash their own robes in the blood of the Lamb before they become white. This distinction is significant. It means that they are saved, but only just barely. They are not saved due to their great faith and are not handed a white robe as the 5th seal martyrs had been. This may also be

---

[161] This verse, depicting millions of souls arriving in heaven, is often cited by many who support a pre-tribulation rapture or pre-wrath rapture of saints. However, both camps skip over vitally important parts of the passage: that these people had been scorched by the sun and died, and that they had to wash their own robes. This is yet another example of what happens when people view every verse through the lens of a preconceived doctrine—as I did for decades—they try to make everything fit within that doctrine.

the reason why they will now be attendants of God, serving in his temple day and night.

7. An unmistakable verification that this view of people in heaven has to occur after the 4th bowl is that these newly arrived Christians have hungered, thirsted, been struck by the sun, and been scorched by the heat of the sun. John intends for us to make the connection that these Christians were killed by the sun in the 4th bowl and ensures that these events would one day be viewed together, as they are here because these are the only two places in the Bible that use the Greek *Kauma* (scorching heat).[162] John intentionally uses that specific word as a 'signet ring' so that someone would one day make the connection between both events. However, he didn't make the connection easy to recognize. It isn't something one would discover just by reading Revelation like a book, because the two events are described nine chapters apart.[163] We're left with the understanding that although it is the sun's intense heat and flames of fire from the 4th bowl that ultimately kills these people, they have also lived through the 3rd trumpet and 3rd seal. We know this because they endured severe hunger and thirst. Hunger began with the 3rd Seal's black horse rider rationing barley and wheat, and thirst likely resulted from the droughts caused by the two witnesses combined with the contamination of the fresh bodies of water

---

[162] "Kauma," which in usage means "burning heat," is only used in Revelation 7:16 (the second view into heaven) and Revelation 16:9 (the 4th bowl). (Bible Hub, "2738. kauma," *Strong's Concordance*, biblehub.com, https://biblehub.com/greek/2738.htm).

[163] In the same way that Zerubbabel was the Lord's signet ring that would tie Mary's line to Joseph's line (as predicted by Haggai 2:23), Zerubbabel was the single ancestor in common to Joseph's line and Mary's line (Matthew 1:12–13 & Luke 3:27). (Jon Gleason, "Zerubbabel and the Genealogies of Christ," *Mind Renewers*, December 31, 2013, https://mindrenewers.com/2013/12/31/zerubbabel-and-the-genealogies-of-christ/).

and springs in the 3$^{rd}$ trumpet. Those details provided in this conversation in heaven help confirm that the first four trumpets and the first four bowls have occurred before this point, which means the trumpet-attack/bowl-countermeasure theory is tracking properly.

8. These new arrivals are allowed to drink from the springs of living water, which means they will have eternal life.

9. God wipes every tear from their eyes, which means they will experience no more sadness, heartache, or pain.

I've re-read this section many times and each time I get emotional. I sigh deeply, and sometimes I cry. My heart grieves for the unnecessary suffering of those hundreds of millions of Christians who, we are told, will be killed by the scorching sun. They had no idea they would go through the Great Tribulation, and as a result, they were just as unprepared as the unbelievers. They didn't see the need to study the end-time prophecies, likely believing, just as I once did, that they would be taken to heaven before it all began, so those thousands of prophetic verses didn't apply to them. Yes, thank God they knew the cardinal basics: they didn't give in to the pressure to accept the mark and kept their faith in Jesus, so they did make it to heaven, but only by the skin of their teeth.

In this next verse, it appears that Paul had this event of the 4$^{th}$ bowl in mind when he warned Christians that their faith must be built on a complete foundation of all the Scripture, not just a portion of it. If not, they may make it to heaven, but it would be without any reward, as though they escaped *"through fire"* with nothing else to their name.

> *But if any person's work is burned up [by the test],*
> *he will suffer the loss [of his reward]; yet he himself*

*will be saved, but only as [one who has barely escaped] through fire.* (1 Corinthians 3:15 Amplified Bible)

These saints, the "arrogant" of Malachi 4:1, confident that they would be whisked away before the bad stuff began, neglected to study the end-time prophecies that could have prepared them. They never fully learned how to use the spiritual armor that God makes available to all believers for this exact time. Like the five foolish virgins who ran out of oil when they needed it most, they found themselves completely unprepared as the Great Tribulation began. Tossed and turned as they reacted to the effects of each devastating trumpet and bowl, they suffered terribly, enduring severe thirst, hunger, and ultimately being scorched to death by the sun. Much of their suffering could have at least been reduced had they heeded Jesus' admonition in the Olivet Discourse, "*See, I have told you ahead of time.*" [164]

These unprepared Christians were welcomed into heaven and consoled as victims of the effects of the 4th bowl, not hailed as victors. They will serve the Lord, and I comfort myself with this Psalm:

> *For a day in your courts is better than a thousand elsewhere. I would rather be a doorkeeper in the house of my God than dwell in the tents of wickedness.* (Psalm 84:10 ESV)

At about this time, an eagle flies over the earth, making an ominous announcement.

---

[164] Matthew 24:25

# 18.1 Woe! The Worst is Yet to Come!

> *Then I looked, and I heard an eagle crying with a loud voice as it flew directly overhead, "Woe, woe, woe to those who dwell on the earth, at the blasts of the other trumpets that the three angels are about to blow!"* (Revelation 8:13 ESV)

Up to this point, circumnavigating angels have been making global announcements to the inhabitants of the earth. While there is a reason that the messenger is an eagle this time, there's no consensus on that reason. I tend to agree with the commentators who believe that, since the 4th beast in heaven is an eagle, and that 4th beast is the one that made the announcement when the 4th seal was opened, then this flying eagle may be that 4th beast.[165]

This eagle announces "woe, woe, woe," one woe for the 5th trumpet, one for the 6th, and one for the 7th, indicating the mental and physical torment of the upcoming trumpets will be much worse than what occurred during the first four trumpets. Up to this point, the trumpets have ushered in disasters, but the next two trumpets will unleash evil spirits. I use the word announces rather than warns because there's not much an unsaved person can do about what's coming, and the hearts of most have been hardened so that they believe the lies of the antichrist and his false Jesus. The surviving Christians, however, should once again put on their spiritual armor

---

[165] ". . . 'an eagle': the symbol of judgment descending fatally from on high; the king of birds pouncing on the prey. Compare this 4th trumpet and the flying eagle with the 4th seal introduced by the fourth living creature, 'like a flying eagle,' Revelation 4:7, 6:7, 6:8. . ." (Bible Hub, "Revelation 8:13," Jamieson-Fausset-Brown Bible Commentary, biblehub.com, https://biblehub.com/commentaries/jfb/revelation/8.htm)

when they hear this announcement because Scripture tells us that their armor will be effective protection against *"the evil day,"* which includes what the antichrist is about to unleash once the 5th trumpet sounds.[166]

At the time specified in the 7-sealed book, after the 4th bowl is poured out and the eagle announces its warning to the world, Satan will approach heaven's gate. This will be his first time returning to heaven's entrance since he was banished for leading a rebellion of the angels back in Chapter 10.3. But this time, he is denied entry.

Forced to remain outside in the darkness, he can only peer through the gate, catching a glimpse of everything he lost. Yet, he must wait humbly for something he needs and was promised, a key, which must be handed to him before the 5th trumpet sounds.

Once he receives the key to the bottomless pit, his humiliation deepens as he is physically thrown back down to earth, likely by the archangel Michael.

---

[166] Ephesians 6:13 ESV: "*Therefore take up the whole armor of God, that you may be able to withstand in the evil day, and having done all, to stand firm.*"

# 19 Trumpet Attack #5 (Demon Locusts Sting Men)

As a result of the recent angelic rebellion he instigated and led, Satan is no longer free to enter heaven. However, according to the rules of the 7-sealed book, Satan will be authorized to use the key to hell for his next trumpet, which means he has to go to heaven to get it because Jesus won it from him during the first half of the contest. This time, though, Satan is stopped at the gate and must wait outside until his cue, the sounding of the 5th trumpet, before he can ask Jesus for the key that unlocks a specific pit in hell. Jesus, following the rules of the 7-sealed book to the letter, will loan him the key to the abyss, and then Michael will summarily cast him back down to earth (like a *"star fallen from heaven"*) like a piece of garbage.

> *And the fifth angel blew his trumpet, and I saw a star fallen from heaven to earth, and he was given the key to the shaft of the bottomless pit.* (Revelation 9:1 ESV)

John describes Satan as that *"star fallen from heaven,"* borrowing language from Isaiah 14:12, *"How art thou fallen from heaven, Lucifer, son of the morning!"*[167] Since the day of the abomination of desolation, the veil between the seen and unseen world was lifted. God's third whispering angel and the flying eagle have been seen by all, and now demonic hordes will also be visible. But these demonic creatures will be more than just terrorizing to behold; the pain they inflict will be felt. They will physically torment people who are not prepared to defend against spiritual warfare.

---

[167] Bible Hub, "Revelation 9:1," Jamieson-Fausset-Brown Bible Commentary, biblehub.com, https://biblehub.com/commentaries/revelation/9-1.htm

Satan was not granted access to the power of this trumpet until after personally visiting heaven's gate, much like in Job chapter 1, when Satan visited heaven and spoke with God to obtain permission to test Job. This visit signals that the trumpet powers he's permitted to wield are granted by God in a manner similar to the limited power Satan was allowed to exercise against Job's family and property. If obtaining permission (the key) from heaven wasn't essential, John wouldn't have emphasized the *"fallen from heaven"* point; he would have simply written, "God sent an angel to give Satan the key." The term *"fallen"* also indicates that this wasn't a cordial visit, as in the past when God tolerated Satan's visits to heaven and even conversed with him at times. It probably can't be classified as a visit but rather an attempted visit consisting of a knock at the gate of heaven, followed by a forceful ejection by Michael after he hands Satan the key.

God permits Satan to unleash demonic, stinging locusts upon the earth, creatures that Satan has been preparing for over a thousand years. He would have released this horde much earlier to terrorize humanity and sway them to his side, but he was restrained by the divine timing set by the rules in the 7-sealed book. Satan required a key from heaven to release them, which means he couldn't cheat and bypass these rules or release the demons prematurely.

Since his victory in the first half of the contest by dying sinless on the cross, descending to Sheol, and resurrecting, Jesus, not Satan, now holds the keys to Sheol. The New Testament translates Sheol as Hades.

> *When I saw him, I fell at his feet as though dead. But he laid his right hand on me, saying, "Fear not, I am the first and the last, 18 and the living one. I died, and behold I am alive forevermore, and I have the keys of Death and Hades.* (Revelation 1:17–18 ESV)

The key which was just handed to Satan at God's direction unlocks the Abyss, which will release a horde of demon-locusts.

> *He opened the shaft of the bottomless pit, and from the shaft rose smoke like the smoke of a great furnace, and the sun and the air were darkened with the smoke from the shaft. 3 Then from the smoke came locusts on the earth, and they were given power like the power of scorpions of the earth. 4 They were told not to harm the grass of the earth or any green plant or any tree, but only those people who do not have the seal of God on their foreheads. 5 They were allowed to torment them for five months, but not to kill them, and their torment was like the torment of a scorpion when it stings someone. 6 And in those days people will seek death and will not find it. They will long to die, but death will flee from them.* (Revelation 9:2–6 ESV)

This 5th trumpet is blood-curdling, but thankfully God places very, very specific limitations on Satan in these rules of engagement. These demonic stinging locusts:

1. are commanded not to harm the grass or any green plant or tree.[168]
2. are prohibited from tormenting those who have the seal of God on their foreheads.[169]

---

[168] We learn three things from this: 1) The grass that was burned up from the 1st trumpet has grown back, so it's probably been at least 1 season. Satan would surely want to cause more starvation and crop failure, but he had his chance in the 1st trumpet and would not be allowed any further damage to grass or trees. 2) These are not normal locusts, because locusts only eat green vegetation, which is why they are called destroyers of crops. 3) These locusts don't eat anything––they sting and cause torment.

[169] We know from Revelation 7:3 that these are the 144,000 sealed Jews. Yet I believe that the full armor of God, when used as God instructed with full faith, will also serve as a type of seal of God.

3. are prohibited from killing.

4. create such intense fear and distress that many people, either suffering from their stings or terrified of being stung, will attempt suicide, but they will be unable to die. Twice, we're told that *"death will flee from them."*[170]

5. are prohibited from remaining on the earth for any longer than five months. But their reign of terror and torment will end once the 6th trumpet sounds.

I'm adding three important observations that are not specifically stated, but can be inferred about this 5th trumpet :

6. Since these are Satan's hordes, it is unlikely that he will unleash them on those who already have his mark because that would be self-defeating.

> *And if Satan casts out Satan, he is divided against himself.*
> *How then will his kingdom stand?* (Matthew 12:26 ESV)

Satan's goal is to win as many converts to his kingdom as possible before the 3½ year timer runs out and Jesus returns. Those with the mark are already his eternal vassals, so there is nothing further he could gain from tormenting them. Therefore, Satan will unleash these demonic stinging locusts only on those who have no mark, which includes the remaining Christians.

---

[170] Imagine what it would mean to be unable to commit suicide. This could mean either that you are somehow prevented from attempting it or that, no matter what you try, you survive. In the latter case, attempts like shooting or stabbing yourself might fail, leaving you with serious wounds but still alive. Now consider other methods, like overdosing, drinking poison, or jumping from a tall building, only to survive with severe injuries. The result could be many people walking around, visibly alive but bearing the shocking evidence of seemingly fatal, yet failed suicide attempts.

7. Points 3 and 4 are restrictions placed by God so that Satan can't just add to his soul count by purposely or calculatingly killing unsaved people who haven't taken the mark. That must be another one of the rules of engagement in the 7-sealed book.

8. This trumpet indicates God's 144,000 Jews are specifically protected against these demonic stinging locusts, but they are also protected from every other trumpet and bowl. Only the full armor of God will protect Christians from these demons, so this should spur us to practice with our armor before that time.

The release of these demonic stinging locusts further supports the *trumpet-attack/bowl-countermeasure theory*, in which each trumpet attack is countered by the witnesses calling down a plague. Without these bowl countermeasures for each of the seven trumpets, which most authors believe occur sequentially, this terrible 5th trumpet, left unchecked by the 5th bowl, would be absolutely unbearable. The demonic locusts would launch a relentless, five-month long stinging assault against everyone without the mark of the beast. With nothing to slow these demon locusts, untold numbers of people would be driven to take the mark, desperate for protection from the unbearable and lasting torment of the scorpion stings.

However, if we accept the *trumpet-attack/bowl-countermeasure theory*, then God has already diminished the impact of these horrific demonic stinging locusts because of the lasting effects of the 1st bowl. During the 1st bowl, the two witnesses inflicted excruciating sores on those who took the mark of the beast. Now, with the coming 5th bowl, the 2 witnesses will cripple the antichrist's entire kingdom even further by plunging it into complete darkness and cutting off transportation, electricity, and communication.

## 19.1 Bowl Countermeasure #5 (The antichrist's Kingdom Plunged into the Dark Ages)

> *The fifth angel poured out his bowl on the throne of the beast, and its kingdom was plunged into darkness. People gnawed their tongues in anguish 11 and cursed the God of heaven for their pain and sores. They did not repent of their deeds.* (Revelation 16:10–11 ESV)

This is not a normal darkness. The dark is so thick that it's described as though it were a liquid that they are *"plunged into."* This plague of darkness is the same as the plague of darkness that two earlier witnesses called down upon Egypt 3500 years ago.

> *Then the LORD said to Moses, "Stretch out your hand toward heaven, that there may be darkness over the land of Egypt, a darkness to be felt."* (Exodus 10:21 ESV)

This utter darkness will cause serious sensory deprivation and panic. But absolute darkness also means that there are no lights of any kind: electric, battery, gas, or even glow sticks. This also means that there is no electricity, no communications, no operational vehicles, or any working weapons because each of those would emit at least a little light, a spark, or a flash, which would break up the total darkness. This is a complete blackout that covers only the antichrist's territory and sky. Civilized life can only survive a few days without electricity before sewer systems, drinking water systems, and climate control systems fail. The effects of this bowl will be harder on those living in cities than in rural areas.

Samuel doesn't tell us how, but he tells us God will protect his faithful during the darkness.

> He will guard the feet of his faithful ones, but the wicked shall be cut off in darkness, for not by might shall a man prevail. 10 The adversaries of the LORD shall be broken to pieces; against them he will thunder in heaven. The LORD will judge the ends of the earth; he will give strength to his king and exalt the horn of his anointed. (1 Samuel 2:9-10 ESV)

Those with the mark throughout the antichrist's kingdom are left alone, isolated and in pitch-black darkness with only their thoughts. And their thoughts go haywire. They can focus on nothing but the pain of their oozing, malignant sores with which they were inflicted during the 1st bowl. We can be certain that they still suffer from these because the sores will never heal. The pain is so bad that they gnaw their tongues to take their minds off *"their pain and sores."* They understand that this plague of darkness came from God and so they *"cursed the God of heaven."* They know it was God who caused this, which means the two witnesses are effective in communicating that fact to the world. Yet, men refuse to repent because God has hardened their hearts.

People living outside of the antichrist's kingdom will not be affected by this darkness because the bowl says it only targets his kingdom. For any Christians who may be living in the antichrist's territory, Micah 7:8 gives this comforting and timeless message that the darkness will be tolerable for them because they have Jesus.

> *"Rejoice not against me, O mine enemy: when I fall, I shall arise; when I sit in darkness, the LORD shall be*

*a light unto me.*" (Micah 7:8 KJV)

And John reminds us that Jesus is *"the light of the world,"* and his followers will *"not walk in darkness."*

> *"Again Jesus spoke to them, saying, "I am the light of the world. Whoever follows me will not walk in darkness, but will have the light of life."* (John 8:12 ESV)

Satan was convinced that his demonic stinging locusts, released from hell during the 5th trumpet, would be his crowning stroke in this contest. He must have assumed that once the antichrist let it be known that taking the mark would serve as a shield against the agonizing sting of these demon locusts, the lines at the mark processing centers would overflow with people anxiously begging to get the mark before one of those demonic stinging locusts stung them. But there was a flaw in Satan's plan. He didn't anticipate that all those who had already taken the mark would still be suffering with painful, oozing sores inflicted on them way back during the 1st bowl. Moaning people with oozing, festering sores that can't heal is not exactly a great advertisement for the benefits of taking the mark.

So those without the mark will have to decide which is the lesser of the two evils: take their chances of getting a long-lasting, unimaginably painful sting, or take the mark knowing that it comes with permanent, oozing, painful sores from the soles of their feet to their scalps. I can't imagine there will be many who will voluntarily choose the mark over scorpion stings at this point.

The 5th bowl countermeasure by the two witnesses together with the lasting effects of their first bowl, deal a significant blow to Satan in this round. Once the five months of horrifying fear and torment are over, the demonic stinging locusts are forced back down into their dungeon in hell and locked back up in accordance with the rules of the 7-sealed book. Satan knows that the next trumpet will be his final opportunity—at least the last one authorized by the 7-sealed book—to win the souls of those who still have no mark, assuming he plans to adhere to the rules of engagement. However, when it comes to Satan and his antichrist, assuming they will follow the rules is never a safe bet.

# 20 Trumpet Attack #6 (1/3rd of Mankind Killed by 200 Million Cavalry)

*Then the sixth angel blew his trumpet, and I heard a voice from the four horns of the golden altar before God, 14 saying to the sixth angel who had the trumpet, "Release the four angels who are bound at the great river Euphrates." 15 So the four angels, who had been prepared for the hour, the day, the month, and the year, were released to kill a third of mankind. 16 The number of mounted troops was twice ten thousand times ten thousand; I heard their number. 17 And this is how I saw the horses in my vision and those who rode them: they wore breastplates the color of fire and of sapphire and of sulfur, and the heads of the horses were like lions' heads, and fire and smoke and sulfur came out of their mouths. 18 By these three plagues a third of mankind was killed, by the fire and smoke and sulfur coming out of their mouths. 19 For the power of the horses is in their mouths and in their tails, for their tails are like serpents with heads, and by means of them they wound.* (Revelation 9:13–19 ESV)

The 6th trumpet unlocks four fallen angels that have been bound under the Euphrates river. We know these are fallen angels because God does not bind his heavenly angels. Jude references the binding of the Nephilim of Genesis 6, who rebelled, so these four are most likely from that group.

*And the angels who did not stay within their own position of authority, but left their proper dwelling, he has kept in eternal chains under gloomy darkness until the judgment of the great day* (Jude 1:6 ESV)

These four newly unchained angels have some significance, but it's difficult to discern because the attention soon turns to the 200 million horses and their riders.[171] 200 million, *"twice ten thousand times ten thousand,"* may seem like an exaggeration, but John adds a confirmation, *"I heard their number,"* to let us know that it wasn't just his own wild estimate, it was an exact count mentioned by some authority in heaven. It's hard to imagine 200 million soldiers and their horses gathered in a single location, let alone the logistical challenge of transporting, arming, and providing enough food, water, and supplies for all of them.[172]

I've always accepted the dominant narrative that these are troops and horses from one of the two countries currently capable

---

[171] Some say "horses" may be an analogy because John didn't know how to describe military vehicles. But if they were vehicles, I think John would have said chariots or wagons or something else with wheels. I think these are horse-type creatures that had been cross-bred in preparation for this very moment.

[172] There has never been an army assembled in one place with even one million soldiers. The closest was probably the cumulative number of Russian conscripts sent in human waves to defend Stalingrad during WWII. They were used as human fodder and were gunned down by the Germans almost as fast as they could be pushed to the front lines. Some accounts say there were a million Soviet casualties over the five months of that brutal and sad battle of Stalingrad, but there were never even close to 1 million of them assembled at any one time. In the entirety of WWII, there were "only" about 100 million soldiers from the 50 nations involved on any side (Nancy Levin, "9 Largest Battles in History," largest.org, December 24, 2018, https://largest.org/culture/battles-in-history/) & (Daniel L. Davis, "The Battle of Stalingrad Left an Incomprehensible 1.9 Million Dead," *The National Interest*, October 9, 2021, https://nationalinterest.org/blog/reboot/battle-stalingrad-left-incomprehensible-19-million-dead-194783)

of fielding such a large number of military-age people: China or India. However, my perspective has evolved for two reasons: the horses described are truly bizarre, and the significance of the four fallen angels has been largely overlooked. Verse 15 states that these angels *"were released to kill a third of mankind."* While they may use the 200 million horsemen to achieve this, the angels are the demonic power behind these horsemen. The fact that these angels had to be unlocked, in the same manner as the demon horde of the 5th trumpet, indicates that these fallen angels would have escaped to unleash their destructive force sooner had God not kept them restrained under lock and key. But it also, in an indirect way, reveals the righteousness of God. Because once freed from their prison and given a second chance, they didn't change their ways. Instead, they immediately returned to their evil ways, proving God was just and right to chain them in the first place.

These horses and horsemen, just like the demonic stinging locusts of the 5th trumpet, are creatures Satan has been *"preparing"* or working on. Satan has been working on this particular weapons system for thousands of years to prepare for this exact moment. I say *working on* because nowhere in the Bible does it say that Satan has the power to create. Rather, it calls him a destroyer.[173] So, it's likely that his infernal team has been crossbreeding and genetically modifying animals to hybridize these horses and maybe even their riders. I infer this because the fallen angels had been preparing something for this exact moment for a long time (*"had been prepared for this hour and day and month and year"*) and because each part of the horse is described as being *"like"* something else that already exists.[174] Specifically, the horses' heads are *like* lions and their tails *like* biting snakes.

---

[173] *The thief's purpose is to steal and kill and destroy. My purpose is to give them a rich and satisfying life.* (John 10:10 NLT)

[174] Several versions, including the New Living Translation cited here, use "this

Joel, who seems to be speaking of this 6ᵗʰ trumpet, tells us that these creatures have *"the appearance of horses,"* yet with abilities far beyond any earthly horse. They scale walls, burn everything in their path to ashes, and, most ominously, are unstoppable by any ordinary weapon (*"they burst through the weapons and are not halted"*).

> . . . *a day of darkness and gloom, a day of clouds and thick darkness! Like blackness there is spread upon the mountains a great and powerful people; their like has never been before, nor will be again after them through the years of all generations. 3 Fire devours before them, and behind them a flame burns. The land is like the garden of Eden before them, but behind them a desolate wilderness, and nothing escapes them. 4 Their appearance is like the appearance of horses, and like war horses they run. 5 As with the rumbling of chariots, they leap on the tops of the mountains, like the crackling of a flame of fire devouring the stubble, like a powerful army drawn up for battle. 6 Before them peoples are in anguish; all faces grow pale. 7 Like warriors they charge; like soldiers they scale the wall. They march each on his way; they do not swerve from their paths. 8 They do not jostle one another; each marches in his path; they burst through the weapons and are not halted. 9 They leap upon the city, they run upon the walls, they climb up into the houses, they enter through the windows. . . like a thief. 10 The earth quakes before them; the heavens tremble. The sun and the moon are darkened, and the stars withdraw their shining.* (Joel 2:2–10 ESV)

---

hour" instead of the more common "the hour". I think "this" adds clarity that they were created for this specific moment.

This freakish cavalry will use some fantastic weaponry to kill 1/3ʳᵈ of mankind, and it's not swords or guns. John and Joel both describe their method of destruction as flame and fire. These weapons are not directly aimed at those with the mark for the same reason the locust stings of the 5ᵗʰ trumpet weren't; *a house divided against itself cannot stand.*[175] That's not to say people with the mark won't be killed, but they're not who Satan will be targeting.

The meaning of this 6th trumpet is difficult to understand because it doesn't speak of war or even who this army of 200 million horsemen will destroy. We are left to think that they will just aimlessly kill a third of mankind for no particular reason. But when the 6ᵗʰ trumpet is followed quickly by the 6ᵗʰ bowl, these two pieces of the puzzle fit together to help answer the questions of why these troops are amassed in Jerusalem and who they are there to destroy.

---

[175] Matthew 12:26

# 20.1 Bowl Countermeasure #6 (Euphrates Dries Up to Make a Road)

> *12 The sixth angel poured out his bowl on the great river Euphrates, and its water was dried up, to prepare the way for the kings from the east.* (Revelation 16:12 ESV)

The following verses are not meant to be part of the 6th bowl, although many Bibles and writers group them together. They should be treated separately from the 6th bowl for the following reasons:

1. verse 13 begins with *"and"*
2. the events in these verses aren't caused by the Euphrates River drying up but are responses to it drying up
3. Jesus is quoted in verse 15, right in the middle of these verses, and he is not quoted in any other bowl or trumpet. This further indicates that these verses are separate from the 6th bowl

> *13 And I saw, coming out of the mouth of the dragon and out of the mouth of the beast and out of the mouth of the false prophet, three unclean spirits like frogs. 14 For they are demonic spirits, performing signs, who go abroad to the kings of the whole world, to assemble them for battle on the great day of God the Almighty. 15 ("Behold, I am coming like a thief! Blessed is the one who stays awake, keeping his garments on, that he may not go about naked and be seen exposed!") 16 And they assembled them at the place that in Hebrew is called Armageddon.* (Revelation 16:13–16 ESV)

When their effects are viewed together, as they are here in the *trumpet-attack/bowl-countermeasure theory* timeline, the 6th trumpet, the 6th bowl, and the subsequent reaction verses reveal that a massive and terrifying army is assembling at Jerusalem near the mountain of Magedon.[176]

The two witnesses must counteract the antichrist's 6th trumpet cavalry of 200 million that has just appeared along with the four fallen angels that had been unchained from below the Euphrates River, so they call down the 6th bowl to dry up the Euphrates. But what's the big deal about the Euphrates drying up? Here are a few reasons it's an effective countermeasure.

1. This strategic move by the two witnesses strips the antichrist of a key element of his natural defense. It creates a critical vulnerability for his massive 200 million man army positioned near Jerusalem. With the river no longer serving as a barrier, his eastern flank is left completely exposed and unguarded. When he learns of large troop movements swiftly advancing toward him, led by *"the kings from the east"* (Revelation 16:12),

---

[176] *Armageddon* is a poor interpretation of the Hebrew *Har-Magedon*. The Amplified Bible translates it more literally "And they (demons) gathered the kings and armies of the world together at the place which in Hebrew is called Har-Magedon (Armageddon)" (Bible Hub, "Revelation 16," *Amplified Bible*, biblehub.com, https://biblehub.com/amp/revelation/16.htm)
Armageddon has been established as the undisputed name and location of the final battle, and it's been reinforced through constant repetition. The name *Armageddon* is a modern adulteration of the Hebrew word *Har-Magedon*. In *The Unseen Realm*, Michael S. Heiser devotes eight pages to the etymology and concludes that Har Magedon is Mount Zion. In other words, it's Jerusalem, not the valley of Magiddo (Armageddon), as every modern author and commentator asserts. Heiser points to Isaiah 14:12–14 as evidence that Satan has grand plans to make himself like God on that mountain (Mount Zion is called the mountain of assembly in that passage) and then in Isaiah verse 15 God tells Satan that when he makes the move to do it, he will be brought down to Sheol. (Michael S. Heiser, *The Unseen Realm*, 368–375).

Daniel gives us insight into his state of mind, describing him as alarmed and furious.

> But news *from the east* and the north shall *alarm him*, and he shall go out with great *fury* to destroy and devote many to destruction. (Daniel 11:44 ESV)

Unless you view the 6ᵗʰ trumpet attack as being immediately countered by the witnesses' 6ᵗʰ bowl, this 44ᵗʰ verse of Daniel 11 is hard to understand. Trying to fit that verse into the timeline has led many authors to look outside the Bible for answers. Many mistakenly concluded the antichrist's forces must be Russian or European. It's only after the Euphrates, the natural eastern border, is dried up that it becomes clear why the antichrist is alarmed.

2.  The antichrist recognizes that this now dry riverbed is acting like a yellow brick road, giving his enemies easy access to his troop staging area around Jerusalem.
3.  All these troops need to drink, and the two witnesses have ensured that at least this part of the world has been in a terrible drought for the past three years. The Euphrates is one of the few sources of fresh water in that hot, desert region. Water can be hauled in from other areas but imagine how much water will be needed to sustain a standing force as large as the combined populations of Turkey, Iraq, and Iran in that sweltering environment. Not to mention the devastating impact it will have on all the countries and cities that obtain their drinking and irrigating water from that river.
4.  While we don't know the exact location of New Babylon, it's likely it will be on the site of the original Tower of Babel. Most think that infamous tower was located in Mesopotamia, modern-

day Iraq, on the banks of the Euphrates River. If so, the loss of water from that river could be a real problem for Babylon.

But the question remains at this point: Who are these enemy troops that are advancing towards the antichrist in Daniel 11:44?

## 20.2 Battle of Har-Magedon: Antichrist Versus Whom?

It's impossible to know how many people have been killed up to this point by the preceding wars, famines, trumpets, bowls, and beheadings. A reasonable guess is that at least half of humanity has been wiped out, which means there could still be 3 or 4 billion people alive when the battle begins. But by the time that battle is over, another third will be killed by the 6th trumpet cavalry.

> . . . *a third of mankind was killed, by the fire and smoke and sulfur coming out of their mouths* (Revelation 9:18 ESV)

Once again, this is God limiting Satan to 1/3rd. If the world population is down to 3 or 4 billion, this means that another 1 to 1.25 billion will be killed by the antichrist's forces. On the battlefront, however, it's still just a one-sided war with the antichrist's troops killing hundreds of millions of people and destroying population centers within range of their weapons.

Several countries must suspect that the antichrist's actions indicate that he's trying to either subjugate or destroy every nation on earth. Some of these nations band together and send their armies to try to preemptively destroy him. The largest, or at least the most concerning of those armies, will come from the east and north (Daniel 11:44).

Let's take a closer look at this massive army stationed near Mount Magedon, likely John's term for what we now call Mt Zion.[177] The

---

[177] The word origin of Harmagedón is Hebrew *har* and *Megiddon*. The definition of "Har-Magedon" is "a mountain of uncertain location." (Bible Hub, "717. Harmagedón," NAS Exhaustive Concordance, biblehub.com, https://biblehub.

Mahdi's forces include 200 million ominous cavalry and four newly released fallen angels. Alongside them are hundreds of thousands of loyal, battle-tested soldiers who have fought beside the Mahdi since the beginning of his rapid rise to power, as well as countless other zealots from far corners of the world. Similar to those who once flocked to ISIS, these fighters will follow willingly, driven by the hope of gaining promised rewards in paradise through service and sacrifice in the Mahdi's cause. [178]

Many commentators and authors suggest these troops are there to fight Israel, but that's only partially correct. While the antichrist believes he is orchestrating these events, Zechariah reveals that it is actually God who gathers them there. As is often the case with prophetic passages, Zechariah moves through multiple phases of the end-times within these two verses.

> *For I will gather all the nations against Jerusalem to battle, and the city shall be taken and the houses plundered and the women raped. Half of the city shall go out into exile, but the rest of the people shall not be cut off from the city.* (Zechariah 14:2 ESV)

---

com/nasec/greek/717.htm). Most people assume the battle will take place in the Valley of Megiddo, known as Armageddon. However, this misunderstanding comes from a mistranslation in the Latin Vulgate that has been repeated in nearly every modern translation. The original text actually says "the mountain of Magedon," or *Har Magedon*. It can't be what we currently think of as the Valley of Megiddo, because there isn't a mountain—or even a hill—in the Valley of Megiddo. The only feature there is an ancient mound of rubble, called a "tell," which is the remains of an old town, now just a pile of stones and earth. Michael S. Heiser asserts Harmegedon must be Mt Zion in Jerusalem. (Michael S. Heiser, *The Unseen Realm*, 368–375).

[178] Muslim men who die during a Jihad are promised 72 virgins in paradise (*About Islam*, "72 Virgins for Men, What Do Women Get in Paradise?" aboutislam. net, November 26, 2018, https://aboutislam.net/counseling/ask-about-islam/72-virgins-men-women-get-paradise/)

The few Jews remaining in occupied Jerusalem have technically been under the antichrist's rule since the moment of the abomination of desolation. Eliminating them would be no challenge if not for two immoveable obstacles protecting them: the two witnesses.

Part of the witnesses' mission is to carry on the role that the Archangel Michael performed for Israel before he was recalled to heaven; they protect the portion of Jerusalem that has not been given over to the Gentiles for the duration of the Great Tribulation, which is forty-two months.

> . . . *but do not measure the court outside the temple; leave that out, for it is given over to the nations, and they will trample the holy city for forty-two months.* (Revelation 11:2 ESV)

So, who does the largest army ever assembled in the history of the world really come to fight? The antichrist has three opponents in mind, plus a secret objective.

1. He may invade or destroy the countries that have rejected his leadership. While he carries out these actions in earnest, their true purpose is actually a cover, a deception operation for his next objective.[179]

---

[179] A military deception is an operation designed to mislead an adversary into taking specific actions (or inaction) that will work to friendly advantage. For example, "As a crucial part of their preparations for D-Day (6 June 1944), the Allies developed a deception plan to draw attention from Normandy." Normandy was the real place the Allies intended to invade (Imperial War Museums, "The Lies and Deceptions that made D-Day possible," https://www.iwm.org.uk/history/the-lies-and-deceptions-that-made-d-day-possible).

2. The antichrist has a top-secret mission, and it's much more important than dealing with the countries who oppose him. We'll discuss that covert operation in the next chapter.

3. As implausible as this sounds, the antichrist and his demon envoys have convinced his allies that he possesses supernatural power and that together, they can fight and defeat God, *"the Lord."*

> *Why do the nations rage and the peoples plot in vain?*
> *2 The kings of the earth set themselves, and the rulers*
> *take counsel together, against the LORD and against*
> *his Anointed, saying, 3 "Let us burst their bonds apart*
> *and cast away their cords from us." 4 He who sits in*
> *the heavens laughs; the Lord holds them in derision.*
> (Psalm 2:1–4 ESV)

To achieve the second objective above, the antichrist needs to buy time, and he thinks that sacrificing some of the troops he has amassed is a worthwhile trade-off for the delay it buys him.

> *But news from the east and the north shall alarm him,*
> *and he shall go out with great fury to destroy and*
> *devote many to destruction.* (Daniel 11:44 ESV)

There are at least two ways he may *"devote many to destruction."*

1. To slow the advancing enemy forces, he takes a page from the Russian defense of Stalingrad, dividing hundreds of thousands of ground troops into carefully spaced waves of attack as a stalling tactic, knowing full well that each subsequent wave of his soldiers will be decimated.

2. Another possibility is that, in his desperate effort to destroy or overwhelm the two witnesses, he throws everything in his weapons arsenal against them at once, fully aware that the troops he sends on this kamikaze mission will be incinerated by the two witnesses.

> *And if anyone would harm them* [the two witnesses], *fire pours from their mouth and consumes their foes. If anyone would harm them, this is how he is doomed to be killed.* (Revelation 11:5 ESV)

However, the second option seems unlikely; he won't try to overpower the two witnesses with sheer force... at least not yet. When the antichrist receives alarming news from the east and north, he abandons secrecy and urgently sends out three demons, who strangely, look like frogs, in full view of everyone. He instructs them to perform miracles and offer whatever incentives necessary to persuade the *"kings of the whole world"* to join him, insisting that his is the side that will prevail.

> *And I saw, coming out of the mouth of the dragon and out of the mouth of the beast and out of the mouth of the false prophet, three unclean spirits like frogs. 14 For they are demonic spirits, performing signs, who go abroad to the kings of the whole world, to assemble them for battle on the great day of God the Almighty.* (Revelation 16:13-14 ESV)

He is trying to convince these kings that he really has the supernatural power necessary to defeat Jesus, so they should throw in their lot with him. He desperately wants those kings to quickly bring more replacement troops or weapons, or maybe he gets them to agree to launch some special weapons against targets he's designated.

The fact that he's now working directly with demons in front of everyone, ordering those demons to travel across the world (Revelation 16:13–14) and openly perform miracles for the kings, tells us several things:

1. It confirms that the unseen world still operates in our visible world as it has been since the abomination of desolation.

2. The antichrist is becoming desperate. He knows he only has at most a month or so left before the Day of the Lord.

3. Driven by desperation, the antichrist will resort to a merciless slaughter for a truly diabolical reason: he knows that some previously "lukewarm" believers are beginning to solidify their faith in Jesus, and he is determined to stop them before they complete that transformation and are counted among the saved.[180] To him, it doesn't matter if, in this mass extermination, during which he is authorized to kill one-third of the remaining population, even those who bear his mark of the beast are killed. Their lives are nothing more than chaff in his ruthless, winner-takes-all campaign.

4. He's no longer confident that even the unique 200 million horsemen he has assembled will be sufficient to take on Jesus and his heavenly army, which he knows will arrive soon, but he's not about to admit that to his allies.

The antichrist and false prophet understand the gravity of losing. Eternal torment awaits them if they are not successful.

---

[180] Revelation 3:15-16 ESV *"I know your works: you are neither cold nor hot. Would that you were either cold or hot! 16 So, because you are lukewarm, and neither hot nor cold, I will spit you out of my mouth."*

Isaiah tells us in this dual prophecy that the thing which had alarmed the antichrist from the east and north is now on its way toward him.

> *He* [this is referring to the Lord] *will raise a signal for nations far away, and whistle for them from the ends of the earth; and behold, quickly, speedily they come! 27 None is weary, none stumbles, none slumbers or sleeps, not a waistband is loose, not a sandal strap broken; 28 their arrows are sharp, all their bows bent, their horses' hoofs seem like flint, and their wheels like the whirlwind. 29 Their roaring is like a lion, like young lions they roar; they growl and seize their prey; they carry it off, and none can rescue.* (Isaiah 5:26–29 ESV)

I like to imagine that the United States is part of this because *"nations far away"* may mean nations on another continent.[181] The fact that nations are coming against him in battle indicates that the antichrist never fully achieves the total world domination he desires, or, if he does for a while, several significant regions rebel. Thankfully, the antichrist's troop reinforcements or foreign weapons don't make it to him in time. Still, the antichrist sets up his headquarters and plants his flag near Mount Zion in Jerusalem.

> *And he* [the antichrist] *shall pitch his palatial tents between the sea and the glorious holy mountain* [Jerusalem]. *Yet he shall come to his end, with none to*

---

[181] I would also like to believe that the United States will stay true to its founding documents and will not buy-in to the antichrist's tempting economic system. But this requires vigilance from citizens to ensure they vote for representatives who will infringe the least on Christian values. Sadly, evidence of Christian values is no longer something most people, including many Christians, consider when voting.

*help him.* (Daniel 11:45 ESV)

He makes this brazen move as a show of confidence to his troops and allies and as an act of defiance to God. But it also adds another layer of believability to his covert operation, which we'll discuss next.

# 20.3 Operation "Deception"

What makes the antichrist confident that he can not only challenge but defeat Jesus? Yes, he has the power of demons and a few fallen angels behind him, but he's well aware of his own limitations. Somewhere along the line, his tactic switched from trying to fight his way out of his "checked" position and win the contest by following the rules, to simply trying to force a stalemate.[182] It's possible he is using his operation centered at Har-Magedon as a massive deceptive maneuver while he attempts something that has a much higher probability of succeeding in causing God to cancel the contest. I think the antichrist is on a covert search-and-destroy mission and must keep its true purpose secret from everyone, especially God.

The antichrist likely felt forced into this deceptive tactic because he had counted on millions of people desperately taking the mark as a way to escape the terror he'd unleashed with the demonic locusts from the 5th trumpet, but it had failed miserably due to the countermeasure plagues of the two witnesses. While the demon locusts' stings were truly horrifying, people dreaded the gruesome, unending pain associated with the mark even more. Anyone contemplating the mark any time after the 1st bowl understood it came with festering, incurable sores, guaranteeing a lifetime of relentless agony. Consequently, the threat of enduring the pain from the locusts was overshadowed by the certainty of perpetual suffering from sores tied to the mark. This miscalculation meant that Satan couldn't sway enough of the unmarked, leaving him no

---

[182] "Stalemate" is a draw in the game of chess. The player has no legal moves left, but the king is not under attack, so the game ends in a draw (**Chess Questions**, "Stalemate in Chess: Rules, Tips and Pieces to Avoid," chessquestions.com, April 8, 2021, https://chessquestions.com/stalemate-in-chess/)

way to legitimately obtain the number of converts necessary to claim victory in this second half of the contest. He will lose for sure if he keeps following the rules of engagement, and that is just not an outcome he can accept.

The 3½-year clock has ticked down to just weeks or even days remaining. He's come to terms with the fact that he can no longer win, and a loss, being chained for 1,000 years in a pit of hell, is unthinkable. So how will he force a stalemate?

Satan has calculated that there is a high probability that many of those who still don't have the mark are not Christians because his forces have beheaded or converted any Christians he could find in the areas he controls. Many of the remaining unmarked people include hundreds of millions from other religions, such as Buddhists and Hindus, as well as unbelieving doomsday preppers and anti-establishment renegades. He couldn't entice them to take the mark with promises of better food and an easier life, nor did the terror of the demonic stinging locusts override their horror of being afflicted with oozing sores that now accompany accepting the mark of the beast. Now, he's just going to kill them all and hope that most are not Christians and will thus count as his dead and not Jesus' dead. [183]

The antichrist's bigger objective, the one that he's calculated has the best chance to force a stalemate, is to find and destroy the supernaturally protected remnant, even though he knows that it's against the rules of the 7-sealed book, because each of the 144,000 are sealed and protected by God. So, he is determined to throw away the rulebook and fall back on his natural strength, the one that has served him well since Eve: deception.

---

[183] All those useless deaths wouldn't be a total loss because any unmarked, non-Christian the antichrist kills can be added to the billions of unbelievers he's holding ransom in Hades, which he thinks, adds to his future bargaining power.

In this dual prophecy, the antichrist consults his mediums and witches (*"taken crafty counsel"*), probably the same ones who helped locate all the hidden Bibles, and tries to divine where God may be hiding the 144,000 Jews.

> *They have taken crafty counsel against thy people, and consulted against thy hidden ones. 4 They have said, Come, and let us cut them off from being a nation; that the name of Israel may be no more in remembrance.* (Psalm 83:3–4 KJV)

Since the establishment of God's covenant with Abraham, Satan has relentlessly attempted to destroy Abraham's blessed offspring. He believes that annihilating God's chosen people is the key to holding on to his kingdom. His logic is simple: if he could exterminate even just one entire tribe, especially Judah, the tribe from which King David descended, it would mean that God had failed to uphold his covenant and, consequently, would be unable to award the 7-sealed book to Jesus, thus postponing the final countdown, perhaps indefinitely.[184]

He came close to achieving this several times in history, but miraculously, a remnant of Jews always survived, each time protected, probably by the archangel Michael.[185] Now, however, it is the two witnesses who stand in his way.

---

[184] Genesis 17:6-8 ESV " *I will make you exceedingly fruitful, and I will make you into nations, and kings shall come from you. 7 And I will establish my covenant between me and you and your offspring after you throughout their generations for an everlasting covenant, to be God to you and to your offspring after you. 8 And I will give to you and to your offspring after you the land of your sojournings, all the land of Canaan, for an everlasting possession, and I will be their God."*

[185] Haman tried to exterminate all Jews in the Persian empire, probably around 460 BC (Jean-Louis Hout, "Xerxes I," *Encyclopedia Britannica*, August 2, 2024, https://www.britannica.com/biography/Xerxes-I).

This time, Satan believes he has devised the perfect plan for his human avatar, the antichrist. He's gathered an overwhelming force, enough to finally make his goal of eradicating the Jews a reality. But for his plan to succeed, he must deceive God into believing he's still following the rules of the 7-sealed book, therefore he keeps most of his forces engaged in battle as a cover for his true objective. However, he has no hope of deceiving God as long as the two witnesses remain alive because he can't get anything past them. The witnesses continuously harass his antichrist, publicly exposing his weaknesses and countering each of his trumpet powers with their own devastating plagues. To succeed, he must find a way to eliminate them.

---

In York, England in 1190, antisemitic rioters killed 150 Jews (History of York, "The 1190 Massacre," historyofyork.org.uk, http://www.historyofyork.org.uk/themes/norman/the-1190-massacre).

In Poland in 1918 and Ukraine from 1918–1921, pogroms killed up to 100,000 Jews (Rich Tenorio, "20 years before the Holocaust, pogroms killed 100,000 Jews – then were forgotten," *The Times of Israel*, December 21, 2021, https://www.timesofisrael.com/20-years-before-the-holocaust-pogroms-killed-100000-jews-then-were-forgotten/)

Stalin had a detailed plan to exterminate 3,000,000 jews, but suddenly died of a stroke on March 5, 1953 before he could implement it (Jewish Telegraphic Agency, "Behind the Headlines: How Stalin's Plan to Annihilate USSR Jews Was Thwarted," jta.org, January 8, 1978, https://www.jta.org/archive/behind-the-headlines-how-stalins-plan-to-annihilate-ussr-jews-was-thwarted).

The German Holocaust claimed the lives of almost 6 million jews (Jewish Virtual Library, "Estimated Number of Jews Killed in the Final Solution," jewishvirtuallibrary.org, https://www.jewishvirtuallibrary.org/estimated-number-of-jews-killed-in-the-final-solution).

## 20.3 (A) The Antichrist Kills His Arch Enemies: Finally, Those Two Old Men Are Dead

By calling down the powers of the plagues *"as often as they wanted,"* these two witnesses use their power to:

1. Serve as firsthand witnesses that the false prophet "Jesus" is an imposter.
2. Cause a 3½-year-long drought on the antichrist's kingdom.
3. Inflict painful sores on those with the mark, first at bowl 1, then probably multiple times since then, since they can call on the plagues *"as often as they desire."*[186]
4. Turn the sea, rivers, and fountains of the earth to blood (bowls 2 & 3).
5. Increase the power of the sun to scorch and kill men with heat and fire (bowl 4).
6. Plunge the antichrist's kingdom back into the Dark Ages (bowl 5).
7. Expose the antichrist's eastern flank to the enemy kings from the East (bowl 6).

The two witnesses wielded the power of these plagues at precisely the right times to counteract many of the effects of each of the antichrist's trumpet powers, disrupting Satan's plan to sway massive numbers of people into taking the mark of the beast, a scheme he has been crafting for eons.

Satan's plan B, to force the contest to a stalemate, requires him to first eliminate the two witnesses because, in their role as

---

[186] Revelation 11:6 ESV *"They have the power to shut the sky, that no rain may fall during the days of their prophesying, and they have power over the waters to turn them into blood and to strike the earth with every kind of plague, as often as they desire."*

restrainers they would discover and obstruct the secret and illegal assault he's planning to launch. He has likely tried over and over to kill the witnesses and has probably lost untold thousands of his troops in the process, but every weapon he's used has failed to harm or even slightly weaken them.

> . . . *no weapon that is fashioned against you shall succeed, and you shall refute every tongue that rises against you in judgment. This is the heritage of the servants of the LORD and their vindication from me, declares the LORD.* (Isaiah 54:17 ESV)

When Satan attempts to kill the two witnesses this time, he succeeds easily, and there's a specific reason for this that I'll explain. The fact that the witnesses "*had been a torment*" and were killable at this precise moment strongly supports the *trumpet-attack/ bowl-countermeasure theory*. I previously explained that the 7th trumpet and 7th bowl are under the Lord's control, whereas the first 6 trumpets were under Satan's control and the first 6 bowls were controlled by the two witnesses. Therefore, the mission of the witnesses was complete after they called down the 6th bowl. More specifically, after they called down the 6th bowl to counter Satan's 6th trumpet, they had no more bowls remaining and thus had "*finished their testimony*" (verse 7), which is the only reason the antichrist, empowered by Satan, could kill them at this moment.

Those with the mark of the beast will revel and rejoice in the death of the two witnesses at the hands of the antichrist and declare a celebration because these troublemakers are finally gone. While their murders will dishearten the Jews that they had been helping to protect, it will not dishearten Christians familiar with end-time prophecies who know that the witnesses were only able to be killed because they had *"finished their testimony."* These knowledgeable Christians will also know that this means the 7ᵗʰ trumpet, their blessed hope, can't be too far away.

> *And when they* [the two witnesses] *have finished their testimony, the beast that rises from the bottomless pit will make war on them and conquer them and kill them, 8 and their dead bodies will lie in the street of the great city that symbolically is called Sodom and Egypt, where their Lord was crucified. 9 For three and a half days some from the peoples and tribes and languages and nations will gaze at their dead bodies and refuse to let them be placed in a tomb, 10 and those who dwell on the earth will rejoice over them and make merry and exchange presents, because these two prophets had been a torment to those who dwell on the earth.* (Revelation 11:7–10 ESV)

Jihadists almost always parade the bodies of their dead victims through the streets, but they won't be allowed to parade the dead bodies of the two witnesses. Which means God must be supernaturally protecting their corpses from desecration. Satan, knowing the prophecy that they will be resurrected after three and a half days, would surely try to completely pulverize their bodies or even ship them somewhere remote, so that no one can witness their resurrection. But we know that after three and a half days lying dead in the street, God very publicly resurrects them, and *"a loud voice from heaven,"* with *loud* indicating that the voice will be unmistakably heard by the entire world, commands them to *"Come up here!"*[187]

---

[187] A *'loud'* voice indicates it will be heard by everyone and there will be no mistaking what is spoken.

*11 But after the three and a half days a breath of life from God entered them, and they stood up on their feet, and great fear fell on those who saw them. 12 Then they heard a loud voice from heaven saying to them, "Come up here!" And they went up to heaven in a cloud, and their enemies watched them.* (Revelation 11:11–12 ESV)

The residents of Jerusalem watch in astonishment as the two witnesses stand on their feet and ascend to heaven. This demonstrates that God has protected their dead bodies from removal or desecration during those 3½ days they lie in the street.

*13 And at that hour there was a great earthquake, and a tenth of the city fell. Seven thousand people were killed in the earthquake, and the rest were terrified and gave glory to the God of heaven. 14 The second woe has passed; behold, the third woe is soon to come.* (Revelation 11:13–14 ESV)

As they witness the two dead bodies being brought back to life, levitated up to heaven, and hear that loud voice, they are struck by a sudden, soul-melting realization: everything the two witnesses preached must have been true. Though this is the only time, up to this point, that non-Christians give *"glory to the God of heaven,"* they know it is too late for them. Their hearts are filled with terror at the inescapable reality that, by their own free will, they rejected the gospel proclaimed by the first whispering angel, instead choosing the seemingly more appealing path and taking the mark. What could have been a moment of celebration has become one of deep regret, as they understand they have sealed their fate through their willful rejection, with the weight of that decision now hanging over them like an omen from which they know there is no escape.

## 20.3 (B) Blast those Hidden Jews

> 13 And when the dragon saw that he had been thrown down to the earth, he pursued the woman [the 144,000 protected Jews] who had given birth to the male child. 14 But the woman was given the two wings of the great eagle so that she might fly from the serpent into the wilderness, to the place where she is to be nourished for a time, and times, and half a time [3½ years]. (Revelation 12:13-14 ESV)

"*The dragon*" represents Satan, who has just lost the war in heaven and has been "*thrown down to the earth*," permanently barred from returning. "*The woman*" symbolizes the Jewish people, because it was through the Jews, specifically Mary, that Jesus, "*the male child*" was born. The Jews specially marked by God are taken to the wilderness, where they are cared for and protected ("*nourished*") during the Great Tribulation, as indicated by the duration of 3½ years ("*a time, times, and half a time*").

With the two witnesses dead and out of his way, the antichrist is free to unleash a level of destruction never before attempted by anyone. He will bomb every known enclave of survivors who refused the mark and will work to kill everyone without it. But this will merely serve as cover for his true mission: to search for and destroy God's hidden, protected Jews. By this point, through the process of elimination and with the aid of his "*crafty counsel*," he has narrowed down the area where he believes they are hiding.

The hordes of his remaining cavalry of 200 hundred million will fan out over the area where his fiendish diviners believe the 144,000 Jews are hidden. I expect he'll focus his search on a several-hundred-mile radius around Jerusalem. Other troops will be sent to all of the suspected enclaves of unmarked people in the region as an elaborate military deception operation, and also to totally annihilate them because there is simply no more time to process them with a mark, even if they beg for one in the face of their death. But the antichrist is doing more than just cavalry maneuvers; he's using potent long-range weaponry to destroy hundreds of millions of people.

By this point in the Great Tribulation, Jesus has opened the first 5 seals, Satan has used the powers of the first 6 trumpets, and the two witnesses have countered each trumpet with the powers of the first 6 bowls. The antichrist's empire, consisting mainly of the countries that used to be part of the Ottoman/Persian Empire, was populated with far less than a billion people before all the deaths began, so to kill 1/3rd of mankind means he's using powerful weapons targeting large population centers outside of his empire. He's probably aiming at parts of the world where he has the fewest marked followers. This is likely where the number of dead will begin to approach 1/3rd of mankind.

Several verses suggest that the antichrist will deploy some intriguing weapons in his search for the supernaturally protected, hidden Jews. As he gets closer to their suspected hiding place, it seems natural that he would use some type of bunker-buster bomb to try to destroy the underground refuge of the 144,000 Jews.[188] But verse 15 implies that he has developed a water cannon or some type of modified fracking device that releases large amounts of water into the ground, *poured water like a river,* with the aim of destroying the Jews protected by Jesus.[189]

[188] It seems the hiding place must be underground or in a cave because Revelation 12:16 indicates that the earth will help protect them by swallowing the river sent by the dragon.

[189] Fracking involves jetting a solution of water and chemicals using high pressure to break through layers of rock deep underground to release trapped oil and gas.

> 15 *The serpent poured water like a river* out of his
> mouth after the woman [the 144,000 Jews], *to sweep*
> *her away with a flood. 16 But the earth came to the*
> *help* of *the woman, and the earth opened its mouth*
> *and swallowed the river* that the dragon had poured
> *from his mouth.* (Revelation 12:15–16 ESV)

As this weapon closes in on the underground refuge where God has supernaturally safeguarded the 144,000, Satan feels victory within his grasp. But just as he believes he is about to triumph, the earth itself intervenes, opening up and *"swallow*[ing] *the river,"* sinking his entire elaborate plan in an instant. I picture the ground spontaneously opening a wide fissure to divert the water away from the hidden Jews.

David seems to be describing this same event in the following dual prophecy:

> For this shall every one that is godly pray unto thee
> in a time when thou mayest be found: surely in the
> *floods of great waters* they shall *not come nigh* unto
> him. 7 Thou art *my hiding place; thou shalt preserve*
> *me* from trouble; thou shalt compass me about with
> songs of deliverance. Selah. (Psalm 32:6–7 KJV)

The earth itself thwarts the antichrist's deceptive and illegal assault, rendering the water weapon impotent. The assault was illegal because Satan had attempted to violate the seal of protection God had placed on each of the 144,000 Jews' foreheads. Yet this is not the first time in the Bible that some type of diabolical device was developed specifically to kill Jews.

*But when Esther came before the king, he commanded by letters that his wicked device, which he devised against the Jews, should return upon his own head, and that he and his sons should be hanged on the gallows.* (Esther 9:25 KJV)

This water fracking weapon may be the *"device"* prophesied in three different areas in Psalms which God supernaturally stops:

*11 For they intended evil against thee: they imagined a mischievous device, which they are not able to perform. 12 Therefore shalt thou make them turn their back, when thou shalt make ready thine arrows upon thy strings against the face of them.* (Psalm 21:11–12 KJV)

*Let all the earth fear the LORD: let all the inhabitants of the world stand in awe of him. 9 For he spake, and it was done; he commanded, and it stood fast. 10 The LORD bringeth the counsel of the heathen to nought: he maketh the devices of the people of none effect.* (Psalm 33:8–10 KJV)

*O GOD the Lord, the strength of my salvation, thou hast covered my head in the day of battle. 8 Grant not, O LORD, the desires of the wicked: further not his wicked device; lest they exalt themselves. Selah. 9 As for the head of those that compass me about, let the mischief of their own lips cover them. 10 Let burning coals fall upon them: let them be cast into the fire; into deep pits* (Psalm 140:7–10 KJV)

Satan will have his excuse ready for God if his plot is discovered and he's called out for violating the rules of engagement defined in the 7-sealed book. In his true deceiver fashion, he'll be prepared to say something like, "I was leading a war. How could I have known you had hidden your precious Jews in that place? Collateral damage is just a part of the fog of war. It's not as if you had a no-trespassing sign over that area to warn me." But, as we'll soon see, he will have no chance to deliver his prepared excuse.

The Battle of Har-Magedon is still raging. The enemy forces that alarmed the antichrist have probably arrived by now and have joined the battle to try to stop the antichrist's forces from destroying the world. The antichrist is still killing anyone without a mark and appears to be on a winning streak, probably getting close to exterminating 1/3$^{rd}$ of mankind, the maximum number of deaths to which the 6th trumpet rules have restricted him. Many of those unmarked people killed will be Christians.

It doesn't matter whether the full number of martyred Christians is reached first—which, as we covered in Chapter 16, 'The 5th Seal,' is how Jesus' success is scored—or whether Satan's audacious act of willfully disrespecting the seal of God on the 144,000 Jews is detected first. Why? Because Satan has once again deceived himself into believing he could slip something past God. Now, a referee under the full authority of God is about to touch down on earth and make the call, not with a mere referee's whistle, but with an unmistakable sound like *"a lion roaring."* Every soldier on each side will immediately freeze and be forced to listen to that giant angel's proclamation.

# 21 The Sound of Seven Thunders: The Infallible Court Makes Its Ruling

*1 Then I saw another mighty angel coming down from heaven, wrapped in a cloud, with a rainbow over his head, and his face was like the sun, and his legs like pillars of fire. 2 He had a little scroll open in his hand. And he set his right foot on the sea, and his left foot on the land, 3 and called out with a loud voice, like a lion roaring. When he called out, the seven thunders sounded. 4 And when the seven thunders had sounded, I was about to write, but I heard a voice from heaven saying, "Seal up what the seven thunders have said, and do not write it down." (Revelation 10:1-4 ESV)*

This mighty, giant angel raised his right hand, pointed to heaven, and said by the authority of God, *"there would be no more delay."* The Seven Thunders continue speaking, but we don't know what they say because John is stopped from writing it down.

*5 And the angel whom I saw standing on the sea and on the land raised his right hand to heaven 6 and swore by him who lives forever and ever, who created heaven and what is in it, the earth and what is in it, and the sea and what is in it, that there would be no more delay, 7 but that in the days of the trumpet call to be sounded by the seventh angel, the mystery of God would be fulfilled, just as he announced to his servants the prophets. 8 Then the voice that I had heard from heaven spoke to me again, saying, "Go, take the scroll that is open in the hand of the angel who is standing on the sea and on the land."* (Revelation 10:5-8 ESV)

This very mysterious piece of the puzzle is solvable now in light of the *trumpet-attack/bowl-countermeasure theory*. The angel touching down with one foot on the sea and one foot on the land indicates that he's a representative of God.[190] The moment that he descends, everyone *"in heaven or on earth or under the earth"* will acknowledge that this angel is under the authority of God. A supernaturally enforced time-out goes into effect for all those fighting and all activity ceases. No soldier will be able to move a muscle as they await the angel's message. The seven thunders, speaking with the full authority of God, then make a decisive proclamation. John is told to *"seal up what the seven thunders have said."* But given the trumpet-attack/bowl-countermeasures that have occurred up to this exact point in this timeline, we have a really good idea about what the angel will proclaim.

It's likely that these seven thunders are the voices of the seven spirits described in four other places in Revelation.[191] They appear to be universally recognized as holy, uncontestable judges for this contest. They declare that the criteria established by the 7-sealed book have been met, and they call the contest in favor of Jesus. I arrive at this conclusion for the following reasons:

1. This announcement falls at a point in the timeline after Satan tries to violate God's mark of protection on the Jews.

---

[190] ". . . when once the seventh trumpet is about to sound; the angel with his right foot on the sea, and his left on the earth, claims both as God's..." (Bible Hub, "Revelation 10:2," Jamieson-Fausset-Brown Bible Commentary, biblehub.com, https://biblehub.com/commentaries/revelation/10-2.htm).

[191] Revelation 1:4, 3:1, 4:5, and 5:6

2. The angel proclaims, *"there would be no more delay,"* which means that there is no reason to continue the contest. In other words, there is a clear winner or there is a clear violator.

3. Daniel tells us 600 years before John that a court will make a judgment and rule against the antichrist after *"time, times, and half a time,"* which is a reference to the 3½ year duration of the Great Tribulation:

> *25 He* [the antichrist] *shall speak words against the Most High, and shall wear out the saints of the Most High, and shall think to change the times and the law; and they shall be given into his hand for a time, times, and half a time. 26 But the court shall sit in judgment, and his dominion shall be taken away, to be consumed and destroyed to the end.* (Daniel 7:25–26 ESV)

John just revealed that the the seven thunders are the same as the court in Daniel's prophecy. The seven thunders will perform the role of impartial judges who sit in judgment over the contest from their *"court,"* as Daniel outlines. What's more, this judgment occurs exactly when Daniel predicted, which is right after God's mighty angel makes his entrance. This is yet another indication that the *trumpet-attack/bowl-countermeasure theory* timing is still working perfectly.

4. The angel concludes by proclaiming in Revelation 12:7, *"But that in the days of the trumpet call to be sounded by the seventh angel, the mystery of God would be fulfilled."* Since the 6th trumpet has already sounded, the 7th is coming very soon, and we know the 7th trumpet announces Jesus' arrival. Thus, this angel just confirmed that Jesus will soon be declared

king (the victor of the contest), which aligns with the passage in Daniel that tells us that Satan's *"dominion shall be taken away."* Daniel also gives us insight into this court's eventual ruling that God will soon award Jesus, the *"son of man. . . an everlasting dominion."*

> *13 I saw in the night visions, and behold, with the clouds of heaven there came one like a son of man, and he came to the Ancient of Days and was presented before him. 14 And to him was given dominion and glory and a kingdom, that all peoples, nations, and languages should serve him; his dominion is an everlasting dominion, which shall not pass away, and his kingdom one that shall not be destroyed.* (Daniel 7:13–14 ESV)

Even though we're not told everything that the mighty angel says, the four reasons above effectively confirm that he proclaims that the contest has been decided in favor of Jesus. It's officially over, and the seven thunders, serving as a heavenly panel of judges for this cosmic contest, unanimously affirm that the mighty angel's pronouncement from God was a fair and just decision. The *"little scroll"* in the hand of the giant angel is likely the official title deed to the kingdoms of the world.

However, and this is an important detail, the angel also mentions that there will still be a few more *"days"* before the 7th trumpet sounds and God officially transfers the kingdom to Jesus.[192]

---

[192] *"In the days"* indicates it will not happen right now, but some number of days in the future. Revelation 10:7 ESV *"but that in the days of the trumpet call to be sounded by the seventh angel, the mystery of God would be fulfilled, just as he announced to his servants the prophets."*

*. . . there would be no more delay, 7 but that in the days of the trumpet call to be sounded by the seventh angel, the mystery of God would be fulfilled.* (Revelation 10:6b-7a ESV)

When the giant angel ascends, the supernatural timeout on earth is lifted, but only for a few more days. In the next chapter, we'll see that Satan will make desperate use of those final "*days.*"

## 21.1 Satan's Final Move: "Now, I am Become Death, the Destroyer of… Earth"

*But woe to you, O earth and sea, for the devil has come down to you in great wrath, because he knows that his time is short!* (Revelation 12:12b ESV)

Though chapter 12 in Revelation comes two chapters after the seven thunders declare Jesus the victor, it's further evidence that John's writing pattern is not linear.

Every intricate plan Satan laid has collapsed in utter failure. His long-schemed plan to rally an angelic uprising in heaven backfired so disastrously that, instead of *"ascending to heaven,"* he lost access to it entirely. His secretive plot to eliminate the 144,000 Jews was thwarted when the earth itself rose against him, diverting the deadly flood meant to destroy them. Now, the 7 Thunders have pronounced his defeat in the second half of the cosmic contest laid out in the 7-sealed book. With thousands of years of plotting and preparation unraveling to nothing, Satan sees the writing on the wall and switches to instinctive survival mode, gripped by the realization that he has, at most, a couple of days before the 7th trumpet sounds and God's angels arrive to chain him.[193] [194] Backed

---

[193] Daniel 5:13-31 describes a chilling incident when fingers appeared and wrote a prophecy on the wall in king Belshazzar's banquet room Babylon. Daniel was called out of retirement to interpret the strange writing and here is a portion of that: *"Then from his presence the hand was sent, and this writing was inscribed. 25 And this is the writing that was inscribed: MENE, MENE, TEKEL, and PARSIN. 26 This is the interpretation of the matter: MENE, God has numbered the days of your kingdom and brought it to an end;"*

[194] *"1 Then I saw an angel coming down from heaven, holding in his hand the key to the bottomless pit and a great chain. 2 And he seized the dragon, that ancient serpent, who is the devil and Satan, and bound him for a thousand years, 3 and threw him*

into a corner like a trapped animal, he is consumed with fury and desperation, frantically searching for any escape from the fate closing in around him.

The only option Satan sees is a completely radical one: to destroy the earth entirely, taking the 144,000 hidden Jews down with it. This would leave God without a Jewish remnant and no place to establish the thousand-year reign of Jesus, so Satan goes all in, betting everything on the astronomically long odds that this will force God to cancel the contest. Even if God doesn't cancel it, Satan knows that he and his demons are immortal. Although, with the earth destroyed, they might drift through space for ages, it's still a far better fate than the lake of fire awaiting them if they do nothing.[195] It would be a Pyrrhic victory, but it would buy them the one thing he is completely out of: time.[196]

Satan, through his antichrist and his frog-like demons, now frantically works to convince the commanders of allied nations to unleash their most powerful weapons on the earth itself, targeting a specific fault line. Each leader believes they are acting alone, unaware that the antichrist is simultaneously persuading other leaders to deploy their own doomsday weapons in the same way

---

*into the pit, and shut it and sealed it over him, so that he might not deceive the nations any longer, until the thousand years were ended."* (Revelation 20:1–3 ESV).

[195] Satan and his demons are immortal, which is why a special place, the lake of fire, had to be made to hold them and punish them: *"Then shall he say also unto them on the left hand, Depart from me, ye cursed, into everlasting fire, prepared for the devil and his angels"* (Matthew 25:41 KJV). Sheol is somewhere inside the earth, as was demonstrated when the God judged Korah, Dathan, and Abiram for challenging Moses' authority and had the earth swallow them and their tents and families, delivering them alive to Sheol inside the earth: *"But if the LORD creates something new, and the ground opens its mouth and swallows them up with all that belongs to them, and they go down alive into Sheol, then you shall know that these men have despised the LORD."* (Numbers 16:30 ESV).

[196] A Pyrrhic victory is a victory, but one with such enormous losses that it becomes questionable whether it was worth it

on the exact same coordinates. If they knew, they'd likely refuse to participate in such a suicidal plan.

Thus, Satan begins his final, desperate attempt to destroy the earth and comes alarmingly close to total annihilation. But once again, God intervenes, ensuring his ultimate plan stays on course.

*When the earth totters, and all its inhabitants, it is I who keep steady its pillars. Selah.* (Psalm 75:3 ESV)

Before Satan and his allies reach the tipping point of destruction, when their weapons are mere moments away from their target and about to destroy the world, God intervenes, bringing a sudden end ("*cut short*") to Satan's attempt and concluding the Great Tribulation a few days earlier than the full 3 ½ years.

As further evidence that the antichrist's weapons are within seconds of reaching their target and achieving his desperate goal of complete and total annihilation of the earth, Jesus said that if he did not "*cut short*" the days of the Great Tribulation, no human would survive.[197] At this critical point in the timeline, Christians are still on earth because the Day of the Lord has not yet occurred. But just when it seems all hope is lost, that Satan's plans have succeeded and the earth is mere seconds away from being destroyed, something extraordinary happens and every eye will see it: God himself steps in.

To protect the plan he ordained, foretold through his prophets, and promised to his people, *"for the sake of his elect,"* God will once again step in to keep his plan from going off track. He will instantly render Satan's doomsday weapons impotent that are mere seconds

---

[197] Christians would be saved one way or another. Jesus is referring to the rest of the humans, those without a mark, who would be destroyed with no opportunity for a second chance in the Millennium.

from destroying the earth and bring the Great Tribulation to an abrupt and decisive end.

> *And if those days had not been* cut short, *no human being would be saved. But for the sake of the elect those days will be cut short.* (Matthew 24:22 ESV)

The military commanders who conspire with Satan and his demons to carry out this doomsday operation will later be called-out on Judgment Day. Those *"destroyers of the earth"* will themselves be destroyed for unleashing these weapons of obliteration.

> *The nations raged, but your wrath came, and the time for the dead to be judged, and for rewarding your servants, the prophets and saints, and those who fear your name, both small and great, and for destroying the destroyers of the earth."* (Revelation 11:18 ESV)

There are many theories about what Matthew meant in chapter 24:22 when he implied that the 3½-year Great Tribulation would be *"cut short."* But now, using this *trumpet-attack/bowl-countermeasure theory* timeline that has been unfolding chapter by chapter, the meaning of this and many other obscure passages become clear. We can now understand not only what they mean, but also why they must happen, and approximately when they occur within the timeline. In the next chapter, we'll witness the spectacular way God will *"cut short"* the Great Tribulation.

# Part Five:

## God Steps In

# 22 Seal 6: "ENOUGH!" All Creation Bows at the Creator's Arrival

*When he opened the sixth seal, I looked, and behold, there was a great earthquake, and the sun became black as sackcloth, the full moon became like blood, 13 and the stars of the sky fell to the earth as the fig tree sheds its winter fruit when shaken by a gale. 14 The sky vanished like a scroll that is being rolled up, and every mountain and island was removed from its place. 15 Then the kings of the earth and the great ones and the generals and the rich and the powerful, and everyone, slave and free, hid themselves in the caves and among the rocks of the mountains, 16 calling to the mountains and rocks, "Fall on us and hide us from the face of him who is seated on the throne, and from the wrath of the Lamb, 17 for the great day of their wrath has come, and who can stand?"* (Revelation 6:12–17 ESV)

When correctly placed in the end-time sequence, as it is here using the *trumpet-attack/bowl-countermeasure theory* timeline, the true purpose of the 6th seal emerges like the final piece of a glorious puzzle: it is not an act of destruction, but an act of salvation! It is God the Creator decisively checkmating, he *"cut short,"* Satan the destroyer. In this breathtaking moment, God makes his appearance in the heavens so that all the world can observe him stepping in to save the earth from annihilation: shattering Satan's lie to Eve that God doesn't truly love humanity.

The 6th seal reveals God's ultimate triumph and infinite love for his entire creation, then portrays creation's breathtaking response as every element rises in its own spectacular way to praise the One who made them! John explains how the heavens and the earth will declare the glory of God and all creation will acknowledge him in total awestruck and celebratory submission in the only way each of the created elements can.

A Psalmist describing what we can now understand is the 6th seal scene, states that the trees will sing for joy and the fields will shout (*"exult"*) before the Lord. It seems so surreal that you may think it's just a writer with a fantastic imagination, but it's no exaggeration. It perfectly describes the physical movements and actions that creation will make when the 6th seal is opened and all of God's handiwork celebrates the arrival of its Lord and creator. As further evidence that this is the 6th seal, the Psalmist adds the critical phrase that it will occur *"before...he comes to judge the earth."* When read in conjunction with the Olivet Discourse framework, it confirms that we have placed the 6th seal precisely in the correct position on the end-times timeline: at the end of the Great Tribulation and before Judgment Day.[198]

> *Worship the LORD in the splendor of holiness; tremble before him, all the earth! 10 Say among the nations, "The LORD reigns! Yes, the world is established; it shall never be moved; he will judge the peoples with equity." 11 Let the heavens be glad, and let the earth*

---

[198] In the Olivet Discourse, Jesus said that: *"Immediately after the tribulation of those days the sun will be darkened, and the moon will not give its light, and the stars will fall from heaven, and the powers of the heavens will be shaken. 30 Then will appear in heaven the sign of the Son of Man, and then all the tribes of the earth will mourn, and they will see the Son of Man coming on the clouds of heaven with power and great glory."* (Matthew 24: 29-30 ESV)

*rejoice; let the sea roar, and all that fills it; 12 let the field exult, and everything in it! Then shall all the trees of the forest sing for joy 13 before the LORD, for he comes, for he comes to judge the earth. He will judge the world in righteousness, and the peoples in his faithfulness.* (Psalm 96:9–13 ESV)

Joel tells us that signs in the sky will foretell the arrival of the Day of the Lord: the sun will grow dark (though not completely extinguished), and the moon will turn the color of blood.

*I will produce portents both in the sky and on the earth--blood, fire, and columns of smoke. 31 The sunlight will be turned to darkness and the moon to the color of blood, before the day of the LORD comes-- that great and terrible day! 32 It will so happen that everyone who calls on the name of the LORD will be delivered. For on Mount Zion and in Jerusalem there will be those who survive, just as the LORD has promised; the remnant will be those whom the LORD will call.* (Joel 2:30–32 NET)

The writer of Hebrews foretold that God would shake not only the earth but also the heavens.

*26 At that time his voice shook the earth, but now he has promised, "Yet once more I will shake not only the earth but also the heavens."* (Hebrews 12:26 ESV)

Isaiah pleaded for God to *"tear apart the sky and come down,"* writing that the mountains would tremble before him:

— 311 —

*If only you would tear apart the sky and come down! The mountains would tremble before you! 2 As when fire ignites dry wood, or fire makes water boil, let your adversaries know who you are, and may the nations shake at your presence!* (Isaiah 64:1–2 NET)

The prophet Nahum let us know that a day will come when the earth and hills and every person and animal will quake at God's presence.

*The mountains quake at him, and the hills are shaken, and the earth recoils at his presence, even the world, and all that dwell in it.*
(Nahum 1:5 Brenton Septuagint Translation)

The prophet Habakkuk foretold that when creation sees the bright light of God's arrival, the mountains would shake, the oceans (*"the deep"*) would shout out, and the sun and moon would stop in their orbits. Yet, if you believed in the three-septet sequence, you would not be able to discern, just by reading the events of the 6th seal, that God is about to appear in the heavens and all creation bows in awe and reverence.

*When the mountains see you, they shake. The torrential downpour sweeps through. The great deep shouts out; it lifts its hands high. 11 The sun and moon stand still in their courses; the flash of your arrows drives them away, the bright light of your lightning-quick spear.*
(Habakkuk 3:10–11 NET)

A song sung in many churches, called "Christ Be Magnified," captures the essence of how each element of creation responds when the 6th Seal is opened.[199] The song suggests that if all of creation could suddenly articulate and express itself, it would praise the Lord in its own unique way, right alongside humans. Here are a few stanzas:

> Were creation suddenly articulate
> With a thousand tongues to lift one cry
> Then from North to South and East to West
> We'd hear Christ be magnified
>
> Were the whole earth echoing His eminence
> His name would burst from sea and sky
> From rivers to the mountain tops
> We'd hear Christ be magnified...
>
> When every creature finds its inmost melody
> And every human heart its native cry
> Oh, then in one enraptured hymn of praise
> We'll sing Christ be magnified

The description of these events makes it unmistakably clear that the 6th seal represents all of God's creation—the sun, moon, earth, seas, sky, and stars—working together in perfect harmony to glorify and praise him. Simultaneously, the earth shakes and compels every human being to bow in reverence, as the God of the universe reveals himself and shows his compassion by saving the world from Satan's attempt to destroy it.

---

[199] Cody Carnes, Cory Asbury, and Ethan Hulse, *Christ Be Magnified*, Cory Asbury Publishing, 2019.

[200] All of mankind is about to see the image of God on his throne as a huge portal in the sky is opened (*"like a scroll that is being rolled up"*). At the bright shining of his light through that opening, every human will instinctively understand with every fiber of their being that they are seeing their creator in all his power and glory, and that something even more spectacular than what they just witnessed is about to take place.

A heavenly ceremony announcing the coronation of Jesus as King of the world is about to take place. It is this assumption of command by Jesus that all of creation has been longing for since Adam forfeited the kingdom to Satan.

> For we know that the whole creation has been groaning together in the pains of childbirth until now. (Romans 8:22 ESV).

Never has there been more pomp and circumstance for a coronation of a king. Creation's tremulous drumroll will direct everyone's attention to the most important declaration in the history of the universe. And there will be no doubt that it is the creator of the world who will make the announcement.

Matthew confirms that we are still following God's intended chronology, and that the 6th seal occurs after the tribulation. He adds a crucial detail: as God appears in the heavens, *"the stars will fall from heaven."* John ties Revelation 6:13 back to this detail, stating, *"the stars of the sky fell to the earth as the fig tree sheds its winter fruit when shaken by a gale."*

---

[200] It seems like Revelation 6:13 ESV, "and the stars of the sky fell to the earth as the fig tree sheds its winter fruit when shaken by a gale", is describing weapons and satellites dropping out of the sky as God cleanses the heavens of manmade space debris before he reveals himself.

These are not literal stars; rather, this represents God supernaturally clearing the skies of satellites, space stations, and space debris because when God appears, he will not share the heavens with anything man has made.

Most significantly, this passage describes the manner in which God intervenes to prevent his creation from spiraling beyond the boundaries he preordained. The phrase *"shaken by a gale"* suggests that God is destroying the space-based weapons or intercontinental missiles the antichrist persuaded the commanders in the previous chapter to launch. In this desperate, last-ditch attempt to annihilate the hidden Jews by destroying the earth, Satan's plan is thwarted as God steps in, shakes the missiles as *"fruit when shaken by a gale,"* and causes them to drop harmlessly to the earth like falling stars before they can cause their intended destruction.

> *Immediately after the tribulation of those days the sun will be darkened, and the moon will not give its light, and the stars will fall from heaven, and the powers of the heavens will be shaken.* (Matthew 24:29 ESV)

Luke also confirms that these wonders in the sky and on earth, the 6th seal events, occur before the Day of the Lord.

> *And I will show wonders in the heavens above and signs on the earth below, blood, and fire, and vapor of smoke; 20 the sun shall be turned to darkness and the moon to blood, before the day of the Lord comes, the great and magnificent day.* (Acts 2:19–20 ESV)

See Exhibit 7 for nine additional reasons why the 6th seal is not destructive. Rather it is when God steps in to his creation to save it from destruction and all creation, from rocks to men, bow to revere and worship him.

And, ominously, all men will soon understand what Jesus meant when he said, *"vengeance is mine."*

> *Beloved, never avenge yourselves, but leave it to the wrath of God, for it is written, "Vengeance is mine, I will repay, says the Lord."* (Romans 12:19 ESV)

The spectacular display of nature's reverence during the 6th seal reaches a crescendo as all doomsday weapons are rendered harmless, and then, as quickly as they began, all of the celestial and earthly actions of praise will cease, and there will be total silence on earth and in heaven for half an hour..

This next verse, which following the 6th seal, tells us that the angels at each of the four corners of the earth have been directed to stop all noise and movement from one end of the earth to the other.t:

> *After this I saw four angels standing at the four corners of the earth, holding back the four winds of the earth, that no wind might blow on earth or sea or against any tree.* (Revelation 7:1 ESV)[201]

At the exact same time, Jesus opens the final seal which directs the silence to apply to heaven too. And we're told it will last for 30 minutes.

---

[201] Verse 7:1 clearly applies to the 6th seal. The fact that it starts a new chapter leads most people to believe it's a new section and new thought, but this is one of the many instances when I think the chapter division has been placed incorrectly. It is one of the few times John uses "after this", which tells us that it occurs immediately after God reveals himself.

# 23 Seal 7: "Shhhh. Be Still and Know that I Am God"

*And when he had opened the seventh seal, there was silence in heaven about the space of half an hour.* (Revelation 8:1 KJV)[202]

To place this in context in the end-time timeline, the 6th seal events have just finished at Revelation 6:17 and the next verse, 7:1, begins with one of those very rare times where John conveys a sequential order: "*After this.*"

---

[202] Many authors assume that the next verse (8:2), which introduces the seven angels with the 7 trumpets, can't commence until the 7th seal is opened, only because the verse comes after 8:1. That blind devotion to following Revelation as though it is a sequential story, is the reason the real order has remained hidden in plain sight for so long.

Strictly from reading this in context, it seems clear that John, in keeping with his normal way of recounting his vision, is *not* telling us that the trumpets must come next. He was just letting us know that the next group of important things he had seen were the seven angels with the 7 trumpets. As usual, he didn't use any words that would indicate a sequence, so he didn't tell us where these 7 trumpets fell in the overall order.

It is for this reason that so many authors have tried to fit every seal, trumpet, and bowl sequentially as three sequential septets. They tie Revelation 8:2 together with 8:1 only because it happens to fall as the next verse. The unquestioning belief that Revelation is written as a story, in order, has forced almost every author and commentator to conclude that none of the 7 trumpets can be sounded until all the seals have been opened. But there is nothing within the context of either 8:1 or 8:2 that would tie them together. The fact that verse 8:2 begins with *kai* [Greek "and"] further indicates that John is just beginning another description of another grouping. He wasn't telling us that 8:2 had to occur after 8:1. It is this confusion which causes the 3 sequential septet fallacy.

*After this I saw four angels standing at the four corners*
*of the earth, holding back the four winds of the earth,*
*that no wind might blow on earth or sea or against*
*any tree.* (Revelation 7:1 ESV)

John is preparing to describe the next event, the opening of
the 7th seal, but then, in keeping with his pattern, breaks from his
sequential narrative to describe the sealing of the 144,000 Jews.[203]
Once he finishes with this aside, he returns to the timeline in
Revelation 8:1 with the 7th seal. This means that verses 7:1 and 8:1
would flow directly in sequence if not for the interjection describing
the144,000. Here's how the 7th seal reads once the aside is removed:

*7:1 After this I saw four angels standing at the four*
*corners of the earth, holding back the four winds of*
*the earth, that no wind might blow on earth or sea*
*or against any tree. 8:1 When the Lamb opened the*
*seventh seal, there was silence in heaven for about half*
*an hour.* (Revelation 7:1 and 8:1 ESV)

Verse 8:1 reveals that a breathtaking, reverential silence will
envelop heaven itself. This means that the upcoming announcement
isn't just for earth this time; it's something the entire host of heaven,
angels and heavenly beings alike, need to witness.

The glorious chorus of praise that erupted after the 6th seal
is suddenly and dramatically halted as the 7th seal is opened. At
that moment, everything across the entire universe falls into a
profound, absolute silence. A silence so intense it can almost be

---

[203] We know this is an aside because the 144,000 are sealed much earlier in the
timeline, at the very beginning of the Great Tribulation. This aside is another
indication that John's account is not sequential.

felt. It's a moment of breathtaking anticipation, a hush signaling that something extraordinary is about to unfold. Zephaniah tells us this is the silence which precedes *"the day of the Lord."*

*Be silent before the Lord GOD! For the day of the LORD is near; the LORD has prepared a sacrifice and consecrated his guests.* (Zephaniah 1:7 ESV)

This is the supernatural hush before the great announcement, the moment the 7th trumpet sounds, declaring the Day of the Lord has come.[204] You may have read over verses 7:1 and 8:1 quickly, as I have many times, but pause for a moment and consider what total silence truly means. Every power plant will stop. Every vehicle and electronic device will go dead. Leaves will no longer rustle, waves will cease, and every body of water will become as smooth as glass. Rivers will stop flowing, waterfalls will stand still, and even the breeze will rest.

Humans and animals, still prostrate from the 6th seal, will remain frozen in place, and not even the smallest mosquito will take flight.[205] God will bring about a silence so complete that, just as he will soon cause every knee to bow at the sound of the 7th trumpet, he will quiet every breath, every heartbeat, until not the faintest sound is heard. No one will speak, nor could they even if they wanted to, for God has decreed this profound half-hour of silence within his 7-sealed book. The 7th seal depicts everything in the universe holding its breath, reverently acknowledging the

---

[204] The only other place in the Bible where "great hush," or Greek *sigē*, is used is in Acts 21:40 ESV: "And when he had given him permission, Paul, standing on the steps, motioned with his hand to the people. And when there was a great hush, he addressed them in the Hebrew language, saying. . ."

[205] I think that everything that makes noise will pause, including mosquitos, waves crashing, water boiling, etc.

presence of their creator, held in suspense in anticipation of a holy proclamation.

> *Come, behold the works of the LORD, how he has brought desolations on the earth. 9 He makes wars cease to the end of the earth; he breaks the bow and shatters the spear; he burns the chariots with fire. 10 "Be still, and know that I am God. I will be exalted among the nations, I will be exalted in the earth!"* (Psalm 46:8–10 ESV)

Thirty minutes of total, unnatural silence will feel like an eternity to the wicked and unsaved, who will be powerless to escape the rising terror that has gripped their minds since they got a glimpse of God's power and majesty at the 6th seal. Unlike when they sat in liquid darkness during the 5th bowl, when they could at least hear others nearby and commiserate about the pain of their oozing sores, the absolute silence imposed by this 7th seal won't allow them to move, speak, or share the horror of what they are experiencing. For the wicked, that half-hour will leave them utterly alone, isolated, and terrified. The silence will haunt them, forcing them to relive every bad deed they've ever done and imagine the punishment awaiting them.

But knowledgeable Christians, those who expected this and know what is coming next, will hardly be able to contain their joy and excitement!

> *Now when these things* [the 6th seal events] *begin to take place, straighten up and raise your heads, because your redemption is drawing near."* (Luke 21:28 ESV)

*And now, little children, remain in him, so that when he appears we may have confidence and not shrink away from him in shame when he comes back.* (1 John 2:28 NET)

Knowledgeable Christians will understand that the 6th seal filled the world with awe as they witnessed an aspect of the majesty and power of God, while the 7th seal, the thirty minutes of utter silence, heightened the anticipation for a proclamation with eternal consequences for "*everyone in heaven or on earth or under the earth.*"

At the end of this sacred half-hour, the silence will be pierced by the triumphant sound of the 7th trumpet.[206] This final trumpet blast, the magnificent third woe, will resound alongside powerful voices from heaven, proclaiming to all the world that Jesus has been declared victorious by the court of the 7 Thunders. Now, at last, Jesus is being installed as the rightful King of the World!

For Christians, it will be a moment of unimaginable joy, for their Savior and Redeemer, Jesus, is coming swiftly!

For those branded with the mark of the beast, this third woe will be a nightmare beyond imagining, for Jesus is returning, and he's coming for them in relentless fury, unleashing the long-foretold Wrath of God. Neither the antichrist, his legions, nor anyone bearing the mark will survive the annihilation this final woe will bring.

---

[206] While the first 6 trumpets each signaled deprivation and destruction was on its way, the 7th trumpet signals the final buzzer of the match, but only for Christians. They have kept the faith and been refined by the fiery trials of the Great Tribulation and now Jesus will take them to heaven. But for those who took the mark or joined forces against him, what comes next for them is the "Woe, Woe, Woe" which the angel warned about.

# 24 Trumpet #7: The Second Coming of Jesus in Two Stages: Air and Ground

*Then the seventh angel blew his trumpet, and there were loud voices in heaven, saying, "The kingdom of the world has become the kingdom of our Lord and of his Christ, and he shall reign forever and ever." 16 And the twenty-four elders who sit on their thrones before God fell on their faces and worshiped God, 17 saying, "We give thanks to you, Lord God Almighty, who is and who was, for you have taken your great power and begun to reign. 18 The nations raged, but your wrath came, and the time for the dead to be judged, and for rewarding your servants, the prophets and saints, and those who fear your name, both small and great, and for destroying the destroyers of the earth." 19 Then God's temple in heaven was opened, and the ark of his covenant was seen within his temple. There were flashes of lightning, rumblings, peals of thunder, an earthquake, and heavy hail.* (Revelation 11:15–19 ESV)

The angel of the 7th trumpet announces something like this: "stand by for the most important message in history." There is no confusion about this message in Scripture.[207] At the blowing of the

---

[207] Many commentators and denominations who subscribe to a specific tribulation theory discount the 7th trumpet. To make their theory work they say that the 7th trumpet is not the last trumpet and that there is at least one additional trumpet. Scripture does not support this argument, as you'll see in the next few sections. Prophets prior to John referred to the "last" or "final" trumpet because they had no indication of the total number of trumpets there would be until John revealed his vision in Revelation. Once John revealed there would be 7 trum-

7th trumpet, loud voices in heaven proclaim that Jesus is the victor of the second half of this contest, and everyone in the universe will hear it! Having triumphed in both the first half and the second half of the contest, those voices declare, *"The kingdom of the world has become the kingdom of our Lord and of his Christ and he shall reign for ever and ever."* The war for souls is over and Jesus is now officially declared King of Kings!

Since this proclamation is preceded by 30 minutes of complete silence, every ear will be fully attuned, unable to miss the most profound declaration ever uttered. Heaven and Christians will burst into joyous celebration, while Satan, along with his pride, will be utterly crushed!

> *And I will put enmity between you and the woman, and between your offspring and hers; he will crush your head, and you will strike his heel.* (Genesis 3:15 NIV)

During the 6th seal, Satan, his demons, and the antichrist had to bow down (*"every knee should bow"*) at the presence of God along with everyone else. Then, they were immediately compelled to observe 30 minutes of total silence during the 7th seal. Imagine how humiliating this announcement that Jesus is King of the World will be for Satan. There is no passing of the royal baton from the old king to the new king and no royal change-of-command ceremony that would show respect for the former king. Satan is completely ignored in the proclamation and is just suddenly and unceremoniously dethroned and, to add to the insult, he must now

---

pets, it became clear that the final or last trumpet is the 7th. God is a God of order. An 8th trumpet would introduce disorder and would cause confusion in the prophecies.

> *For if the trumpet give an uncertain sound, who shall prepare himself to the battle?* (1 Corinthians 14:8 KJV)

pay homage to Jesus and bow down and confess that Jesus is now the King of the Earth.

> *Therefore God has highly exalted him and bestowed on him the name that is above every name, 10 so that at the name of Jesus every knee should bow, in heaven and on earth and under the earth, 11 and every tongue confess that Jesus Christ is Lord, to the glory of God the Father.* (Philippians 2:9–11 ESV)

This is the long-awaited Day of the Lord. Jesus is crowned King, and so much must unfold that this day will extend far beyond 24 hours. God will make this extraordinary day last as long as necessary. Isaiah even suggests that this *"day of vengeance"* could span an entire year.

> *For the day of vengeance was in my heart, and my year of redemption had come.* (Isaiah 63:4 ESV)

# 25 Trumpet 7 Stage One: In the Air

Jesus will return to earth in exactly the manner the angels told the disciples he would: on a cloud.

> *And when he had said these things, as they were looking on, he was lifted up, and a cloud took him out of their sight. 10 And while they were gazing into heaven as he went, behold, two men stood by them in white robes, 11 and said, "Men of Galilee, why do you stand looking into heaven? This Jesus, who was taken up from you into heaven, will come in the same way as you saw him go into heaven."* (Acts 1:9–11 ESV)

As Jesus descends through that cloud-covered day of darkness, there will be no missing his arrival. Jesus told us there would be no excuse to fall for a fake Jesus. We would know it was him because his very presence will illuminate the whole world with unimaginable brightness!

> *For as the lightning comes from the east and shines as far as the west, so will be the coming of the Son of Man.* (Matthew 24:27 ESV)

When Jesus ascended to heaven in a cloud as a resurrected man 2,000 years ago, he did so as the victor of the first half of the contest, having made *"the way"* for believers to one day follow him there.

*Jesus said to him, "I am the way, and the truth, and the life. No one comes to the Father except through me."* (John 14:6 ESV)

Now that glorious, long-awaited day has arrived! As he descends toward the earth on a cloud, the golden crown on his head proclaims to the world that he is the victor of the second half of the contest. And absolutely every eye in the world will see this glorious arrival.

*Behold, he is coming with the clouds, and every eye will see him, even those who pierced him, and all tribes of the earth will wail on account of him. Even so. Amen. (Revelation 1:7 ESV)*

Yet, there is something so vital and urgent that he cannot wait even a second longer to act. So he swiftly carries out this long-awaited deed even before his feet touch the ground.

# 25.1 The First Harvest: Jesus Brings in the Sheaves

What is so pressing that it cannot wait until he arrives on earth? His deep longing to gather the souls of all who belong to him and send them, escorted by angels, to the rooms he has prepared for them in heaven!

> ... so *Christ, having been offered once to bear the sins of many, will appear a second time, not to deal with sin but to save those who are eagerly waiting for him.* (Hebrews 9:28 ESV)

With his newly won authority as King, he acts immediately, during the brief moments of his descent from heaven, completing his urgent task before he steps foot on earth.

John tells us Jesus' first royal act, the First Harvest, will unfold in two rapid but distinct phases.

Phase one: releasing the souls of believers held captive in Sheol by the now-dethroned king, Satan. Some of these souls have been waiting in Paradise for this moment since Adam originally sinned.

Phase two: the gathering of believers who survived the Great Tribulation and are still alive on earth.

Here is the specific language used to describe this First Harvest:

> *Then I looked, and behold, a white cloud, and seated on the cloud one like a son of man, with a golden crown on his head, and a sharp sickle in his hand.*[208]

---

[208] For those who think that this "*son of man*" is just an angel and can't be Jesus because Jesus wouldn't take orders from an angel, observe that this angel had just emerged from the temple. He was not giving an order to Jesus; he was relaying

*15 And another angel came out of the temple, calling with a loud voice to him who sat on the cloud, "Put in your sickle, and reap, for the hour to reap has come, for the harvest of the earth is fully ripe." 16 So he who sat on the cloud swung his sickle across the earth, and the earth was reaped.* (Revelation 14:14–16 ESV)

Paul explains this act in terms of "firstfruits," a farming metaphor that signifies the first and best of the harvest. By dying sinless on the cross, descending to Sheol, and rising to heaven, Jesus became the firstfruits, making the way for believers to follow him *"at his coming."* Now, at Jesus' coming, he reaps his crop, *"those who belong to Christ,"* because the harvest is fully ripe.

*20 But in fact Christ has been raised from the dead, the firstfruits of those who have fallen asleep. 21 For as by a man came death, by a man has come also the resurrection of the dead. 22 For as in Adam all die, so also in Christ shall all be made alive. 23 But each in his own order: Christ the firstfruits, then at his coming those who belong to Christ. 24 Then comes the end, when he delivers the kingdom to God the Father after destroying every rule and every authority and power.* (1 Corinthians 15:20–24 ESV)

an order which he had just received as part of his duties serving God. It was God inside the temple who gave the order.

## 25.1 (A) First Harvest Phase One: Dead Christians Released to Meet the Lord in the Air

Phase one: Now that he's been proclaimed King of the Earth, Jesus' first act will be to command Satan to free the dead in Christ that he has been holding captive. As Jesus descends from heaven, he will command an archangel to shout the order to release the believers from Sheol. This will happen as the 7th trumpet sounds.

> *For this we declare to you by a word from the Lord, that we who are alive, who are left until the coming of the Lord, will not precede those who have fallen asleep. 16 For the Lord himself will descend from heaven with a cry of command, with the voice of an archangel, and with the sound of the trumpet of God. And the dead in Christ will rise first.* (1 Thessalonians 4:15–16 ESV)

Jesus is making good on the promise that all believers who have died before this time would not be forgotten and would one day be released from the Paradise section of Sheol.

> *For you will not abandon my soul to Sheol, or let your holy one see corruption.* (Psalm 16:10 ESV)

The Psalmists, for example, looked forward to the day when Jesus would raise them from Sheol.

> *But God will rescue my life from the power of Sheol; certainly he will pull me to safety. (Selah)*
> (Psalm 49:15 NET)

> *Though you have allowed me to experience much trouble and distress, revive me once again! Bring me up once again from the depths of the earth! 21 Raise me to a position of great honor! Turn and comfort me!* (Psalm 71:20–21 NET)

But Jesus is also fulfilling his own promise to believers that he would one day return and bring them to live with him in the rooms he prepared for them in heaven.

> *In my Father's house are many rooms. If it were not so, would I have told you that I go to prepare a place for you? 3 And if I go and prepare a place for you, I will come again and will take you to myself, that where I am you may be also.* (John 14:2-3 ESV)

If you are still saying to yourself that the Paradise part of Sheol only applied to the Old Testament and that believers today don't go there but instead go directly to heaven, then listen to John. Writing long after Jesus was resurrected, John affirmed that Jesus will not lose track of any believer (in Sheol) and would *"raise them all up at the last day."*

> *Now this is the will of the one who sent me––that I should not lose one person of every one he has given me, but raise them all up at the last day. 40 For this is the will of my Father––for everyone who looks on the Son and believes in him to have eternal life, and I will raise him up at the last day."* (John 6:39–40 NET)

Paul rejoiced with his followers, assuring them that believers who had died (he refers to death as *"sleep"*) would have their souls raised when the last trumpet sounds. Remember, John revealed that what Paul had referred to as the *"last trumpet"* is the 7th trumpet.

> *Now this I say, brethren, that flesh and blood cannot inherit the kingdom of God; neither doth corruption inherit incorruption. 51 Behold, I shew you a mystery; We shall not all sleep, but we shall all be changed, 52 In a moment, in the twinkling of an eye, at the last trump: for the trumpet shall sound, and the dead shall be raised incorruptible, and we shall be changed. 53 For this corruptible must put on incorruption, and this mortal must put on immortality.* (1 Corinthians 15:50–53 KJV)

> *For as in Adam all die, so also in Christ shall all be made alive.* (1 Corinthians 15:22 ESV)

John continues the metaphor often used by Jesus, describing those ready for eternal life as crops ripe for the harvest:

> *Even now the harvest workers are receiving their reward by gathering a harvest that brings eternal life. Then everyone who planted the seed and everyone who harvests the crop will celebrate together.* (John 4:36 Contemporary English Version)

Both phases of the First Harvest will be completed supernaturally fast, *"in the twinkling of an eye."*

*"in a moment, in the twinkling of an eye, at the last trumpet. For the trumpet will sound, and the dead will be raised imperishable, and we shall be changed. (1 Corinthians 15:52 ESV)*

The phrase *"Raised incorruptible"* is quite specific. Many translations use *"imperishable,"* but *"incorruptible"* better captures the essence of John's message. This isn't so much about the body's physical form when it goes to heaven; it's about whether it's clean or unclean according to the Jewish Levitical law. Specifically, human bodies are considered corrupted and, therefore, cannot enter heaven without purification, so God clothes the souls in clean, incorruptible forms as they rise to meet the Lord in the air. As we'll explore in the Judgment Day chapter, those raised in this First Harvest will undergo their final transformation at that time.

## 25.1 (B) First Harvest Phase Two: Christian Survivors Meet the Lord in the Air

Phase two: The souls of the Christians who survived up to this point will also be harvested. They will be raised up and clothed with their incorruptible bodies to meet Jesus, who has remained in a cloud above the earth, waiting to receive them all.[209]

> "...Put in your sickle, and reap, for the hour to reap has come, for the harvest of the earth is fully ripe." (Revelation 15:15b ESV)

What does "fully ripe" mean? John's readers would recognize it as a reference to the "mystery" Paul wrote about a few years earlier.

> For I do not want you to be ignorant of this mystery, brothers and sisters, so that you may not be conceited: A partial hardening has happened to Israel until the full number of the Gentiles has come in. (Romans 11:25 NET)

It means that everyone who will turn to Christ has now done so. As Paul explained, once "the full number of Gentiles" is reached, the harvest is as full and ripe as it will ever be. This "fully ripe" harvest of Christians alive on earth is now ready to be gathered into heaven.

> 1 And he will send out his angels with a loud trumpet call [this is the 7th trumpet, the First Harvest], and they will gather his elect from the four winds, from one end of heaven to the other. (Matthew 24:31 ESV)

---

[209] "waiting" is a relative term. Phase one and phase two are over in "the twinkling of an eye."

*Then we who are alive, who are left, will be caught*
*up together with them in the clouds to meet the Lord*
*in the air, and so we will always be with the Lord.*
(1 Thessalonians 4:17 ESV)

The Bible doesn't specify what happens to our physical bodies once our immortal souls are clothed with an incorruptible form and called up to be with Jesus. The old physical bodies may vaporize, or they may remain where they fall, like the bodies of the two witnesses that lay in the street for three and a half days after their assassination.[210] What we do know is that our earthly bodies cannot enter heaven because nothing unclean can ever enter that sanctified place.

Most of us have heard that those who are brought to heaven in the First Harvest, both the dead and those alive in Christ, will be *"raised incorruptible."*

*in a moment, in the twinkling of an eye, at the last*
*trump: for the trumpet shall sound, and the dead*
*shall be raised incorruptible, and we shall be changed.*
(1 Corinthians 15:52 ESV)

However, here's a profound insight I had never grasped until I carefully arranged all the end-time Scriptures in chronological order: it's not until Judgment Day, specifically during the second resurrection, that they will receive their final, eternal bodies and

---

[210] Revelation 11:7-9 ESV *"And when they have finished their testimony, the beast that rises from the bottomless pit will make war on them and conquer them and kill them, 8 and their dead bodies will lie in the street of the great city that symbolically is called Sodom and Egypt, where their Lord was crucified. 9 For three and a half days some from the peoples and tribes and languages and nations will gaze at their dead bodies and refuse to let them be placed in a tomb,"*

come fully to life.[211] This passage in Isaiah now makes sense in light of this new understanding.

> *But your dead will live, LORD; their bodies will rise--*
> *let those who dwell in the dust wake up and shout for*
> *joy--your dew is like the dew of the morning; the*
> *earth will give birth to her dead. 20 Go, my people,*
> *enter your rooms and shut the doors behind you; hide*
> *yourselves for a little while until his wrath has passed*
> *by. 21 See, the LORD is coming out of his dwelling to*
> *punish the people of the earth for their sins. The earth*
> *will disclose the blood shed on it; the earth will conceal*
> *its slain no longer.* (Isaiah 26:19–21 NIV)

This means that those who have been waiting in Abraham's Bosom (the Paradise section of Sheol) will be *"raised"* into incorruptible bodies during the First Harvest on the Day of the Lord, but they won't fully *"come to life"* just yet.[187] Isaiah describes this by explaining that they will be raised (*"the earth will give birth to the dead"*), but their incorruptible bodies will be somehow incomplete. Their complete resurrection occurs on Judgment Day, during the second resurrection when they will finally come to life and will assemble in an orderly manner before Jesus' throne. This process resembles the stages of Jesus' own resurrection, where his body was not entirely ready to interact with humanity until he ascended to the Father.[212]

---

[211] *(The rest of the dead did not come to life until the thousand years were finished.)* (Revelation 20:5a ESV). *And many of them that sleep in the dust of the earth shall awake, some to everlasting life, and some to shame and everlasting contempt.* (Daniel 12:2 KJV)

[212] "16 Jesus said to her, 'Mary.' She turned and said to him in Aramaic, '*Rabboni*' (which means 'Teacher') 17 Jesus replied, 'Do not touch me, for I have not yet

This means that until Judgment Day, which occurs after *"his wrath has passed by,"* they will remain in their *"rooms"* in the New Jerusalem until the Lord's vengeance (*"his wrath"*) is finished.[213][214][215]

That's a lot to take in, so here's a simple recap: the souls raised and gathered by Jesus at the 7th trumpet are clothed in incorruptible bodies, escorted into the New Jerusalem in the sky, and assigned their rooms. They are then told to wait in their rooms while Jesus takes out his wrath on those who rejected him. Some of the believers may even be selected to ride white horses behind Jesus and witness him take vengeance on those who rejected him and remain alive on earth. Then, on Judgment Day, they will receive their fully complete, immortal bodies and come to life.

The First Harvest is complete, and all believers are rejoicing in heaven, secure in their incorruptible bodies. But for Jesus, the day has only just begun. Once he touches down on earth, he has one more very important thing to do and then he will unleash the Wrath of God.

---

ascended to my Father. Go to my brothers and tell them, 'I am ascending to my Father and your Father, to my God and your God." (John 20:16–17 NET).

[213] Isaiah 26:20 NIV: *Go, my people, enter your rooms and shut the doors behind you; hide yourselves for a little while until his wrath has passed by.*
There may be an implication here that by shutting oneself in a room, that they are not able to yet have the full heaven experience. They may be limited to certain areas or activities of heaven until the Marriage Supper of the Lamb occurs (right after Judgment Day). This is somewhat evident in each of the five scenes depicting humans in heaven, where none of them are shown engaging in activities that most would consider fun or indicative of how Jesus described heaven.

214 John 14:2–3 ESV: *In my Father's house are many rooms. If it were not so, would I have told you that I go to prepare a place for you? 3 And if I go and prepare a place for you, I will come again and will take you to myself, that where I am you may be also."*

[215] The New Jerusalem is heaven. It's where Jesus went to "prepare a place" for us (John 14:3). It will descend to earth after the Millennium.

# Part Six:

# "Woe, Woe, Woe": The Wrath of God Unleashed[216]

---

[216] *"I will get revenge and pay them back at the time their foot slips; for the day of their disaster is near, and the impending judgment is rushing upon them."* (Deuteronomy 32:35 NET) and more specifically, *"Do not avenge yourselves, dear friends, but give place to God's wrath, for it is written, "Vengeance is mine, I will repay," says the Lord."* (Romans 12:19 NET)

# 26 Trumpet 7 Stage Two: On the Ground

At this point, only non-Christians remain on earth, and they are gripped with overwhelming terror. They have just witnessed the spectacular glory of God during the 6th seal, been struck silent for 30 minutes in awe and fear, and then experienced the deafening blast of the 7th trumpet accompanied by blinding flashes of light.[217] The resurrection of the dead in Christ and the gathering of the living believers happened in the blink of an eye, so quickly that it likely passed by unnoticed except for all the newly dead bodies in prisons and homeless camps.

But now they behold something that makes them quake in their shoes: Jesus himself is descending to earth. And yes, every eye, no matter where they are, will somehow witness that glorious yet terrifying moment when his feet touch the ground. It's likely everyone in the world will feel the earth react to Jesus' touch as it splits to form a channel of escape for the Jews. With "*eyes... like a flame of fire*," Jesus comes to execute divine vengeance upon the wicked across the world.[218] He's been patiently waiting for this moment for a couple of thousand years, and it will begin with those still holding their weapons at the battle of Har-Magedon. When he's finished with those, he has targeted a particularly heinous group of people that he's going to personally slice to pieces. When that's through, he'll mount a white horse and turn his attention to annihilating those who took the mark of the beast and will root them out no matter where in the world they try to hide. He has so

---

[217] Matthew 24:27 (ESV): For as the lightning comes from the east and shines as far as the west, so will be the coming of the Son of Man.

[218] Revelation 19:12 (ESV): "His eyes are like a flame of fire, and on his head are many diadems, and he has a name written that no one knows but himself."

much wrath to unleash on so many people that the Day of the Lord will last much longer than 24 hours. From this list of what must be accomplished on that day, it looks like it will last at least weeks.

1. Weather Forecast for the Day of the Lord
2. Jesus leads the Remnant Jews to a Safe Haven to Exclude Them from His Coming Wrath
3. Jesus' Second Harvest: The Grapes of Wrath
   A. Stomping Grapes with a Vengeance
4. Jesus Rides a White Horse Wielding His Sword of Wrath Against:
   B. The Remaining Armies at Har-Magedon
   C. The antichrist and false prophet
   D. Unbelievers with the Mark
   E. Former Believers with the Mark
5. 3rd Time Eavesdropping on Humans in Heaven: Singing the Victory Song of Moses
6. The Great Feast of the Unclean

# 26.1 Weather Forecast for the Day of the Lord

The Day of the Lord will be unlike any other. The sun and moon, still frozen in their orbits from the 6th seal, cast a dim and eerie light over the earth. The moon remains red, an ominous sign of the blood that will soon flow as Jesus carries out the Wrath of God.

As Jesus descends from the air to the ground, Zechariah, Ezekiel, and Amos each describe this day as foreboding, gloomy, cloudy, and dimly lit. Yet, some daylight still shines in the evenings, confirming that the earth's rotation is still affected by the 6th seal. This likely allows Jesus to carry out his terrible vengeance continuously, both day and night, until his work is finished.

> On that day there shall be no light, cold, or frost. 7 And there shall be a unique day, which is known to the LORD, neither day nor night, but at evening time there shall be light. (Zechariah 14:6-7 ESV)

> For the day is near, even the day of the LORD is near, a cloudy day; it shall be the time of the heathen. (Ezekiel 30:3 KJV)

> Woe to you who desire the day of the LORD! Why would you have the day of the LORD? It is darkness, and not light, 19 as if a man fled from a lion, and a bear met him, or went into the house and leaned his hand against the wall, and a serpent bit him. 20 Is not the day of the LORD darkness, and not light, and gloom with no brightness in it? (Amos 5:18–20 ESV)

The Day of the Lord begins with a brief, dazzling moment of blinding brightness and indescribable joy for Christians as they are swept up to heaven instantly. But for those who remain on the earth, there will be no joy and the bright light will be short-lived, as everything is soon enveloped in a heavy, foreboding gloom. The skies will darken, shrouded in thick clouds and deep shadows, *"with no brightness in it."*

The rest of this overcast day is dedicated to divine justice, a reckoning against those who have persecuted Jews and Christians. The antichrist and his army, and all who bear the mark of the beast will be destroyed. For those who have opposed God, what follows will be truly blood curdling and terrifying.

## 26.2 Jesus Shelters the Surviving Jews from His Coming Wrath

Once the believers have met Jesus in the air and are ushered to heaven by his angels, Jesus descends the rest of the way to earth. When his feet come to rest on Mt. Zion, the earth reacts in obedience to his touch. Mt. Zion splits and forms a long valley, which will serve as an escape passage for the Jews who remain in Jerusalem.

> *3 Then the LORD will go out and fight against those nations as when he fights on a day of battle. 4 On that day his feet shall stand on the Mount of Olives that lies before Jerusalem on the east, and the Mount of Olives shall be split in two from east to west by a very wide valley, so that one half of the Mount shall move northward, and the other half southward. 5 And you shall flee to the valley of my mountains, for the valley of the mountains shall reach to Azal. And you shall flee as you fled from the earthquake in the days of Uzziah king of Judah. Then the LORD my God will come, and all the holy ones with him.* (Zechariah 14:3–5 ESV)

Micah tells us the *"valleys will split open"* at his touch, which is how this supernatural valley appears and provides a sheltered avenue through which the remnant of surviving Jews in Jerusalem will make their escape to *"Azal."*[219]

---

[219] *Azal* refers to a town that must have been known during Zechariah's time. Jamieson-Fausset-Brown Commentary says that the newly cleaved valley provides a quick means of egress from Jerusalem, but does not imply it's a specific location

For behold, *the LORD is coming* out of his place, and will come down and tread upon the high places of the earth. 4 And the mountains will melt under him, and the *valleys will split open*, like wax before the fire, like waters poured down a steep place. (Micah 1:4 ESV)

Then the Jews (*"those who pierced him"*) will recognize that Jesus is, and has always been, the Messiah they had been waiting for, and they will instantly regret never accepting him. They will wail and beat their chests in anguish over how blind and ignorant they and their forefathers have been for these past two thousand years.

> *Behold, he is coming with the clouds, and every eye will see him, even those who pierced him, and all tribes of the earth will wail on account of him. Even so. Amen. 8 "I am the Alpha and the Omega," says the Lord God, "who is and who was and who is to come, the Almighty."* (Revelation 1:7–8 ESV)

With the surviving Jews safely sheltered and all believers secure in their rooms in heaven, Jesus will now unleash the wrath he has been holding himself back from during the entire church age. This is personal, and so he will personally carry out the first phase of his wrath: the dreadful Second Harvest.

---

of refuge (Bible Hub, "Zechariah 14:5," biblehub.com, https://biblehub.com/commentaries/zechariah/14-5.htm).

## 26.3 Second Harvest: The Grapes of Wrath: Jesus Avenges His Brothers!

Jesus has been holding back his wrath until the surviving Jews were in a safe place and Christians had been brought to heaven. All believers have been safely removed from the earth to heaven in the First Harvest, including *"the dead in Christ"* from Paradise in Sheol and the Christians who survived the Great Tribulation, *"we who are alive."*[220] This is exactly what Paul said Jesus would do: take us to heaven before he unleashes his coming wrath on the world.

> and to *wait for his Son* from heaven, whom he raised from the dead, Jesus who *delivers us from the wrath to come.* (1 Thessalonians 1:10 ESV)

> For *God has not destined us for wrath,* but to obtain salvation through our Lord Jesus Christ (1 Thessalonians 5:9 ESV)

Behold the Wrath of the Lord. Now the remaining inhabitants of earth will experience what the writer of Hebrews, the prophet Isaiah, and now John warned:

> *It is a dreadful thing to fall into the hands of the living God.* (Hebrews 10:31 NIV)

---

[220] *For the Lord himself will descend from heaven with a cry of command, with the voice of an archangel, and with the sound of the trumpet of God. And the dead in Christ will rise first. 17 Then we who are alive, who are left, will be caught up together with them in the clouds to meet the Lord in the air, and so we will always be with the Lord.* (1 Thessalonians 4:16-17 ESV)

*For behold, the LORD is coming out from his place to punish the inhabitants of the earth for their iniquity.* (Isaiah 26:21 ESV)

*So the angel swung his sickle across the earth and gathered the grape harvest of the earth and threw it into the great winepress of the wrath of God.* (Revelation 14:19 ESV)

This *"wrath of God"* is the wrath that has long been prophesied, the one Christians were promised to be spared from. It will surpass any display of divine wrath the world has ever experienced, far exceeding even the wrath of the last six plagues. This is the moment when Jesus himself fulfills his promise: *"Vengeance is mine."* And what a staggering, awful vengeance it will be!

*Beloved, never avenge yourselves, but leave it to the wrath of God, for it is written, "Vengeance is mine, I will repay, says the Lord."* (Romans 12:19 ESV)

Jesus, now standing alone on the ground outside the city of Jerusalem, begins the gruesome but fully justified Second Harvest. While the First Harvest was a harvest of love, salvation, and homecoming, this Second Harvest is purely of vengeance and wrath. If you've ever wondered why Jesus hasn't punished evil doers sooner, it's because he allowed everyone the freedom to choose. Now, however, decision time is over. Those who freely chose to reject his many overtures to accept the salvation he offers will now reap the consequences of their choice. He no longer needs to hold back, and he won't. Now, he will unleash his full fury.

Here's the Second Harvest Scripture:

> *Then another angel came out of the temple in heaven,
> and he too had a sharp sickle. 18 And another angel
> came out from the altar, the angel who has authority
> over the fire, and he called with a loud voice to the
> one who had the sharp sickle, "Put in your sickle and
> gather the clusters from the vine of the earth, for its
> grapes are ripe." 19 So the angel swung his sickle* [this
> is reference to the Second Harvest] *across the earth
> and gathered the grape harvest of the earth and threw
> it into the great winepress of the wrath of God. 20 And
> the winepress was trodden outside the city, and blood
> flowed from the winepress, as high as a horse's bridle,
> for 1,600 stadia.* (Revelation 14:17–20 ESV)

Up to this point in Revelation, the only physical action we've
seen Jesus take is to hold the 7-sealed book and break open each
seal one by one. With the exception of his two witnesses, it has
been God's angels who have done the physical work of releasing
the bowls, sounding the trumpets, proclaiming his warnings, and
even reaping the believers in the First Harvest and bringing them
to Jesus in the clouds. But this Second Harvest is different; this
time, it's personal. Jesus has been storing up this vengeance (*"I have
long...restrained myself"*), and he will not delegate his vengeance to
an angel or anyone else.

> *The LORD will march forth like a mighty hero; he
> will come out like a warrior, full of fury. He will shout
> his battle cry and crush all his enemies. 14 He will say,
> "I have long been silent; yes, I have restrained myself.*

*But now, like a woman in labor, I will cry and groan and pant.(Isaiah 42:13-14 NLT)*

Isaiah tells us that Jesus has to do this deed alone, it is his day, the Day of the Lord. What this group in the Second Harvest has done is so egregious that Jesus will personally cut them down and stomp them in the winepress in his fury. The physical evidence (*"their lifeblood"*) is *"splattered"* all over his garments.

*Who is this who comes from Edom, in crimsoned garments from Bozrah, he who is splendid in his apparel, marching in the greatness of his strength? "It is I, speaking in righteousness, mighty to save." 2 Why is your apparel red, and your garments like his who treads in the winepress? 3 "I have trodden the winepress alone, and from the peoples no one was with me; I trod them in my anger and trampled them in my wrath; their lifeblood spattered on my garments, and stained all my apparel. 4 For the day of vengeance was in my heart, and my year of redemption had come. 5 I looked, but there was no one to help; I was appalled, but there was no one to uphold; so my own arm brought me salvation, and my wrath upheld me. 6 I trampled down the peoples in my anger; I made them drunk in my wrath, and I poured out their lifeblood on the earth." (Isaiah 63:1–6 ESV)*

I can envision two groups that may qualify for this extreme level of Jesus' personal anger:

1. A people who were particularly heinous and barbaric to the Jews, Christians, or children.
2. Christians who forsook Jesus and took the mark.

Since Jesus is on foot and the winepress is *"outside the city"* of Jerusalem, it must be the first group: people living near Jerusalem who did unspeakable things to the Jews.[221] [222] Zechariah affirms it is the first group.

> And on *that day* I will seek to destroy all the nations
> that come against *Jerusalem. (Zechariah 12:9 ESV)*

Jesus is coming for the nations surrounding Jerusalem who abused and killed his people, and he is holding nothing back.

> For my sword has drunk its fill in the heavens; behold,
> it descends for *judgment upon Edom,* upon the people
> *I have devoted to destruction.* (Isaiah 34:5 ESV) [223] [224]

Jesus will swing the sword himself and cut down this vile group of people, much like the Jews in the Book of Esther cut down the Persians whom the vile Haman, advisor to King Xerxes, had

---

[221] Revelation 14:20

[222] Behavior such as that of the Hamas of Gaza, who raped Israeli women and young girls until it killed them on October 7, 2023, would definitely merit this personal wrath of Jesus. And that is just a foretaste of what the Jews who live near Jerusalem will experience when the covenant is broken, so the anger of Jesus could certainly be directed toward those abusers.

[223] Jesus' sword drank its fill in the heavens. This may be a reference to the very recent war in heaven. If it is, it implies that Jesus fought alongside his loyal angels as they battled to put down the rebellion of Satan and his traitorous angels.

[224] Edom is the general area east of Jerusalem, which includes Jordan (Joel Richardson, *Mideast Beast*, 18).

incited to exterminate them.[225] None of these wicked people stand a chance against the wrath of Jesus, who will completely annihilate those who had tortured, imprisoned, or killed the Jews before and during the Great Tribulation.

When viewed through the lens of the *trumpet-attack/bowl-countermeasure theory* timeline, it becomes clear that God's wrath was not demonstrated through the seals, trumpets, or bowls. With this new timeline, it is now unmistakable that the Wrath of God, Jesus' vengeance, occurs at the Second Harvest, when Jesus cuts down the *"grapes"* of his wrath.

> *...for the great day of their wrath has come, and who can stand?"* (Revelation 6:17 ESV)

> *Vengeance is Mine, and retribution, In due time their foot will slip; For the day of their disaster is at hand, And their doom hurries to meet them.*
> (Deuteronomy 32:35 Amplified)

> *... when I whet my flashing sword, and my hand takes hold on judgment; I will take vengeance on my adversaries, and will repay those who hate me. 42 I will make my arrows drunk with blood, and my sword shall devour flesh- with the blood of the slain and the captives, from the long-haired enemy. 43 Praise, O heavens, his people, worship him, all you gods! For he will avenge the blood of his children, and take vengeance on his adversaries; he will repay those*

---

[225] "Now the rest of the Jews who were in the king's provinces also gathered to defend their lives, and got relief from their enemies and killed 75,000 of those who hated them, but they laid no hands on the plunder" (Esther 9:16).

*who hate him, and cleanse the land for his people.*
(Deuteronomy 32:41–43 NRSV)

*For we know him who said, "Vengeance is mine; I will repay." And again, "The Lord will judge his people."* (Hebrews 10:30 ESV)

*Beloved, never avenge yourselves, but leave it to the wrath of God, for it is written, "Vengeance is mine, I will repay, says the Lord."* (Romans 12:19 ESV)

*"The hand of our God is for good on all who seek him, and the power of his wrath is against all who forsake him."* (Ezra 8:22b ESV)

Joel chapter 3 ties beautifully to John's description of the Second Harvest. In just a few verses, Joel summarizes the Day of the Lord: nations are gathered to fight, Jesus provides shelter for the Jewish survivors during the harvest (creating a valley, according to Zechariah 14:5), the day is dark after the 6th seal events shake the heavens and the earth, and Jesus personally oversees the Second Harvest, the harvest of the grapes of his wrath.

*11 Hasten and come, all you surrounding nations, and gather yourselves there. Bring down your warriors, O LORD. 12 Let the nations stir themselves up and come up to the Valley of Jehoshaphat; for there I will sit to judge all the surrounding nations. 13 Put in the sickle, for the harvest is ripe. Go in, tread, for the winepress is full. The vats overflow, for their evil is great.* (Joel 3:11–13 ESV)

*15 The sun and the moon are darkened, and the stars withdraw their shining. 16 The LORD roars from Zion, and utters his voice from Jerusalem, and the heavens and the earth quake. But the LORD is a refuge to his people, a stronghold to the people of Israel. (Joel 3:15-16 ESV)*

By an improvident choice of words, modern translators of verse 14 left us with the mistaken impression that people may still be able make a decision to accept Jesus Christ, "*in the valley of decision.*"

*14 Multitudes, multitudes, in the valley of decision! For the day of the LORD is near in the valley of decision.* (Joel 3:14 ESV)

Modern translators selected the word *decision* over more contextually fitting meanings of the Hebrew word *charuwts*, which can also mean a threshing or cutting instrument.[226]

*Valley of decision* implies that there is a choice or decision to be made by someone in this valley. But when read in context, it's clearly too late to decide to follow Christ. The Hebrew word *charuwts* can mean "strict decision," but its other meaning, threshing or sharp cutting instrument, makes much more sense in the context of Jesus using a sword to harvest these heinous sinners. Interestingly, it was translated more precisely as *threshing* in one of the earliest English translations from 1587.

---

[226] *Charuwts* was translating as "threshing sledge" or "threshing instrument" in Isaiah 41:15 & 28:27, Amos 1:3, and Job 41:22 (Bible Hub, s.v. "2742. charuwts," Strong's Concordance, biblehub.com, https://biblehub.com/hebrew/2742.htm).

*O multitude, O multitude, come into the valley of threshing: for the day of the Lorde is neere in the valley of threshing.* (Joel 3:14 Geneva Bible of 1587)

It was also translated well in the Catholic Public Domain Bible, which provides a more literal translation:

*Nations, nations in the valley of being cut to pieces: for the day of the Lord fittingly takes place in the valley of being cut to pieces.* (Joel 3:14 Catholic Public Domain Bible)

There is simply no decision that can be made once the Day of the Lord begins; by then, it's far too late. The Lord himself will be wielding his sword of righteousness to *"thresh"* this group of people *"to pieces,"* with no opportunity for last-minute repentance. And consider this: the very valley where Jesus is cutting down these oppressors will soon, as we learn in the next chapter, be flooded, not with water but with blood, rising to the height of a horse's bridle. Does that sound like Jesus is offering people an opportunity to repent, or does it sound like he is wielding his sword in vengeance to cut down those who barbarically abused his brothers?

This is not a cordial harvest with Jesus carefully placing the grapes into the winepress. Revelation 14:19 says Jesus *"threw"* the harvest into the great winepress. Which means he's doing it with righteous indignation, much like when he whipped the money changers in the temple.[227]

---

[227] "And making a whip of cords, he drove them all out of the temple, with the sheep and oxen. And he poured out the coins of the money-changers and overturned their tables" (John 2:15).

## 26.3 (A) Stomping Grapes with a Vengeance

Once this harvest of rotten grapes is cut with his sickle, Jesus throws their flesh into the great winepress of God's wrath. He throws in so many bodies that the wine vats overflow and blood runs about five feet deep for a length of about 150 miles.[228]

> *And the winepress was trodden outside the city, and blood flowed from the winepress, as high as a horse's bridle, for 1,600 stadia.* (Revelation 14:20 ESV)

This measurement is very specific. If it seems like a five-foot-deep valley over a hundred and fifty miles long filled with blood of those slain by Jesus is a wild exaggeration, Isaiah provides the explanation: the earth will no longer soak up the blood of the dead but instead *"will display the blood"* for all to see.

> *For look, the LORD is coming out of the place where he lives, to punish the sin of those who live on the earth. The earth will display the blood shed on it; it will no longer cover up its slain.* (Isaiah 26:21 NET)

There will be no survivors left when Jesus is finished with his personal vendetta against the people of the countries surrounding Israel who abused the Jews at every opportunity.

---

[228] 1,600 stadia = 252 Km = 156 miles (convertunits.com, "Convert stadion to mile," https://www.convertunits.com/from/stadia/to/miles)

*Your warriors will be shattered, O Teman, so that everyone will be destroyed from Esau's mountain! 10 "Because you violently slaughtered your relatives, the people of Jacob, shame will cover you, and you will be destroyed forever. 11 You stood aloof while strangers took his army captive, and foreigners advanced to his gates. When they cast lots over Jerusalem, you behaved as though you were in league with them. 12 You should not have gloated when your relatives suffered calamity. You should not have rejoiced over the people of Judah when they were destroyed. You should not have boasted when they suffered adversity. 13 You should not have entered the city of my people when they experienced distress. You should not have joined in gloating over their misfortune when they suffered distress. You should not have looted their wealth when they endured distress. 14 You should not have stood at the fork in the road to slaughter those trying to escape. You should not have captured their refugees when they suffered adversity. 15 "For the day of the LORD is approaching for all the nations! Just as you have done, so it will be done to you. You will get exactly what your deeds deserve. 16 For just as you have drunk on my holy mountain, so all the nations will drink continually. They will drink, and they will gulp down; they will be as though they had never been.* (Obadiah 1:9–16 NET)

We're not told how Jesus will make the transition from walking on foot, personally treading the winepress filled with those who tortured and killed the Jews, to mounting his white horse to bring retribution on everyone who took the mark, no matter where in the world they are located. However, at some point, he mounts his white horse and does so without returning to heaven.[229]

---

[229] Heaven is immaculate and pure, and I can't imagine that Jesus would return to heaven splattered in the blood of evil people and not first cleanse himself in the same way Levitical priests must first cleanse themselves before they enter in to the Holy of Holies in the temple (Isaiah 63:2-3). We know his clothes are unclean because he is still wearing the same blood-stained clothes when we see him on the white horse in Revelation 19:13.

# 26.4 Jesus Rides a White Horse Unleashing His Vengeance on Those with the Mark

> *Then I saw heaven opened, and behold, a white horse!*
> *The one sitting on it is called Faithful and True, and in*
> *righteousness he judges and makes war. 12 His eyes are*
> *like a flame of fire, and on his head are many diadems,*
> *and he has a name written that no one knows but*
> *himself. 13 He is clothed in a robe dipped in blood, and*
> *the name by which he is called is The word of God.*
> (Revelation 19:11–13 ESV)

This is the royal arrival on the white horse that the antichrist was trying to impersonate when the 1st seal was opened. It's also the portion of the Day of the Lord that takes the longest amount of time.

One possibility of how Jesus transitions from the Second Harvest to riding his white horse is that the heavenly host comes down from heaven to meet Jesus. That group would be holding the reigns of Jesus' horse in a manner reminiscent of when Jesus sent two disciples to untie a colt and bring it to him to ride into Jerusalem.[230]

We know that Jesus does not change his garments after taking out his vengeance during the Second Harvest because they are still

---

[230] *"Now when they drew near to Jerusalem, to Bethphage and Bethany, at the Mount of Olives, Jesus sent two of his disciples 2 and said to them, "Go into the village in front of you, and immediately as you enter it you will find a colt tied, on which no one has ever sat. Untie it and bring it. 3 If anyone says to you, 'Why are you doing this?' say, 'The Lord has need of it and will send it back here immediately.'" 4 And they went away and found a colt tied at a door outside in the street, and they untied it. 5 And some of those standing there said to them, "What are you doing, untying the colt?" 6 And they told them what Jesus had said, and they let them go. 7 And they brought the colt to Jesus and threw their cloaks on it, and he sat on it"* (Mark 11:1–7 ESV).

stained with blood when we see him riding on a white horse with his *"holy ones"* trailing behind him on their own white horses. He's still wearing the same white robe splattered with blood. This blood is not his own.[231] There's no need for Jesus to change his garments because he still has much more wrath to unleash.

> *Then the LORD my God will come, and all the holy ones with him.* (Zechariah 14:5b ESV)

> *14 And the armies of heaven, arrayed in fine linen, white and pure, were following him on white horses. 15 From his mouth comes a sharp sword with which to strike down the nations...* (Revelation 19:14–15a ESV)

---

[231] Joel Richardson, *Mideast Beast*, p.

## 26.4 (A) Jesus' Sword of Wrath Against Remaining Troops

Jesus doesn't perform this next task alone as he did during the Second Harvest. For this task he begins working with the surviving Jews to destroy what remains of the antichrist's army that had been fighting at Har-Magedon. Isaiah seems to indicate that the Jews will "*thresh*" and "*winnow*" the mountains and the hills, which are metaphors for their enemies' kingdoms, and the Lord will help.[232]

> . . . 14 Don't be afraid, despised insignificant Jacob, men of Israel. I am helping you," says the LORD, your protector, the Holy One of Israel. 15 "Look, I am making you like a sharp threshing sledge, new and double-edged. You will thresh the mountains and crush them; you will make the hills like straw. 16 You will winnow them and the wind will blow them away; the wind will scatter them. You will rejoice in the LORD; you will boast in the Holy One of Israel. (Isaiah 41:14–16 NET)

The Jewish soldiers fighting alongside Jesus will have plenty of light, but those fighting against him (the wicked) will be left in gloomy darkness. These Jewish soldiers will immediately recognize this as the same way God protected their ancestors during their

---

[232] "Just like such a threshing machine would Israel thresh and grind to powder from that time forth both mountains and hills. This is evidently a figurative expression for proud and mighty foes, just as wind and tempest denote the irresistible force of Jehovah's aid. The might of the enemy would be broken down to the very last remnant, whereas Israel would be able to rejoice and glory in its God" (Bible Hub, "Isaiah 41:15," Keil and Delitzsch Biblical Commentary on the Old Testament, biblehub.com, https://biblehub.com/commentaries/isaiah/41-15.htm).

Exodus from Egypt: illuminating their path with a pillar of fire in front and protectively shielding them with a cloud behind.[233] No matter how strong the enemy soldiers or how powerful their weapons, they will not stand a chance against Jesus and his Jewish army.

> *He will guard the feet of his faithful ones, but the wicked shall be cut off in darkness, for not by might shall a man prevail. 10 The adversaries of the LORD shall be broken to pieces; against them he will thunder in heaven. The LORD will judge the ends of the earth; he will give strength to his king and exalt the horn of his anointed.* (1 Samuel 2:9–10 ESV)

Without firing a single shot, Jesus will render every weapon useless, fulfilling the prophecy, *"not by might shall a man prevail."* The antichrist, who's vast army that began 200 million strong, supported by demons and four unshackled fallen angels from the 6th trumpet, has brought all his forces to bear against Jesus and his heavenly army. But Zechariah reveals the astonishing fate of this ungodly force: their flesh, eyes, and tongues will dissolve while they stand, leaving them like blind, decaying zombies. The same devastating plague will strike their demonically bred horses, leaving them to rot in place.

This image of rotting bodies, enemies of God's people whose flesh is melting away, is a graphic reversal of Ezekiel's chapter 37 vision, where God took the dry bones of the Israelites, clothed them in new

---

[233] "And the LORD went before them by day in a pillar of cloud to lead them along the way, and by night in a pillar of fire to give them light, that they might travel by day and by night" (Exodus 13:21 ESV).

flesh and brought them back to life.[234] Here, in stark contrast, the flesh and life of the enemy army dissolve, providing a grisly visual of God's unmatched power to restore life, or to take it away.

> *And this shall be the plague with which the LORD will strike all the peoples that wage war against Jerusalem: their flesh will rot while they are still standing on their feet, their eyes will rot in their sockets, and their tongues will rot in their mouths. 13 And on that day a great panic from the LORD shall fall on them, so that each will seize the hand of another, and the hand of the one will be raised against the hand of the other. 14 Even Judah will fight at Jerusalem. And the wealth of all the surrounding nations shall be collected, gold, silver, and garments in great abundance. 15 And a plague like this plague shall fall on the horses, the mules, the camels, the donkeys, and whatever beasts may be in those camps.* (Zechariah 14:12–15 ESV)

---

[234] *"Then he said to me, "Prophesy over these bones, and tell them: "Dry bones, hear the word of the Lord. 5 This is what the Sovereign LORD says to these bones: Look, I am about to infuse breath into you and you will live. 6 I will put tendons on you and muscles over you and will cover you with skin; I will put breath in you and you will live. Then you will know that I am the LORD."' 7 So I prophesied as I was commanded. There was a sound when I prophesied – I heard a rattling, and the bones came together, bone to bone. 8 As I watched, I saw tendons on them, then muscles appeared, and skin covered over them from above, but there was no breath in them"* (Ezekiel 37:4-11 NET).
*""He said to me, "Prophesy to the breath,––prophesy, son of man––and say to the breath: 'This is what the Sovereign LORD says: Come from the four winds, O breath, and breathe on these corpses so that they may live."' 10 So I prophesied as I was commanded, and the breath came into them; they lived and stood on their feet, an extremely great army. 11 Then he said to me, "Son of man, these bones are all the house of Israel. Look, they are saying, 'Our bones are dry, our hope has perished; we are cut off"* (Ezekiel 37:9-11 NET).

According to Zechariah 12, when the soldiers' eyes dissolve, they will go mad, and their horses, which also go blind, will bolt away. He also tells us that Jesus will enhance the Jews fighting alongside him with extraordinary abilities, saying, *"the feeblest among them... shall be like David."*

> On that day I will make Jerusalem a heavy stone for all the peoples. All who lift it will surely hurt themselves. And all the nations of the earth will gather against it. 4 On that day, declares the LORD, I will strike every horse with panic, and its rider with madness. But for the sake of the house of Judah I will keep my eyes open, when I strike every horse of the peoples with blindness. 5 Then the clans of Judah shall say to themselves, 'The inhabitants of Jerusalem have strength through the LORD of hosts, their God.' 6 "On that day I will make the clans of Judah like a blazing pot in the midst of wood, like a flaming torch among sheaves. And they shall devour to the right and to the left all the surrounding peoples, while Jerusalem shall again be inhabited in its place, in Jerusalem. 7 "And the LORD will give salvation to the tents of Judah first, that the glory of the house of David and the glory of the inhabitants of Jerusalem may not surpass that of Judah. 8 On that day the LORD will protect the inhabitants of Jerusalem, so that the feeblest among them on that day shall be like David, and the house of David shall be like God, like the angel of the LORD, going before them. 9 And on that day I will seek to destroy all the nations that come against Jerusalem. (Zechariah 12:3–9 ESV)

Even those enemy troops who think they are safe in their hardened bunkers will not escape from the pestilence Jesus sends. Their flesh, too, will rot.

> *According to the days of thy coming out of the land of Egypt will I shew unto him marvelous things. 16 The nations shall see and be confounded at all their might: they shall lay their hand upon their mouth, their ears shall be deaf. 17 They shall lick the dust like a serpent, they shall move out of their holes like worms of the earth: they shall be afraid of the LORD our God, and shall fear because of thee.* (Micah 7:15–17 KJV)

> *Say this to them, Thus says the Lord GOD: As I live, surely those who are in the waste places shall fall by the sword, and whoever is in the open field I will give to the beasts to be devoured, and those who are in strongholds and in caves shall die by pestilence. 28 And I will make the land a desolation and a waste, and her proud might shall come to an end, and the mountains of Israel shall be so desolate that none will pass through. 29 Then they will know that I am the LORD, when I have made the land a desolation and a waste because of all their abominations that they have committed.* (Ezekiel 33:27–29 ESV)

Their defeat is so complete that there will be no coming back from it, *"no easing your hurt."*

> *Your shepherds are asleep, O king of Assyria; your nobles slumber. Your people are scattered on the*

*mountains with none to gather them. 19 There is no easing your hurt; your wound is grievous. All who hear the news about you clap their hands over you. For upon whom has not come your unceasing evil?* (Nahum 3:18–19 ESV)

Nahum gives us a clue that the antichrist's *"unceasing evil"* extends to the entire world. We know that he never gains complete control over every government, as evidenced by the large armies deployed against him at Har-Magedon. However, he likely had economic control over everyone through his closed economic system, with his currency becoming the world's reserve currency.

Now Jesus will turn his wrath on the antichrist and the fake Jesus.

## 26.4 (B) The Antichrist and his False Prophet are Unceremoniously Dumped

As soon as Jesus, still *"sitting on the* [his white] *horse,"* finishes taking out his wrath on the nations he's fighting, angels capture the false prophet and the antichrist and unceremoniously cast them alive into the lake of fire, like discarded pieces of trash.

> *And I saw the beast and the kings of the earth with their armies gathered to make war against him who was sitting on the horse and against his army. 20 And the beast was captured, and with it the false prophet who in its presence had done the signs by which he deceived those who had received the mark of the beast and those who worshiped its image. These two were thrown alive into the lake of fire that burns with sulfur* (Revelation 19:19–20 ESV)

Satan is then bound in chains and cast into the abyss, likely in a way similar to how the angels released at the 6th trumpet had been restrained beneath the Euphrates River. This indicates heaven is once again in possession of the keys to hell. Though Satan had been allowed to use them briefly, under the terms of 7-sealed book, to release his 5th trumpet demonic stinging locusts, those keys were retrieved back to heaven.

> *Then I saw an angel descending from heaven, holding in his hand the key to the abyss and a huge chain. 2 He seized the dragon––the ancient serpent, who is the devil and Satan – and tied him up for a thousand*

*years. 3 The angel then threw him into the abyss and locked and sealed it so that he could not deceive the nations until the one thousand years were finished. (After these things he must be released for a brief period of time.)* (Revelation 20:1–3 NET)

Now that the antichrist, his false prophet, and all their fighting forces are destroyed, Jesus will move to the next phase of his wrath: cutting down those who chose to reject him by worshipping the antichrist and taking his mark.

## 26.4 (C) Jesus' Sword of Wrath Against Unbelievers with the Mark

Once Jesus and the Jewish fighters eliminate the enemy forces around Har-Magedon and cast the souls of the antichrist and his false prophet into the lake of fire, Jesus, still on horseback and accompanied by his heavenly army, will go throughout the world to "*convict all the ungodly,*" which is all those who took the mark and are still alive. He'll travel to wherever they live in the world to destroy them.

The number of people who rejected Jesus and took the mark, possibly in the billions, is so massive that when Jesus pours out his wrath on them, the scale of the slaughter will be staggering.

This will be no quick event. The sheer number of people that must be eliminated is so mindboggling that it could take weeks or even months for Jesus to complete.

Joel and John both prophesied about this White Horse judgment and the destruction of those who rejected the warning of the prophets and the angels and accepted the mark instead.

> "*Behold, the Lord comes with ten thousands of his holy ones, 15 to execute judgment on all and to convict all the ungodly of all their deeds of ungodliness that they have committed in such an ungodly way, and of all the harsh things that ungodly sinners have spoken against him.*" (Jude 1:14b–15 ESV)

Paul says Jesus will use a sword to take out his wrath on "*wrongdoers.*"

*. . . for he is God's servant for your good. But if you do wrong, be afraid, for he does not bear the sword in vain. For he is the servant of God, an avenger who carries out God's wrath on the wrongdoer.* (Romans 13:4 ESV)

Paul implies his sword of wrath used against those who don't know God will be *"flaming."* This sounds like he'll use a weapon much like the flaming swords the cherubim brandished to prevent the fallen Adam from returning to Eden.[235]

*. . . since indeed God considers it just to repay with affliction those who afflict you, 7 and to grant relief to you who are afflicted as well as to us, when the Lord Jesus is revealed from heaven with his mighty angels 8 in flaming fire, inflicting vengeance on those who do not know God and on those who do not obey the gospel of our Lord Jesus. 9 They will suffer the punishment of eternal destruction, away from the presence of the Lord and from the glory of his might, 10 when he comes on that day to be glorified in his saints, and to be marveled at among all who have believed, because our testimony to you was believed.* (2 Thessalonians 1:6–10 ESV)

Ezekiel says that Jesus will blow fire so hot on those he's destroying that it will blaze like a metalworking furnace. There will be no mistaking it's Jesus doing the fire blasting.

---

[235] *"He drove out the man, and at the east of the garden of Eden he placed the cherubim and a flaming sword that turned every way to guard the way to the tree of life"* (Genesis 3:24 ESV).

*As one gathers silver and bronze and iron and lead and tin into a furnace, to blow the fire on it in order to melt it, so I will gather you in my anger and in my wrath, and I will put you in and melt you. 21 I will gather you and blow on you with the fire of my wrath, and you shall be melted in the midst of it. 22 As silver is melted in a furnace, so you shall be melted in the midst of it, and you shall know that I am the LORD; I have poured out my wrath upon you."* (Ezekiel 22:20–22 ESV)

Isaiah confirms that Jesus will use his sword and fire to slay, and there will *"be many"* slain.

*For by fire will the LORD enter into judgment, and by his sword, with all flesh; and those slain by the LORD shall be many.* (Isaiah 66:16 ESV)

## 26.4 (D) Jesus' Sword of Wrath Against Former Believers with the Mark

One reason why Jesus is so angry is that many of those with the mark were once Christians or Jews. They were unwilling to give up the comforts of their lives and so chose to take the mark. Lacking a strong understanding of Scripture and unaccustomed to listening to the Holy Spirit, they were easily deceived by the antichrist's convincing miracles and the elaborate lies of his false Jesus.

> *Jesus said to them, "Is this not the reason you are wrong, because you know neither the scriptures nor the power of God?* (Mark 12:24 ESV)

These Christians shared fatal flaws with the Christians of the churches of Ephesus, Pergamum, Thyatira, Sardis, and Laodicea, churches Jesus rebuked for tolerating false teachings, embracing false teachers, or having only a shallow understanding of or relationship with him. They epitomized fair-weather faith: following Jesus when it was convenient but abandoning him when the pressure mounted. They may have taken the mark to escape the antichrist's sword, but they met their end by the *"terrible swift sword"* of Jesus.[236]

As he cuts these former Christians down, one can imagine Jesus thinking, *"What more could I have done? I sent my prophets; I came in person and gave my life to show you the way back to me. I warned you in my Word, sent my two witnesses, and even dispatched my messenger angels. Yet you still chose to listen to that deceiver instead of*

---

[236] Isaiah 27:1 New Living Translation *"In that day the LORD will take his terrible, swift sword and punish Leviathan, the swiftly moving serpent, the coiling, writhing serpent. He will kill the dragon of the sea."*

*me.*" Now, with no way to conceal their rejection of Jesus, because it's emblazoned on their right hands or foreheads, Jesus unleashes his righteous wrath and cuts them down.

By taking the mark, those Christians committed the unpardonable sin. They rejected their salvation or '*looked back*' to their old ways in the same way Lot's wife "*looked back*" at Sodom, thus they gave up their place in the Kingdom of God.

> *But Lot's wife, behind him, looked back, and she became a pillar of salt.* (Genesis 19:26 ESV)

> *Jesus said to him, "No one who puts his hand to the plow and looks back is fit for the kingdom of God."* (Luke 9:62 ESV)

It didn't have to end like this for them if only they had listened to the Holy Spirit. They had free will up to the point they rejected Jesus and took the mark, but now their fate will be the same as every other person who took the mark; they will be cut to pieces.

Jesus utterly destroys his enemies and the enemies of the Jews, just as he had completely destroyed Midian thousands of years earlier. Now, as he cuts down the final person who took the mark, the Wrath of God is finished.

> The *Almighty LORD of Armies will carry out this destruction throughout the world* as he has determined. (Isaiah 10:23 God's Word Translation)

# 26.5 Third Time Eavesdropping on People in Heaven: The Victory Song

> *2 And I saw what appeared to be a sea of glass mingled with fire-and also those who had conquered the beast and its image and the number of its name, standing beside the sea of glass with harps of God in their hands. 3 And they sing the song of Moses, the servant of God, and the song of the Lamb, saying, "Great and amazing are your deeds, O Lord God the Almighty! Just and true are your ways, O King of the nations! 4 Who will not fear, O Lord, and glorify your name? For you alone are holy. All nations will come and worship you, for your righteous acts have been revealed."* (Revelation 15:2–4 ESV)

John sees a remarkable group of people in heaven, people who had been killed for refusing to recant their belief in Jesus and *"had conquered the beast, its image, and the number of its name."* These were the martyrs first seen in the 5th seal as souls under the altar, who had apparently been given the high honor of riding on white horses to accompany Jesus. Now, as firsthand witnesses to his ultimate triumph, having seen him cut down every single one of his enemies, they are singing in celebration.

In their hands are the harps of God, and their voices rise singing the *Song of Moses,* a significant yet overlooked clue.[237] This song, last sung in Exodus 15, was Moses' tribute to God's supernatural destruction of Pharaoh's army. It was the Jews' victory anthem,

---

[237] These souls behave as though they have bodies: they stand, wear linens, sing, hold harps, and ride horses.

celebrating their miraculous escape through the Red Sea. God had parted and dried its waters to make a way of salvation for them but then closed it back to drown their enemies, the Pharaoh and his entire army. Just as God unleashed his *"burning wrath"* on Pharaoh and his followers, these martyrs had just witnessed Jesus unleash his burning wrath on the antichrist and all those who bore his mark. Here's a portion of the *Song of Moses*:

> *I will sing to the LORD,*
> *for He is highly exalted.*
> *The horse and rider*
> *He has thrown into the sea.*
> *The LORD is my strength and my song,*
> *and He has become my salvation.*
> *He is my God, and I will praise Him,*
> *my father's God, and I will exalt Him....*
>
> *Your right hand, O LORD,*
> *is majestic in power;*
> *Your right hand, O LORD,*
> *has shattered the enemy.*
> *You overthrew Your adversaries*
> *by Your great majesty.*
> *You unleashed Your burning wrath;*
> *it consumed them like stubble.*
> *my hand will destroy them.'...*
>
> *With loving devotion You will lead*
> *the people You have redeemed;*
> *with Your strength You will guide them*
> *to Your holy dwelling.*

*The nations will hear and tremble;*
*anguish will grip the dwellers of Philistia.*
*Then the chiefs of Edom will be dismayed;*
*trembling will seize the leaders of Moab;*
*those who dwell in Canaan will melt away,*
*and terror and dread will fall on them.*
*By the power of Your arm*
*they will be as still as a stone*
*until Your people pass by, O LORD,*
*until the people You have bought pass by.*

*You will bring them in and plant them*
*on the mountain of Your inheritance-*
*the place, O LORD, You have prepared for Your dwelling,*
*the sanctuary, O Lord, Your hands have established.*

*The LORD will reign forever and ever!" (Exodus 15:*
*selected stanzas, Berean Standard Bible)*

The singing of the Song of Moses by this multitude in heaven is a powerful confirmation that Jesus has just triumphed over the antichrist and his armies. Just as God overthrew Pharaoh and his army, Jesus has defeated the antichrist and his army of followers. [238]

John paints an unmistakable picture of victory and celebration. These saints have returned to heaven after witnessing Jesus and the tribes of Judah annihilate the antichrist and his warriors at Har-Magedon and all his followers. Their song is a declaration of triumph, confirming that they are the same saints mentioned in Revelation 19:14, clothed in white robes, riding white horses, and

---

[238] Recall that the 7th of each seal, trumpet, and bowl (plague) is set aside for the Lord. The witnesses controlled and have released the first 6 bowls at this point.

part of the heavenly army that followed Jesus as he cut down the antichrist's followers. These are the witnesses in white linen who had been executed for their faith, now returning fully vindicated by Jesus, celebrating the righteous retribution, justice, and power of their King.

> And the armies of heaven, arrayed in fine linen, white and pure, were following him on white horses. 15 From his mouth comes a sharp sword with which to strike down the nations and he will rule them (Revelation 19:14–15a ESV)

This evidence strongly suggests that John used this view of people in heaven, together with the other four views, as clues to reveal the true sequence of events unfolding simultaneously on earth. Although John doesn't describe Jesus riding his white horse and leading the host of heaven until chapter 19, he gives us this glimpse of the end result in chapter 15 so that those who seek to understand it may discern the true order.

> And I tell you, ask, and it will be given to you; seek, and you will find; knock, and it will be opened to you.10 For everyone who asks receives, and the one who seeks finds, and to the one who knocks it will be opened. (Luke 11:9–10 ESV)

The Wrath of God is finished, and Jesus' vengeance has run its course. The presence of this group of witnesses in heaven, who rode with Jesus, confirms that the sun has finally set on that long Day of the Lord. However, Jesus is notably absent from the scene because he still has an important task to complete on earth before he rests.

One stanza of the Song of Moses indicates the 144,000 Jews marked by God will be led back to Jerusalem by Jesus.

*With loving devotion You will lead*
*the people You have redeemed;*
*with Your strength You will guide them*
*to Your holy dwelling.*

These Jewish survivors must now contend with the grim task of disposing of the countless human remains and animal carcasses left in Jesus' wake.

## 26.6 Calling all Beasts to a Banquet of Decay. The "Just Deserts" of taking the Mark

> 24 *"And they shall go out and look on the dead bodies of the men who have rebelled against me. For their worm shall not die, their fire shall not be quenched, and they shall be an abhorrence to all flesh."* (Isaiah 66:24 ESV)

You may recall from the *Stomping Grapes with a Vengeance* chapter that Isaiah foretold the earth will keep the dead bodies displayed for all to see. As a result of this massive world war, in which the antichrist leads his forces against Jesus and his heavenly host, there will be hundreds of millions of the antichrist's dead covering nearly every inch of Israel and spilling over into neighboring lands. It will take the Jewish survivors seven months of nearly non-stop work to cleanse their land from the corpses and toss them into mass graves. The human remains of the antichrist, referred to as Gog in Ezekiel's prophecy, will be treated as just another one of the corpses and unceremoniously shoveled into a mass grave as the surviving Jews *"cleanse the land"* of this filth.

> *You shall fall* on the mountains of Israel, you and all your hordes and the peoples who are with you. I will give you to birds of prey *of every sort and to the beasts of the field to be devoured. 5 You shall fall in the open field, for I have spoken, declares the Lord GOD.* (Ezekiel 39:4-5 ESV)

> 11 *"On that day I will give to Gog a place for burial in Israel, the Valley of the Travelers, east of the sea. It will block the travelers, for there Gog and all his multitude will*

*be buried. It will be called the Valley of Hamon-gog. 12 For seven months the house of Israel will be burying them, in order to cleanse the land.* (Ezekiel 39:11–12 ESV)

For a Jew, having your dead body defiled by unclean vultures and animals is a fate worse than death itself. Burial with dignity is nearly as sacred as living a righteous life. To be denied this final honor, to have your corpse left to vultures and scavengers is an affront to all that is decent. The prophecy of such a disgraceful end is not merely justice but a righteous reckoning and fitting end for those who mercilessly tortured, raped, and murdered Jewish men, women and children.

*17 Then I saw an angel standing in the sun, and with a loud voice he called to all the birds that fly directly overhead, "Come, gather for the great supper of God, 18 to eat the flesh of kings, the flesh of captains, the flesh of mighty men, the flesh of horses and their riders, and the flesh of all men, both free and slave, both small and great."* (Revelation 19:17–18 ESV)

*And the dead bodies of this people will be food for the birds of the air, and for the beasts of the earth, and none will frighten them away.* (Jeremiah 7:33 ESV)

The cleanup effort to clear the trail of hundreds of millions of dead horses and dead humans left in the wake of Jesus' wrath is underway. With Jesus' 7th seal opened and his 7th trumpet complete, only his 7th bowl remains, and when it is poured out, the effect on each of the continents will be astonishing.

# Part Seven

# Making Things Right with the World Again

# 27 Pouring of Bowl #7: Restoring Eden

> *17 The seventh angel poured out his bowl into the air, and a loud voice came out of the temple, from the throne, saying, "It is done!" 18 And there were flashes of lightning, rumblings, peals of thunder, and a great earthquake such as there had never been since man was on the earth, so great was that earthquake. 19a The great city was split into three parts, and the cities of the nations fell* (Revelation 16:17–19a ESV)

A loud voice from the temple in heaven announces the end of Jesus' wrath: "*It is done!*" accompanied by the most extensive earthquake mankind has ever witnessed. The people who are alive on the earth at this point are not Christians, and if you accept this *trumpet-attack/bowl-countermeasure theory*, all those with the mark have just been personally destroyed by Jesus. The only people left alive on earth are therefore unbelievers who refused to take the mark, and the remnant of Jews.

Jerusalem is separated into three sections, an unusual effect that can't be explained by mere violent tremors. Ordinary tremors would cause it to crumble like other cities. Instead, this suggests that the ground is shifting directionally, and as it slides, Jerusalem is divided into three parts.

The 7ᵗʰ bowl earthquake is no ordinary seismic event; it has no epicenter from which it radiates. In other words, this won't be an earthquake centered in Chili or Israel, but rather one that will affect "*the cities of the nations*," meaning it will be felt across every region of the planet. It is a worldwide movement of the earth's surface layer, but the ground does not shake back and forth as in a typical earthquake. Instead, the tremors convulse the surface of the earth with immense force, yet only in one direction.

When viewed from the heavens, each continent appears as a large island. John writes, *"every island fled."* If all islands move or *"flee"* toward each other until they touch, they will no longer appear as separate islands, but rather one giant landmass. This sounds as if God is returning the continents to their original unified position, what geologists call Pangea, when the earth was one single landmass surrounded by one great sea (see Exhibit 8).[239] This means God is terraforming the world, reshaping the face of the earth in preparation for the coming Millennium.

> 20 And every island fled away, and no mountains were to be found. (Revelation 16:20 ESV)

During these convulsing movements, all mountains will be brought level to the ground except for a single, very important mountain.[240] The mountain of God, Mount Zion, will be raised up even higher than it currently stands because it will serve as a foundation point for the New Jerusalem that Jesus will bring to earth after the Millennium.

---

[239] Pangea is the name of the single large landmass of ancient times which was broken up into the separated continents we see today. See map in Exhibit 2.

[240] Mountains made level? It sounds like the reverse of how mountains are formed will be happening. Mountain ranges were formed when tectonic plates crashed into one another at a high speed, forcing up folds of the earth's crust. Other mountains are formed from volcanic activity. Revelation 16:20 seems to indicate that the tectonic plates will be reversing direction, heading back to their starting position, and in the process, letting those mountains sink back into the mantle from which they came (Charles Q. Choi, "How do mountains form?" Live Science, November 12, 2023, https://www.livescience.com/planet-earth/how-do-mountains-form).

Isaiah provides more evidence that there are enormous tectonic shifts occurring:

*He who flees at the sound of the terror shall fall into the pit, and he who climbs out of the pit shall be caught in the snare. For the windows of heaven are opened, and the foundations of the earth tremble. 19 The earth is utterly broken, the earth is split apart, the earth is violently shaken. 20 The earth staggers like a drunken man; it sways like a hut; its transgression lies heavy upon it, and it falls, and will not rise again.* (Isaiah 24:18–20 ESV)

That *"the foundations of the earth tremble. . . broken"* adds further support for the Pangea theory. God is reversing the direction of the tectonic plates, which are currently moving away from each other, though their movement is measured in centimeters per year. God breaks their normal movement to push the islands and continents back to their original, single mass.[241]

---

[241] "Earth's crust, called the lithosphere, consists of 15 to 20 moving tectonic plates. The plates can be thought of like pieces of a cracked shell that rest on the hot, molten rock of Earth's mantle and fit snugly against one another. The heat from radioactive processes within the planet's interior causes the plates to move, sometimes toward and sometimes away from each other. This movement is called plate motion, or tectonic shift" (NOAA, "What is Tectonic Shift?" National Geodetic Survey, Last Modified October 25, 2019, https://geodesy.noaa.gov/INFO/facts/tectonic-shift.shtml).

Most mountain ranges were formed when tectonic plates rammed into each other buckling the crust into giant folds of crust material (Matt Williams, "Mountains: How Are They Formed?" *Universe Today*, https://www.universetoday.com/29833/how-mountains-are-formed/).

When those plates begin to reverse direction in the 7th bowl, it's not hard to imagine those mountain ranges subsuming back into the magma from which they originally formed.

This terraforming will probably take weeks as every tectonic plate under each continent scurries rapidly back to its place of origin. We're told the rotating earth would appear to *"sway like a hut"* as it seeks a new equilibrium from this shifting mass. There will also be storms over the entire world that drop a lot more than just torrential rain: they will throw 100-pound hailstones.

> *21 And great hailstones, about one hundred pounds each, fell from heaven on people; and they cursed God for the plague of the hail, because the plague was so severe.* (Revelation 16:21 ESV)

A hailstone that heavy would be about 45 centimeters (18 inches) in diameter, roughly the size of a beach ball.[242] With these deadly ice bombs screaming down from the sky, slamming into the earth with such force that they smash craters into the shifting ground, it's no wonder John says that men "cursed God."

Between the first worldwide earthquake and the largest hailstones humans have experienced, Isaiah 24 indicates that it doesn't matter whether people "fall into the pit" or "climb[s] out of the pit," there is nowhere safe from the danger.[243]

---

[242] Information on circumference and weight of large hailstones proved impossible to find. So I calculated the circumference as follows for a 100 lb (45.36 Kg) hailstone. Assuming the hail has a standard density of ice (920 kg/m3 ) then the volume would be found using mass/density = 45.36/920 = .0493. The Radius would be $r=(3V/4\pi)1/3 =(3*0.493/4\pi)1/3$ = .2275 meters or 22.75 cm, which means the Diameter =45.5 cm (17.9 inches). Using $C=\pi\times d$, the circumference would be almost 57 inches or 144 cm.

[243] The largest earthquake recorded was 9.5 on the Richter scale (in Chili), so this one is at least 9.6 (Tia Ghose, "The 20 largest recorded earthquakes in history," Live Science, January 27, 2023, https://www.livescience.com/largest-recorded-earthquakes-in-history).

The cataclysm of the 7$^{th}$ bowl will thin out the world's remaining population, but it is not an extinction-level event. We can be sure of that because we'll see many survivors straggling-in to Jerusalem, irresistibly drawn there to present themselves before the upcoming Sheep and Goat Separation. Yet while this great terraforming is underway, God deals with Babylon.

# 27.1 Babylon Destroyed Without a Trace

*. . . and God remembered Babylon the great, to make her drain the cup of the wine of the fury of his wrath.* (Revelation 16:19b ESV)

As part of the plague of the 7th bowl, Babylon will be destroyed. But it won't just crumble to its foundations like every other city of the world during the great earthquake; it will be utterly burned up without a trace, just as Sodom was when God annihilated it with fire and brimstone thousands of years earlier.

Jeremiah's prophecy was fulfilled the first time God destroyed Babylon, and it will attain its ultimate fulfillment when God destroys it for good.

*Therefore wild beasts shall dwell with hyenas in Babylon, and ostriches shall dwell in her. She shall never again have people, nor be inhabited for all generations. 40 As when God overthrew Sodom and Gomorrah and their neighboring cities, declares the LORD, so no man shall dwell there, and no son of man shall sojourn in her.* (Jeremiah 50:39–40 ESV)

In the same way Lot was warned by angels to flee Sodom, this time it's a voice from heaven that gives a warning to the Jews left in Babylon to flee before the city is destroyed.[244]

---

[244] Christians are also called "my people", but they have already been taken to heaven in the First Harvest of Revelation 14:15

*Then I heard another voice from heaven saying, "Come out of her, my people, lest you take part in her sins, lest you share in her plagues; 5 for her sins are heaped high as heaven, and God has remembered her iniquities.* (Revelation 18: 4–5 ESV)

*Flee from the midst of Babylon; let every one save his life! Be not cut off in her punishment, for this is the time of the LORD's vengeance, the repayment he is rendering her. 7 Babylon was a golden cup in the LORD's hand, making all the earth drunken; the nations drank of her wine; therefore the nations went mad. 8 Suddenly Babylon has fallen and been broken; wail for her! Take balm for her pain; perhaps she may be healed.* (Jeremiah 51:6–8 ESV)

*Pay her back as she herself has paid back others, and repay her double for her deeds; mix a double portion for her in the cup she mixed. 7 As she glorified herself and lived in luxury, so give her a like measure of torment and mourning, since in her heart she says, 'I sit as a queen, I am no widow, and mourning I shall never see.' 8 For this reason her plagues will come in a single day, death and mourning and famine, and she will be burned up with fire; for mighty is the Lord God who has judged her.' 9 And the kings of the earth, who committed sexual immorality and lived in luxury with her, will weep and wail over her when they see the smoke of her burning. 10 They will stand far off, in fear of her torment, and say, "Alas! Alas! You great city, you mighty city, Babylon! For in a single hour your*

*judgment has come." 11 And the merchants of the earth weep and mourn for her, since no one buys their cargo anymore, 12 cargo of gold, silver, jewels, pearls, fine linen, purple cloth, silk, scarlet cloth, all kinds of scented wood, all kinds of articles of ivory, all kinds of articles of costly wood, bronze, iron and marble, 13 cinnamon, spice, incense, myrrh, frankincense, wine, oil, fine flour, wheat, cattle and sheep, horses and chariots, and slaves, that is, human souls. 14 "The fruit for which your soul longed has gone from you, and all your delicacies and your splendors are lost to you, never to be found again!"*
(Revelation 18: 6–14 ESV)

These next verses provide another reason why the Battle of Har-Magedon seems primarily regional: these merchants are still trading in luxury goods. If the battle were worldwide, the manufacturing of non-war-related items would have been a low priority, and shipping would have been too dangerous, likely ceasing almost entirely before this point.

*15 The merchants of these wares, who gained wealth from her, will stand far off, in fear of her torment, weeping and mourning aloud, 16 "Alas, alas, for the great city that was clothed in fine linen, in purple and scarlet, adorned with gold, with jewels, and with pearls! 17 For in a single hour all this wealth has been laid waste." And all shipmasters and seafaring men, sailors and all whose trade is on the sea, stood far off 18 and cried out as they saw the smoke of her burning, "What city was like the great city?" 19 And they threw dust on their heads as they wept and mourned, crying out, "Alas, alas, for the great city where all who had ships at sea grew rich by her wealth! For in a single hour she has been laid waste.* (Revelation 18:15–19 ESV)

This affirms that Babylon is the headquarters that directed the effort to behead the saints of the world, because verses 20 and 24 indicate that it has their blood on its hands.

*"20 Rejoice over her, O heaven, and you saints and apostles and prophets, for God has given judgment for you against her!" 21 Then a mighty angel took up a stone like a great millstone and threw it into the sea, saying, "So will Babylon the great city be thrown down with violence, and will be found no more; 22 and the sound of harpists and musicians, of flute players and trumpeters, will be heard in you no more, and a craftsman of any craft will be found in you no more, and the sound of the mill will be heard in you no more, 23 and the light of a lamp will shine in you no more, and the voice of bridegroom and bride will be heard in you no more, for your merchants were the great ones of the earth, and all nations were deceived by your sorcery. 24 And in her was found the blood of prophets and of saints, and of all who have been slain on earth."* (Revelation 18:20–24 ESV)

After Babylon is utterly annihilated, like Sodom, without a trace, we are given another glimpse into heaven. [245] This time, we hear those who were martyred for their faith express satisfaction that their murders, orchestrated by Babylon, *"the great prostitute,"* have been avenged.

---

[245] "Then the LORD rained on Sodom and Gomorrah sulfur and fire from the LORD out of heaven" (Genesis 19:24 ESV).

## 27.2 Fourth Time Eavesdropping on Heaven: The Martyrs Celebrate Babylon's Annihilation

*After this I heard what seemed to be the loud voice of a great multitude in heaven, crying out, "Hallelujah! Salvation and glory and power belong to our God, 2 for his judgments are true and just; for he has judged the great prostitute who corrupted the earth with her immorality, and has avenged on her the blood of his servants." 3 Once more they cried out, "Hallelujah! The smoke from her goes up forever and ever." 4 And the twenty-four elders and the four living creatures fell down and worshiped God who was seated on the throne, saying, "Amen. Hallelujah!" 5 And from the throne came a voice saying, "Praise our God, all you his servants, you who fear him, small and great."* (Revelation 19:1–5 ESV)

In our fourth opportunity to eavesdrop on a conversation in heaven, we hear saints rejoicing over the long-awaited fall of Babylon, the great prostitute.

*And the woman that you saw is the great city [Babylon] that has dominion over the kings of the earth.* (Revelation 17:18 ESV)

This fourth view of people in heaven reveals two major fulfillments of prophecy:

1. This confirms that Jesus now has the authority to save the souls, *"salvation and glory belong to our God,"* who have been held captive by Satan all these millennia, and

2. God has finally judged and destroyed Babylon and has thus "has avenged. . . the blood of his servants." [246] [247] But this celebration is also very interesting in that it further supports that the *trumpet-attack/bowl-countermeasure theory* timeline is accurate, and that Revelation is not presented in chronological order.

John presents many events out of order, and this becomes obvious when we examine how he reveals the manner of death of the martyrs and Babylon's fall.

1. In Chapter 6, John introduces the martyrs in heaven, but he doesn't explain how or why they died, or who (what city) was behind it.

2. In Chapter 19, those same saints in heaven are shown rejoicing over Babylon's destruction, but still, John hasn't revealed the cause of their deaths.

3. It isn't until Chapter 20, one chapter after the celebration of Babylon's fall that John finally tells us why those saints died: They were beheaded for refusing the mark of the beast.

4. The confusion continues with John's announcements about Babylon's fall. In Chapter 14, a flying angel declares, "Babylon is fallen!" But at this point in the narrative, the reader has no

---

[246] Jesus' power was attained when the 7th Trumpet sounded, officially announcing the kingdoms of the earth were now the kingdoms of our Lord

[247] *"They cried out with a loud voice, "O Sovereign Lord, holy and true, how long before you will judge and avenge our blood on those who dwell on the earth?" 11 Then they were each given a white robe and told to rest a little longer, until the number of their fellow servants and their brothers should be complete, who were to be killed as they themselves had been"* (Revelation 6:10–11 ESV)

idea whether Babylon's fall is a good or bad thing, because John hasn't yet explained Babylon's role in the end-times.

5. We don't find out for sure that Babylon was the evil headquarters behind the antichrist and the mark of the beast until Chapter 20, which is oddly placed two chapters after John describes Babylon's destruction Chapter 18.

It's as though John is telegraphing, *"this isn't the real order, look for the clues I left."*

The grids below, expanded from the one shown in Chapter 4.1, "Revelation is a Catalog of Events," list the events around Babylon and its destruction and will help demonstrate that Revelation is not conveyed in chronological order.

By comparing the two grids, one listing events in the order they will actually happen and the other listing them in the order John presents them in Revelation, it provides further support that that Revelation is not a straightforward timeline. John arranged the prophecy like a catalog, breaking the story into pieces and presenting events from different angles and groupings rather than in a simple step-by-step sequence.

Most people expect Revelation to read like a linear prophecy, but it is really a puzzle, one meant to be understood when the time is right using clues John provided.

| Order event will happen | Babylon and Martyr Verses Listed in the **Order in Which the Events will Happen** | Order verse Appears in Revelation | |
|:---:|---|:---:|:---:|
| ⬇ | | | |
| 1 | The third Whispering Angel warns everyone not to get the mark of the beast. | 14:9-10 | 4th |
| 2 | The mark of the beast is forced upon everyone. | 13:16-17 | 2nd |
| 3 | We find out what happens to those who refused the mark: they are beheaded. | 20:04 | 9th |
| 4 | The 5th seal martyrs arrive in heaven. They have been "*slain. . . for the witness they had borne*," (but we don't yet know how or why they were slain) | 6:09 | 1st |
| 5 | In the final part of the 7th bowl judgment, "...*God remembers Babylon*" but doesn't yet say what was done to it. | 16:19 | 5th |
| 6 | John devotes two chapters-one-eighth of his entire letter-to identifying Babylon as the evil city responsible for the murder of the saints and describing its well-deserved, total annihilation. | Chapters 17 & 18 | 6th |
| 7 | The second Whispering Angel proclaims that "*Babylon is fallen*" | 14:08 | 3rd |
| 8 | Another angel shouts, "*Babylon the great is fallen*" | 18:1-2 | 7th |
| 9 | John uses five verses to describe the celebration in heaven over Babylon's annihilation. | 19:1-5 | 8th |

| Order event will happen | Babylon and Martyr Verses Listed in the **Order** in Which the Verses Appear in Revelation | Order verse Appears in Revelation | |
|---|---|---|---|
| 4 | The 5th seal martyrs arrive in heaven. They have been "*slain. . . for the witness they had borne*," (but we don't yet know how or why they were slain) | 6:09 | 1st |
| 2 | The mark of the beast is forced upon everyone. | 13:16-17 | 2nd |
| 7 | The second Whispering Angel proclaims that "*Babylon is fallen*" | 14:08 | 3rd |
| 1 | The third Whispering Angel warns everyone not to get the mark of the beast. | 14:9-10 | 4th |
| 5 | In the final part of the 7th bowl judgment, "...*God remembers Babylon*" but doesn't yet say what was done to it. | 16:19 | 5th |
| 6 | John devotes two chapters-one-eighth of his entire letter-to identifying Babylon as the evil city responsible for the murder of the saints and describing its well-deserved, total annihilation. | Chapters 17 & 18 | 6th |
| 8 | Another angel shouts, "*Babylon the great is fallen*" | 18:1-2 | 7th |
| 9 | John uses five verses to describe the celebration in heaven over Babylon's annihilation. | 19:1-5 | 8th |
| 3 | We find out what happens to those who refused the mark: they are beheaded. | 20:04 | 9th |

## Part Eight:

# Thy Kingdom Has Come: The Thousand Year Reign of Jesus

# 28 Preparing for The Millennium

During the transition between the completion of the Day of the Lord and the start of the Millennium, several important events transpire. We'll devote a section to each event in the order in which they will occur:

1. Jesus personally gathers the Jews back to Israel in two phases: first, the marked 144,000, second the rest of the Jewish survivors
2. All non-Jewish survivors of every nation are supernaturally drawn to walk to Jerusalem
3. The promise to the martyrs: the First Resurrection occurs
4. Jesus will determine who gets to continue living and thus enter the Millennium

# 28.1 Gathering the Surviving Jews

All three of Jesus' 7's—his $7^{th}$ seal, $7^{th}$ trumpet, and $7^{th}$ bowl, are complete. Now, Jesus personally leads the procession of the 144,000 Jews whom he has kept protected in an undisclosed place during the Great Tribulation and the time of his wrath. When he leads them in an orderly procession back to Mount Zion, Isaiah tells us he's still wearing the same robe he wore while he stomped the grapes of his wrath in the $2^{nd}$ Harvest, because it still shows the blood stains.

> *Who is this who comes from Edom, in crimsoned garments from Bozrah, he who is splendid in his apparel, marching in the greatness of his strength? "It is I, speaking in righteousness, mighty to save." 2 Why is your apparel red, and your garments like his who treads in the winepress? 3 "I have trodden the winepress alone, and from the peoples no one was with me; I trod them in my anger and trampled them in my wrath; their lifeblood spattered on my garments, and stained all my apparel. 4 For the day of vengeance was in my heart, and my year of redemption had come.* (Isaiah 63:1–4 ESV)

Though Benjamin was the last tribe listed to have the seal of God applied by his angel in Revelation 7, the writer of Psalms tells us that by the time Jesus leads the 144,000 back to Jerusalem, Benjamin is now the closest, *"in the lead,"* to him.

> *The Lord said, "I will bring them back from Bashan, I will bring them back from the depths of the sea, 23*

*that you may strike your feet in their blood, that the tongues of your dogs may have their portion from the foe." 24 Your procession is seen, O God, the procession of my God, my King, into the sanctuary-25 the singers in front, the musicians last, between them virgins playing tambourines: 26 "Bless God in the great congregation, the LORD, O you who are of Israel's fountain!" 27 There is Benjamin, the least of them, in the lead, the princes of Judah in their throng, the princes of Zebulun, the princes of Naphtali.* (Psalm 68:22–27 ESV)

Jesus, whom they once considered a blasphemer and heretic, will now be looked upon by the surviving Jews with reverence, awe, and appreciation. The returning Jewish refugees will now consider Jesus to be their crown of glory.

*In that day the LORD of hosts will be a crown of glory, and a diadem of beauty, to the remnant of his people, 6 and a spirit of justice to him who sits in judgment, and strength to those who turn back the battle at the gate.* (Isaiah 28:5–6 ESV)

John echoes what Isaiah told us about the exuberance of the 144,000 Jews returning to Jerusalem: They will be singing a song of joy that only they know.

*Then I looked, and behold, on Mount Zion stood the Lamb, and with him 144,000 who had his name and his Father's name written on their foreheads. 2 And I heard a voice from heaven like the roar of many waters and like the sound of loud thunder. The voice I heard was like the sound of harpists playing on their harps, 3 and they were singing a new song before the throne and before the four living creatures and before the elders. No one could learn that song except the 144,000 who had been redeemed from the earth.* (Revelation 14:1–3 ESV)

Isaiah tells us that those whom Jesus ransomed, the 144,000, will enter Jerusalem and this time, they won't be afraid.

*Therefore the redeemed of the LORD shall return, and come with singing unto Zion; and everlasting joy shall be upon their head: they shall obtain gladness and joy; and sorrow and mourning shall flee away. 12 I, even I, am he that comforteth you: who art thou, that thou shouldest be afraid of a man that shall die, and of the son of man which shall be made as grass; 13 And forgettest the LORD thy maker, that hath stretched forth the heavens, and laid the foundations of the earth; and hast feared continually every day because of the fury of the oppressor, as if he were ready to destroy? and where is the fury of the oppressor?* (Isaiah 51:11–13 KJV)

This remnant of Jews has learned their lesson and will never again trust, *"lean on"* men who claimed to have their best interests in mind but turned on them. Instead, they will now trust in the Lord.

*In that day the remnant of Israel and the survivors of the house of Jacob will no more lean on him who struck them, but will lean on the LORD, the Holy One of Israel, in truth. 21 A remnant will return, the remnant of Jacob, to the mighty God. 22 For though your people Israel be as the sand of the sea, only a remnant of them will return. Destruction is decreed, overflowing with righteousness.* (Isaiah 10:20–22 ESV)

You might think that after Jesus leads the marked 144,000 back to Mount Zion, having protected them for 3 ½ years, his work would be finished. However, instead, he goes out "*a second time*" to gather every Jewish survivor, wherever they may have been scattered, "*from the four corners*" of Pangea. Survivors from the nations will assist Jesus in his gleaning effort.

*In that day the Lord will extend his hand yet a second time to recover the remnant that remains of his people, from Assyria, from Egypt, from Pathros, from Cush, from Elam, from Shinar, from Hamath, and from the coastlands of the sea. 12 He will raise a signal for the nations and will assemble the banished of Israel, and gather the dispersed of Judah from the four corners of the earth.* (Isaiah 11:11–12 ESV)

These Jews who survived were those who heeded God's warning to flee at the beginning of the Great Tribulation. Most were killed, but some were imprisoned in different countries. Jesus will free them and bring them to Israel from wherever they were sheltering, imprisoned, or "*trapped in holes.*"

*But this is a people plundered and looted; they are all of them trapped in holes and hidden in prisons; they have become plunder with none to rescue, spoil with none to say, "Restore!"* (Isaiah 42:22 ESV)

The survivors of all nations will come and see the glory of Jesus and Jesus will send some of those survivors to nations around the world to search for and gather any surviving Jews that may have been in hiding or wasting in prisons. Some Jews will be in such bad condition they have to be brought to Jerusalem in wagons or litters.

> *"For I know their works and their thoughts, and the time is coming to gather all nations and tongues. And they shall come and shall see my glory, 19 and I will set a sign among them. And from them I will send survivors to the nations, to Tarshish, Pul, and Lud, who draw the bow, to Tubal and Javan, to the coastlands far away, that have not heard my fame or seen my glory. And they shall declare my glory among the nations. 20 And they shall bring all your brothers from all the nations as an offering to the LORD, on horses and in chariots and in litters and on mules and on dromedaries* [camels], *to my holy mountain Jerusalem, says the LORD, just as the Israelites bring their grain offering in a clean vessel to the house of the LORD.* (Isaiah 66:18–20 ESV)

The Jews who survive will no longer bicker among themselves and will be in unity.

> *The jealousy of Ephraim shall depart, and those who harass Judah shall be cut off; Ephraim shall not be jealous of Judah, and Judah shall not harass Ephraim.* (Isaiah 11:13 ESV)

We won't know how many of these salvaged Jews will now choose to acknowledge Jesus as their Lord and Savior, but after all they've been through and all they saw Jesus do for them, there will surely be a large number of them who will accept Jesus as their Lord.

> *Lest you be wise in your own sight, I do not want you to be unaware of this mystery, brothers: a partial hardening has come upon Israel, until the fullness of the Gentiles has come in. 26 And in this way all Israel will be saved, as it is written, "The Deliverer will come from Zion, he will banish ungodliness from Jacob"; 27 "and this will be my covenant with them when I take away their sins." (Romans 11:25–27 ESV)*

Israel should be ripe for salvation, but it doesn't sound like they will be taken to heaven just because they accepted Jesus as their Savior at that moment. They will live in the camp of Jesus until they die at some point during the Millennium.

Apparently, the temple, or the *"tent of David,"* built just before the Great Tribulation had been destroyed, because now Jesus rebuilds it.

> *After this I will return, and I will rebuild the tent of David that has fallen; I will rebuild its ruins, and I will restore it, 17 that the remnant of mankind may seek the Lord, and all the Gentiles who are called by my name, says the Lord, who makes these things 18 known from of old. (Acts 15:16–18 ESV)*

Jesus will select some of the remnant to serve before him as priests, because there will be a temple during the Millennium.

*And some of them also I will take for priests and for Levites, says the LORD. 22 "For as the new heavens and the new earth that I make shall remain before me, says the LORD, so shall your offspring and your name remain. 23 From new moon to new moon, and from Sabbath to Sabbath, all flesh shall come to worship before me, declares the LORD.* (Isaiah 66:21–23 ESV)

## 28.2 Non-Jewish Survivors Trek to Jerusalem

Once the Jews are restored to Israel, they will take control of all the territories around them, including Palestine and Jordan. There will even be a highway directly from Assyria to Israel, and a passage over a dry river from Egypt.[248] The Jews will also reclaim their wealth that had been carried off by the nations during the Great Tribulation.

> But they shall swoop down on the shoulder of the Philistines in the west, and together they shall plunder the people of the east. They shall put out their hand against Edom and Moab, and the Ammonites shall obey them. 15 And the LORD will utterly destroy the tongue of the Sea of Egypt, and will wave his hand over the River with his scorching breath, and strike it into seven channels, and he will lead people across in sandals. 16 And there will be a highway from Assyria for the remnant that remains of his people, as there was for Israel when they came up from the land of Egypt. (Isaiah 11:14–16 ESV)

Before the Millennial Reign of Christ can begin, all the survivors of the world will be gathered to Jerusalem. Transport ships won't be necessary because, due to the terraforming in the 7th bowl, the continents have returned to their original position as a single

---

[248] Assyria is now northern Iraq and southeastern Turkey (Encyclopedia Britannica, "Assyria," britannica.com, July 29, 2024, https://www.britannica.com/place/Assyria)

massive continent. The *"coastlands far away"* refers to the farthest ends of the unified landmass.[249]

> *. . . and the time is coming to* gather all nations *and tongues. And they shall come and shall* see my glory, *19 and I will set a sign among them. And from them I will send survivors to the nations, to Tarshish, Pul, and Lud, who draw the bow, to Tubal and Javan, to the* coastlands *far away, that have not heard my fame or seen my glory. And they shall declare my glory among the nations.* (Isaiah 66:18b–19 ESV)

While there is some debate about whether the Philistines are the progenitors of Palestinians, the following passage indicates that Philistia was rejoicing that their archenemy, Israel, was destroyed. But they were warned that after the great battle, their own remnant would die out from starvation, while Israel would return and find refuge in the Lord.

> *In the year that King Ahaz died came this oracle: 29 Rejoice not, O* Philistia, *all of you, that the rod that struck you is broken, for from the serpent's root will come forth an adder, and its fruit will be a flying fiery serpent. 30 And the firstborn of the poor will graze, and the needy lie down in safety;* but I will kill your root with famine, and your remnant it will slay. *31 Wail, O gate; cry out, O city; melt in fear, O Philistia,*

---

[249] *"Coastlands far away."* That the furthest points away from Jerusalem, which is probably now positioned at the center of this giant landmass, are called *coastlands* is further evidence that the world is now in Pangea form. Coastlands are the edges, the coasts, of Pangea. See Exhibit 8 for a Map of Pangea

*all of you! For smoke comes out of the north, and there is no straggler in his ranks. 32 What will one answer the messengers of the nation? "The LORD has founded Zion, and in her the afflicted of his people find refuge."* (Isaiah 14:28–32 ESV)

# 28.3 First Resurrection: The Martyrs' Reward

*This is the first resurrection.* (Revelation 20:5b ESV).

Those beheaded during the 70th week of Daniel for refusing to recant their faith in Jesus have a special place in God's heart and are promised a very distinguished role in Jesus' Millennial kingdom. We saw the first group of them in heaven when the 5th seal was opened:

> *When he opened the fifth seal, I saw under the altar the souls of those who had been slain for the word of God and for the witness they had borne. 10 They cried out with a loud voice, "O Sovereign Lord, holy and true, how long before you will judge and avenge our blood on those who dwell on the earth?"* (Revelation 6:9–10 ESV)

God considers these martyred believers special because they loved Jesus more than they loved their own lives.

> *And they have conquered him by the blood of the Lamb and by the word of their testimony, for they loved not their lives even unto death.* (Revelation 12:11 ESV)

They were told that because they remained faithful right up until they were beheaded, they would receive a crown. A crown indicates that these martyrs will be rulers and have authority over the nations:

> *Do not fear what you are about to suffer. Behold, the devil is about to throw some of you into prison, that*

*you may be tested, and for ten days you will have tribulation. Be faithful unto death, and I will give you the crown of life. 11 He who has an ear, let him hear what the Spirit says to the churches. The one who conquers will not be hurt by the second death.'* (Revelation 2:10–11 ESV)

*Only hold fast what you have until I come. 26 The one who conquers and who keeps my works until the end, to him I will give authority over the nations,* (Revelation 2:25–26 ESV)

These martyrs will receive a twofold reward. First, they have the unique privilege of being the first to return to earth and receive a resurrected, immortal body. Second, they will rule during the Millennium alongside Jesus.

For some unexplained reason, these martyred saints existed in heaven only as souls, *"under the altar the souls of those who had been slain for the word of God."*[250] The fact that they did not have incorruptible bodies is evident because they couldn't wear robes, as the rest of the humans in heaven do. Instead, they were *"given"* their robes and told to wait.

*Each of them was given a long white robe and they were told to rest for a little longer, until the full number was reached of both their fellow servants and their brothers who were going to be killed just as they had been.* (Revelation 6:11 NET)

---

[250] Revelation 6:9 ESV: "When he opened the fifth seal, I saw under the altar the souls of those who had been slain for the word of God and for the witness they had borne."

Just before the Sheep and Goat Separation occurs, the souls of these martyrs will be sent to earth and will *"come to life"* into resurrected bodies. They will live and reign with Christ during the Millennium. This is the First Resurrection, and it fits perfectly here, at this point in the *trumpet-attack/bowl-countermeasure theory* timeline.

> *Then I saw thrones, and seated on them were those to whom the authority to judge was committed. Also I saw the souls of those who had been beheaded for the testimony of Jesus and for the word of God, and those who had not worshiped the beast or its image and had not received its mark on their foreheads or their hands. They came to life and reigned with Christ for a thousand years.* (Revelation 20:4 ESV)

> *This is the first resurrection.* (Revelation 20:5b ESV).

The second resurrection, which is the resurrection of the remainder of humanity, will not occur for another thousand years, at the conclusion of the Millennium. In the meantime, there are survivors being drawn to Jerusalem who must be dealt with.

## 28.4 Who shall Enter His Gates?
## The Sheep and Goat Separation

> *When the Son of Man comes in his glory, and all the*
> *angels with him, then he will sit on his glorious throne.*
> *32 Before him will be gathered all the nations. . .*
> (Matthew 25:31-32a ESV)

All believers have been taken to heaven, and all those with the
mark have been destroyed by Jesus as he carried out the wrath of
God, so the Day of the Lord is complete. Now, the long-awaited
Millennial Reign of Christ is about to begin. In preparation, Jesus
has personally shepherded all surviving Jews to Jerusalem. All non-
Jewish survivors have also arrived, and for many, it may have been
a long journey from the distant edges of Pangea.

Will these survivors simply be welcomed into Jesus' glorious
Millennial kingdom? Absolutely not! While there may be millions
of survivors gathered there, merely surviving to this point doesn't
make them worthy to enter the Millennial Kingdom.

God does not want outright bad individuals benefiting from
the blessings of the Millennium, so Jesus must separate the wicked
survivors from those whose most recent actions demonstrated they
have some redeeming qualities. This second group, those deemed
worthy, will have the privilege of becoming subjects in his Kingdom,
partaking in his 1,000-year era of peace and justice.

As the newly crowned King of the World, Jesus takes his seat
on a glorious throne surrounded by angels. Now try to picture
what Jesus sees before him.

On his right are the martyred saints, many of whom we saw when
the 5th seal was opened. They have just been resurrected and are

now clothed in immortal bodies. Nearby in a place of honor stand the 144,000 sealed Jews, together with any other surviving Jews.

In front of him stands  a vast assembly of the last surviving people from every nation. They have endured the trials of the Great Tribulation, resisted taking the mark of the beast, and somehow survived to this moment. Many will know little of the Bible except what they had heard from the whispering angels, and they may have never heard of the Millennial Reign of Christ, leaving them apprehensive about what is coming next.

The process Jesus has established to vet these survivors is unique and beautifully simple; it doesn't involve Jesus opening the Book of Life or these survivors making a profession of faith in Jesus Christ. Instead, to determine which among them deserves a  second chance, Jesus will act as the Good Shepherd, separating the worthy from the unworthy in a process known as the Sheep and Goat Separation. This process, described in Matthew 25, involves a straightforward test. [251]

> 31 *"When the Son of Man comes in his glory, and all the angels with him, then he will sit on his glorious throne. 32 Before him will be gathered all the nations, and he will separate people one from another as a shepherd separates the sheep from the goats. 33 And he will place the sheep on his right, but the goats on the left. 34 Then the King will say to those on his right, 'Come, you who are blessed by my Father, inherit the kingdom prepared for you from the foundation of the world.* (Matthew 25:31–34 ESV)

---

[251] To cull is to separate something from a group or lot for not being as good as the others. For example, the unbruised apples will be packed in bags, and the *culls* will be used for cider (Merriam-Webster, s.v. "cull," merraimwebster.com, https://www.merriam-webster.com/thesaurus/cull).

This test question is remarkably simple and straightforward—it's not a trick question. It focuses solely on how each of these survivors treated Jesus' *"brothers."*

> *40 And the King will answer them, 'Truly, I say to you, as you did it to one of the least of these my brothers, you did it to me.'* (Matthew 25:40 ESV)

But who are these *"brothers"* Jesus is referring to? I struggled for days to understand verse 40. Jesus was answering the questions posed by the sheep, who had just made the cut and so will be allowed to live and enjoy his Millennial Kingdom, and in his response, he referred to another, unknown group as *"my brothers."* *"Brother"* usually identifies someone who believes in Jesus, which is why Christians call each other brother and sister. But all of Jesus' "brothers and sisters" have already been taken to heaven at the 7th trumpet. Jesus is not calling the sheep *"my brothers,"* because that would imply they had accepted him as Savior, which they have not. He clearly wouldn't call the goats, those who failed the test question and so are rejected, his brothers, nor would he refer to the angels present as brothers. So, if *"my brothers"* doesn't refer to the sheep, the goats, or the angels, then who is this group Jesus acknowledges with that title?

It became clear to me that the people Jesus refers to as *"my brothers"* are the martyrs who had faced persecution and hardship and ultimately gave their lives to uphold their testimony of Jesus. Just moments before this they received the priceless reward promised to them during the 5th seal. They have been resurrected, given immortal bodies, and are now getting ready to take their places as co-regents with Jesus as the Millennium begins. [252] During this

---

[252] The group Jesus is referring to may also include some of the remnant Jews he

Sheep and Goat Separation, this group will sit in a place of honor near him. As Jesus answers the questions posed by the sheep, he will acknowledge this special group, so dear to his heart, with a nod and refer to them as *"my brothers."*

> *35 For I was hungry and you gave me food, I was thirsty and you gave me drink, I was a stranger and you welcomed me, 36 I was naked and you clothed me, I was sick and you visited me, I was in prison and you came to me.' 37 Then the righteous will answer him, saying, 'Lord, when did we see you hungry and feed you, or thirsty and give you drink? 38 And when did we see you a stranger and welcome you, or naked and clothe you? 39 And when did we see you sick or in prison and visit you?' 40 And the King will answer them, 'Truly, I say to you, as you did it to one of the least of these my brothers, you did it to me.'* (Matthew 25:35-40 ESV)

The test question Jesus asks each survivor assembled before him is simple: "When you encountered my people, the Jews and Christians who were imprisoned or fleeing persecution and the threat of execution, how did you respond?"

If a survivor answers that they provided shelter, food, water, or any form of relief to ease the suffering of these refugees who had endured abuse, imprisonment, or starvation during the Great Tribulation, or if they voted for leaders who sought to protect or help them, they will be deemed sheep. Those who showed compassion to Jesus' people during the tribulation will be counted as sheep and led to Jesus' right side, near his "brothers". However, few of the survivors before him will be counted as sheep.

---

had just gathered from prisons and "holes" around the world.

But woe to those who answer that they ignored his refugees or, worse, did something that made their plight more difficult. If they went along with the crowd by persecuting or shaming the refugees, casting their ballots and voting for a politician who made the lives of these refugees more difficult, or if they neglected to vote for a leader who would have improved their plight, they won't make the cut. If Jesus cannot find anything redemptive that they did to lessen the suffering of his people, they will be classified as goats and sent to his left, which means they are not worthy of a second chance. And if you think some might lie to save their lives, remember they are now in the presence of Jesus, who cannot be deceived.

The Sheep and Goat Separation is not part of the final judgment as many teach. Instead, it is a vetting process through which Jesus determines who among the survivors will be allowed to remain alive and granted the privilege of a second chance to know him and accept him as their Savior.

Final Judgment occurs on Judgment Day, after life is over. It is reserved for the resurrected, and the Book containing everything they did or thought during their entire life is opened. But these people standing before Jesus now are very much alive, so their Book of Life is not yet complete, which is why Jesus does not open and judge them using it.[253]

But, and this is an important distinction, the sheep are not "saved" for eternity just because they made the cut. Making the cut gives them a second chance by allowing them to live during the Millennial Reign of Christ, but it's not for an eternity. In verse 46, the word *eternal* is the Greek *aionios* which means 'agelong' or

---

[253] *"And if anyone's name was not found written in the book of life, he was thrown into the lake of fire"* (Revelation 20:15 ESV).

'lasts for an age,' which is a more literal translation.[254] An 'age' in this context is 1,000 years.

> And these shall go away into age-lasting punishment,
> but the righteous into age-lasting life.
> (Matthew 25:46 Worrell translation)[255]

This wording indicates that when these sheep eventually die at some point during the Millennium or the rebellion at the end of the Millennium, and they will be resurrected to face the real Judgment Day.

> And just as it is appointed for man to die once, and
> after that comes judgment, (Hebrews 9:27 ESV)

But what, then, is the fate of the goats? It's dreadful. Verse 46 states they are thrown into hell for an age.[256] They will be killed and cast into hell, the bad side of Hades, where they will remain until Judgment Day, which will take place after the 1,000-year reign of Christ is over. Isaiah seems to confirm this fate, telling us that those who *"strive against"* God's people will ultimately get what they deserve; they will *"perish."*

> Behold, all who are incensed against you shall be put

---

[254] Bible Hub, "Matthew 25:46," Weymouth New Testament Translation, https://biblehub.com/matthew/25-46.htm. "And these shall go away into the Punishment of the Ages, but the righteous into the Life of the Ages."

[255] (Bible Hub, "Matthew 25:46," Worrell New Testament, biblehub.com, https://biblehub.com/parallel/matthew/25-46.htm)

[256] I used the Morrell translation for Matthew 25:46 because it's the only version that captured this essence of the Greek in its translation. Most other versions translated it "for eternity," which is another way the Greek can be interpreted.

*to shame and confounded; those who strive against you
shall be as nothing and shall perish.* (Isaiah 41:11 ESV)

Since everyone deserves their day in court, with all the books of their lives opened, on Judgment Day, these goats will be resurrected from Hades to face a full judgment. This time, it is not only for how they treated Christians and Jews but for everything they did in life. [257]

---

[257] The goats will be resurrected on Judgment Day along with everyone else existing in deprivation in hell, the uncomfortable side of Sheol. When they are resurrected on Judgment Day, Sheol will be empty because the Paradise side of Sheol was already emptied by Jesus during the First Harvest.

# 29 The Millennial Reign of Christ: The God of Second Chances

The only mortals remaining alive when the Millennial reign of Christ begins on earth will be those few unbelievers who were just declared *"sheep"* and all the surviving Jews, including the 144,000. This means that if you are reading this and are a Christian, you will not, as many teach, be alive during the Millennium. You may be a resurrected martyr helping Jesus administer it, but there will be no Christian mortals present at the start of the 1,000 years.

What is the Millennium? It's an interim span of 1,000 years between the old world and the time when the world will be reborn. It's not heaven, but it's much better than our current world, because the Lord will be the head of the government, the resurrected martyrs will help him rule, and Satan will be chained in hell until the very end.

God is fulfilling his covenant promise to the Jews, granting them a second chance to know him and accept him as their Lord and Savior. In the same way that we Gentiles get to share in the blessing of salvation originally offered to the Jews, those counted as sheep will now share in the second chance surviving Jews are given to learn about Jesus and accept him as their Savior. These two groups will be given an opportunity to get to know the Lord under these nearly idyllic conditions and either accept him as their Savior or rebel against him. Sadly, we know from Revelation 20:8 that many will reject Jesus at the end of the 1,000-year reign and join forces with Satan soon after he's temporarily paroled from the bottomless pit..

What will the Millennial Reign of Christ be like? Isaiah tells us that during the Millennium, people will have no stress or tears. Their lifespans will be long but will not last forever.

*I will rejoice in Jerusalem and be glad in my people; no more shall be heard in it the sound of weeping and the cry of distress. 20 No more shall there be in it an infant who lives but a few days, or an old man who does not fill out his days, for the young man shall die a hundred years old, and the sinner a hundred years old shall be accursed.* (Isaiah 65:19–20 ESV)

People will work. Yes, you read that correctly. Humans were designed to care for God's creation, and now they will fulfill their destiny.[258] They will farm, fish, build their own homes, and gather wood for heat. There will be no army or training for war, so they'll convert weapons of war into farming tools, and then personally use those tools and *"enjoy the work of their hands."*

*21 They shall build houses and inhabit them; they shall plant vineyards and eat their fruit. 22 They shall not build and another inhabit; they shall not plant and another eat; for like the days of a tree shall the days of my people be, and my chosen shall long enjoy the work of their hands. 23 They shall not labor in vain or bear children for calamity, for they shall be the offspring of the blessed of the LORD, and their descendants with them.* (Isaiah 65:21–23 ESV)

Micah tells us that Mount Zion, currently at an elevation of around 2,500 feet, will become *"the highest of mountains"* after the worldwide earthquakes of the 7th bowl bring all other mountains

---

[258] Genesis 2:15 (ESV): "The LORD God took the man and put him in the garden of Eden to work it and keep it."

low. It will be the site where the new temple, *"the house of the Lord,"* will be built.

> *1 It shall come to pass in the latter days that the mountain of the house of the LORD shall be established as the highest of the mountains, and it shall be lifted up above the hills; and peoples shall flow to it, 2 and many nations shall come, and say: "Come, let us go up to the mountain of the LORD, to the house of the God of Jacob, that he may teach us his ways and that we may walk in his paths." For out of Zion shall go forth the law, and the word of the LORD from Jerusalem. 3 He shall judge between many peoples, and shall decide disputes for strong nations far away; and they shall beat their swords into plowshares, and their spears into pruning hooks; nation shall not lift up sword against nation, neither shall they learn war anymore;*
> (Micah 4:1–3 ESV)

Isaiah 2:2-3 says the same exact thing, which is not too surprising since they were contemporaries and were apparently referencing some older text known to both of them.[259]

> *It shall come to pass in the latter days that the mountain of the house of the LORD shall be established as the highest of the mountains, and shall be lifted up above the hills; and all the nations shall flow to it, 3 and*

---

[259] "The question as to which prophecy, (Micah 4:1-3 or Isaiah 2:2-3) is the earlier cannot be settled. Possibly both prophets [Micah and Isaiah] borrowed the language of some earlier work, as Isaiah is thought to have done on other occasions" (Bible Hub, "Micah 4:1," Pulpit Commentary, biblehub.com, https://biblehub.com/commentaries/micah/4-1.htm)

> *many peoples shall come, and say: "Come, let us go up*
> *to the mountain of the LORD, to the house of the God*
> *of Jacob, that he may teach us his ways and that we*
> *may walk in his paths." For out of Zion shall go forth*
> *the law, and the word of the LORD from Jerusalem.*
> (Isaiah 2:2–3 ESV)

Jesus will teach the people his ways. It's hard to imagine how amazing that will be for those sheep and Jews. They will enjoy the fruits of their own labor, and no one will break into their houses or steal their possessions. They will have children, and their children will not be killed or die of disease, and they will be taught by Jesus himself!

Jesus will know their prayers and answer them before they can even formulate the words!

> *24 Before they call I will answer; while they are yet*
> *speaking I will hear.* (Isaiah 65:24 ESV)

But this implies that there will still be things that people will need to pray about, which is something I had never considered would be necessary in the Millennium.

# 29.1 All the Kings of the Earth will Respect Zion and Hold Jesus in Awe.

> But you, O LORD, are enthroned forever; you are remembered throughout all generations. 13 You will arise and have pity on Zion; it is the time to favor her; the appointed time has come. 14 For your servants hold her stones dear and have pity on her dust. 15 Nations will fear the name of the LORD, and all the kings of the earth will fear your glory. 16 For the LORD builds up Zion; he appears in his glory; (Psalm 102:12–16 ESV)

Jesus will be with us and sit as judge over all the nations, but his justice will be swift.

> He shall judge between the nations, and shall decide disputes for many peoples;... (Isaiah 2:4a ESV)

This is truly fascinating. Even in a world of near-perfect conditions, with Jesus reigning as King and Satan no longer present, nations and their kings will still exist, and there will still be conflicts and disagreements among them. Jesus himself will step in to resolve these disputes, demonstrating his wisdom and justice. But he won't do it alone. This is where the resurrected martyrs come into play. Just as Moses appointed tribal elders to help settle disputes, these martyrs will serve as co-regents of Jesus, acting as trusted judges to help maintain peace and harmony in his Kingdom. [260]

---

[260] *"Now obey my voice; I will give you advice, and God be with you! You shall represent the people before God and bring their cases to God, 20 and you shall warn them about the statutes and the laws, and make them know the way in which they*

*. . . then a throne will be established in steadfast love,
and on it will sit in faithfulness in the tent of David
one who judges and seeks justice and is swift to do
righteousness."* (Isaiah 16:5 ESV)

Can you imagine going before a judge who can see into your
thoughts and discern your motives, distinguishing truth from lies?
If you take someone before Jesus' court, you'd better be justified
because Jesus will rule with a *"rod of iron,"* as emphasized in
multiple verses.

*. . . and he will rule them with a rod of iron...*
(Revelation 19:15a ESV)

*She gave birth to a male child, one who is to rule all the
nations with a rod of iron* (Revelation 12:5a ESV)

*. . . and he will rule them with a rod of iron, as when
earthen pots are broken in pieces, even as I myself
have received authority from my Father.*
(Revelation 2:27 ESV)

This is no ceremonial rod of gold, nor a flexible rod of steel;
it's a rod of stiff, unbendable iron. This suggests that during the
Millennium, there will be no more mercy. And why should there
be? Everyone will be living under the perfect ruler, without Satan

---

*must walk and what they must do. 21 Moreover, look for able men from all the people,
men who fear God, who are trustworthy and hate a bribe, and place such men over
the people as chiefs of thousands, of hundreds, of fifties, and of tens. 22 And let them
judge the people at all times. Every great matter they shall bring to you, but any small
matter they shall decide themselves. So it will be easier for you, and they will bear the
burden with you"* (Exodus 18:19-22 ESV)

or demons constantly working to undermine them? There will be only right and wrong, with no gray areas left for interpretation. A rod of iron means Jesus will rule with ultimate fairness and justice, being "*swift to do righteousness.*" The kings are, therefore, warned to be wise, or else Jesus will "*dash them in pieces like a potter's vessel.*"

> *Ask of me, and I will make the nations your heritage, and the ends of the earth your possession. 9 You shall break them with a rod of iron and dash them in pieces like a potter's vessel." 10 Now therefore, O kings, be wise; be warned, O rulers of the earth.* (Psalm 2:8–10 ESV)

The Millennium will be a time of great peace and long lifespans. There will be no threats or dangers from nature, including natural disasters, and people will have direct access to Jesus. And did I mention there will be no temptation from Satan? At least not until the very end of the thousand years. You would think people would love this idyllic, farm-to-table existence, yet astonishingly, many will not.

## 29.2 Trouble in Paradise

At the end of the thousand years, as unlikely as it seems, there will be many people, *"as numerous as the grains of sand in the sea,"* who become disenchanted with this utopian life with Jesus. It will be history repeating itself. Just as when God led his people to the land of Canaan, a land *"flowing with milk and honey,"* where they had everything they could have wanted, they inexplicably turned to other gods, just as he had foretold.

> For after *I have brought them to the land I promised* to their ancestors—one flowing with milk and honey— and they eat their fill and become fat, *then they will turn* *to other gods* and worship them; they will reject me and break my covenant. (Deuteronomy 31:20 NET)

The fact that people will rebel after living in the physical presence of Jesus for 1,000 years breaks my heart. I can't imagine what it does to Jesus.

It may be because Jesus *"rules with a rod of iron,"* or perhaps because people resist living as God originally intended in the Garden of Eden, in harmony with the rest of nature. But for whatever reason, many will rebel... again. [261]

Just as the survivors of the Great Tribulation who were deemed worthy (the *"sheep"*) were granted a second chance to change their ways and accept Jesus as their Savior, Satan is released into the new Garden of Eden and given a chance to change his ways and

---

[261] There is no mention of any manufacturing or technology. In fact, people are repurposing swords by hammering them into plowshares. So, I suspect the memory of the days of technology will be brought back by Satan when he is paroled.

acknowledge God as Lord. Yet, he cannot resist his old ways. His actions lay bare his true nature to the angels, dispelling any remaining doubts they might have had about God's treatment of him. They now see with undeniable clarity that God has been right and just all along. Even after 1,000 years of reflecting on the suffering he has inflicted *"in heaven and on earth and under the earth,"* Satan feels no remorse and has no intention of changing his ways.

Instead, he remains hell-bent on his rebellion against God. Seizing his newfound parole from his chains in the depths of hell, Satan uses his powers of persuasion to exploit the underlying dissatisfaction simmering within many, swiftly convincing them to rise in rebellion against the camp of Jesus.

> *After these things he* [Satan] *must be released for a brief period of time.* (Revelation 20:3b NET)

> *Now when the thousand years are finished, Satan will be released from his prison 8 and will go out to deceive the nations at the four corners of the earth, Gog and Magog, to bring them together for the battle. They are as numerous as the grains of sand in the sea.* (Revelation 20:7–8 NET)

The rebellion will be quickly extinguished. Just as fire and brimstone destroyed Sodom and every one of its people, fire comes down from heaven and *"devoured"* the millions of rebels who surround the camp of the saints.

*They went up on the broad plain of the earth and encircled the camp of the saints and the beloved city, but fire came down from heaven and devoured them completely.* (Revelation 20:9 NET)[262]

*"Devoured"* implies that their bodies will be vaporized, sparing the faithful survivors from having to locate and bury the rebels' bodies as they did after the battle of Har-Magedon. [263]

You may wonder why Satan was allowed to tempt the people living in this nearly perfect world. The reason becomes clear when you consider that these people are either survivors or the children of survivors who were not Christians when the Millennium began. Living each day in the physical presence of Jesus would likely convince most people to accept him as their Savior, and it's reasonable to assume that most, if not all, do. However, with hunger, disease, homelessness, war, and premature death nearly eliminated, their faith has never truly been tested by hardship. As discussed in Chapter 3, Jesus desires more than fair-weather followers. When God releases Satan, he knows that Satan will remain unchanged and will do what he always does: challenge believers' faith through deception. Tragically, a vast number, *"..as numerous as the grains of sand in the sea,"* fail this test.

Millions of these sheep and their descendants, despite getting a second chance at eternal life and the privilege of living in a virtual paradise alongside their Creator, now, incredibly, reject their salvation by siding with the newly released Satan.

---

[262] This is further support that the 7th bowl brought the tectonic plates back together and leveled the mountains. The earth is now a broad plain, or one continuous and relatively level landmass.

[263] Interestingly, we're not told if their souls were sent into the lake of fire with Satan. Wherever they go, they will soon be resurrected to face Judgment Day, which occurs almost immediately after this tragic event.

Even though Jesus knows these millions of people will turn on him, just as God knew Adam would choose Satan's offer of the knowledge of good and evil, the pain of betrayal is no less real. Foreknowledge doesn't soften the sting of rejection.

But this rebellion will be Satan's last.

> *. . . and the devil who had deceived them was thrown into the lake of fire and sulfur where the beast and the false prophet were, and they will be tormented day and night forever and ever.* (Revelation 20:10 ESV)

# Part Nine:

# Judgment Day

# 30 The Day of Reckoning

*And just as it is appointed for man to die once, and
after that comes judgment, (Hebrews 9:27 ESV)*

The Millennium is over. The survivors of the Great Tribulation
and their offspring have had their opportunity for a second chance
to accept Jesus. Now everyone *"in heaven and on earth and under
the earth"* must face their day of reckoning.[264]

*Rise up, O God, and execute judgment on the earth!
For you own all the nations.* (Psalm 82:8 NET)

All the books will be opened, and everyone's deeds, even their
thoughts, will be laid bare. It will begin with God judging the
demons and end with Jesus judging humans.

The term *"judgment"* is interesting for several reasons:

1.  Didn't God make a judgment that Adam and Eve were not
    worthy to continue occupying Eden?
2.  Wasn't a judgment already made when each person died,
    determining which part of Sheol their temporary body would
    reside in, the pleasant or the miserable side?
3.  Didn't Jesus also make a judgment during the First Harvest,
    choosing only those he deemed worthy to go to heaven in the
    Blessed Hope?
4.  Furthermore, *"on the day of his wrath,"* during the Second
    Harvest and the subsequent white-horse slaughter, doesn't

---

[264] Revelation 5:13b ESV

Jesus use his judgment to kill ("*shatter*") only those who bore the mark of the beast or had mercilessly persecuted the Jews?

> *The Lord is at your right hand; he will shatter kings on the day of his wrath. 6 He will execute judgment among the nations, filling them with corpses; he will shatter chiefs over the wide earth. (Psalm 110:5–6 ESV)*

Since a form of judgment has been ongoing throughout history, Judgment Day serves as the formal demonstration that every decision and action God makes has always been completely just. As with all formal proceedings, the books of evidence are opened, and what is revealed within them will bring all creation, *"in heaven and on earth and under the earth,"* to understand that God's judgments are truly just and fair and have always been so. Judgment Day is not just about delivering a verdict for each defendant; it is the ultimate display of God's righteousness, openly and undeniably confirming he is just for all creation to witness.

# 30.1 Judgment of Demons

Jesus will preside over the judgment of humanity, while God, the *"Ancient of Days,"* will preside over the judgment of the demons.[265] God, who keeps meticulous and perfect records, will open some of these books before tens of thousands of angels, placing Satan and his demons on trial at last.

God holds this event in front of all creation and conducts these formal proceedings so that his holy angels, along with anyone who was part of the Council of God, can see and understand that he is following an orderly set of rules. He wants to show that he does not take lightly what he is about to do. God will demonstrate how Jesus adhered to all the requirements of the 7-sealed book and fairly won the Kingdom from Satan. He will show them that Satan not only lost the contest for his kingdom but also disqualified himself by breaking at least two rules: attempting to kill God's marked 144,000 Jews and trying to destroy the earth. However, it's likely that God will provide evidence that he violated many other rules of the 7-sealed book. All of this will be deliberately revealed before God's angels so that they will understand that God is just.

Remember that Satan had convinced at least 1/3rd of God's angels that God was being unreasonable in refusing to forgive the Watcher angels, even after they had served thousands of years of imprisonment in hell. Therefore, it is essential for God to demonstrate to the remaining angels that his decision to destroy these fallen angels, along with Satan and his demons, is fully justified. The undeniable proof will come when God presents evidence before the assembled witnesses, showing Satan's unwillingness to change. God will explain

---

[265] John 5:22 (ESV): "For the Father judges no one, but has given all judgment to the Son,"

that he sentenced Satan to 1,000 years of solitary confinement in hell to calm his rage and give him time to reflect on how far he had fallen by rebelling. Yet Satan, as soon as he was paroled and set free in paradise, proving that he is irredeemable, returns immediately to his old ways of rebellion and chaos. If the previous evidence did not already convince the angels that God's treatment of Satan was just, this last example will be impossible to deny.

> 9 *"While I was watching, thrones were set up, and the Ancient of Days took his seat. His attire was white like snow; the hair of his head was like lamb's wool. His throne was ablaze with fire and its wheels were all aflame. 10 A river of fire was streaming forth and proceeding from his presence. Many thousands were ministering to him; many tens of thousands stood ready to serve him. . .* (Daniel 7:9–10a NET)

But right up to the end, Satan (or there's a possibility this is his antichrist) is mouthy and *"arrogant."*

> 10b *...many tens of thousands stood ready to serve him. The court convened and the books were opened. 11 "Then I kept on watching because of the arrogant words of the horn that was speaking. I was watching until the beast was killed and its body destroyed and thrown into the flaming fire.* (Daniel 7:10b–11 NET)

This next portion is interesting in that it reveals that there was more than one beast. The antichrist and his false prophet were each referred to as beasts and they had already been thrown into the lake of fire. So *"the rest of the beasts"* indicates that there were more.

*12 As for the rest of the beasts, their dominion was taken away, but their lives were prolonged for a season and a time.* (Daniel 7:12 ESV)

So, who are these other beasts in Daniel 7:12? It's possible they are some of the *"sons of God,"* the supernatural beings that had been assigned to specific regions of the world soon after the Tower of Babel incident.[266]

*When the Most High gave to the nations their inheritance, when he divided mankind, he fixed the borders of the peoples according to the number of the sons of God.* (Deuteronomy 32:8 ESV)

We haven't heard anything about these principalities since Gabriel described his personal battles with the King of Persia and the King of Greece in the book of Daniel. Additionally, Paul tells us in Ephesians 6 that there are unseen principalities with whom we wrestle. For some unexplained reason, God allows these specific principalities to continue a little longer, for *"a season and a time."*

Satan, however, will not be granted this extension, as God's holy angels will end his freedom, and he will never again be paroled.

*And the devil who deceived them was thrown into the lake of fire and sulfur, where the beast and the false prophet are too, and they will be tormented there day and night forever and ever.* (Revelation 20:10 ESV)

After this will come Judgment Day for every human who has ever lived.

---

[266] Michael S. Heiser, *The Unseen Realm*, 112–113.

## 30.2 The 'Second' Resurrection: ALL Rise

*"At the set time that I appoint I will judge with equity"*
(Psalm 75:2 ESV)

The First Resurrection was a reward exclusively for those martyred during the Great Tribulation, and it took place just before the Millennium. Then, at the sound of the 7th trumpet, Jesus commanded Satan to release the souls of those who died as believers, the *"dead in Christ,"* as well as believers who were alive. Both groups were given incorruptible, though not yet fully complete, bodies and then escorted to their rooms in heaven.

The second resurrection, though not explicitly called that, is for everyone else. The *"rest of the dead"* refers to every unbeliever who has ever died. This includes everyone who remained in Sheol after Jesus raised the *"dead in Christ"* from Paradise.

> *(The rest of the dead did not come to life until the thousand years were finished.)* (Revelation 20:5a NET)

To bring the rest of the souls to judgment, he will now command "Death and Hades" to release the rest of the souls, those who were not Christians.

> *And many of them that sleep in the dust of the earth shall awake, some to everlasting life, and some to shame and everlasting contempt.* (Daniel 12:2 KJV)

It may surprise some to learn that Judgment Day includes every believer and every non-believer.[267] Yes, those who were taken up to meet the Lord in the air during the First Harvest, who received incorruptible bodies and have been awaiting his return in their glorious rooms in heaven, will also face Judgment Day. Though they were given incorruptible bodies, these were not fully complete. Now, as they descend to earth for Judgment Day, they will undergo their final transformation, receiving eternal, physical, immortal bodies.

Judgment Day is not like the earlier Sheep and Goat Separation, where survivors were asked a simple question and those who answered correctly were deemed worthy of a second chance and allowed to enter the Millennial Kingdom. This is the final judgment, and its verdict cannot be appealed. It will stand for eternity.

Interestingly, we also learn that Hades (or Sheol in Hebrew) isn't the only place where souls are held, as the sea also releases some souls.

> 13 And the sea gave up the dead who were in it, Death and Hades gave up the dead who were in them, and they were judged, each one of them, according to what they had done. 14 Then Death and Hades were thrown into the lake of fire. This is the second death, the lake of fire. 15 And if anyone's name was not found written in the book of life, he was thrown into the lake of fire. (Revelation 20:13–15 ESV)

Every person who has ever lived will be resurrected into an eternal body and come face-to-face with Jesus simultaneously to face their judgment.[268]

---

[267] All except the martyrs, who were resurrected at the First Resurrection.

[268] Except those resurrected during the First Resurrection, the martyred saints

*For we must all appear before the judgment seat of Christ, so that each one may receive what is due for what he has done in the body, whether good or evil.*
(2 Corinthians 5:10 ESV)

But how many people are we talking about? It's impossible to know for certain, but the World Economic Forum estimates that over 100 billion people have lived and died throughout human history. [269]

If you thought the 200 million cavalry was unimaginably large, consider what it will be like when 100 billion resurrected people are gathered together. How could such an enormous crowd possibly fit in one place? What better location than somewhere above the earth, where Jesus will have the immense space needed to accommodate tens of billions.

To make room for everyone, it is said that the earth *"fled away"* from beneath them, leaving this massive assembly of resurrected humans *"standing"* in the heavens before Jesus.

*11 Then I saw a great white throne and him who was seated on it. From his presence earth and sky fled away, and no place was found for them. 12 And I saw the dead, great and small, standing before the throne, and books were opened. Then another book was opened, which is the book of life. And the dead were judged by what was written in the books, according to what they had done. (Revelation 20:11–12 ESV)*

---

of the Great Tribulation.

[269] The WEF estimates that 109 billion people have lived and died over the course of 192,000 years (Nick Routley, "This is how many humans have ever existed, according to researchers," April 4, 2022, World Economic Forum, https://www.weforum.org/agenda/2022/04/quantifying-human-existence/).

# 30.3 Why Isn't God Our Judge?

God gets everything ready for Judgment Day. He *"raises all the dead and gives them life,"* clothes them in their eternal bodies, and assembles them above the earth. Then, he entrusts the process of judging to Jesus, who will sit as the Judge of all mankind.

> *For as the Father raises the dead and gives them life, so also the Son gives life to whom he will. 22 For the Father judges no one, but has given all judgment to the Son, 23 that all may honor the Son, just as they honor the Father. Whoever does not honor the Son does not honor the Father who sent him.* (John 5:21–23 ESV)

There are two main reasons why Jesus *"the Son,"* not God *"the Father,"* is the one who judges humanity.

1. First, God's perfect standards:

   If God judged us by his own perfect standards, none of us would stand a chance. Every human being has fallen short of God's perfection.

   *". . . for all have sinned and fall short of the glory of God."* (Romans 3:23 ESV)

   Recognizing that it was impossible for humans to meet his perfect standards, and that he could not just water-down those standards, God provided another way of salvation by sending his Son to live and die fully as a human.

*"For God so loved the world, that he gave his only Son, that whoever believes in him should not perish but have eternal life." (John 3:16 ESV)*

A key part of Satan's power as ruler of this world is his authority to hold every sinner captive in Sheol. Every person who has died since humanity began has died a sinner except Jesus. Living fully as a human, Jesus resisted every temptation and remained sinless, the only one to meet God's perfect standard. Because he died without sin, Satan was powerless to detain him in Sheol. Thus, Jesus walked free from Sheol and ascended to take his place at the right hand of God.

*". . . through the resurrection of Jesus Christ, who has gone into heaven and is at the right hand of God, with angels, authorities, and powers having been subjected to him."* (1 Peter 3:21b–22 ESV)

2.  Second, Jesus' personal relationship with his sheep:

Jesus is the one who judges because he personally knows those who have made a covenant with him. As he says, *"My sheep hear my voice, and I know them"* (John 10:27 ESV). God, who demands perfection, accepts Jesus' perfect sacrifice as a substitute for the failings of his flock. On Judgment Day, Jesus will vouch for each of his sheep before the Father, ensuring their place in heaven.

*but you do not believe because you are not among my sheep. 27 My sheep hear my voice, and I know them, and they follow me. 28 I give them eternal life, and they will never perish, and no one will snatch them out of my hand. 29 My Father, who has given them to me, is greater than all, and no one is able to snatch them out of the Father's hand. 30 I and the Father are one. (John 10:26–30 ESV)*

But woe to those who never entered into a covenant with Jesus.

# 30.4 By What Standard are we Judged?

On Judgment Day, Jesus will publicly show everyone, "*every creature in heaven and on earth and under the earth and in the sea,*" that God is the God of order and justice. It's Jesus' moment to present the evidence and prove to each person, and to every angel witnessing the judgment, that his decisions are fair and perfect.[270]

While we all live under grace now, on Judgment Day, Jesus will judge everyone ("*the world*") by a set standard.

> *Therefore, although God has overlooked such times of ignorance, he now commands all people everywhere to repent, 31 because he has set a day on which he is going to judge the world in righteousness, by a man whom he designated, having provided proof to everyone by raising him from the dead.* (Acts 17:30–31 NET)

Each person's actions and thoughts will be measured against a specific standard. For Christians, this standard will be the teachings of the Bible and the guidance of the Holy Spirit. For non-Christians and non-Jews (Gentiles) who never had the opportunity to hear the gospel, their judgment will depend on whether they followed the innate sense of right and wrong that God has placed in every human heart.

> *Even Gentiles, who do not have God's written law, show that they know his law when they instinctively obey it, even without having heard it. 15 They demonstrate that God's law is written in their hearts, for their own conscience and thoughts either accuse them or tell them*

---

[270] Revelation 5:13b ESV

*they are doing right.* (Romans 2:14-15 NLT)

Some verses suggest that judgment will be far more complex than we might think. God understands each of us fully. He knows the unique gifts and talents he gave us and the opportunities each of us had or didn't have in life. He knows whether the gospel was presented to us and whether we truly grasped it. In Luke, we see that Jesus will consider all of these factors, ensuring that everyone is judged fairly.

> *But the one who did not know, and did what deserved a beating, will receive a light beating. Everyone to whom much was given, of him much will be required, and from him to whom they entrusted much, they will demand the more.* (Luke 12:48 ESV)

Remember, the judgment process will reveal that Jesus is perfectly fair and just. Every verdict he delivers based on the evidence presented in the books will be undeniable and beyond question. But it won't just be humans who witness and affirm the justice of Jesus—his angels will also observe his perfect fairness. When the judgment is complete, no one *"in heaven and on earth and under the earth"* will be able to challenge or claim that Jesus was unjust. [271] His decisions will be universally recognized as righteous.

In the parable of the talents, in Matthew 25:14-30, Jesus teaches that we will be judged not only on whether we use our God-given gifts but also on how we choose to apply them, whether for good, evil, or selfish purposes. For example, consider someone with a gift for creativity. If they used it to design addictive games that ultimately influenced children toward violence, their judgment would be starkly different from that of someone who used the same talent to

---

[271] Revelation 5:13b ESV

create games that are both entertaining and educational, guiding children toward positive growth. This parable emphasizes that it's not just what we do but the impact of our actions that matters.

For his sheep, those who are in a covenant relationship with him, Jesus will grant eternal life in heaven.

> *Jesus answered them, "I told you, and you do not believe. The works that I do in my Father's name bear witness about me, 26 but you do not believe because you are not among my sheep. 27 My sheep hear my voice, and I know them, and they follow me. 28 I give them eternal life, and they will never perish, and no one will snatch them out of my hand. 29 My Father, who has given them to me, is greater than all, and no one is able to snatch them out of the Father's hand. 30 I and the Father are one." (John 10: 25–30 ESV)*

John affirms that those in Christ have nothing to fear on Judgment Day. They rest securely in the confidence that Jesus will never leave them or forsake them.

> *By this is love perfected with us, so that we may have confidence for the day of judgment, because as he is so also are we in this world. (1 John 4:17 ESV)*

Jesus will stand as the advocate for each of his sheep, serving as their sole defense. After the books are opened, and every thought and action of your life is read aloud, you will fully grasp the depth of your failures, the countless ways you fell short of God's perfect standard, and the punishment that awaits those who have done so. As one of his sheep, Jesus, standing beside you as your advocate, will turn to his Father, and in the hearing of all his angels, he will say your name and declare, "He (or she) is mine; I've covered it all."

Only in that moment will you truly grasp the immeasurable depth of what Jesus' life and death has done for you. He relinquished his divine throne in heaven, achieved the impossible by living a human life without sinning, voluntarily poured out his absolutely pure lifeblood as a sacrificial offering on the cross, and rose in triumph from Sheol to make a way for you to follow. Then, the depth of your gratitude for Jesus will surpass all description which will render to God what he has desired *"since the foundation of the world:"* your true, heartfelt love, adoration, and worship.

> *The one who conquers will be clothed thus in white garments, and I will never blot his name out of the book of life. I will confess his name before my Father and before his angels. (Revelation 3:5 ESV)*

The believer passes from death to life the moment he or she *"believes him who sent me."* This confirms that those in Christ have nothing to fear on Judgment Day.

> *Truly, truly, I say to you, whoever hears my word and believes him who sent me has eternal life. He does not come into judgment, but has passed from death to life. 25 "Truly, truly, I say to you, an hour is coming, and is now here, when the dead will hear the voice of the Son of God, and those who hear will live. 26 For as the Father has life in himself, so he has granted the Son also to have life in himself. (John 5:24–26 ESV)*

Jesus will hand out crowns to his saints who have *"works"* that warrant rewards.

*And when the chief Shepherd appears, you will receive the unfading crown of glory.* (1 Peter 5:4 ESV)

*6 He will reward each one according to his works: 7 eternal life to those who by perseverance in good works seek glory and honor and immortality* (Romans 2:6–7 NET)

But if you are not one of his sheep you will stand there alone, with no one to speak in your defense.[272]

Picture this utterly horrifying moment: as you cower there, exposed, with every hidden thought and secret deed laid bare, you will finally realize that your choice to reject Jesus—despite all the times he placed someone in your path to reach you—has brought you to this point. When you lift your forlorn head toward your Judge, desperate for a glimmer of mercy, Jesus will meet your gaze and utter these soul-shattering words: *'I never knew you; depart from me.'*[273]

Then, you will understand that your verdict—the Second Death, spending eternity in that dreadful Lake of Fire—was the inevitable destination of the road you recklessly and stubbornly chose. You ignored and avoided the God of order during your life, so you will be granted your foolish wish in death as you are ushered from God's presence and cast out into chaos.

---

[272] This is yet another tragic, yet inevitable, consequence of free will. By choosing to reject what Christ freely offered during life, these people have, by definition, chosen to waive their right of "counsel" during the trial of their life. They have rejected their one and only opportunity for an advocate.

[273] *And then will I declare to them, 'I never knew you; depart from me, you workers of lawlessness. (Matthew 7:23 ESV)*

# 30.5 Is it a Judgment Seat or Great White Throne?

The prevailing view among Christian teachers is that there is a special judgment for believers (the "*Judgment Seat of Christ*") and a separate and terrible judgment for unbelievers (the "*Great White Throne*"). However, a close examination of all verses related to Judgment Day reveals no clear evidence for two separate judgments. Instead, Scripture points to a single, comprehensive judgment in which all people, both saved and unsaved, are judged at the same time.[274] Sometimes, this judgment is referred to as the Great White Throne and sometimes as the Judgment Seat of Christ. You should think of it as one judgment, with Jesus seated on a white throne.

Here is the rationale for understanding them as the same judgment. Revelation 20:11–15, often cited as a judgment solely for those who die without Christ, actually provides evidence to the contrary. In this passage, John describes the judgment scene:

> *Then I saw a great white throne and him who was seated on it*. From his presence earth and sky fled away, and no place was found for them. 12 And I saw the dead, great and small, standing before the throne, and books were opened. Then another book was opened, which is the book of life. And *the dead* were *judged by what was written in the books, according to what they had done*. 13 And the sea gave up the dead who were in it, Death and Hades

---

[274] This verse from Ezekiel is the only one I found that might be construed to indicate a judgment of just Christians, or "*sheep*", but it doesn't sound like it applies to Judgment Day. *I will rescue my flock; they shall no longer be a prey. And I will judge between sheep and sheep.* (Ezekiel 34:22 ESV)

gave up the dead who were in them, and they were judged, each one of them, according to what they had done. 14 Then Death and Hades were thrown into the lake of fire. This is the second death, the lake of fire. 15 *And if anyone's name was not found written in the book of life, he was thrown into the lake of fire.* (Revelation 20:11–15 ESV)

The key phrase here is, "*if anyone's name was not found in the Book of Life,*" which implies that some names were indeed found in the Book of Life at this judgment. If the judgment were solely for unbelievers, it would likely state, "none of their names were found written in the book of life." This strongly suggests that both saved and unsaved individuals are present at the Great White Throne Judgment, and that it is not exclusively for those who died without Christ.

So what about the Judgment Seat of Christ, which many say is only for believers? Paul writes that "*all*" will appear before that seat.

"*For we must all appear before the judgment seat of Christ, so that each one may receive what is due for what he has done in the body, whether good or evil.*"
(2 Corinthians 5:10 ESV)

The use of "*all*" indicates that every person must appear before Christ's judgment seat. If "*all*" must appear before the judgment seat, then both the saved and the unsaved are included in this single judgment event, suggesting that this judgment seat of Christ is the Great White Throne Judgment.

The language in both Revelation 20 and 2 Corinthians 5 supports the idea that all will appear together before Christ for a single judgment. Therefore, the Judgment Seat of Christ and the Great White Throne Judgment are best understood as the same event. On Judgment Day, Jesus will sit upon this great white throne, and everyone, both saved and unsaved, will stand before him to be judged for what they have done, whether good or evil.

John, Paul, and Peter provide further evidence that all the dead, both those who have "*done good*" and those who have "*done evil*," will hear his voice and come out to appear before him at the same time on judgment day.

> And he has given him authority to execute judgment, because he is the Son of Man. 28 Do not marvel at this, for an hour is coming when all who are in the tombs will hear his voice 29 and come out, those who have done good to the resurrection of life, and those who have done evil to the resurrection of judgment. (John 5:27–29 ESV)

Though verse 29 makes it seem as though the good and the evil will be called out of their tombs at the same time, as we see in many other prophetic verses, there is often a significant span of time between listed events. We know there is a long interval between when the "*good*" are called out of their tombs and those who have "*done evil*" are called out of theirs. The good are called out during the First Harvest at the sound of the 7th trumpet, while the evil are not called out of their tombs until 1,000 years later on Judgment Day. Paul's language here applies to both the good and the evil: we will all "*stand*," we will all "*bow*" to Jesus, and we will all "*confess*" that Jesus is Lord of all.

This means that the saved, together with the unsaved, will stand in one great assembly before the Lord, each giving an account of their actions or inactions to God.

*Why do you pass judgment on your brother? Or you, why do you despise your brother? For we will all stand before the judgment seat of God; 11 for it is written, "As I live, says the Lord, every knee shall bow to me, and every tongue shall confess to God." 12 So then each of us will give an account of himself to God.* (Romans 14:10–12 ESV)

Everyone, "*the living*" (those alive at the end of the Millennium), and "*the dead*" will give an account of their lives to Jesus.

*. . . but they will give account to him who is ready to judge the living and the dead.* (1 Peter 4:5 ESV)

## 30.6 What About Those Who Don't Meet Standards?

Good works warrant rewards, but bad works warrant wrath.

> *but wrath and anger to those who live in selfish ambition and do not obey the truth but follow unrighteousness.* (Romans 2:8 NET)

Some Christians will just barely (*"scarcely"*) make it in, presumably because they barely *"persevered in good works."*

> *For it is time for judgment to begin at the household of God; and if it begins with us, what will be the outcome for those who do not obey the gospel of God? 18 And "If the righteous is scarcely saved, what will become of the ungodly and the sinner?"* (1 Peter 4:17–18 ESV)

If you've ever harbored ulterior motives or bad thoughts during your life, now is the time to ask for forgiveness because nothing will be concealed on Judgment Day. Every thought and motive (*"purposes of the heart"*) will be exposed before all when the books are opened.

> *For I am not aware of anything against myself, but I am not thereby acquitted. It is the Lord who judges me. 5 Therefore do not pronounce judgment before the time, before the Lord comes, who will bring to light the things now hidden in darkness and will disclose the purposes of the heart. Then each one will receive his commendation from God.* (1 Corinthians 4:4–5 ESV)

Honesty, integrity, bravery, and morality are highly valued, but God holds special disdain for cowards, liars, the sexually immoral, and witches.

> He also said to me, "It is done! I am the Alpha and the Omega, the beginning and the end. To the one who is thirsty I will give water free of charge from the spring of the water of life. 7 The one who conquers will inherit these things, and I will be his God and he will be my son. 8 But as for the cowards, unbelievers, detestable persons, murderers, the sexually immoral, and those who practice magic spells, idol worshipers, and all those who lie, their place will be in the lake that burns with fire and sulfur. That is the second death." (Revelation 21:6–8 NET)

What about Christians who can't stop deliberately sinning after being saved? Things don't look good for them. The writer of Hebrews addresses pre-meditated (deliberate) sins here:

> For if we deliberately keep on sinning after receiving the knowledge of the truth, no further sacrifice for sins is left for us, 27 but only a certain fearful expectation of judgment and a fury of fire that will consume God's enemies. (Hebrews 10:26–27 NET)

What about someone who was once saved or made holy by "*the blood of the covenant*" but later rejects or "*profanes*" it? Things look even worse for them. "*Terrifying*," in fact.

*28 Someone who rejected the law of Moses was put to death without mercy on the testimony of two or three witnesses. 29 How much greater punishment do you think that person deserves who has contempt for the Son of God, and profanes the blood of the covenant that made him holy, and insults the Spirit of grace? 30 For we know the one who said, "Vengeance is mine, I will repay," and again, "The Lord will judge his people." 31 It is a terrifying thing to fall into the hands of the living God.* (Hebrews 10:28–31 NET)

What about people who have never heard the gospel but are not wicked? God is a God of justice, so if a person has never been presented with the gospel in a way they could understand, Jesus will judge them not according to the Bible but according to whether they followed the natural law he placed within the heart of every person. Paul seems to suggest here that there is a way for them: as long as they follow the law of their conscience, their inner sense of right and wrong, and have works (as *"doers"*) that reflect this, God will know their *"secrets."* In other words, God will know their true heart and judge them accordingly, which is in keeping with God being the God of justice and order.

But by no stretch would this apply to someone who was presented with the gospel and chose to reject it.

*For all who have sinned without the law will also perish without the law, and all who have sinned under the law will be judged by the law. 13 For it is not the hearers of the law who are righteous before God, but the doers of the law who will be justified. 14 For when Gentiles, who do not have the law, by nature do what the law requires, they are a law to themselves, even though they do not have the law. 15 They show that the work of the law is written on their hearts, while their conscience also bears witness, and their conflicting thoughts accuse or even excuse them 16 on that day when, according to my gospel, God judges the secrets of men by Christ Jesus.* (Romans 2:12–16 ESV)

What happens to those who are judged and whose names are not found in the Lamb's Book of Life? They are counted as wicked.

*The wicked plots against the righteous and gnashes his teeth at him, 13 but the Lord laughs at the wicked, for he sees that his day is coming.* (Psalm 37:12–13 ESV)

*... whoever does not obey the Son shall not see life, but the wrath of God remains on him.* (John 3:36b ESV)

The wicked are unworthy to enter the gates of God's Kingdom and will go to their second death.

# 30.7 The Second Death: The Fate of Unbelievers

*Blessed and holy is the one who shares in the first resurrection! Over such the second death has no power* (Revelation 20:6a ESV)

*But as for the cowardly, the faithless, the detestable, as for murderers, the sexually immoral, sorcerers, idolaters, and all liars, their portion will be in the lake that burns with fire and sulfur, which is the second death."* (Revelation 21:8 ESV)

Everyone understands that the first death is our physical death, as *"it is appointed for man to die once, and after that comes judgment."* But few are familiar with the term *"second death."*[275] The second death is a simple yet sobering concept: it occurs when those who are judged and found unworthy are thrown into the lake of fire. No one desires the second death, but if your name is not written in the Lamb's Book of Life, I'm afraid Scripture is clear: that is where you will go.

Since all the souls have now been released from Hades (Sheol), the righteous souls from the Paradise portion during the First Harvest and the unrighteous souls from the place of torment just now on Judgment Day, Hades is now empty and has fulfilled its purpose. Hades itself is then *"thrown into the lake of fire,"* and from this point forward, no one will ever go to Hades again.

*Then Death and Hades were thrown into the lake of fire. This is the second death, the lake of fire. 15 And*

---

*if anyone's name was not found written in the book of life, he was thrown into the lake of fire.* (Revelation 20:14–15 ESV)

# Part Ten:

## Heaven At Last!

# 31 Restoration Day: New Heavens and New Earth

After the Millennium and Judgment Day, God will completely burn up the heavens and the earth, remaking them to serve as our renewed, purified, eternal home. It's likely that God will carry out this massive transformation in the background while everyone is still above the earth being judged and thus out of the way.

Peter says every vestige of evidence of man, *"every deed done on it,"* will be destroyed as the earth is burned up and reborn.

> *10 But the day of the Lord will come like a thief; when it comes, the heavens will disappear with a horrific noise, and the celestial bodies will melt away in a blaze, and the earth and every deed done on it will be laid bare. 11 Since all these things are to melt away in this manner, what sort of people must we be, conducting our lives in holiness and godliness, 12 while waiting for and hastening the coming of the day of God? Because of this day, the heavens will be burned up and dissolve, and the celestial bodies will melt away in a blaze!* (2 Peter 3:10–12 NET)

That means all buildings, ancient structures, roads, tunnels, bridges, and, most importantly, pollution will be completely gone. The earth, now in its Pangea form, will once again have virgin soil, as it did when God created the Garden of Eden.

*Of old you laid the foundation of the earth, and the heavens are the work of your hands. 26 They will perish, but you will remain; they will all wear out like a garment. You will change them like a robe, and they will pass away,* (Psalm 102:25–26 ESV)

The heavens are renewed, the earth is renewed, and the sea *"was no more."* This doesn't mean the world is now all dry land; it means there will no longer be seas separating the nations as there are now. This provides further evidence of a return to Pangea, a single landmass surrounded by one sea.

*Then I saw a new heaven and a new earth, for the first heaven and the first earth had passed away, and the sea was no more. (Revelation 21:1 ESV)*

But how do we square this with Zechariah, who said there will be an eastern sea and a western sea?

*On that day living waters shall flow out from Jerusalem, half of them to the eastern sea and half of them to the western sea...* (Zechariah 14:8a ESV)

Zechariah's prophecy further indicates that during the terraforming of the 7th bowl, the earth's landmasses were shifted back together into a single supercontinent, like the original Pangea. On such a large landmass, referring to the surrounding ocean by directional points rather than specific names would make sense. For instance, people might say, "I live near the western sea" or "I'm heading to the eastern sea," indicating different parts of the unified ocean around them.

# 31.1 The Bride of the Lamb: The New Jerusalem

> *Then came one of the seven angels who had the seven bowls full of the seven last plagues and spoke to me, saying, "Come, I will show you the Bride, the wife of the Lamb." 10 And he carried me away in the Spirit to a great, high mountain, and showed me the holy city Jerusalem coming down out of heaven from God,* (Revelation 21:9b-10 ESV)

Paul uses marriage as an analogy at least twice to make a point. In 2 Corinthians, he teaches that Christians should strive to remain pure, just as a young woman strives to remain pure for her future marriage and, after marriage, strives to remain faithful to her husband.

> *For I am jealous for you with godly jealousy, because I promised you in marriage to one husband, to present you as a pure virgin to Christ.* (2 Corinthians 11:2 NET)

Paul uses the marriage analogy again to say that husbands should love their wives in the same way that Christ loves and devotes himself to the church.

> *But as the church submits to Christ, so also wives should submit to their husbands in everything. 25 Husbands, love your wives just as Christ loved the church and gave himself for her* (Ephesians 5:24–25 NET)

By using the marriage metaphor, Paul is not suggesting that Christians will literally marry Jesus. Instead, he uses the image of marriage to illustrate the purity and faithfulness Christians should maintain in their relationship with Christ. While Revelation 19 may initially seem to imply that Christians are *"permitted to be dressed"* as the bride, the passage points more toward a symbolic union, emphasizing the purity, devotion, and readiness expected of believers. The focus is on being spiritually prepared and remaining faithful, not on a literal marriage to Jesus.

> *Let us rejoice and exult and give him glory, because the wedding celebration of the Lamb has come, and his bride has made herself ready. 8 She was permitted to be dressed in bright, clean, fine linen"* (for the fine linen is the righteous deeds of the saints). (Revelation 19:7–8 NET)

But two chapters later, in Revelation 21, John clarifies that the bride of Christ is not the church but is actually the New Jerusalem, into which the church is invited. This clears up the confusion.

> *And I saw the holy city, new Jerusalem, coming down out of heaven from God, prepared as a bride adorned for her husband. 3 And I heard a loud voice from the throne saying, "Behold, the dwelling place of God is with man. He will dwell with them, and they will be his people, and God himself will be with them as their God.* (Revelation 21:2–3 ESV)

When the New Jerusalem comes down to earth, we're told that *"the wedding celebration of the Lamb has come."* This timing indicates that the marriage occurs when Jesus brings the New Jerusalem to earth, which we now know occurs after the Millennium and Judgment Day. At this point, all whose names are written in the

PART TEN: HEAVEN AT LAST!


Lamb's Book of Life, those redeemed by Jesus on Judgment Day, are now ready with their new bodies to attend the wedding celebration.

This means that Christians are not the bride of Christ; rather, they are the honored guests invited to the wedding supper. Jesus told us that there are many rooms in his Father's house and that he would prepare a place for each of us. This indicates that believers are not ordinary guests; they are highly honored, so much so that they are given lodging in the groom's own home.

> *In my Father's house are many rooms. If it were not so, would I have told you that I go to prepare a place for you? 3 And if I go and prepare a place for you, I will come again and will take you to myself, that where I am you may be also.* (John 14:2–3 ESV)

Next, we learn that *"many rooms"* is a wild understatement, as the New Jerusalem is massive. Shaped like a cube or possibly a pyramid, it likely appears as a colossal, jewel-covered structure. [276]

> *16 The city lies foursquare, its length the same as its width. And he measured the city with his rod, 12,000 stadia. Its length and width and height are equal. 17 He also measured its wall, 144 cubits by human measurement, which is also an angel's measurement. 18 The wall was built of jasper, while the city was*

---

[276] Revelation is silent on the shape of the New Jerusalem. Purely from the measurements, it seems like a cube, but it could be a square base with lots of buildings on it, the tallest of which is 12,000 stadia. It could also be a three-dimensional triangle (pyramid shaped). I lean towards that, because the ancient megalithic pyramids in Iraq, China, Mexico, Bosnia, and of course Egypt were probably pre-flood structures trying to imitate or even recreate the abode of God. They may have been based on oral traditions passed down from Adam or, more likely, from the Watcher angels.

*pure gold, like clear glass. 19 The foundations of the wall of the city were adorned with every kind of jewel. The first was jasper, the second sapphire, the third agate, the fourth emerald, 20 the fifth onyx, the sixth carnelian, the seventh chrysolite, the eighth beryl, the ninth topaz, the tenth chrysoprase, the eleventh jacinth, the twelfth amethyst. 21 And the twelve gates were twelve pearls, each of the gates made of a single pearl, and the street of the city was pure gold, like transparent glass.* (Revelation 21:16–21 ESV)

12,000 Stadia is roughly 1,900 kilometers, or 1,200 miles in length, width, and height.[277] From ground level, you'd only be able to see a small part of an object that massive. To take in the entire thing at once, you would need to view it from high up in the sky.

*22 And I saw no temple in the city, for its temple is the Lord God the Almighty and the Lamb. 23 And the city has no need of sun or moon to shine on it, for the glory of God gives it light, and its lamp is the Lamb. 24 By its light will the nations walk, and the kings of the earth will bring their glory into it, 25 and its gates will never be shut by day-and there will be no night there. 26 They will bring into it the glory and the honor of the nations.* (Revelation 21:22–26 ESV)

For those who thought heaven was above the clouds, they were right. The New Jerusalem has always been somewhere in

---

[277] 12,000 stadia = 1,892 Km = 1,176 miles (convertunits.com, "Convert stadion to mile," https://www.convertunits.com/from/stadia/to/miles).

the "*heavens*," but now it will come down to the earth.[278] The New Jerusalem, which houses God's throne, will now be with men. There will be no need for the temple or priests that we had before and during the Millennium. And there will be no need for artificial lights inside because "*the glory of God gives it light.*" It will never be dark ("*no night*") in the New Jerusalem because the light from God's glory never dims.

Can you imagine how spectacular and awe-inspiring the New Jerusalem will appear when the light emanating from the Glory of God within shines through its walls made of Jewels, refracting rainbow-colored light in every direction?[279] This is will serve as a lasting sign that God has fulfilled his covenant.[280]

This magnificent superstructure will be so vast and breathtaking that when kings first catch sight of it descending toward Mt Zion, they will run away "*in panic.*"

> *Great is the LORD and greatly to be praised in the city of our God! His holy mountain, 2 beautiful in elevation, is the joy of all the earth, Mount Zion, in the far north, the city of the great King. 3 Within her*

---

[278] Revelation 3:12b ESV, "...the new Jerusalem, which comes down from my God out of heaven, and my own new name. "

[279] The foundation walls are not just covered in these jewels, they *are* these jewels. The light from God will shine right through them refracting light in the full color spectrum like a rainbow. Though most versions translate it "*adorned*", the Contemporary English Version translates it "*was,*" which means was made of. Revelation 21:18-19 (Contemporary English Version): "*19 Each of the twelve foundations was a precious stone. The first was jasper, the second was sapphire, the third was agate, the fourth was emerald, 20 the fifth was onyx, the sixth was carnelian, the seventh was chrysolite, the eighth was beryl, the ninth was topaz, the tenth was chrysoprase, the eleventh was jacinth, and the twelfth was amethyst.*"

[280] Genesis 9:16 (NIV): "*Whenever the rainbow appears in the clouds, I will see it and remember the everlasting covenant between God and all living creatures of every kind on the earth.*"

*citadels God has made himself known as a fortress. 4*
*For behold, the kings assembled; they came on together.*
*5 As soon as they saw it, they were astounded; they*
*were in panic; they took to flight. 6 Trembling took*
*hold of them there, anguish as of a woman in labor.*
(Psalm 48:1–6 ESV)

As the enormous New Jerusalem descends, a voice from the throne of God announces, *"the dwelling place of God is with man."*

*And I heard a loud voice from the throne saying, "Behold,*
*the dwelling place of God is with man. He will dwell*
*with them, and they will be his people, and God himself*
*will be with them as their God.* (Revelation 21:3 ESV)

We're told that the New Jerusalem doesn't actually touch the earth; it will *"remain aloft"* and *"lifted up above"* Mount Zion, which became the tallest point on earth after the 7th bowl reshaped the landscape. You may recall that during this tectonic event, Mount Zion was the only mountain raised while all others were brought low. Now, Mount Zion acts as a long, natural earthen ramp leading up to the base of the New Jerusalem.

*But Jerusalem shall remain aloft on its site from the*
*Gate of Benjamin to the place of the former gate, to the*
*Corner Gate, and from the Tower of Hananel to the*
*king's winepresses* (Zechariah 14:10b ESV)

This next passage is puzzling, considering that by this point, everyone has been judged, the heavens are new, and the earth is renewed as a true paradise. But it seems to suggest that nothing will ever disrupt this paradise again. [281]

> 27 But nothing unclean will ever enter it, nor anyone who does what is detestable or false, but only those who are written in the Lamb's book of life. (Revelation 21:27 ESV)

The New Jerusalem will be glorious and will be a joy for its inhabitants forever.

> 18 But be glad and rejoice forever in that which I create; for behold, I create Jerusalem to be a joy, and her people to be a gladness. (Isaiah 65:18 ESV)

---

[281] This is puzzling because by stating nothing unclean will ever be allowed to enter the New Jerusalem, it implies that there may be beings of some kind existing outside its gates that will be prevented entry. Conversely, it may be just another way of saying that everyone will forever remain faithful and clean, in the Levitical sense.

# 31.2 Fifth and Final Time John Eavesdrops on Heaven: The Marriage Supper of the Lamb

*Then I heard what seemed to be the voice of a great multitude, like the roar of many waters and like the sound of mighty peals of thunder, crying out, "Hallelujah! For the Lord our God the Almighty reigns. 7 Let us rejoice and exult and give him the glory, for the marriage of the Lamb has come, and his Bride has made herself ready; 8 it was granted her to clothe herself with fine linen, bright and pure"- for the fine linen is the righteous deeds of the saints. 9 And the angel said to me, "Write this: Blessed are those who are invited to the marriage supper of the Lamb." And he said to me, "These are the true words of God."* (Revelation 19:6–9 ESV)

In the final scene of people interacting in heaven, John describes the breathtaking moments after judgment has ended, as those deemed worthy stand on the threshold of eternal glory.

He sees a vast multitude in their radiant, immortal bodies, filled with joyous anticipation as they prepare to enter their eternal abode, the New Jerusalem. Each is about to be welcomed back into their glorious, personally customized room within the city, like guests of honor at a royal celebration. John captures the scene as they await entrance into the magnificent wedding banquet, where endless joy and fulfillment await in the presence of King Jesus.

This last glimpse we have of humans in heaven reaffirms that this *trumpet-attack/bowl-countermeasure theory timeline works perfectly because:*

1. A great multitude of people are celebrating that "*The Lord...reigns.*"
2. Since Jesus reigns, it confirms the kingdoms of the world have become the kingdoms of Jesus.
3. All humans have been judged and now these, the worthy, are about to be invited-in to the New Jerusalem in their fully resurrected bodies.
4. It also confirms that the New Jerusalem has come down to earth because "*The marriage of the Lamb has come,*" which is when the Christians, now in their immortal bodies and having been judged "*worthy*", are invited to partake in the marriage supper and stay in the groom's home, the New Jerusalem.

# 31.3 Paradise Found

The arrival of the New Jerusalem marks the ultimate end of death, sorrow, and rebellion. This is not merely an extension of the near-perfect life experienced during the Millennial Reign of Christ; this is the fulfillment of every promise, the long-awaited heaven itself, finally here in all its glory!

> *He will wipe away every tear from their eyes, and death shall be no more, neither shall there be mourning, nor crying, nor pain anymore, for the former things have passed away." 5 And he who was seated on the throne said, "Behold, I am making all things new." Also he said, "Write this down, for these words are trustworthy and true." 6 And he said to me, "It is done! I am the Alpha and the Omega, the beginning and the end. To the thirsty I will give from the spring of the water of life without payment.* (Revelation 21:4–6 ESV)

The prophecy of Isaiah 9:6 about Jesus' birth, which we often recite at Christmas, is now complete. The Government now rests *"upon his* [Jesus'] *shoulder."* How wonderful that will be! No more elections, politicians, dictators, or wars. Jesus is our king and there will be peace on earth *"forevermore."*

> *For to us a child is born, to us a son is given; and the government shall be upon his shoulder, and his name shall be called Wonderful Counselor, Mighty God, Everlasting Father, Prince of Peace. 7 Of the increase of his government and of peace there will be no end, on*

*the throne of David and over his kingdom, to establish it and to uphold it with justice and with righteousness from this time forth and forevermore. The zeal of the LORD of hosts will do this.* (Isaiah 9:6–7 ESV)

In the next passage, it seems as if Isaiah is saying that everyone will speak the same language, just as they did in the days before Babel.

*19 You will see no more the insolent people, the people of an obscure speech that you cannot comprehend, stammering in a tongue that you cannot understand.* (Isaiah 33:19 ESV)

The New Jerusalem, the City of Zion, will never leave ("*an immovable tent*") or be damaged by storms. Jesus will make the laws, serve as judge, and reign as king.

*20 Behold Zion, the city of our appointed feasts! Your eyes will see Jerusalem, an untroubled habitation, an immovable tent, whose stakes will never be plucked up, nor will any of its cords be broken. 21 But there the LORD in majesty will be for us a place of broad rivers and streams, where no galley with oars can go, nor majestic ship can pass. 22 For the LORD is our judge; the LORD is our lawgiver; the LORD is our king; he will save us.* (Isaiah 33:20–22 ESV)

We won't remember the old world and won't remember our earthly lives because even the good memories would contain some hint of the bad memories. Jesus told us that even pondering sin is as bad as the sin itself.[282] Cleansing or renewing our minds is the only way to keep those thoughts of former sins out of heaven.

> *"For behold, I create new heavens and a new earth, and the former things shall not be remembered or come into mind.* (Isaiah 65:17 ESV)

Isaiah confirms several important details in this next passage. The heavens and the earth are remade, but God promises that this will be the last time. He will never again destroy the heavens, the earth, or its inhabitants, *"your offspring."*

Though the moon has been renewed, it remains in orbit around the new earth, with its phases marking the times to worship the Lord. It's fascinating that we'll still measure the passage of time in a world where no one ages. Though there will be a new sun, the earth will continue to rotate around it, giving us day and night. The Sabbath, a day of rest and worship, will remain, restored to the day God always intended: Saturday. [283]

> *"For as the new heavens and the new earth that I make shall remain before me, says the LORD, so shall your offspring and your name remain. 23 From new moon to new moon, and from Sabbath to Sabbath, all flesh shall come to worship before me, declares the LORD."* (Isaiah 66:22–23 ESV)

---

[282] *"But I say to you that everyone who looks at a woman with lustful intent has already committed adultery with her in his heart"* (Matthew 5:28 ESV).

[283] *"You shall remember that you were a slave in the land of Egypt, and the LORD your God brought you out from there with a mighty hand and an outstretched arm. Therefore the LORD your God commanded you to keep the Sabbath day"* (Deuteronomy 5:15 ESV).

Zechariah assures us that there will still be seasons and that the water of life will begin to flow from the New Jerusalem into the sea. [284] The entire landmass of the earth will be relatively level (*"a plain"*) except for Mount Zion. This mountain, reshaped during the 7th bowl to stand taller than it did when it overlooked old Jerusalem, now serves as a connection between the New Jerusalem and the new earth. The New Jerusalem will float (*"remain aloft"*) above the earth, anchored to the top of Mount Zion.

God then gives us a promise beyond that of his rainbow covenant, which assured us the earth would never again be destroyed by water. This time, he guarantees that no one will ever threaten to destroy the world in any way, as the late Satan had once attempted.

> On that day *living waters shall flow* out from Jerusalem, half of them to the eastern sea and half of them to the western sea. It shall continue in *summer* as in *winter.* 9 And the LORD will be king over all the earth. On that day the LORD will be one and his name one. 10 The whole land shall be turned into *a plain* from Geba to Rimmon south of Jerusalem. But *Jerusalem* shall *remain aloft* on its site from the Gate of Benjamin to the place of the former gate, to the Corner Gate, and

---

[284] To have winter and summer implies that the earth still tilts from its axis by 23.5 degrees. That amazing tilt, along with an elongated orbit, is what allows us to have the wonderful season changes (Anne Helmenstine, "Why Do We Have Seasons On Earth?" Sciencenotes.org, November 4, 2023, https://sciencenotes. org/why-do-we-have-seasons-on-earth/). However, that also implies we still have a sun, but 2 Peter 3:12 says *"the celestial bodies will melt away in a blaze."* This means the sun, if not the rest of the celestial bodies, will have been renewed. Also, Revelation 21:23 ESV says, *"And the city has no need of sun or moon to shine on it, for the glory of God gives it light, and its lamp is the Lamb."* I think this means there is still a sun, but within Jerusalem, there is no need for artificial lights because Jesus and God will emanate light, because they are light.

*from the Tower of Hananel to the king's winepresses. 11
And it shall be inhabited, for there shall never again be
a decree of utter destruction. Jerusalem shall dwell in
security.* (Zechariah 14:8–11 ESV)

The curse on creation will be lifted. Everything will once
again be under our dominion and will no longer pose a threat to
us. Interestingly, however, the serpent still carries its curse. The
legs it had in Eden will never be restored, so it will still occupy
the lowest place, eating *"dust."*

*The wolf and the lamb shall graze together; the
lion shall eat straw like the ox, and dust shall be the
serpent's food. They shall not hurt or destroy in all my
holy mountain," says the LORD.* (Isaiah 65:25 ESV)

After thousands of years of rebellion and wandering, and
thousands more of Jesus making way for humanity to return to him,
mankind will, at last, have the privilege of eating from the Tree of
Life and drinking from the water of life once again. Those who chose
to love Jesus and kept their faith even through life's hardest trials,
the believers (the *"one who conquers"*), will live forever with him.

# Part Eleven

# Before It's Too Late

# 32 Choose a Side

Congratulations on getting this far and learning about the contest for souls, which could go into overdrive at any moment. You may think you can remain a bystander in this war, but you can't. If you believe you can watch this contest from the sidelines without committing yourself to a side, you're mistaken. Until you proactively choose Jesus, you are on the other side by default. You either choose to follow Jesus actively, or you passively fall into Satan's camp. You might not be cheering for Satan, and you may even try to work against him, but by default, until you accept Jesus and actively follow him, you're still on Satan's team.

> *And if it seem evil unto you to serve the LORD, choose you this day whom ye will serve; whether the gods which your fathers served that were on the other side of the flood, or the gods of the Amorites, in whose land ye dwell: but as for me and my house, we will serve the LORD.* (Joshua 24:15 KJV)

And if you think you have all the time in the world to choose a team, you don't. No one knows when their own last day will come.

> *19 And I will say to my soul, Soul, thou hast much goods laid up for many years; take thine ease, eat, drink, and be merry. 20 But God said unto him, Thou fool, this night thy soul shall be required of thee: then whose shall those things be, which thou hast provided?* (Luke 12:19–20 KJV)

If you are ready to join Jesus' side, the first step is simple. All you have to do is ask him. Pray something like this:

"Jesus, I now understand that there is more to this world and life than just pursuing what makes me happy in the moment.

I realize that there is no way I can live up to God's expectations on my own, and that you are the only way I can be reconciled to God, your Father.

Lord, I also understand that bad things happen because God allowed us free will, and we are all living with the consequences of rebelling against you.

I see now that we are still free to choose how we live and whom we worship, and I am freely choosing to follow you and worship only you.

Jesus, I'm a sinner and am sorry for the life I've lived outside of your will. I now commit to devoting the rest of my life to you, to continuously learning how you created me to live, and to helping lead others into a saving relationship with you.

Thank you, Jesus, for making a way for me to be with you for eternity." [285]

The next step is to find a church that does not exclude any part of God's word or add anything to it and start learning and worshipping with that body of Christ.[286] As soon as you can meet that church's requirements for baptism, boldly make that step to publicly and joyfully confess your faith to all *"in heaven and on earth*

---

[285] Romans 5:8 (KJV): *"But God commendeth his love toward us, in that, while we were yet sinners, Christ died for us."*
Romans 10:9-10 (ESV): *"because, if you confess with your mouth that Jesus is Lord and believe in your heart that God raised him from the dead, you will be saved. 10 For with the heart one believes and is justified, and with the mouth one confesses and is saved."*

[286] Hebrews 10:24-25 (ESV): *"And let us consider how to stir up one another to love and good works, 25 not neglecting to meet together, as is the habit of some, but encouraging one another, and all the more as you see the Day drawing near."*

*and under the earth*."[287] Baptism announces to both heaven and hell that you have switched sides. It's much more than just a verbal or mental decision; it is a physical proclamation that you now stand proudly and fearlessly with Jesus and love him unconditionally.[288]

---

[287] Revelation 5:13b (ESV): *"And I heard every creature in heaven and on earth and under the earth and in the sea, and all that is in them, saying, "To him who sits on the throne and to the Lamb be blessing and honor and glory and might forever and ever!"*

[288] Romans 6:3-5 (ESV): *"Do you not know that all of us who have been baptized into Christ Jesus were baptized into his death? 4 We were buried therefore with him by baptism into death, in order that, just as Christ was raised from the dead by the glory of the Father, we too might walk in newness of life. 5 For if we have been united with him in a death like his, we shall certainly be united with him in a resurrection like his."*

# | 33 Conclusion

My prayer is that this book has helped you understand how important it is to Jesus that you know what is to come. Even if you don't fully agree with using the conversations of humans in heaven, the Olivet Discourse, and the 7-sealed book to establish the timing of events, I trust you have gleaned some helpful insights you can use to prepare yourself.

Since God devoted about one-sixth of the Bible to explaining the end-times, it's essential to study these passages as seriously as the rest of Scripture, preparing your armor and your family for what may occur, possibly within their lifetimes. If you are a Christian, I pray that you won't be among the hundreds of millions of Christians who arrive in heaven suddenly, having died a terrible death because they were unprepared for the 4th bowl plague of scorching fire from the sun.

I welcome your constructive criticism, knowing there is always more to be learned from God's Word. Although there is much more I wish to share, once I reached 75,000 words in drafting the main points of the timeline, I realized that many details and additional Scriptures would have to be saved for a future book or article. For example, I barely touched on the demonic activity that will intensify before and during the Great Tribulation.

As for the question, *"When will these things be?"* Events continue to align just as the prophets foretold, but no one knows the exact timing.

So, what does God want you to do? Plan for the future as if you will live a long and fruitful life but strive daily to memorize key Scriptures and practice using the armor of God as if that infamous, infernal covenant could be signed tomorrow and every Bible confiscated soon after.

> *Since all these things are to melt away in this manner, what sort of people must we be, conducting our lives in holiness and godliness, 12 while waiting for and hastening the coming of the day of God? Because of this day, the heavens will be burned up and dissolve, and the celestial bodies will melt away in a blaze!* (2 Peter 3:11–12 NET)

Since you now have a better understanding of what will happen, ask yourself the question Peter asked his readers, *"what sort of people must we be?"* I hope you recognize that Peter's answer is the only answer. We should each *"conduct our lives in holiness and godliness, while we wait for and hasten the coming of the day of God."*

The next time you recite The Lord's Prayer, I hope you will pray with an added sense of urgency since you now understand how important it is to *"hasten"* the coming of his kingdom.

> *Pray then like this: "Our Father in heaven, hallowed be your name. 10 Your kingdom come, your will be done, on earth as it is in heaven. 11 Give us this day our daily bread, 12 and forgive us our debts, as we also have forgiven our debtors. 13 And lead us not into temptation, but deliver us from evil. 14 For if you forgive others their trespasses, your heavenly Father will also forgive you, 15 but if you do not forgive others their trespasses, neither will your Father forgive your trespasses.* (Matthew 6:9–15 ESV)

His kingdom will come when the fullness of time has come.

> *For still the vision awaits its appointed time; it hastens to the end-it will not lie. If it seems slow, wait for it; it will surely come; it will not delay* (Habakkuk 2:3 ESV).

# 34 Epilogue

I've truly enjoyed immersing deeply in God's Word, trying to place myself in the middle of the conversations, so much so that I could hardly pull myself away. Over the past three years, I spent every possible moment methodically analyzing every word in every verse in the Bible, organizing them into categories. My sole objective was to uncover any potential references to end-time events and understand their meaning within the context of the big picture I had uncovered while eavesdropping on the conversations in heaven.

Every word of every verse was scrutinized with a level of detail that reversed the usual approach—I analyzed every branch of every tree and deliberately resisted getting distracted by the forest. Though I went through it all a second time, I am certain there are still more references to the end-times that God does not intend to be discovered. . . yet.

> *"The secret of the LORD is with them that fear him; and he will shew them his covenant."* (Psalm 25:14 KJV)

As I carefully categorized each verse even remotely related to end-time prophecy, building a database of more than 5,000 entries, I experienced at least four powerful "aha" moments that I instantly wanted to shout to the world. When I began grouping these verses within the framework of the big picture, the beauty and ultimate justice of God's meticulous plan came into view, and it was breathtaking! That's when I realized this was more than just a personal study, because I couldn't possibly keep such an astonishing discovery to myself.

A sense of urgency ignited within me to share this message, and I found it difficult to concentrate on anything else until this research was complete. This book is my shout to the world: the key to understanding the order in which end-time events will unfold is to first understand why they must unfold.

God's plan to spend eternity in heaven with only the people and angels who truly love him was established from the very beginning and is perfection itself. On Judgment Day, when every being *"in heaven and on earth and under the earth"* is assembled to receive their own personal verdict about where they will spend eternity, no one will have an excuse to doubt his love for them or the perfection of his plan.[289] Though many will then despise themselves and bitterly regret the bad choices they made during their existence that led them ever further away from God, no one will be able to deny that God is, and has always been, completely and absolutely just.

---

[289] *For ever since the world was created, people have seen the earth and sky. Through everything God made, they can clearly see his invisible qualities—his eternal power and divine nature. So they have no excuse for not knowing God.*

# Exhibit 1:

---

## John's Sparing Use of "And When" (*hote*) to Denote Order

John began his thoughts with *hote* or *hotan* only 14 times (out of over 400 verses), so whenever it occurs, it merits paying particular attention.

1:17 And **when** [Greek *hote*] I saw him, I fell at his feet as dead. And he laid his right hand upon me, saying unto me, Fear not; I am the first and the last:

4:9 And **when** [Greek *hotan*] those beasts give glory and honour and thanks to him that sat on the throne, who liveth for ever and ever,

5:8 And **when** [Greek *hote*] he had taken the book, the four beasts and four and twenty elders fell down before the Lamb, having every one of them harps, and golden vials full of odours, which are the prayers of saints.

6:1 And I saw **when** [Greek *hote*] the Lamb opened one of the seals, and I heard, as it were the noise of thunder, one of the four beasts saying, Come and see.

6:3 And **when** [Greek *hote*] he had opened the second seal, I heard the second beast say, Come and see.

6:5 **When** [Greek *hote*] he opened the third seal, I heard the third living creature say, "Come!" And I looked, and behold, a black horse! And its rider had a pair of scales in his hand.

6:7 And **when** [Greek *hote*] he had opened the fourth seal, I heard the voice of the fourth beast say, Come and see.

6:9 And **when** [Greek *hote*] he had opened the fifth seal, I saw under the altar the souls of them that were slain for the word of God, and for the testimony which they held:

6:12 And I beheld **when** [Greek *hote*] he had opened the sixth seal, and, lo, there was a great earthquake; and the sun became black as sackcloth of hair, and the moon became as blood

8:1 And **when** [Greek *hotan*] he had opened the seventh seal, there was silence in heaven about the space of half an hour.

10:4 And **when** [Greek *hote*] the seven thunders had uttered their voices, I was about to write: and I heard a voice from heaven saying unto me, Seal up those things which the seven thunders uttered, and write them not.

11:7 And **when** [Greek *hotan*] they [two witnesses] shall have finished their testimony, the beast that ascendeth out of the bottomless pit shall make war against them, and shall overcome them, and kill them.

12:13 And **when** [Greek *hote*]the dragon saw that he was cast unto the earth, he persecuted the woman which brought forth the man child.

20:7 And **when** [Greek *hotan*] the thousand years are expired, Satan shall be loosed out of his prison,

# Exhibit 2:

---

## John's Sparing Use of "After This" (*meta*) to Denote Order

When John meant to say, "after this" he used *meta*. Here are the 8 verses where he began his thoughts with *meta*.

4:1 **After** [Greek *meta*] this I looked, and, behold, a door was opened in heaven: and the first voice which I heard was as it were of a trumpet talking with me; which said, Come up hither, and I will shew thee things which must be hereafter.

7:1 **After** [ Greek *meta*] this I saw four angels standing at the four corners of the earth, holding back the four winds of the earth, that no wind might blow on earth or sea or against any tree.

7:9 **After** [Greek *meta*] this I beheld, and, lo, a great multitude, which no man could number, of all nations, and kindreds, and people, and tongues, stood before the throne, and before the Lamb, clothed with white robes, and palms in their hands;

11:11 But **after** [Greek *meta*] the three and a half days a breath of life from God entered them, and they stood up on their feet, and great fear fell on those who saw them.

15:5 **After** this [ Greek *meta*] I looked, and the sanctuary of the tent of witness in heaven was opened,

17:2 **with whom** [Greek *meta*] the kings of the earth have committed sexual immorality, and with the wine of whose sexual immorality the dwellers on earth have become drunk." (the use of "with whom" is another instance of not the best choice of words).

18:1 **After this** [Greek *meta*] I saw another angel coming down from heaven, having great authority, and the earth was made bright with his glory.

19:1 **After this** [Greek *meta*] I heard what seemed to be the loud voice of a great multitude in heaven, crying out, "Hallelujah! Salvation and glory and power belong to our God,

# Exhibit 3:

---

## Harmonizing the Olivet Discourse between Matthew, Mark, and Luke

Using the King James Version. In this comparative format, the similarities are easy to see. But it's also an easy way to quickly see something only one writer captured.

| Event | Matthew 24 | Mark 13 | Luke 21 |
|---|---|---|---|
| Herod's Temple will be destroyed and dismantled | *1 And Jesus went out, and departed from the temple: and his disciples came to him for to shew him the buildings of the temple. 2 And Jesus said unto them, See ye not all these things? verily I say unto you, There shall not be left here one stone upon another, that shall not be thrown down.* | *1 And as he went out of the temple, one of his disciples saith unto him, Master, see what manner of stones and what buildings are here! 2 And Jesus answering said unto him, Seest thou these great buildings? there shall not be left one stone upon another, that shall not be thrown down.* | *5 And as some spake of the temple, how it was adorned with goodly stones and gifts, he said, 6 As for these things which ye behold, the days will come, in the which there shall not be left one stone upon another, that shall not be thrown down* |

| Event | Matthew 24 | Mark 13 | Luke 21 |
|---|---|---|---|
| When will the end begin? And how will we know when it begins? What will be the signs? | *3 And as he sat upon the mount of Olives, the disciples came unto him privately, saying, Tell us, when shall these things be? and what shall be the sign of thy coming, and of the end of the world?* | *3 And as he sat upon the mount of Olives over against the temple, Peter and James and John and Andrew asked him privately, 4 Tell us, when shall these things be? and what shall be the sign when all these things shall be fulfilled?* | *7 And they asked him, saying, Master, but when shall these things be? and what sign will there be when these things shall come to pass?* |
| Let no man deceive you | *4 And Jesus answered and said unto them, Take heed that no man deceive you.* | *5 And Jesus answering them began to say, Take heed lest any man deceive you:* | *8a And he said, Take heed that ye be not deceived:* |
| There will be many false Jesuses, and they will fool many | *5 For many shall come in my name, saying, I am Christ; and shall deceive many.* | *6 For many shall come in my name, saying, I am Christ; and shall deceive many.* | *... 8b for many shall come in my name, saying, I am Christ; and the time draweth near: go ye not therefore after them.* |

| Event | Matthew 24 | Mark 13 | Luke 21 |
|---|---|---|---|
| There will be wars and lots of talk about future wars | *6 And ye shall hear of wars and rumours of wars: see that ye be not troubled: for all these things must come to pass, but the end is not yet. 7a For nation shall rise against nation, and kingdom against kingdom:* | *7 And when ye shall hear of wars and rumours of wars, be ye not troubled: for such things must needs be; but the end shall not be yet. 8a For nation shall rise against nation, and kingdom against kingdom:* | *9 But when ye shall hear of wars and commotions, be not terrified: for these things must first come to pass; but the end is not by and by. 10 Then said he unto them, Nation shall rise against nation, and kingdom against kingdom:* |
| There will be famines, plagues, fearful sights, and great signs from heaven | *. . . 7b and there shall be famines, and pestilences, and earthquakes, in divers places. 8 All these are the beginning of sorrows.* | *. . . 8b and there shall be earthquakes in divers places, and there shall be famines and troubles: these are the beginnings of sorrows.* | *11 And great earthquakes shall be in divers places, and famines, and pestilences; and fearful sights and great signs shall there be from heaven.* |

| Event | Matthew 24 | Mark 13 | Luke 21 |
|---|---|---|---|
| You will be persecuted, hated by all nations, and delivered to the courts. When that happens, allow the Holy Spirit to speak for you | *9 Then shall they deliver you up to be afflicted, and shall kill you: and ye shall be hated of all nations for my name's sake.* | *9 But take heed to yourselves: for they shall deliver you up to councils; and in the synagogues ye shall be beaten: and ye shall be brought before rulers and kings for my sake, for a testimony against them...... 11 But when they shall lead you, and deliver you up, take no thought beforehand what ye shall speak, neither do ye premeditate: but whatsoever shall be given you in that hour, that speak ye: for it is not ye that speak, but the Holy Ghost* | *12 But before all these, they shall lay their hands on you, and persecute you, delivering you up to the synagogues, and into prisons, being brought before kings and rulers for my name's sake. 13 And it shall turn to you for a testimony. 14 Settle it therefore in your hearts, not to meditate before what ye shall answer: 15 For I will give you a mouth and wisdom, which all your adversaries shall not be able to gainsay nor resist.* |

| Event | Matthew 24 | Mark 13 | Luke 21 |
|---|---|---|---|
| Many will be betrayed and hated by their family and friends and be put to death | *10 And then shall many be offended, and shall betray one another, and shall hate one another.* | *12 Now the brother shall betray the brother to death, and the father the son; and children shall rise up against their parents, and shall cause them to be put to death. 13a And ye shall be hated of all men for my name's sake* | *16 And ye shall be betrayed both by parents, and brethren, and kinsfolks, and friends; and some of you shall they cause to be put to death. 17 And ye shall be hated of all men for my name's sake.* |
| There will be many false prophets | *11 And many false prophets shall rise, and shall deceive many. 12 And because iniquity shall abound, the love of many shall wax cold.* | | |
| If you endure to the end, you'll be saved | *13 But he that shall endure unto the end, the same shall be saved.* | *. . . 13b but he that shall endure unto the end, the same shall be saved* | *18 But there shall not an hair of your head perish. 19 In your patience possess ye your souls.* |
| The Gospel will be preached to all nations | *14 And this gospel of the kingdom shall be preached in all the world for a witness unto all nations; and then shall the end come.* | *. . . 10 And the gospel must first be published among all nations* | |

| Event | Matthew 24 | Mark 13 | Luke 21 |
|---|---|---|---|
| When Jerusalem is surrounded by armies, the desecration of the temple will be soon | | | *20 And when ye shall see Jerusalem compassed with armies, then know that the desolation thereof is nigh.* |
| The desecration of the temple will occur | *15 When ye therefore shall see the abomination of desolation, spoken of by Daniel the prophet, stand in the holy place, (whoso readeth, let him understand:)* | *14a But when ye shall see the abomination of desolation, spoken of by Daniel the prophet, standing where it ought not, (let him that readeth understand,)* | |
| When the desolation occurs, those in Judaea flee to the mountains | *16 Then let them which be in Judaea flee into the mountains:* | *. . . 14b then let them that be in Judaea flee to the mountains:* | *21 Then let them which are in Judæa flee to the mountains; and let them which are in the midst of it depart out; and let not them that are in the countries enter thereinto.* |

| Event | Matthew 24 | Mark 13 | Luke 21 |
|---|---|---|---|
| "Flee" means don't grab any belongings | *17 Let him which is on the housetop not come down to take any thing out of his house: 18 Neither let him which is in the field return back to take his clothes.* | *15 And let him that is on the housetop not go down into the house, neither enter therein, to take any thing out of his house 16 And let him that is in the field not turn back again for to take up his garment* | |
| The days of vengeance will be fulfilled | | | *22 For these be the days of vengeance, that all things which are written may be fulfilled.* |
| The Great Tribulation will be more terrible than the worst things that have ever occurred since the beginning of the world | *19 And woe unto them that are with child, and to them that give suck in those days! 20 But pray ye that your flight be not in the winter, neither on the sabbath day: 21 For then shall be great tribulation, such as was not since the beginning of the world to this time, no, nor ever shall be.* | *17 But woe to them that are with child, and to them that give suck in those days! 18 And pray ye that your flight be not in the winter. 19 For in those days shall be affliction, such as was not from the beginning of the creation which God created unto this time, neither shall be.* | *23 But woe unto them that are with child, and to them that give suck, in those days! For there shall be great distress in the land, and wrath upon this people. 24a And they shall fall by the edge of the sword, and shall be led away captive into all nations:* |

| Event | Matthew 24 | Mark 13 | Luke 21 |
|---|---|---|---|
| The 3½ year Great Tribulation will be shortened to save believers | *22 And except those days should be shortened, there should no flesh be saved: but for the elect's sake those days shall be shortened.* | *20 And except that the Lord had shortened those days, no flesh should be saved: but for the elect's sake, whom he hath chosen, he hath shortened the days* | *24b and Jerusalem shall be trodden down of the Gentiles, until the times of the Gentiles be fulfilled.* |
| There will be many false Jesuses. Don't believe anyone who says Christ is here | *23 Then if any man shall say unto you, Lo, here is Christ, or there; believe it not. 24 For there shall arise false Christs, and false prophets, and shall shew great signs and wonders; insomuch that, if it were possible, they shall deceive the very elect.* | *21 And then if any man shall say to you, Lo, here is Christ; or, lo, he is there; believe him not: 22 For false Christs and false prophets shall rise, and shall shew signs and wonders, to seduce, if it were possible, even the elect.* | |
| Jesus has warned us, so we have no excuse for not being prepared | *25 Behold, I have told you before.* | *23 But take ye heed: behold, I have foretold you all things.* | |
| Don't believe it if they say that Jesus is somewhere | *26 Wherefore if they shall say unto you, Behold, he is in the desert; go not forth: behold, he is in the secret chambers; believe it not.* | | |

| Event | Matthew 24 | Mark 13 | Luke 21 |
|---|---|---|---|
| Jesus' return will be unmistakable, marked by signs in the sky | 27 For as the lightning cometh out of the east, and shineth even unto the west; so shall also the coming of the Son of man be. | | |
| | 28 For wheresoever the carcase is, there will the eagles be gathered together. | | |
| Immediately after the Tribulation, there will be signs in the sky and earth (the 6th Seal) | 29 Immediately after the tribulation of those days shall the sun be darkened, and the moon shall not give her light, and the stars shall fall from heaven, and the powers of the heavens shall be shaken: | 24 But in those days, after that tribulation, the sun shall be darkened, and the moon shall not give her light, 25 And the stars of heaven shall fall, and the powers that are in heaven shall be shaken | 25a And there shall be signs in the sun, and in the moon, and in the stars; and upon the earth 25b distress of nations, with perplexity; the sea and the waves roaring; 26 Men's hearts failing them for fear, and for looking after those things which are coming on the earth: for the powers of heaven shall be shaken. |

| Event | Matthew 24 | Mark 13 | Luke 21 |
|---|---|---|---|
| Then everyone will see Jesus coming in the clouds (the 7th trumpet) | *30 And then shall appear the sign of the Son of man in heaven: and then shall all the tribes of the earth mourn, and they shall see the Son of man coming in the clouds of heaven with power and great glory.* | *26 And then shall they see the Son of man coming in the clouds with great power and glory.* | *27 And then shall they see the Son of man coming in a cloud with power and great glory.* |
| Look up, because Jesus is coming to take you to heaven! | | | *28 And when these things begin to come to pass, then look up, and lift up your heads; for your redemption draweth nigh.* |
| Jesus will send his angels with the sound of a great trumpet (the 7th trumpet) and gather his elect | *31 And he shall send his angels with a great sound of a trumpet, and they shall gather together his elect from the four winds, from one end of heaven to the other.* | *27 And then shall he send his angels, and shall gather together his elect from the four winds, from the uttermost part of the earth to the uttermost part of heaven* | |

| Event | Matthew 24 | Mark 13 | Luke 21 |
|---|---|---|---|
| Watch for the signs that summer (the tribulation) is about to begin | *32 Now learn a parable of the fig tree; When his branch is yet tender, and putteth forth leaves, ye know that summer is nigh:* | *28 Now learn a parable of the fig tree; When her branch is yet tender, and putteth forth leaves, ye know that summer is near:* | *29 And he spake to them a parable; Behold the fig tree, and all the trees; 30 When they now shoot forth, ye see and know of your own selves that summer is now nigh at hand.* |
| When you see these signs, know that the events of the end-time are about to begin | *33 So likewise ye, when ye shall see all these things, know that it is near, even at the doors.* | *29 So ye in like manner, when ye shall see these things come to pass, know that it is nigh, even at the doors.* | *31 So likewise ye, when ye see these things come to pass, know ye that the kingdom of God is nigh at hand.* |
| This generation won't pass away until all is fulfilled | *34 Verily I say unto you, This generation shall not pass, till all these things be fulfilled.* | *30 Verily I say unto you, that this generation shall not pass, till all these things be done.* | *32 Verily I say unto you, This generation shall not pass away, till all be fulfilled.* |
| Jesus' word and these prophecies are true | *35 Heaven and earth shall pass away, but my words shall not pass away.* | *31 Heaven and earth shall pass away: but my words shall not pass away.* | *33 Heaven and earth shall pass away: but my words shall not pass away.* |
| Only God knows the day and hour the events leading up to the end-times will begin | *36 But of that day and hour knoweth no man, no, not the angels of heaven, but my Father only.* | *32 But of that day and that hour knoweth no man, no, not the angels which are in heaven, neither the Son, but the Father.* | |

| Event | Matthew 24 | Mark 13 | Luke 21 |
|---|---|---|---|
| Watch and pray, because you don't know when the end-time events will begin | *37 But as the days of Noe were, so shall also the coming of the Son of man be.* | *33 Take ye heed, watch and pray: for ye know not when the time is.* | *34 And take heed to yourselves, lest at any time your hearts be overcharged with surfeiting, and drunkenness, and cares of this life, and so that day come upon you unawares.* |

# Exhibit 4:

---

## There are several problems with calling the 7-sealed book a scroll, not a book:

1. A single scroll doesn't have a back side. An additional indication that it's a book and not a rolled-up scroll is that Revelation 5:1 describes that it is *". . . written within and on the back. . ."* A tubular, rolled-up scroll has no front or back, but a book does. Some commentators say this means there is writing on both sides of the scroll, but if that was the case, why didn't John just say that as clearly as other biblical writers did when they referred to both sides of a scroll? Ezekiel used very clear language in chapter 2:10 "[the scroll] *which he unrolled before me. On both sides of it were written words of lament. . ."* So why didn't John use those same words if he meant a scroll? I think it's because he was describing a book, not a scroll.

2. Opening the 7-sealed book and the act of breaking the seals were identified as separate steps: *"Who is worthy to open the scroll and break its seals."* This phrase in 5:2 is backwards if it's a scroll. Seals must first be cut or broken before the scroll could be opened (unrolled). But the first section of a book or introduction could be opened before other sealed sections if the writer chose to apply the seals that way.

3. A seal does not convey information; its purpose is to authenticate a document and provide evidence of tampering. Seals served as tamper indicators for thousands of years. They were melted

onto a document to give the recipient confidence that the document had not been opened before it reached the rightful recipient or owner. The dilemma with thinking of this as a scroll that can't be unrolled and read until all 7 seals are broken is that we're provided with information, sometimes paragraphs of information, as each seal is broken.

4.  Books have been around since at least the time of John, so he would be familiar with and have the language to describe a book.

This is why I'm confident that John is not describing a scroll. He's describing a unique book with 7 seals. I think those seals are along the edge of the book, with each seal offset from the next in a diagonal pattern from front pages to back pages. Each seal unlocks a different chapter of the book. There are likely several pages released as each seal is broken, which could then be read. The next seal would loosen the next section of pages, and so on. One possibility is that the book has 7 distinctive, slightly protruding dividers separating one section from the next so that there is a defined border between each seal.

Each of the 7 divisions of the book contains a page or more of information, but a division or chapter can't be accessed until its corresponding seal is broken, which is the way the seals are described as being opened in Revelation.

# Exhibit 5:

---

## The Case for Paradise – Continued
## from Chapter 6.3

Peter supports the idea of Paradise, telling us that Christ died to make a way (*"that he might bring us to God"*). In this verse, *"might bring"* means to open a way of access. By sacrificing his sinless life, Jesus secured the victory in the first half of this contest, opening 'the way of access' to heaven! Absolutely no one else in the universe embodied all the intricate, detailed, prophesied qualifications necessary to create this path, as we'll see when the 7-sealed book is opened.

When he triumphs in the second half, Jesus will wield his authority as the rightful King and liberate all believers, the dead in Christ, from Paradise in Sheol at the First Harvest. We cover the overlooked First Harvest in the chapter of the same name.

Here's why understanding Paradise is so important: From the passage about the thief on the cross, we know that when they both died that day, Jesus accompanied the thief to Paradise. But Jesus didn't stay there long. He left the thief in Paradise, and as Peter reveals, Jesus then descended into the terrible part of Sheol, to proclaim a message to certain fallen angels imprisoned there.[290]

This is where it gets exciting for us: Because Jesus did the impossible and lived without ever sinning, Satan had no right to claim his soul and hold him in the Paradise part of Sheol as he does with every other Christian who has died. Satan never imagined that

---

[290] 1 Peter 3:19 ESV "in which he went and proclaimed to the spirits in prison."

Jesus would be uncontrollable until he arrived and began moving freely from place to place. Can you picture Satan's horror when he realized that he *"ha*[d] *no claim"* on him?[291]

At that moment, pure panic set in. Satan had been outmaneuvered. Expecting to gloat over Jesus' defeat, Satan suddenly understood that he was the one who had actually lost. He had acted step by step exactly as God knew he would.

So how did seminaries and commentaries get this wrong? Revelation is the only place in the Bible that describes people living in heaven, and they assumed that what is described in Revelation is applicable before the end-times. This is one of the dangers of drawing conclusions from the Bible without understanding the end-times. In Chapter 11.3 I describe the *'Special Blessing'* which grants believers who die *"from now on"* the privilege of bypassing Sheol and going directly to heaven. But the reason it is *"special"* is because it is not what currently happens when a believer dies. See Chapter 11.3 for a more comprehensive description.

The usual message of comfort from church graveside services today is that believers go immediately to heaven upon death. Many quote 2 Corinthians 5:8-9 as support.

> *8 Yes, we are of good courage, and we would rather be away from the body and at home with the Lord. 9 So whether we are at home or away, we make it our aim to please him. (2 Corinthians 5:8-9 ESV)*

Many interpret verses 8 and 9 as suggesting we immediately join the Lord in in heaven at death, but this reflects preconceived beliefs rather than what the text actually says. The passage could

---

[291] John 14:30 ESV. *"I will no longer talk much with you* [his disciples], *for the ruler of this world is coming. He has no claim on me.*

equally indicate we will be *"at home with the Lord"* in Paradise. For a more complete understanding, these verses should be read in context with the very next verse, which refers to Judgment Day.

> *10 For we must all appear before the judgment seat of Christ, so that each one may receive what is due for what he has done in the body, whether good or evil. (2 Corinthians 5:10 ESV)*

Other passages clarify that Judgment Day occurs for everyone at the end of the Millennium, not immediately after death, which may be why pastors almost always stop quoting before verse 10, because including that context would change the meaning they intend. If they were to read all three verses together, it becomes clear that if believers go directly to heaven after death, it means they would have to experience Judgment Day, or that they would have to return to earth on Judgment Day.

Why is it so bad to wait in comfort in Paradise like Lazarus or the thief on the cross? Revelation 2:7 tells us the Tree of Life is there, so the implication is that the rest of the Garden of Eden is there too.

Jesus and God are omnipresent and nothing can separate us from their love, which means we are not separated from their love while in Paradise or anywhere else.

Paul celebrates that neither height nor depth can separate us from the love of God. I think "depth" refers to Paradise.

*"For I am convinced that neither death nor life, neither angels nor demons, neither the present nor the future, nor any powers, 39 neither height nor depth, nor anything else in all creation, will be able to separate us from the love of God that is in Christ Jesus our Lord. (Romans 8:38-39 NIV).*

Further evidence supporting this Paradise is presented throughout the book.

# Exhibit 6:

---

## Map of Ancient Ottoman Empire
## and Areas it Influenced.

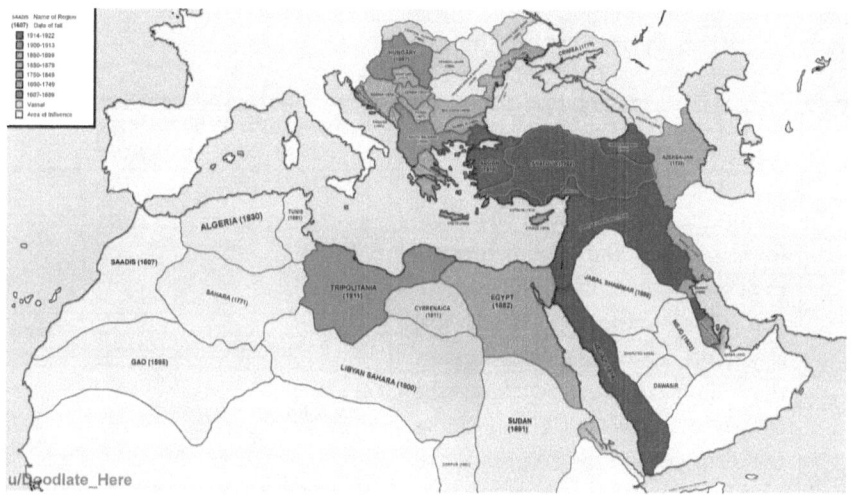

# Exhibit 7:

## Nine Additional Reasons Why the 6th Seal is Not Destructive

It is Creation Worshipping Its Creator

| # | 9 Reasons Why the 6th Seal is All of Creation Worshipping Its Creator | Scriptures Which Describe the 6th Seal Events |
|---|---|---|
| 1 | Because the two "great earthquakes" (of the 6th seal and 7th bowl) occur too close together in this timeline. If you still subscribe to the traditional sequential septet judgment order of the end times, the earthquakes of the 6th seal occur at least a year before the earthquake of the 7th trumpet, so another great earthquake a year later might make sense. However, according to the order that came together in this book, the 7th of each seal, trumpet, and bowl are reserved for Jesus and they occur in rapid succession right after the 6th seal. That quick succession really makes the idea of a great earthquake during the 6th seal, which is soon followed by an even greater earthquake in the 7th Trumpet, seem redundant and confusing. | |

| # | 9 Reasons Why the 6th Seal is All of Creation Worshipping Its Creator | Scriptures Which Describe the 6th Seal Events |
|---|---|---|
| 2 | Because the 6th seal doesn't describe any damage or death. When I examined all the prophesies that referred to earthquakes in the latter days, I tried to sort them into whether they were referring to the 6th seal earthquake or the 7th trumpet earthquake, a task that proved impossible. However, once I understood that the 6th seal earthquake is really the earth shaking just enough to force everyone to the ground in reverent submission, that meant most of the damaging earthquake prophecies refer to the greater earthquake of the 7th bowl. There is a great shaking of the earth and every mountain and every island were "moved out of their places," and Luke tells us that Jesus said the sea and waves will roar, but we're not told about a single person dying or a single city crumbling as we will be a little later during the great earthquake of the 7th bowl. Prophecies that refer to the 6th seal refer to spectacular celestial events and movement of the earth and sea, but not damage. For example, the following verses are now easy to align with the 6th seal. | *18 And the idols he shall utterly abolish. 19 And they shall go into the holes of the rocks, and into the caves of the earth, for fear of the LORD, and for the glory of his majesty, when he ariseth to shake terribly the earth.* (Isaiah 2:18–19 KJV)<br><br>*17 And the loftiness of man shall be bowed down, and the haughtiness of men shall be made low: and the LORD alone shall be exalted in that day.* (Isaiah 2:17 KJV)<br><br>*And there will be signs in sun and moon and stars, and on the earth distress of nations in perplexity because of the roaring of the sea and the waves* (Luke 21:25 ESV) |
| 3 | Because of what the 6th seal does not say. When John tells us something is "great" his pattern is to usually add corroborating information to help us understand why he called it great. He did that for the 7th bowl great earthquake, but not for the 6th seal great earthquake. | *For comparison, here is how John describes the great earthquake of the 7th bowl: "And there were voices, and thunders, and lightnings; and there was a great earthquake, such as was not since men were upon the earth, so mighty an earthquake, and so great. And the great city was divided into three parts, and the cities of the nations fell..."* (Revelation 16:18–19a KJV) |

| # | 9 Reasons Why the 6<sup>th</sup> Seal is All of Creation Worshipping Its Creator | Scriptures Which Describe the 6<sup>th</sup> Seal Events |
|---|---|---|
| 4 | Because God already showed via the 5th bowl that he could make anyplace pitch black, so why does he want the sun to go partially dark now? In the 5th bowl God was depriving followers of the beast of their ability to see and function at all. The liquid-like darkness was not just to hinder their nefarious activities, it was a way to force them to sit alone and focus on their pain and terrifying thoughts. But now, by making the sun "black as sackcloth of hair" and making the moon "as blood," he's not making the world totally pitch dark. Remember the sun had just been in overdrive in the 4th bowl and no one could look at it; now God is turning the brightness of the sun down low and directing everyone to look at something important in the sky. | The sun must still be producing a little light lower on the spectrum, because that dim light is reflecting off the moon as red. A normal blood moon is caused by a lunar eclipse and can only be observed as red from people on a portion of the earth. Since this blood moon will be visible to the whole world, it's probably caused by a lower light output of the sun. (Nineplanets. org, "What Causes a Blood Moon?" November 5, 2019. https://nineplanets.org/questions/what-causes-a-blood-moon/). |

| # | 9 Reasons Why the 6th Seal is All of Creation Worshipping Its Creator | Scriptures Which Describe the 6th Seal Events |
|---|---|---|
| 5 | Because the heavens orchestrate in harmony to set the stage for their creator. The sun goes dim and the full moon in turn goes blood red as their way of bowing in deference to the glorious light emanating from their creator. A light so glorious against which these luminary bodies understand they are not worthy to even hold a candle. The magnificent light of God on his throne will outshine all when he reveals himself. No one will have any doubt who it is or why he's there. | *Revelation 6:12–16 ESV* |
| | The sun and moon dim the lighting. | *. . . the sun became black as sackcloth, the full moon became like blood* (Revelation 6:12 ESV) |
| | The upper atmosphere is cleared of all manmade space objects. All satellites and space pollution will be cast from earth's orbit and will burn up in the atmosphere like shooting stars. | *. . . stars of the sky fell to the earth* (Revelation 6:13a ESV) |
| | Then the curtains of heaven are pulled open to reveal God on his throne. | *The sky vanished like a scroll that is being rolled up* (Revelation 6:14a ESV) |
| 6 | Because planet earth responds to the events in the heavens by shaking every living being to the ground and exposing them to their creator. | *. . . and every mountain and island was removed from its place.* (Revelation 6:14b ESV) |
| | The kings, commanders and slaves all understand it's God and all they want to do is try to crawl into a hole and hide | *15 Then the kings of the earth and the great ones and the generals and the rich and the powerful, and everyone, slave and free, hid themselves* (Revelation 6:15a ESV) |

| # | 9 Reasons Why the 6ᵗʰ Seal is All of Creation Worshipping Its Creator | Scriptures Which Describe the 6ᵗʰ Seal Events |
|---|---|---|
| | The image petrified everyone to the point of wanting to die because they couldn't face his glory | *. . . calling to the mountains and rocks, "Fall on us and hide us from the face of him who is seated on the throne* (Revelation 12:16a ESV) |
| | Every person understands with every fiber of their being that the wrath of Jesus is about to be released and they don't stand a chance | *. . . and from the wrath of the Lamb, 17 for the great day of their wrath has come, and who can stand?* (Revelation 12:16b-17 ESV) |
| | When God reveals himself in all his glorious splendor, everyone, including the antichrist and his false Jesus, is petrified and the earth purposely shakes to toss them to the ground. No man or beast will be able to stand while the earth is swaying and they will have no other option, but to lay prostrate in submission in the presence of their creator, who is about to be revealed. Every human will understand this is their creator and those with the mark will want to crawl into a hole and hide in the same way Adam and Eve wanted to hide from God after they disobeyed by eating the forbidden fruit. In the presence of perfection, all men will be acutely aware of how far they are from the glory of God. | *. . . for all have sinned and fall short of the glory of God (Romans 3:23 ESV)*<br><br>*My hand laid the foundation of the earth, and my right hand spread out the heavens; when I call to them, they stand forth together. (Isaiah 48:13 ESV)*<br><br>*The heavens proclaim his righteousness, and all the peoples see his glory. (Psalm 97:6 ESV)*<br><br>*He bowed the heavens and came down; thick darkness was under his feet. (2 Samuel 22:10 also Psalm 18:9 ESV)*<br><br>*5 Why do you flee, O sea? Why do you turn back, O Jordan River? 6 Why do you skip like rams, O mountains, like lambs, O hills? 7 Tremble, O earth, before the Lord--before the God of Jacob (Psalm 114:5-7 NET)* |

| # | 9 Reasons Why the 6th Seal is All of Creation Worshipping Its Creator | Scriptures Which Describe the 6th Seal Events |
|---|---|---|
| | These leaders know what's about to happen, that the wrath of Jesus is coming but hasn't yet been unleashed (Revelation 6:16). They know it's coming because they can't help but remember the words of the first circumnavigating angel who proclaimed the gospel, which surely included an explanation of what was going to happen. They chose to ignore that warning, but they can't choose to forget it. How humiliating this must be for the antichrist and his false Jesus. | *10 Go up into the rocky cliffs, hide in the ground. Get away from the dreadful judgment of the LORD, from his royal splendor! 11 Proud men will be brought low, arrogant men will be humiliated; the LORD alone will be exalted in that day. 12 Indeed, the LORD of Heaven's Armies has planned a day of judgment, for all the high and mighty, for all who are proud – they will be humiliated; (Isaiah 2:10-12 NET)* |
| 7 | Because the kings want to die but can't. As further evidence the 6th seal is not destructive, the kings of the earth and leaders hiding in bunkers are begging for rocks to fall on them to hide them from God, but the rocks don't fall on them. | *And people shall enter the caves of the rocks and the holes of the ground, from before the terror of the LORD, and from the splendor of his majesty, when he rises to terrify the earth. (Isaiah 2:19 ESV)* |
| 8 | Because Jesus told us that if men wouldn't acknowledge him as king that the very rocks would cry out and proclaim him king. The earth and sea are swaying and trembling in reverence as a way of praising their creator and part of that process is shaking the ground to force humans to bend their knee in reverence to God. | *36 And as he rode along, they spread their cloaks on the road. 37 As he was drawing near—already on the way down the Mount of Olives—the whole multitude of his disciples began to rejoice and praise God with a loud voice for all the mighty works that they had seen, 38 saying, "Blessed is the King who comes in the name of the Lord! Peace in heaven and glory in the highest!" 39 And some of the Pharisees in the crowd said to him, "Teacher, rebuke your disciples." 40 He answered, "I tell you, if these were silent, the very stones would cry out." (Luke 19:36-4 ESV)* |

| # | 9 Reasons Why the 6ᵗʰ Seal is All of Creation Worshipping Its Creator | Scriptures Which Describe the 6ᵗʰ Seal Events |
|---|---|---|
| 9 | Because this interpretation aligns perfectly with the Olivet Discourse. Matthew and Mark both described the 6th seal events as happening immediately after the tribulation and before the sign of Jesus would appear in heaven. Neither of them described it as destructive, just fear and foreboding about what is about to come on the earth. We'll soon see what men are fearful about when the final trumpet sounds. | *Immediately after the tribulation of those days the sun will be darkened, and the moon will not give its light, and the stars will fall from heaven, and the powers of the heavens will be shaken. 30 Then will appear in heaven the sign of the Son of Man, and then all the tribes of the earth will mourn, and they will see the Son of Man coming on the clouds of heaven with power and great glory. (Matthew 24:29-30 ESV)* *But in those days, after that tribulation, the sun will be darkened, and the moon will not give its light, 25 and the stars will be falling from heaven, and the powers in the heavens will be shaken. 26 And then they will see the Son of Man coming in clouds with great power and glory. (Mark 13:24-26 ESV)* *And there will be signs in sun and moon and stars, and on the earth distress of nations in perplexity because of the roaring of the sea and the waves, 26 people fainting with fear and with foreboding of what is coming on the world. For the powers of the heavens will be shaken. 27 And then they will see the Son of Man coming in a cloud with power and great glory. (Luke 21:25-27 ESV)* |

# Exhibit 8:

## Map of Pangea

(Alex, "**Map of Pangea** with current International borders," Vivid Maps, March 14, 2015, https://vividmaps.com/map-of-pangea/).

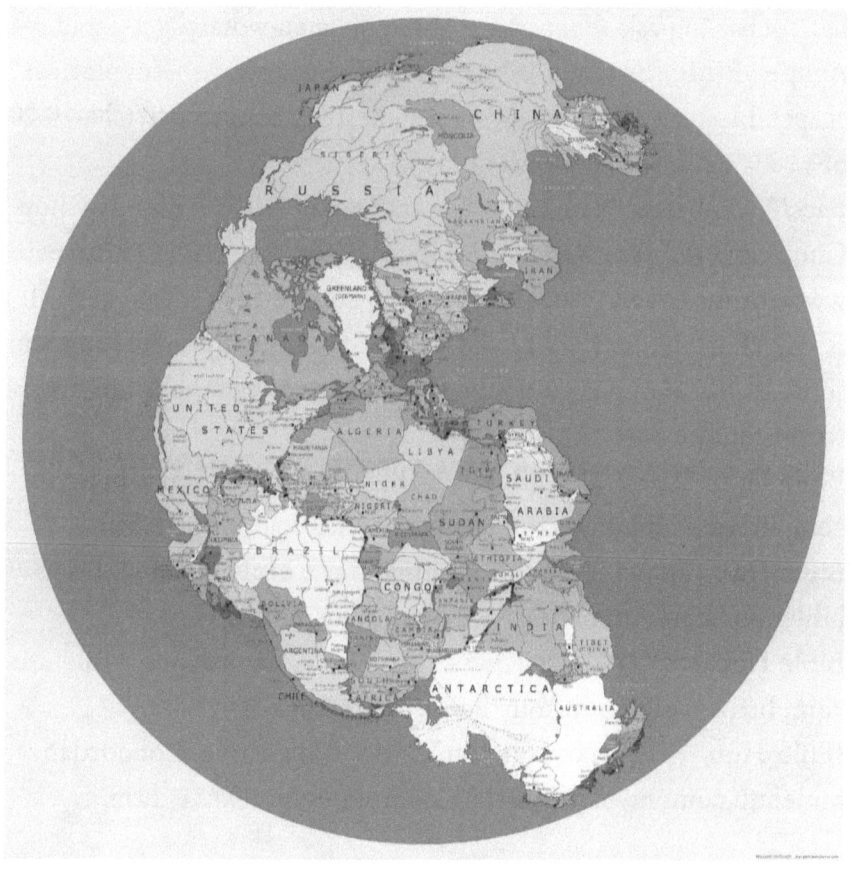

# Bibliography

Abdou, Alaa M. "What does the Quran say about the Bible?" Explore Islam, November 26, 2023, https://explore-islam.com/what-does-the-quran-say-about-the-bible/.

About Islam, "72 Virgins for Men, What Do Women Get in Paradise?" aboutislam.net, November 26, 2018, https://aboutislam.net/counseling/ask-about-islam/72-virgins-men-women-get-paradise/.

Agape Bible Study. "The List of Sevens in Revelation." agapebiblestudy.com, https://agapebiblestudy.com/charts/Chart%20of%207s%20in%20Revelation.htm.

Bacchi, Umberto. "Execution Central: Saudi Arabia's Bloody Chop-Chop Square." *International Business Times*, April 3, 2013, https://www.ibtimes.co.uk/saudi-arabia-chop-square-beheading-453240.

BBC, "The rise and fall of the Islamic State group: The long and short story." March 23, 2019, bbc.com, https://www.bbc.com/news/world-middle-east-47210891.

Bible Hub, "Amos 8," Keil and Delitzsch Commentary, biblehub.com, https://biblehub.com/commentaries/kad/amos/8.htm.

Bible Hub, "Amos 8," Pulpit Commentary, biblehub.com, https://biblehub.com/commentaries/pulpit/amos/8.htm.

Bible Hub, s.v. "2742. charuwts," Strong's Concordance, biblehub.com, https://biblehub.com/hebrew/2742.htm.

Bible Hub, "717. Harmagedón," NAS Exhaustive Concordance, biblehub.com, https://biblehub.com/nasec/greek/717.htm.

Bible Hub, "Isaiah 41:15," Keil and Delitzsch Biblical Commentary on the Old Testament, biblehub.com, https://biblehub.com/commentaries/isaiah/41-15.htm.

Bible Hub, "2738. kauma," *Strong's Concordance,* biblehub.com, https://biblehub.com/greek/2738.htm.

Bible Hub, "Luke 23," Vincent's Word Studies, https://biblehub.com/commentaries/vws/luke/23.htm.

Bible Hub, "Matthew 25:46," Weymouth New Testament Translation, https://biblehub.com/matthew/25-46.htm.

Bible Hub, "Matthew 25:46," Worrell New Testament, biblehub.com, https://biblehub.com/parallel/matthew/25-46.htm.

Bible Hub, "Micah 4:1," Pulpit Commentary, biblehub.com, https://biblehub.com/commentaries/micah/4-1.htm.

Bible Hub, "Revelation 5," Pulpit Commentary, https://biblehub.com/commentaries/pulpit/revelation/5.htm.

Bible Hub. "Revelation 5:1." Jamieson-Fausset-Brown Bible Commentary, https://biblehub.com/commentaries/revelation/5-1.htm.

Bible Hub, "Revelation 5:13," Pulpit Commentary, biblehub.com, https://biblehub.com/commentaries/pulpit/revelation/5.htm.

Bible Hub, "Revelation 6," Cambridge Bible for Schools and Colleges, biblehub.com, https://biblehub.com/commentaries/cambridge/revelation/6.htm.

Bible Hub, "Revelation 6," Clarke's Commentary, biblehub.com, https://biblehub.com/commentaries/clarke/revelation/6.htm.

Bible Hub, "Revelation 6," Ellicott's Commentary for English Readers, biblehub.com, https://biblehub.com/commentaries/ellicott/revelation/6.htm.

Bible Hub, "Revelation 6," Geneva Study Bible, biblehub.com, https://biblehub.com/commentaries/gsb/revelation/6.htm.

Bible Hub, "Revelation 6," Gill's Exposition, biblehub.com, https://biblehub.com/commentaries/gill/revelation/6.htm.

Bible Hub, "Revelation 6," Jamieson-Fausset-Brown Bible Commentary, biblehub.com, https://biblehub.com/commentaries/jfb/revelation/6.htm.

Bible Hub, "Revelation 6:1–2," Gaebelein's Annotated Bible, biblehub.com, https://biblehub.com/commentaries/gaebelein/revelation/6.htm.

Bible Hub, "Revelation 8:13," Jamieson-Fausset-Brown Bible Commentary, biblehub.com, https://biblehub.com/commentaries/jfb/revelation/8.htm.

Bible Hub, "Revelation 9:1," Jamieson-Fausset-Brown Bible Commentary, biblehub.com, https://biblehub.com/commentaries/revelation/9-1.htm.

Bible Hub, "Revelation 10:2," Jamieson-Fausset-Brown Bible Commentary, biblehub.com, https://biblehub.com/commentaries/revelation/10-2.htm.

Bible Hub, "Revelation 16," *Amplified Bible*, biblehub.com, https://biblehub.com/amp/revelation/16.htm.

Bible Hub, "STRONGS NT 3857: παράδεισος," Thayer's Greek Lexicon, https://biblehub.com/greek/3857.htm.

Bible Hub, "Zechariah 14:5," biblehub.com, https://biblehub.com/commentaries/zechariah/14-5.htm.

Blue Letter Bible. "*meta*," Strong's Greek Lexicon (kjv). Accessed 12 Apr, 2024. https://www.blueletterbible.org/lexicon/g3326/kjv/tr/66-1/#lexResults.

Blue Letter Bible. "*Meta*," Strong's #G3326. Accessed 12 Apr, 2024. https://www.blueletterbible.org/lexicon/g3326/kjv/tr/66-1/#lexResults.

Blue Letter Bible. "Ὅτε," Accessed 12 Apr, 2024. https://www.blueletterbible.org/lexicon/g3753/kjv/tr/66-1/#lexResults.

Blue Letter Bible. Strong's G975, "βιβλίον," or *"biblion,"* blueletterbible. org, https://www.blueletterbible.org/lexicon/g975/niv/mgnt/0-1/.

Blue Letter Bible. Vine's Expository Dictionary of New Testament Words, "Kai," https://www.blueletterbible.org/search/Dictionary/viewTopic.cfm?topic=VT0003445.

Carnes, Cody, Cory Asbury, and Ethan Hulse. *Christ Be Magnified.* Cory Asbury Publishing, 2019.

Chabad.org, "Introduction: How Jews Approach Death," https://www.chabad.org/library/article_cdo/aid/282496/jewish/How-Jews-Approach-Death.htm.

Chess Questions, "Stalemate in Chess: Rules, Tips and Pieces to Avoid," chessquestions.com, April 8, 2021, https://chessquestions.com/stalemate-in-chess/.

Choi, Charles Q. "How do mountains form?" Live Science, November 12, 2023, https://www.livescience.com/planet-earth/how-do-mountains-form.

"Christian Views on Hades." *Wikipedia: The Free Encyclopedia.* Accessed 12/1/2024. https://en.wikipedia.org/wiki/Christian views on Hades.

Christianity Today. "Topic: Denominations," https://www.christianitytoday.com/ct/topics/d/denominations/.

Coffey, Donavyn. "Why does Christianity have so many denominations?" *Live Science,* July 29, 2022, https://www.livescience.com/christianity-denominations.html.

convertunits.com, "Convert stadion to mile." https://www.convertunits.com/from/stadia/to/miles.

convertunits.com, "Convert stadion to mile," https://www.convertunits.com/from/stadia/to/miles

Cuffie, Pastor Darryl T. "The 4 Greek Words for 'Love' Used In The New Testament," Blessing of Heaven, February 14, 2023, http://

www.blessingofheaven.org/blog/the-4-greek-words-for-love-used-in-new-testament.

Davis, Daniel L. "The Battle of Stalingrad Left an Incomprehensible 1.9 Million Dead," *The National Interest,* October 9, 2021, https://nationalinterest.org/blog/reboot/battle-stalingrad-left-incomprehensible-19-million-dead-194783.

Encyclopedia Britannica, "Assyria," britannica.com, July 29, 2024, https://www.britannica.com/place/Assyria.

Foxe, John. Foxe's Book of Martyrs. N.p.: n.p., n.d. https://ia600802.us.archive.org/14/items/foxesbookofmartyrs_201708/Foxes-Book-of-Martyrs.pdf.

Ghose, Tia. "The 20 largest recorded earthquakes in history," Live Science, January 27, 2023, https://www.livescience.com/largest-recorded-earthquakes-in-history.

Gleason, Jon. "Zerubbabel and the Genealogies of Christ," *Mind Renewers,* December 31, 2013, https://mindrenewers.com/2013/12/31/zerubbabel-and-the-genealogies-of-christ/.

Goddard, Taegan. "Fifth Column," Political Dictionary, https://politicaldictionary.com/words/fifth-column/.

Got Questions. "Question: Who divided the Bible into chapters and verses?" last updated January 4, 2022. https://www.gotquestions.org/divided-Bible-chapters-verses.html.

Heiser, Michael S. *The Unseen Realm: Recovering the Supernatural Worldview of the Bible* (Lexham Press, 2015), 112–113, 243, 368–375.

Helmenstine, Anne. "Why Do We Have Seasons On Earth?" Sciencenotes.org, November 4, 2023, https://sciencenotes.org/why-do-we-have-seasons-on-earth/.

History of York, "The 1190 Massacre," historyofyork.org.uk, http://www.historyofyork.org.uk/themes/norman/the-1190-massacre.

Hout, Jean-Louis. "Xerxes I," *Encyclopedia Britannica,* August 2, 2024, https://www.britannica.com/biography/Xerxes-I.

Irenaeus. *Against Heresies*. Translated by Alexander Roberts and W.H. Rambaut. In *Ante-Nicene Fathers, Vol. 1*, edited by Alexander Roberts and James Donaldson. Buffalo, NY: Christian Literature Publishing Co., 1885. Revised and edited for New Advent by Kevin Knight. Accessed 12/1/2024. https://www.newadvent.org/fathers/0103.htm.

Jewish Telegraphic Agency, "Behind the Headlines: How Stalin's Plan to Annihilate USSR Jews Was Thwarted," jta.org, January 8, 1978, https://www.jta.org/archive/behind-the-headlines-how-stalins-plan-to-annihilate-ussr-jews-was-thwarted.

Jewish Virtual Library, "Estimated Number of Jews Killed in the Final Solution," jewishvirtuallibrary.org, https://www.jewishvirtuallibrary.org/estimated-number-of-jews-killed-in-the-final-solution.

Klein, Christopher. "A Perfect Solar Superstorm: The 1859 Carrington Event," *History*, August 4, 2023, https://www.history.com/news/a-perfect-solar-superstorm-the-1859-carrington-event.

Koinegreek.com, "homologeo," "orge," "orgizo," & "thumos," https://www.koinegreek.com/koine-greek-dictionary.

Levin, Nancy. "9 Largest Battles in History," largest.org, December 24, 2018, https://largest.org/culture/battles-in-history/.

List of Protestant Martyrs of the English Reformation." Wikipedia. https://en.wikipedia.org/wiki/List_of_Protestant_martyrs_of_the_English_Reformation.

Long, Phillip J. "The Fallen Angels – 1 Enoch 6–8," Reading Acts, readingacts.com, May 31, 2016, https://readingacts.com/2016/05/31/the-fallen-angels-1-enoch-6-8/.

McCallum, Dennis. *Satan and His Kingdom: What the Bible Says and How It Matters to You* (Bethany House Publishers, 2009), 30.

Merriam-Webster, s.v. "cull," merraimwebster.com, https://www.merriam-webster.com/thesaurus/cull.

Merriam-Webster, s.v. "dark web" https://www.merriam-webster.com/dictionary/dark%20web.

Muscat, Emma. "Hidden In Plain Sight: The Fascinating Huguenot Practice Of Bible Concealment." Huguenot Museum. April 26, 2018. https://huguenotmuseum.org/about/news/hidden-in-plain-sight-the-fascinating-huguenot-practice-of-bible-concealment/.

NOAA, "What is Tectonic Shift?" National Geodetic Survey, Last Modified October 25, 2019, https://geodesy.noaa.gov/INFO/facts/tectonic-shift.shtml.

Richardson, Joel. *Mideast Beast: The Scriptural Case for an Islamic Antichrist* (WND Books, 2012), 18, 82–83.

Richardson, Joel. *The Islamic Antichrist: The Shocking Truth about the Real Nature of the Beast* (WND Books, 2015), 12, 30, 96, 98.

Routley, Nick. "This is how many humans have ever existed, according to researchers," April 4, 2022, World Economic Forum, https://www.weforum.org/agenda/2022/04/quantifying-human-existence/.

Saint John Orthodox Church. *What Happens After We Die?* Accessed 12/1/2024. https://www.saintjohnchurch.org/what-happens-after-death.

Small Biz Viewpoints, "The History of Currency – What is a Denarius Worth?" April 4, 2017, https://www.smallbizviewpoints.com/2017/04/04/the-history-of-currency-what-is-a-denarius-worth/.

Smith, Jay. "Job Summary," biblehub.com, https://biblehub.com/summary/job/1.htm.

Smith, Jay. "Job," Bible Book Summary, biblehub.com, https://biblehub.com/summary/job/1.htm.

Strongs Concordance: Toxon.

Tenorio, Rich. "20 years before the Holocaust, pogroms killed 100,000 Jews – then were forgotten," *The Times of Israel,* December

21, 2021, https://www.timesofisrael.com/20-years-before-the-holocaust-pogroms-killed-100000-jews-then-were-forgotten/.

Thakker, Anjana Sahney. "Unveiling The Deeper Meaning Behind The Coexist Symbol: A Message Of Unity And Tolerance," shunspirit.com, July 19, 2023, https://shunspirit.com/article/coexist-symbol-meaning.

Thayer's Greek Lexicon, "Biblion," Strong's G975, biblehub.com, https://biblehub.com/thayers/975.htm.

The Refusenik Project, "Historical Overview," refusenikproject.org, https://www.refusenikproject.org/history/.

The Temple Institute, "About the Temple Institute," https://templeinstitute.org/about-us/.

Williams, Matt. "Mountains: How Are They Formed?" *Universe Today,* https://www.universetoday.com/29833/how-mountains-are-formed/.

Wilson, James. "Converting Old Testament Shekel To Dollar Amounts," Chronicle Collectibles, September 29, 2023, https://www.chroniclecollectibles.com/old-testament-shekel-to-dollar/.